THE ULTIMATES

story **MARK MILLAR**

pencils **BRYAN HITCH**   inks **ANDREW CURRIE**

PAUL MOUNTS
colors

CHRIS ELIOPOULOS
letters

C.B. CEBULSKI
associate editor

BRIAN SMITH
associate editor

RALPH MACCHIO
editor

JOE QUESADA
editor in chief

BILL JEMAS
president

THE ULTIMATES VOL. 1: SUPER-HUMAN. Contains material originally published in magazine form as THE ULTIMATES #1-6. Second printing 2002. ISBN# 0-7851-0960-9. Published by MARVEL COMICS, a division of MARVEL ENTERTAINMENT GROUP, INC. OFFICE OF PUBLICATION: 10 East 40th Street, New York, NY 10016. Copyright © 2002 Marvel Characters, Inc. All rights reserved. $12.99 per copy in the U.S. and $21.00 in Canada (GST #R127032852); Canadian Agreement #40668537. All characters featured in this issue and the distinctive names and likenesses thereof, and all related indicia are trademarks of Marvel Characters, Inc. No similarity between any of the names, characters, persons, and/or institutions in this magazine with those of any living or dead person or institution is intended, and any such similarity which may exist is purely coincidental. Printed in the U.S.A. STAN LEE, Chairman Emeritus. For information regarding advertising in Marvel Comics or on Marvel.com, please contact Russell Brown, Executive Vice President, Consumer Products, Promotions and Media Sales at 212-576-8561 or rbrown@marvel.com

10 9 8 7 6 5 4 3 2

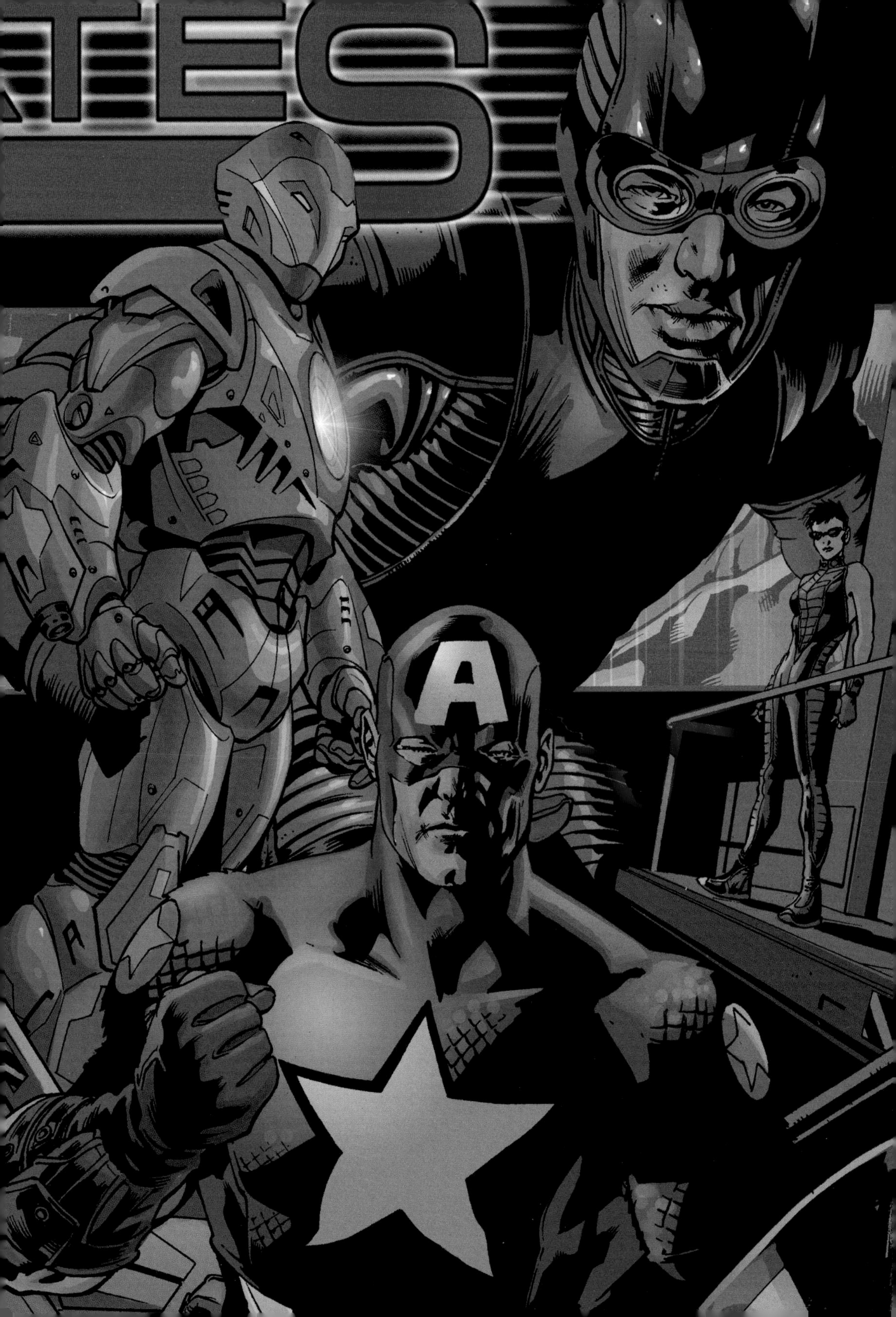
TES

CHAPTER ONE
SUPER-HUMAN

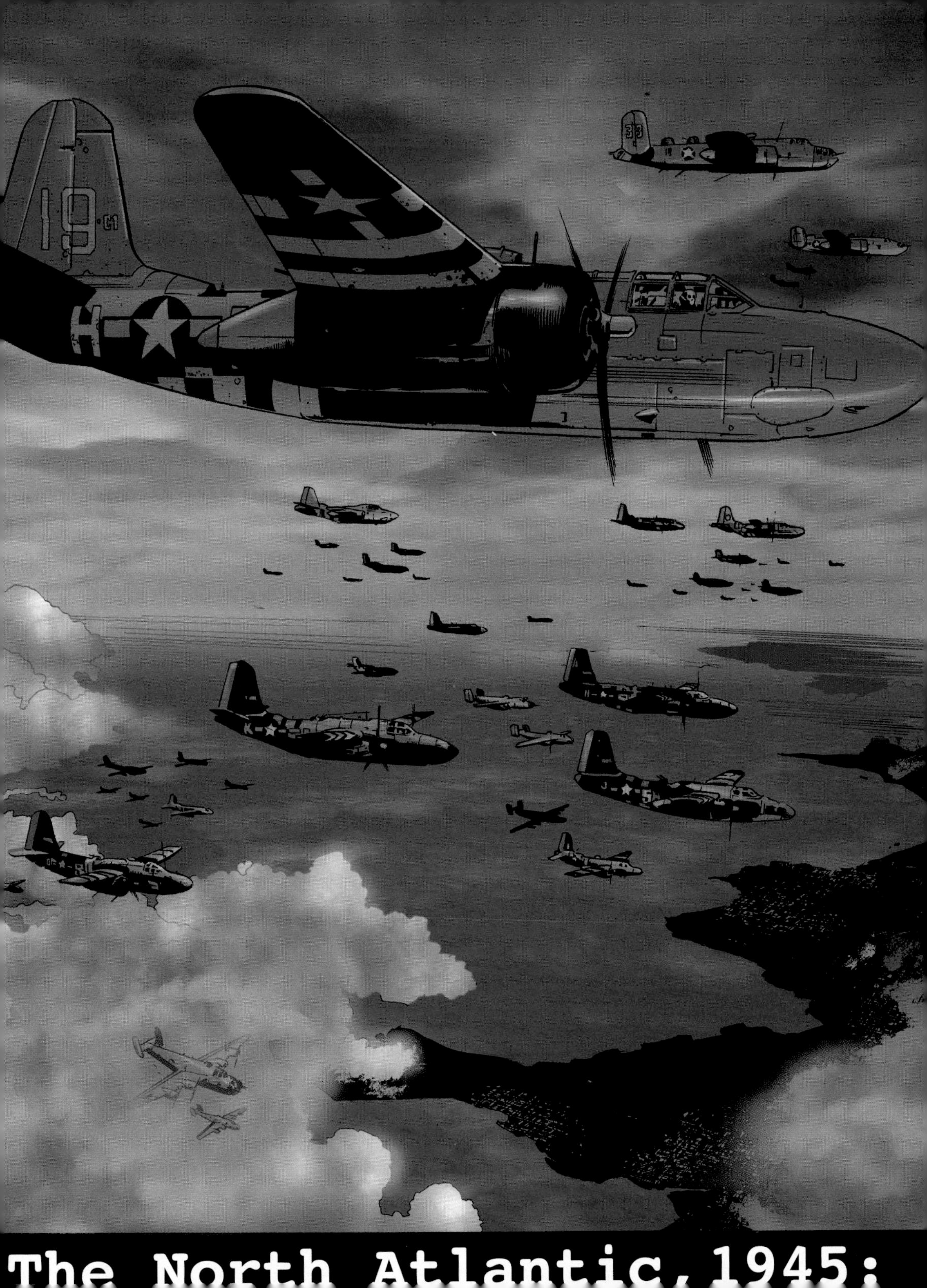
The North Atlantic, 1945:

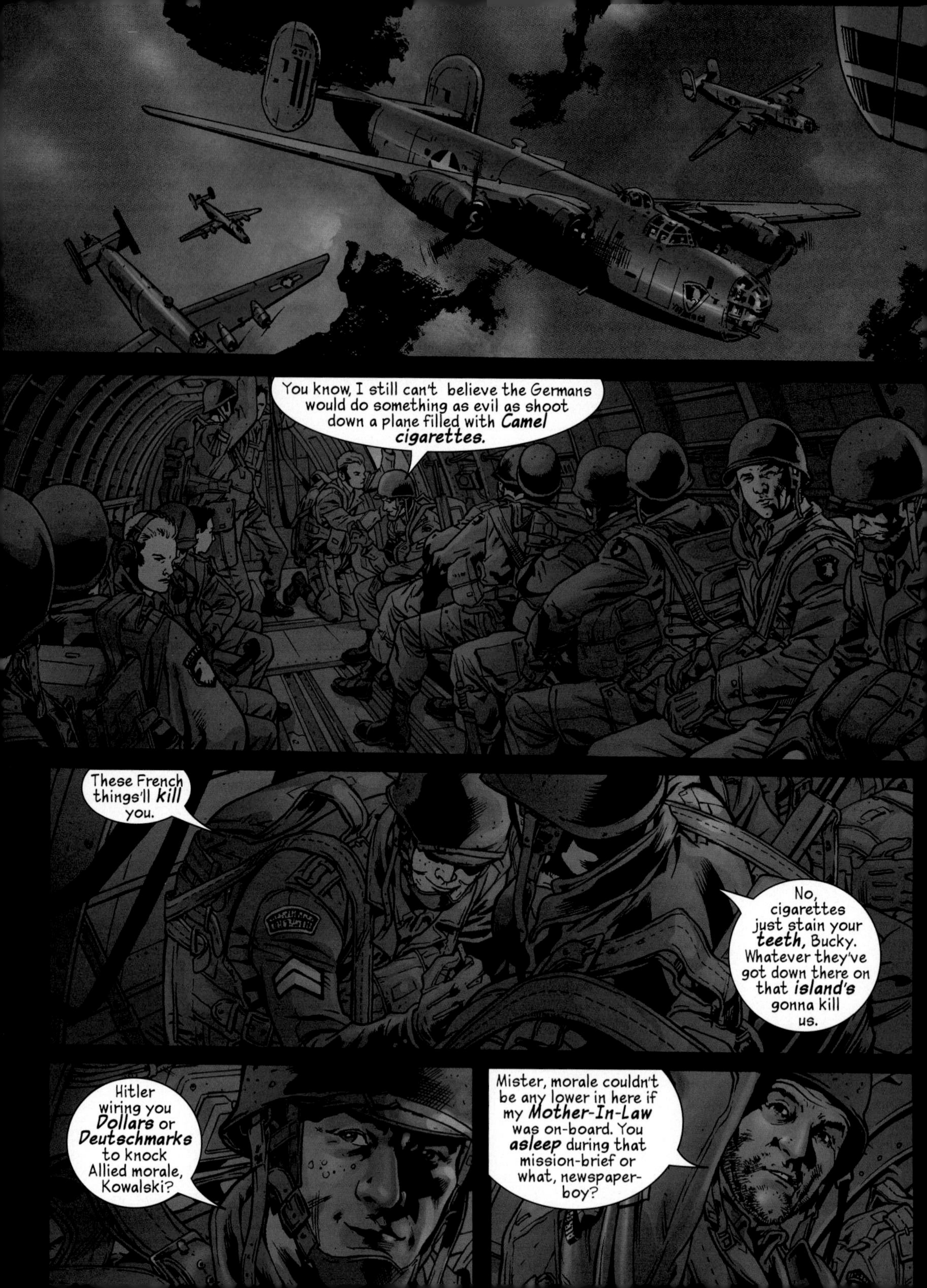
You know, I still can't believe the Germans would do something as evil as shoot down a plane filled with *Camel cigarettes.*
These French things'll *kill* you.
No, cigarettes just stain your *teeth,* Bucky. Whatever they've got down there on that *island's* gonna kill us.
Hitler wiring you *Dollars* or *Deutschmarks* to knock Allied morale, Kowalski?
Mister, morale couldn't be any lower in here if my *Mother-In-Law* was on-board. You *asleep* during that mission-brief or what, newspaper-boy?

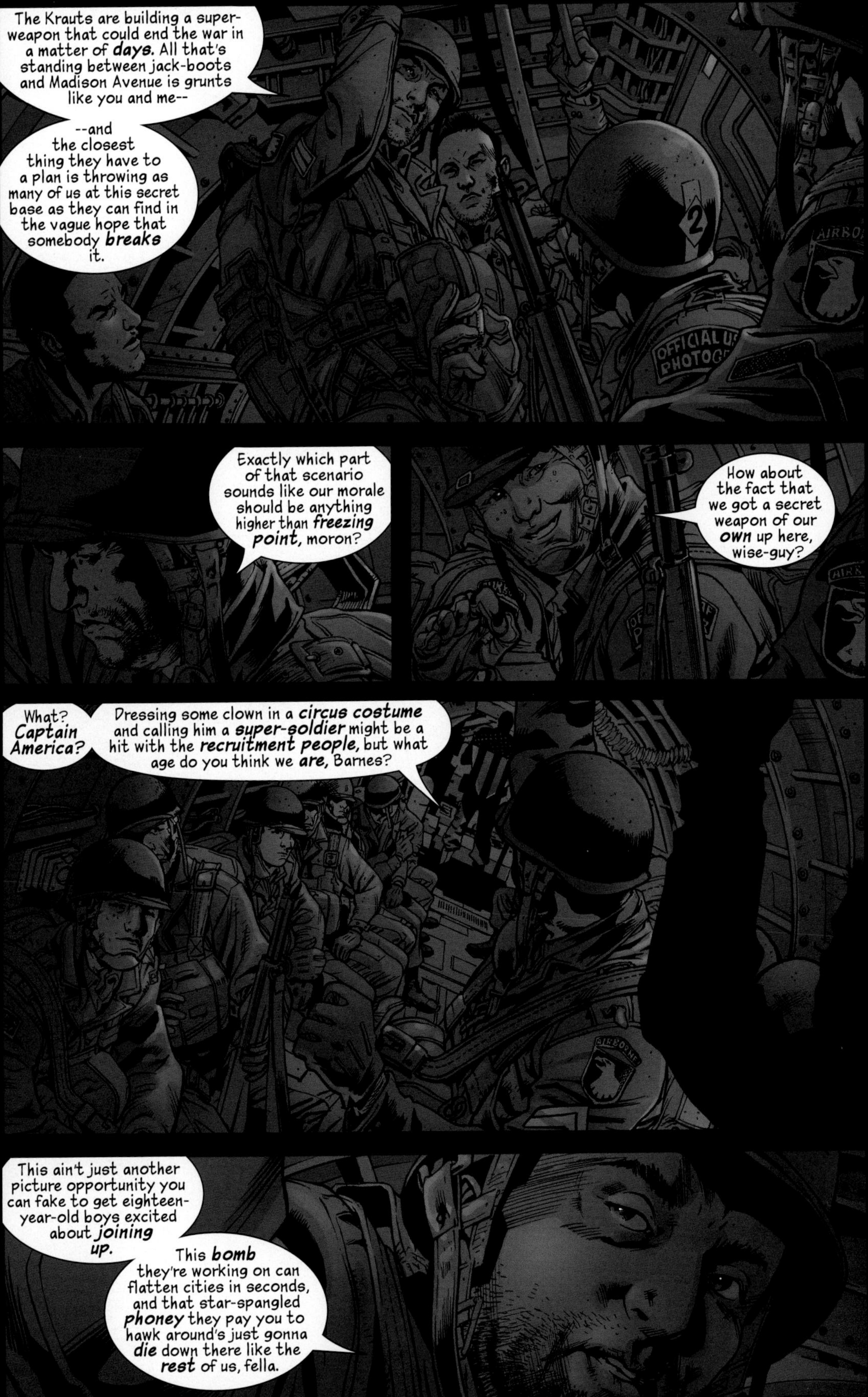
The Krauts are building a super-weapon that could end the war in a matter of **days.** All that's standing between jack-boots and Madison Avenue is grunts like you and me--
--and the closest thing they have to a plan is throwing as many of us at this secret base as they can find in the vague hope that somebody **breaks** it.
Exactly which part of that scenario sounds like our morale should be anything higher than **freezing point,** moron?
How about the fact that we got a secret weapon of our **own** up here, wise-guy?
What? **Captain America?**
Dressing some clown in a **circus costume** and calling him a **super-soldier** might be a hit with the **recruitment people,** but what age do you think we **are,** Barnes?
This ain't just another picture opportunity you can fake to get eighteen-year-old boys excited about **joining up.**
This **bomb** they're working on can flatten cities in seconds, and that star-spangled **phoney** they pay you to hawk around's just gonna **die** down there like the **rest** of us, fella.

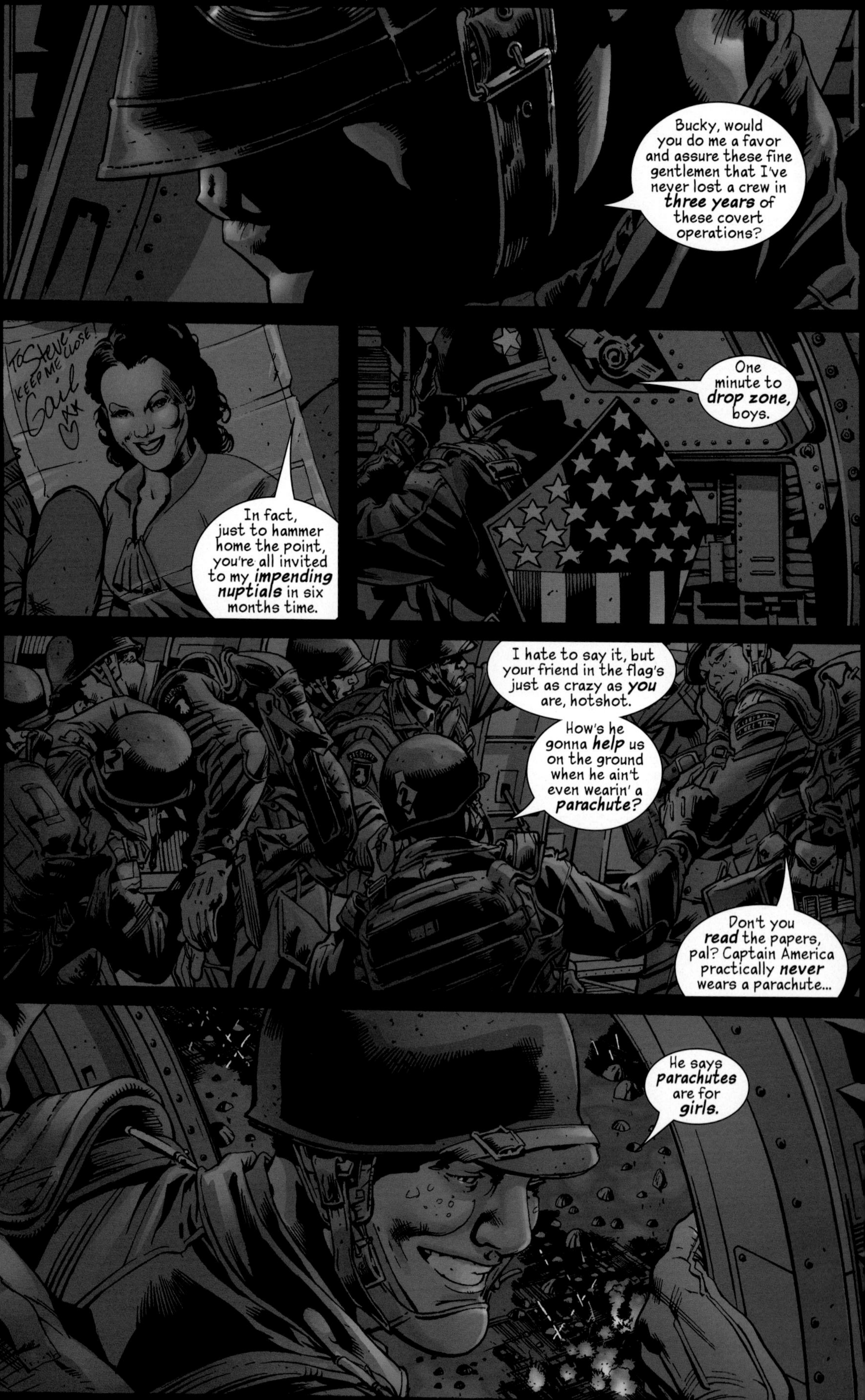
Bucky, would you do me a favor and assure these fine gentlemen that I've never lost a crew in **three years** of these covert operations?
To Steve- KEEP ME CLOSE! Gail xx
In fact, just to hammer home the point, you're all invited to my **impending nuptials** in six months time.
One minute to **drop zone,** boys.
I hate to say it, but your friend in the flag's just as crazy as **you** are, hotshot.
How's he gonna **help** us on the ground when he ain't even wearin' a **parachute?**
Don't you **read** the papers, pal? Captain America practically **never** wears a parachute...
He says **parachutes** are for **girls.**

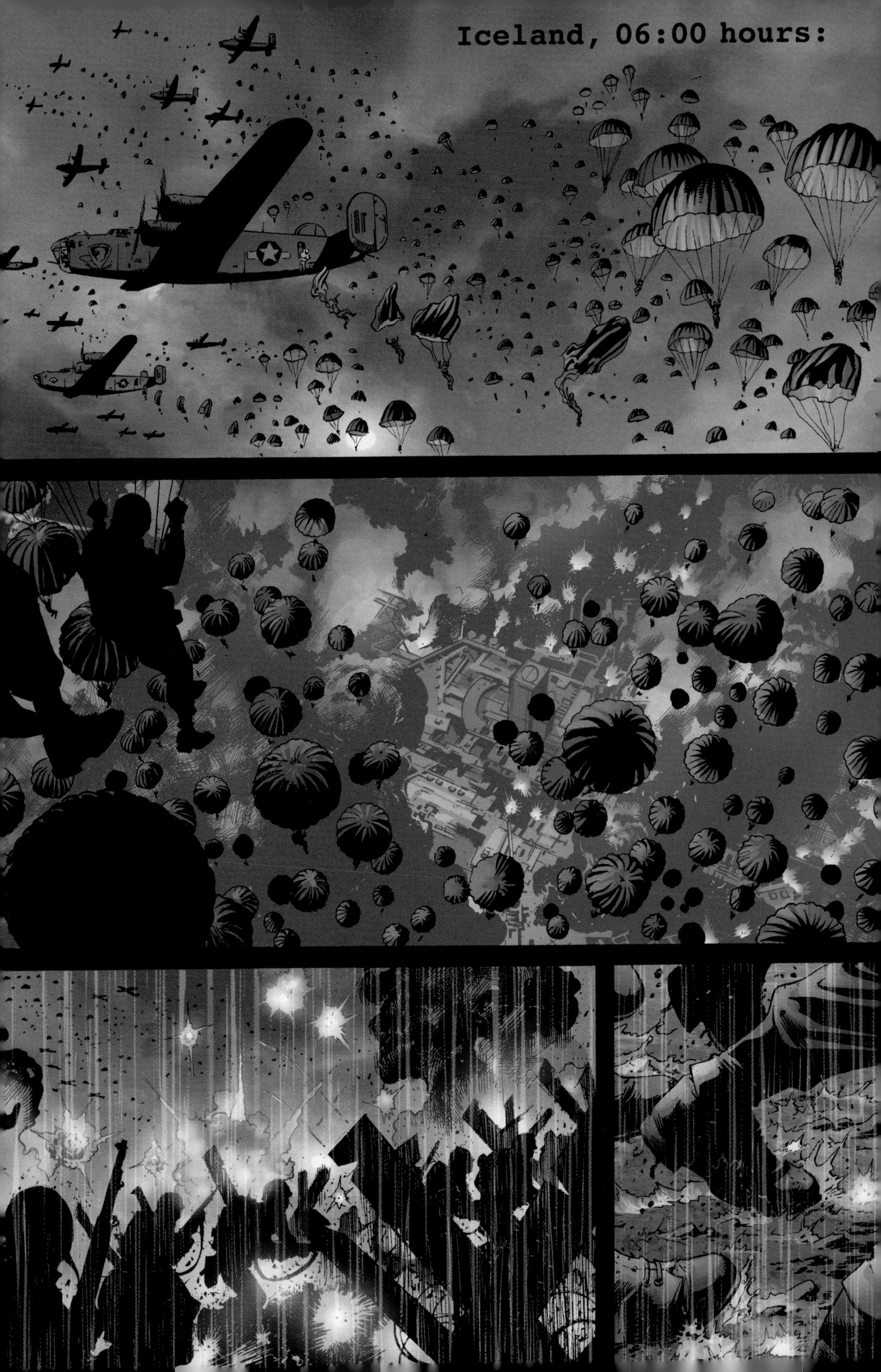
Iceland, 06:00 hours:

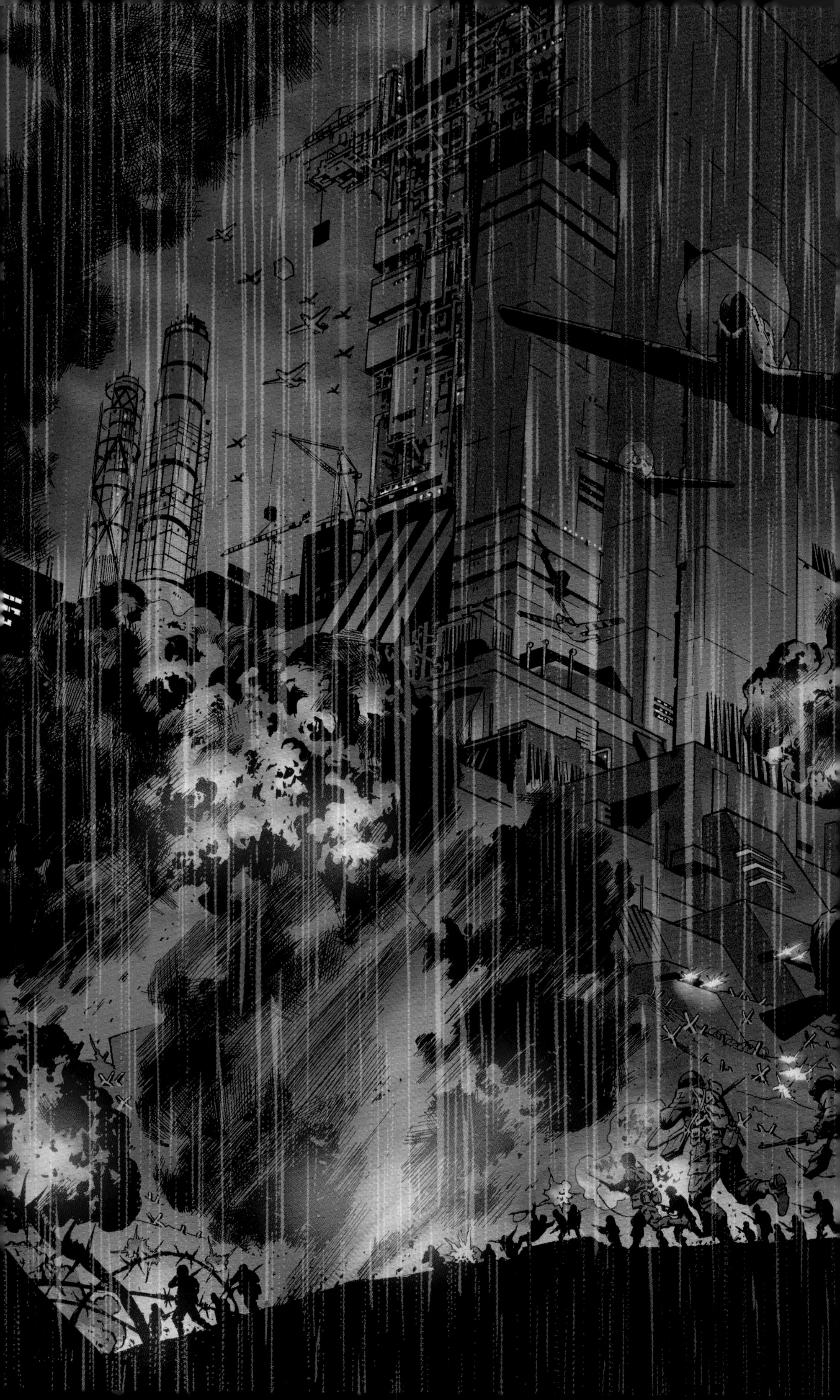

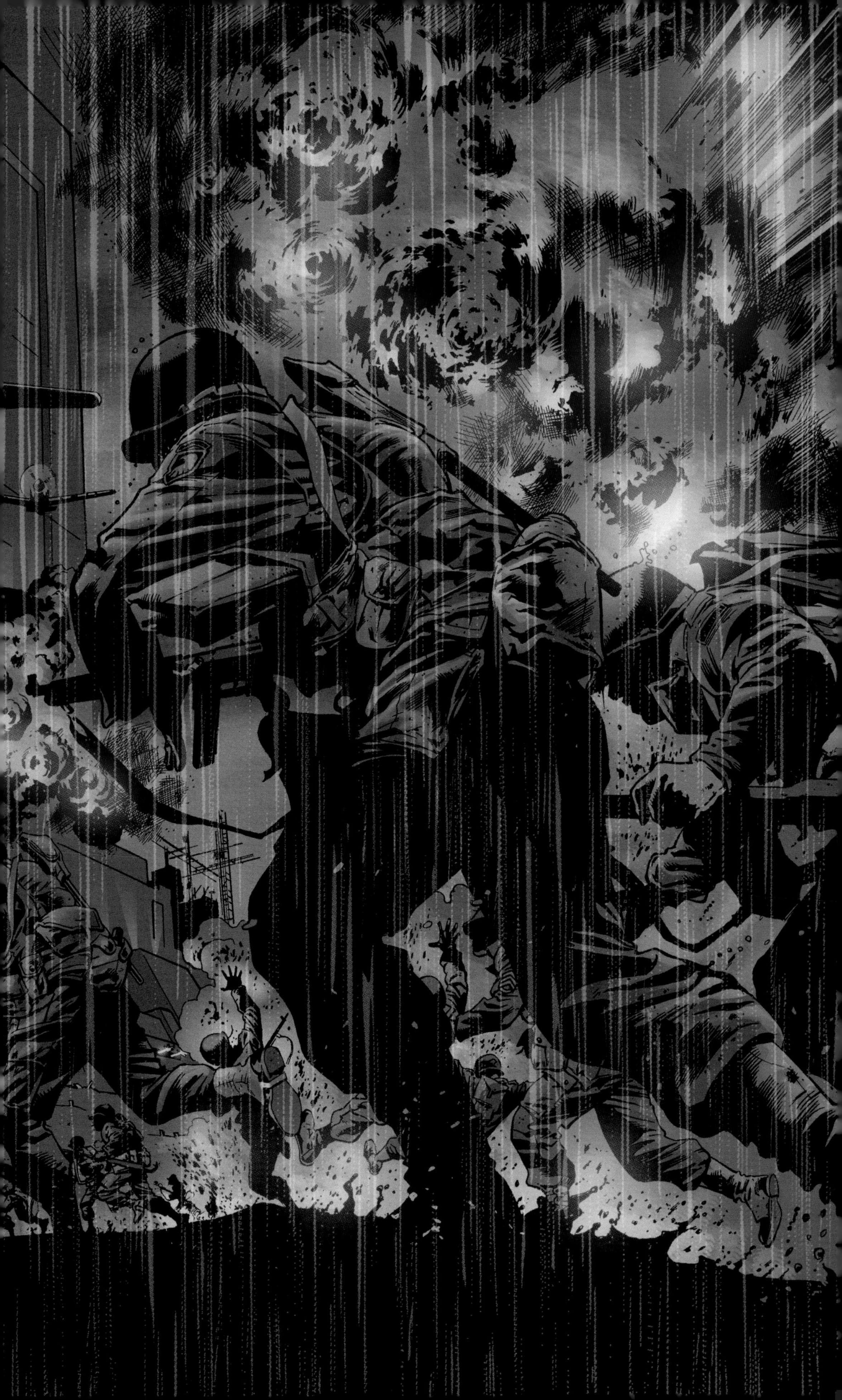

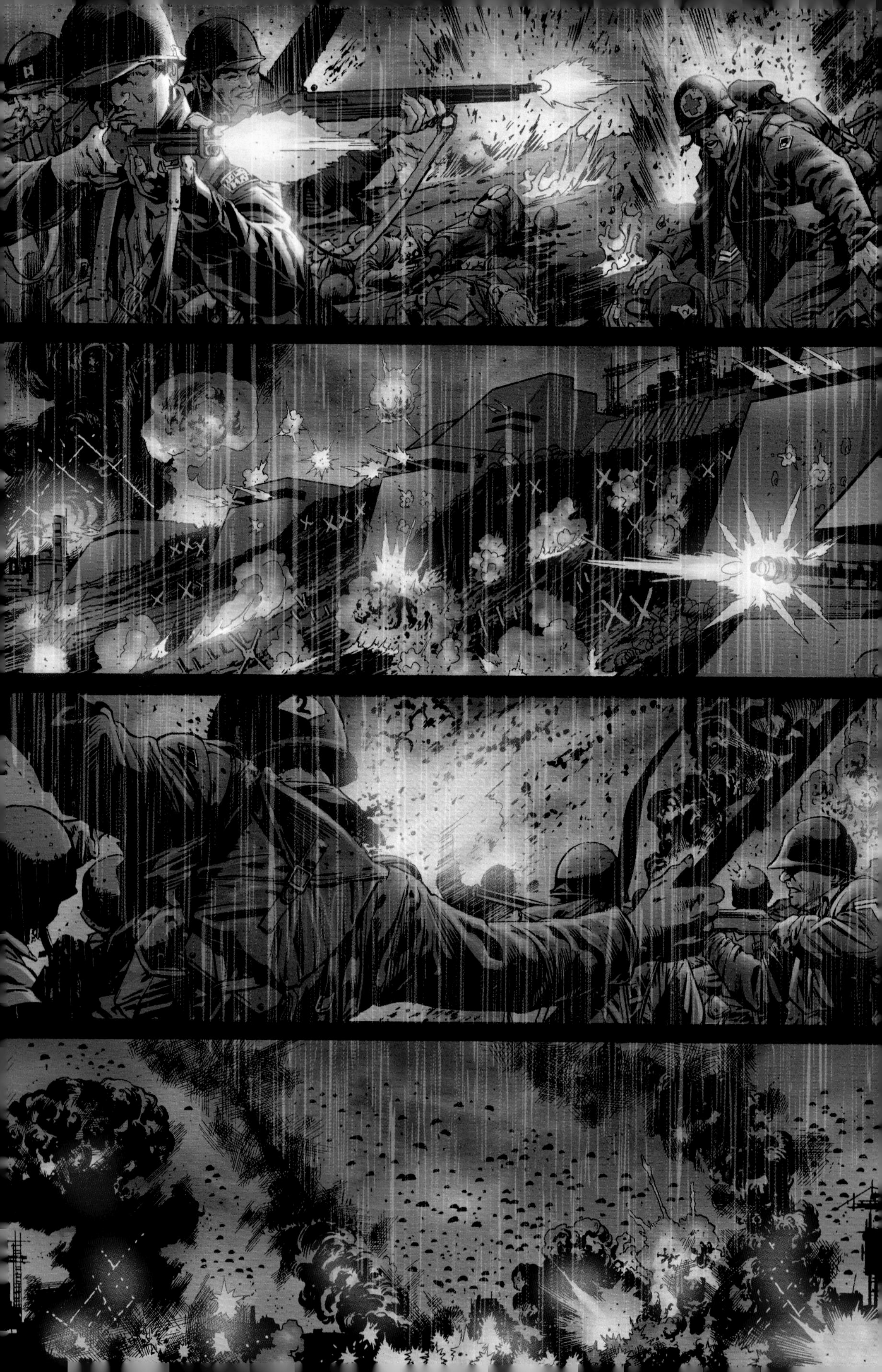

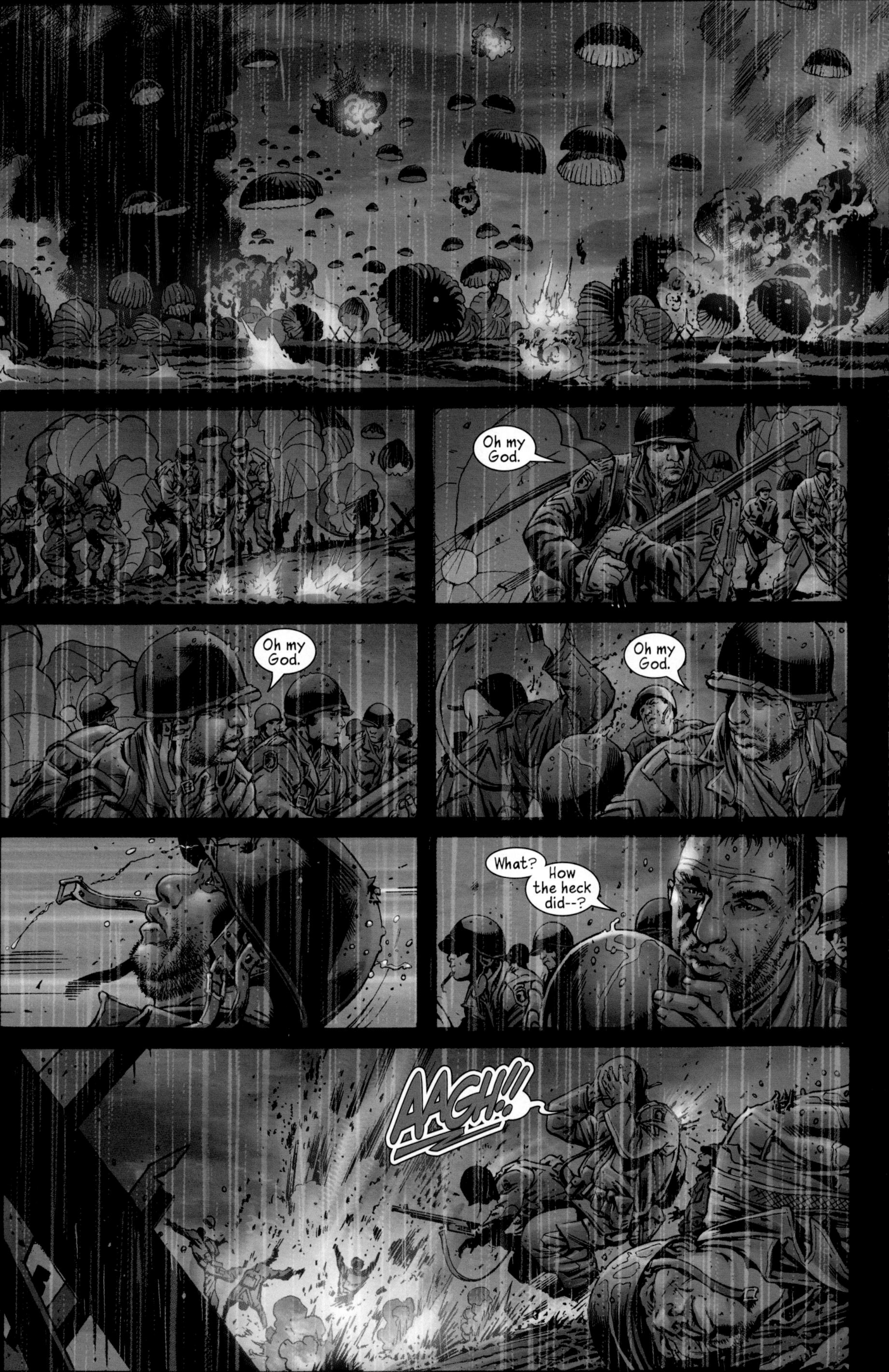
Oh my God.
Oh my God.
Oh my God.
What?
How the heck did--?
AAGH!!

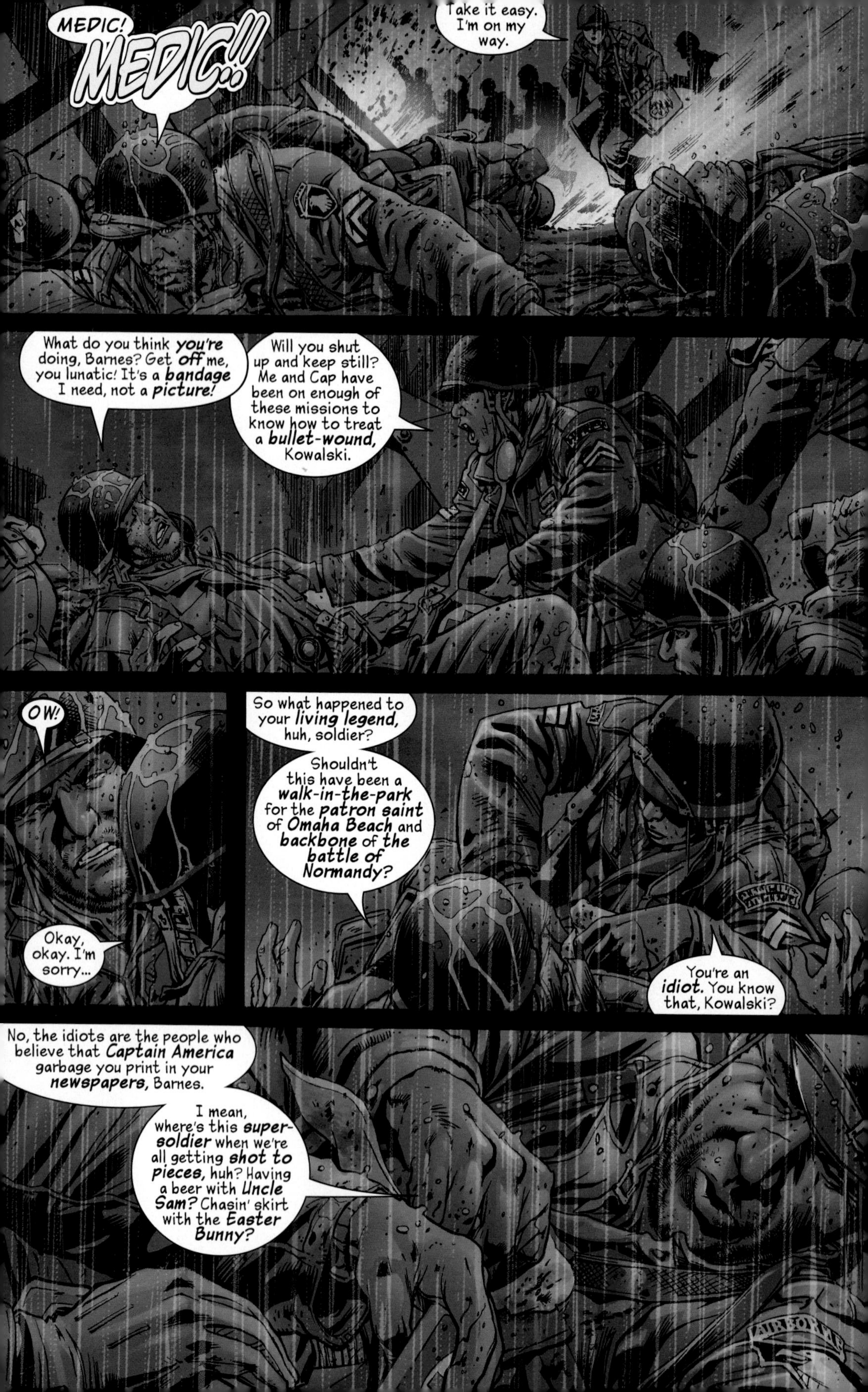
MEDIC!
MEDIC!!
Take it easy. I'm on my way.
What do you think you're doing, Barnes? Get off me, you lunatic! It's a bandage I need, not a picture!
Will you shut up and keep still? Me and Cap have been on enough of these missions to know how to treat a bullet-wound, Kowalski.
OW!
Okay, okay. I'm sorry...
So what happened to your living legend, huh, soldier?
Shouldn't this have been a walk-in-the-park for the patron saint of Omaha Beach and backbone of the battle of Normandy?
You're an idiot. You know that, Kowalski?
No, the idiots are the people who believe that Captain America garbage you print in your newspapers, Barnes.
I mean, where's this super-soldier when we're all getting shot to pieces, huh? Having a beer with Uncle Sam? Chasin' skirt with the Easter Bunny?
AIRBORNE

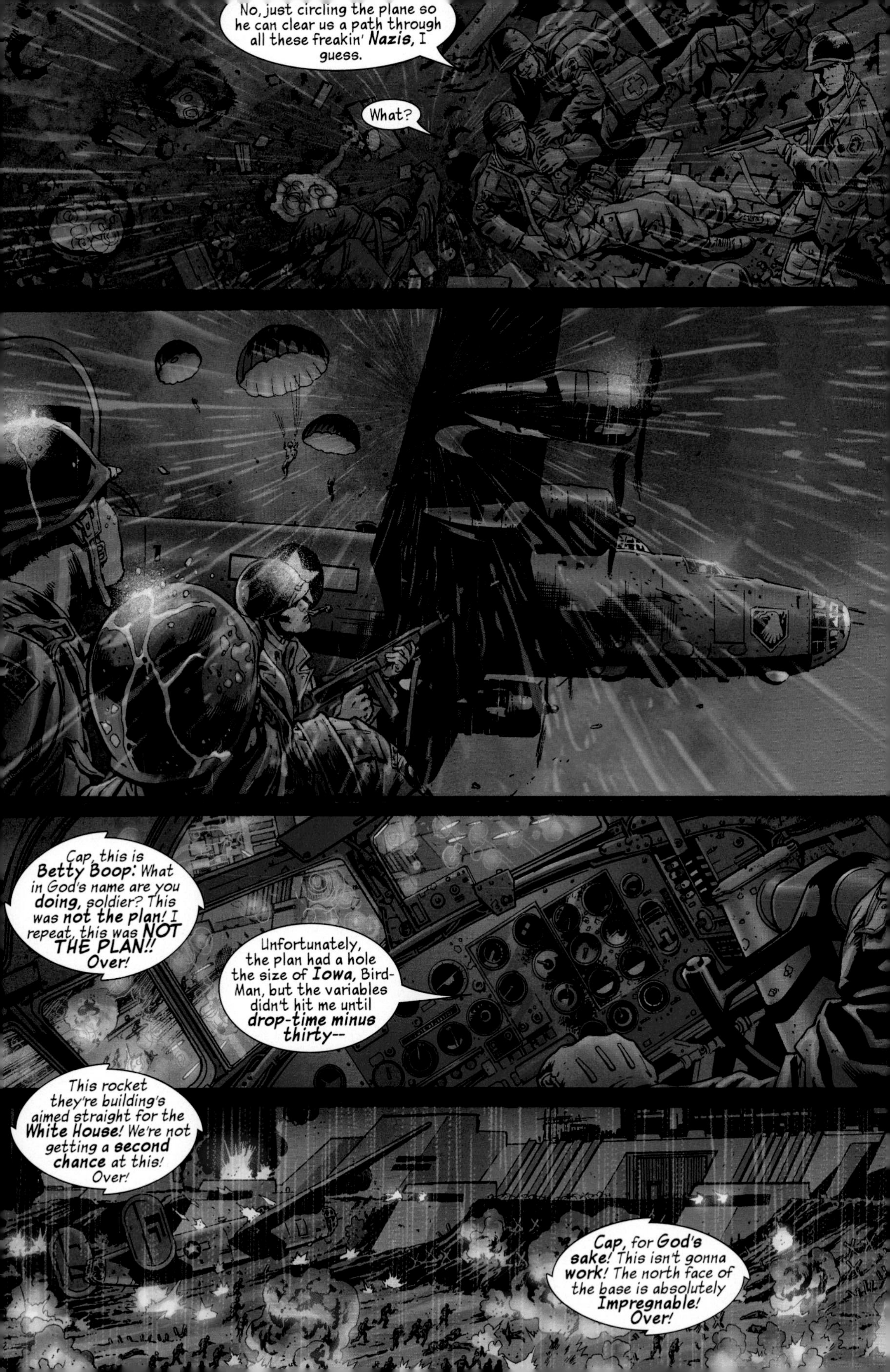
No, just circling the plane so he can clear us a path through all these freakin' **Nazis,** I guess.
What?
Cap, this is **Betty Boop:** What in God's name are you **doing,** soldier? This was **not the plan!** I repeat, this was **NOT THE PLAN!!** Over!
Unfortunately, the plan had a hole the size of **Iowa,** Bird-Man, but the variables didn't hit me until **drop-time minus thirty--**
This rocket they're building's aimed straight for the **White House!** We're not getting a **second chance** at this! Over!
Cap, for **God's sake!** This isn't gonna **work!** The north face of the base is absolutely **Impregnable! Over!**

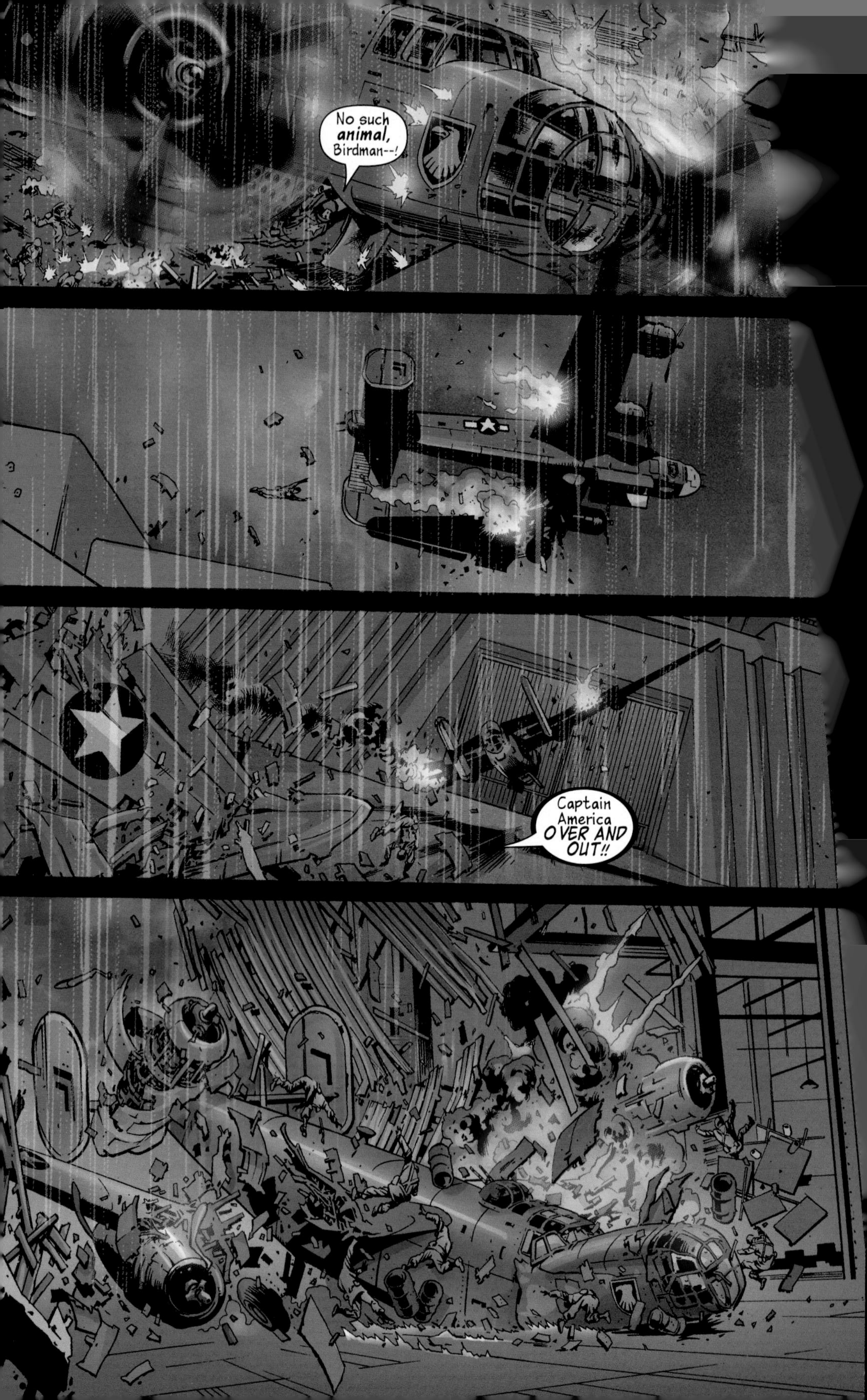
No such animal, Birdman--!
Captain America OVER AND OUT!!

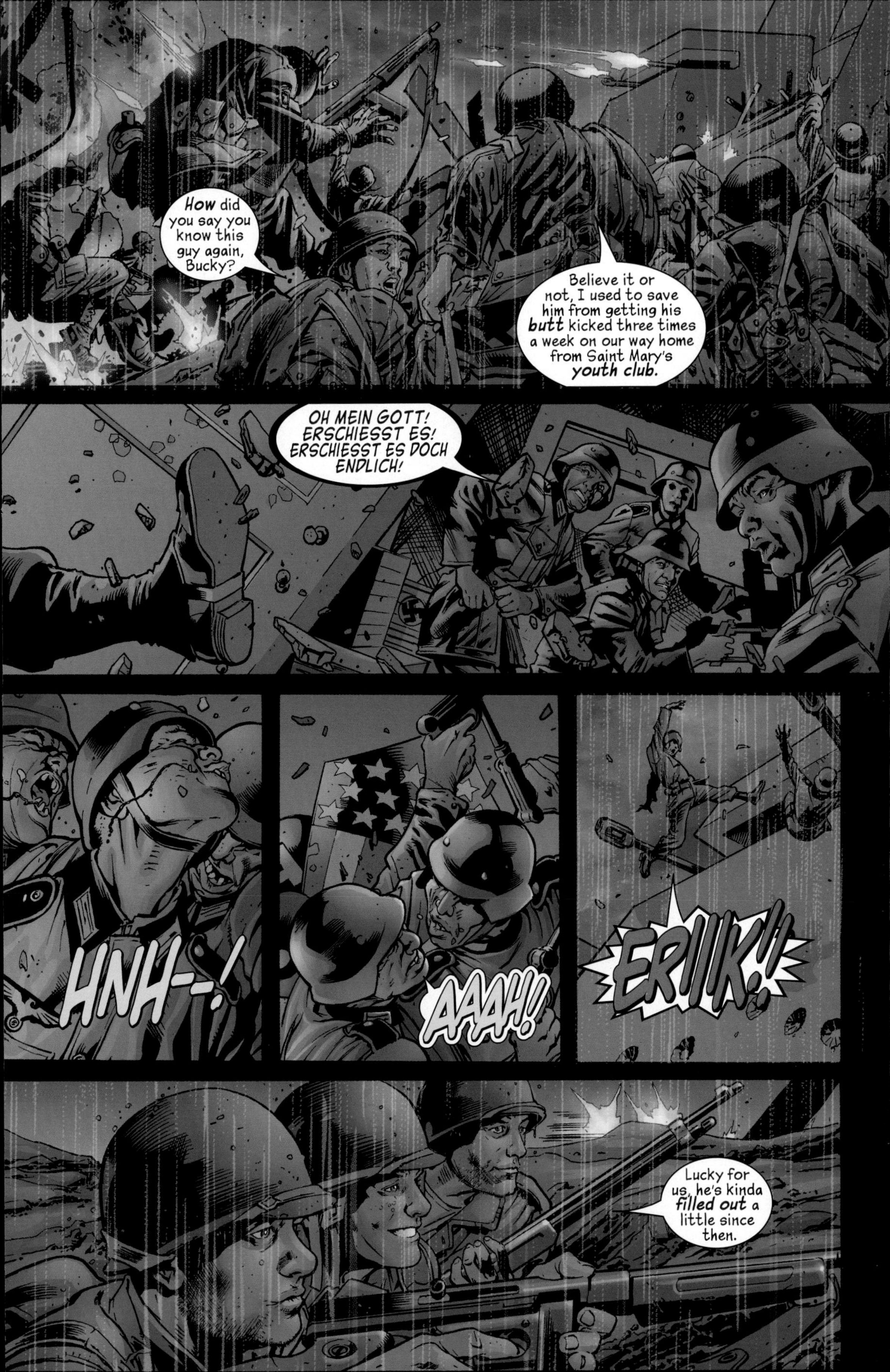
How did you say you know this guy again, Bucky?
Believe it or not, I used to save him from getting his butt kicked three times a week on our way home from Saint Mary's youth club.
OH MEIN GOTT! ERSCHIESST ES! ERSCHIESST ES DOCH ENDLICH!
HNH--!
AAAH!
ERIIK!!
Lucky for us, he's kinda filled out a little since then.

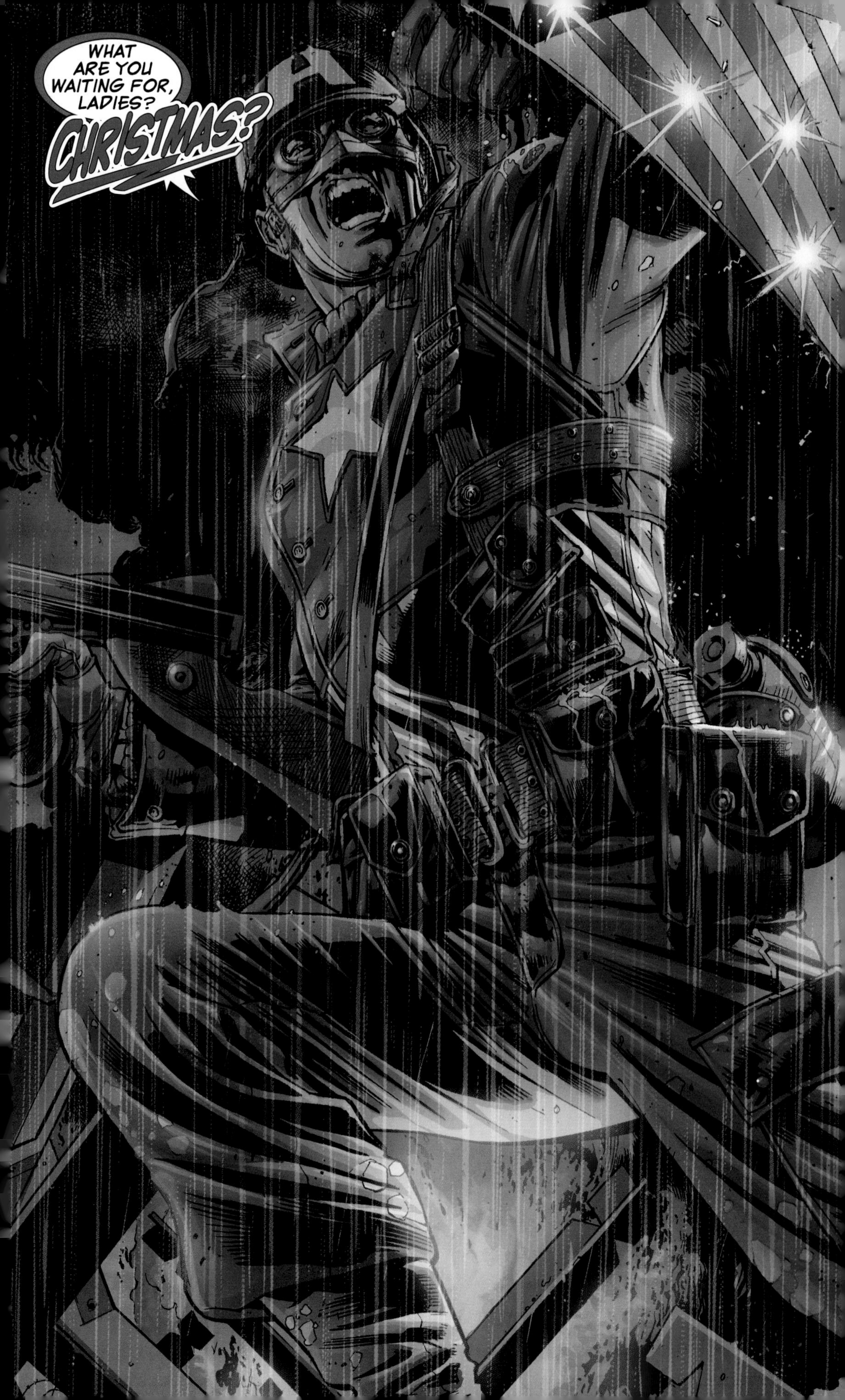
WHAT ARE YOU WAITING FOR, LADIES? CHRISTMAS?

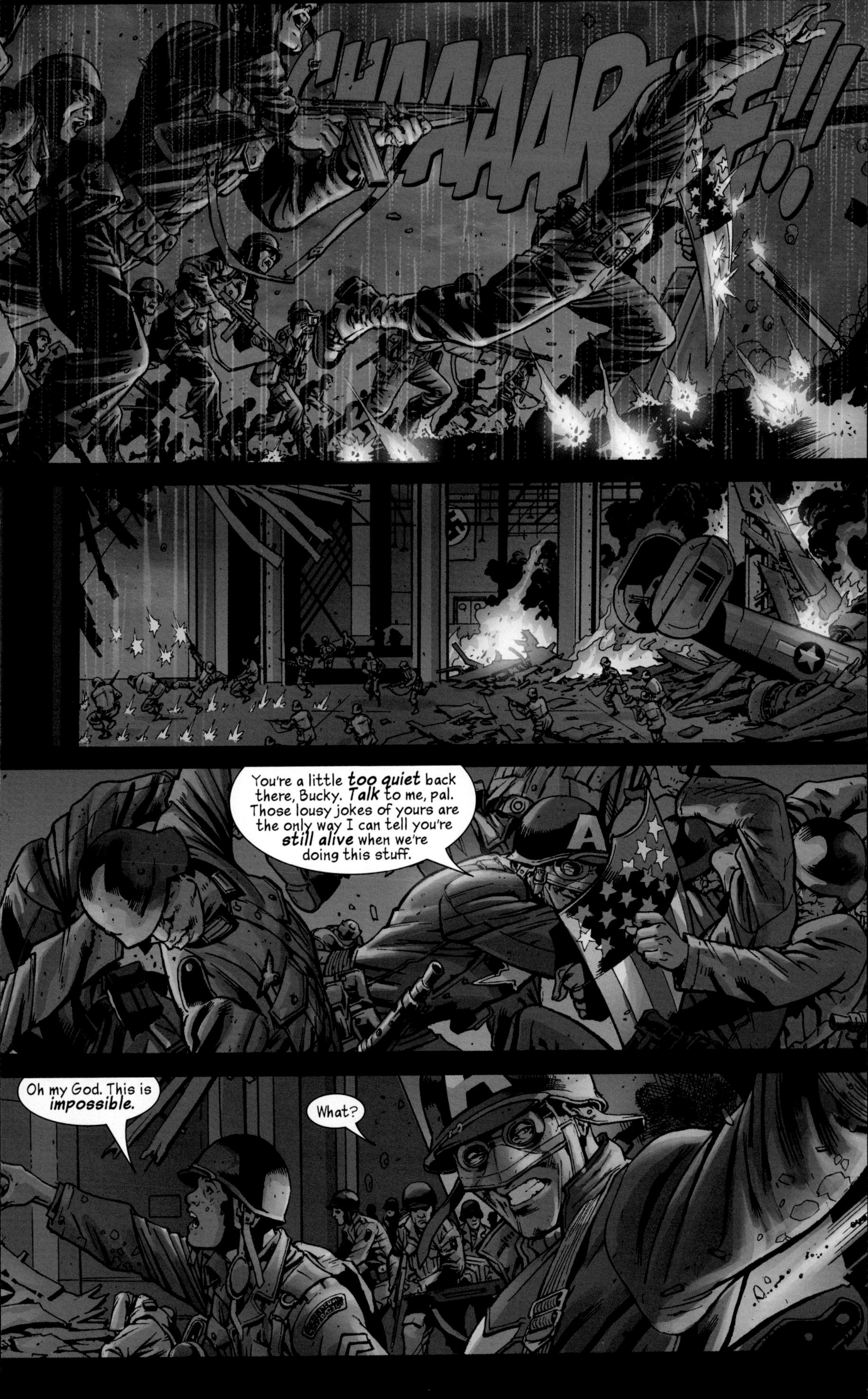
CHAAAARGE!!
You're a little too quiet back there, Bucky. Talk to me, pal. Those lousy jokes of yours are the only way I can tell you're still alive when we're doing this stuff.
Oh my God. This is impossible.
What?

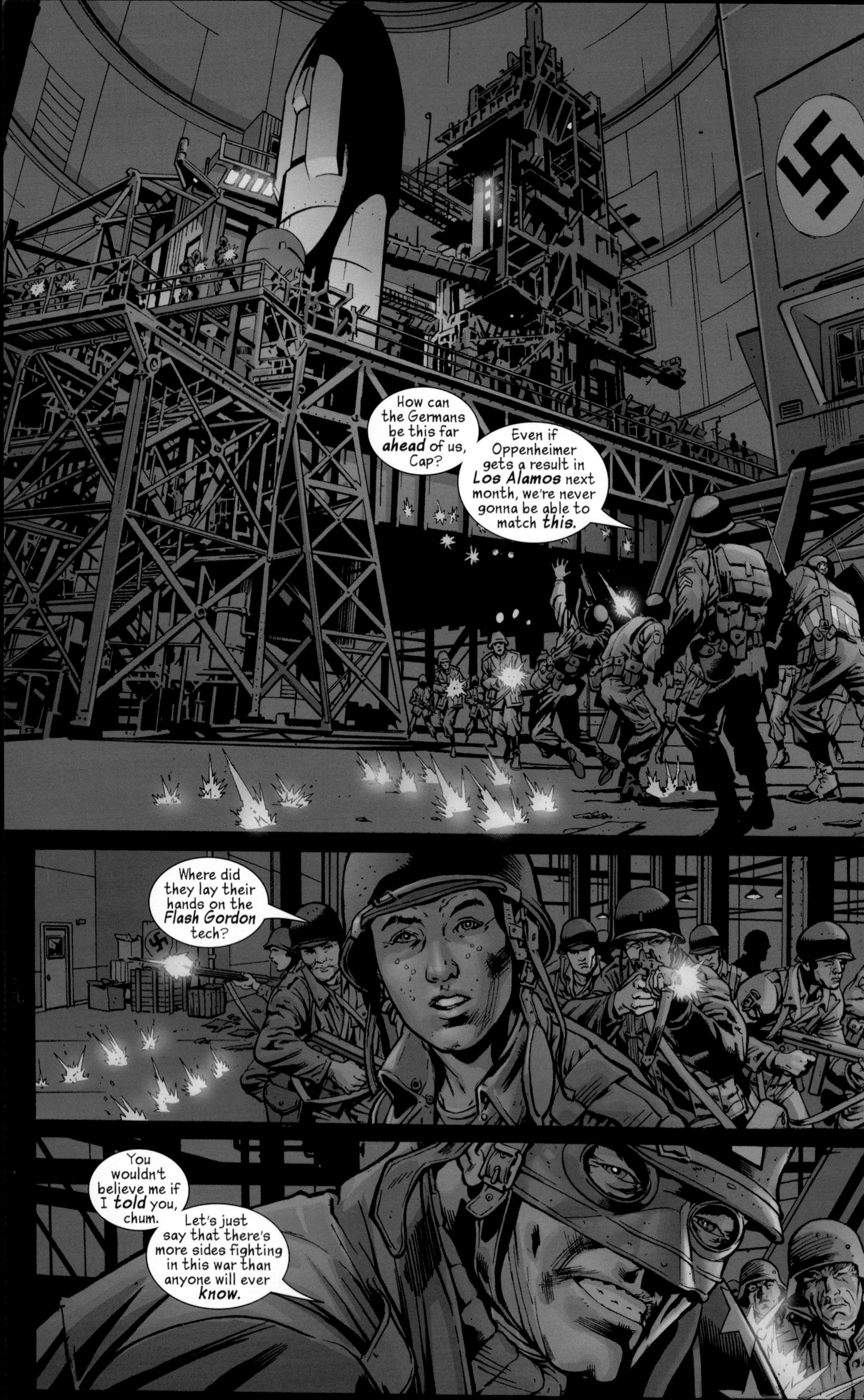
How can the Germans be this far **ahead** of us, Cap?
Even if Oppenheimer gets a result in **Los Alamos** next month, we're never gonna be able to match **this.**
Where did they lay their hands on the **Flash Gordon** tech?
You wouldn't believe me if I **told** you, chum.
Let's just say that there's more sides fighting in this war than anyone will ever **know.**

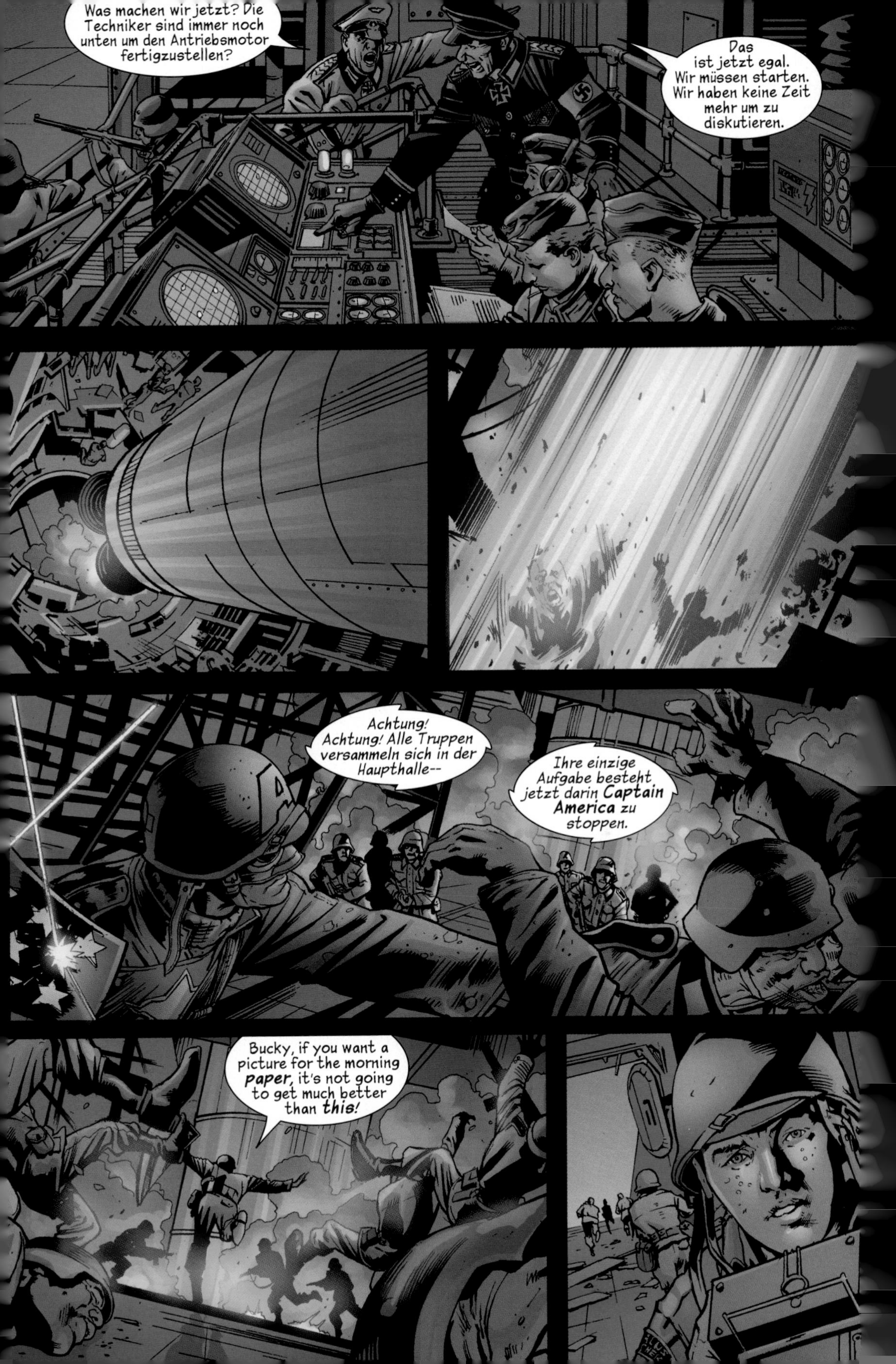
Was machen wir jetzt? Die Techniker sind immer noch unten um den Antriebsmotor fertigzustellen?
Das ist jetzt egal. Wir müssen starten. Wir haben keine Zeit mehr um zu diskutieren.
Achtung! Achtung! Alle Truppen versammeln sich in der Haupthalle--
Ihre einzige Aufgabe besteht jetzt darin **Captain America** zu stoppen.
Bucky, if you want a picture for the morning ***paper***, it's not going to get much better than ***this***!

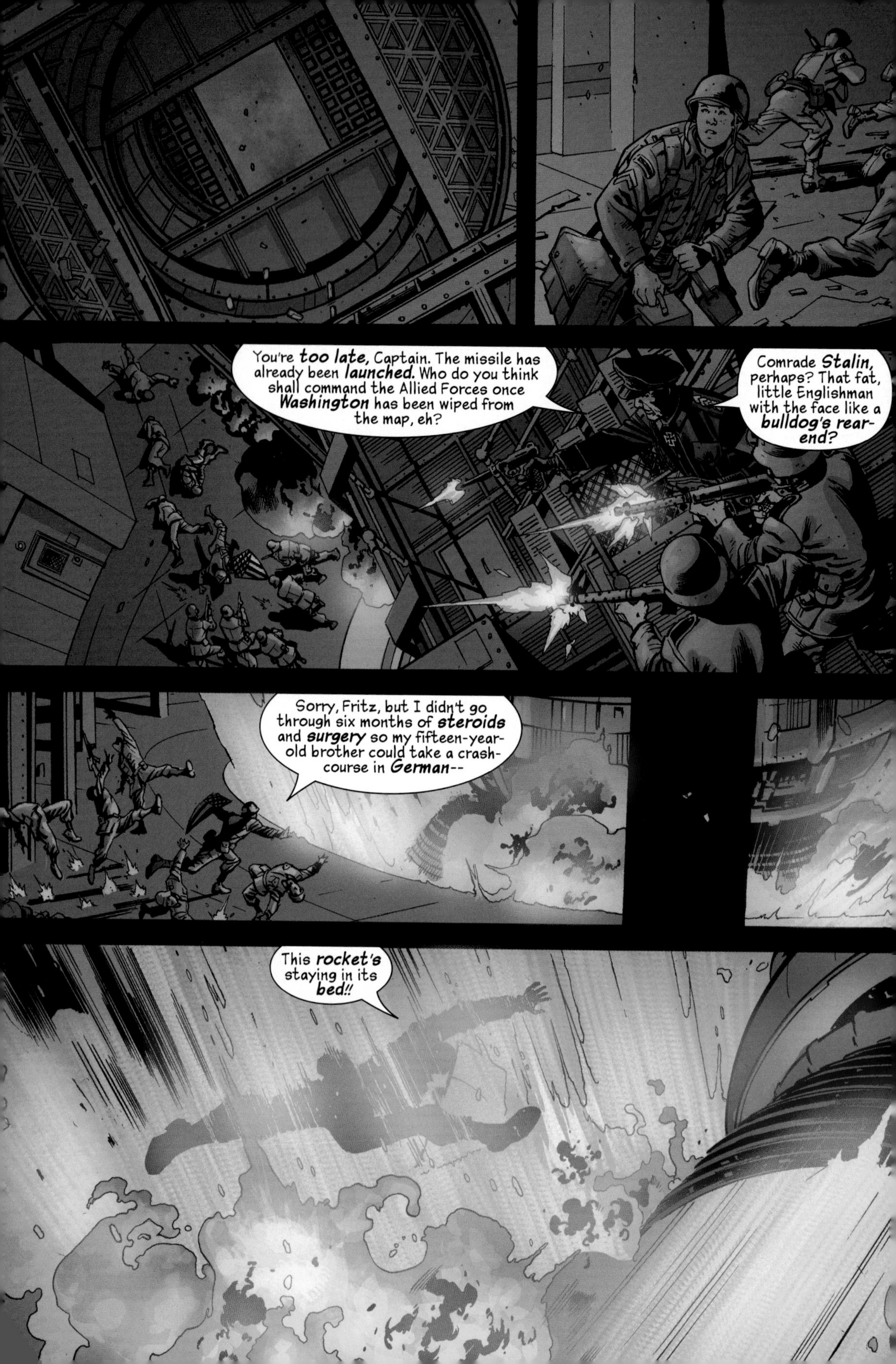
You're too late, Captain. The missile has already been launched. Who do you think shall command the Allied Forces once Washington has been wiped from the map, eh?
Comrade Stalin, perhaps? That fat, little Englishman with the face like a bulldog's rear-end?
Sorry, Fritz, but I didn't go through six months of steroids and surgery so my fifteen-year-old brother could take a crash-course in German--
This rocket's staying in its bed!!

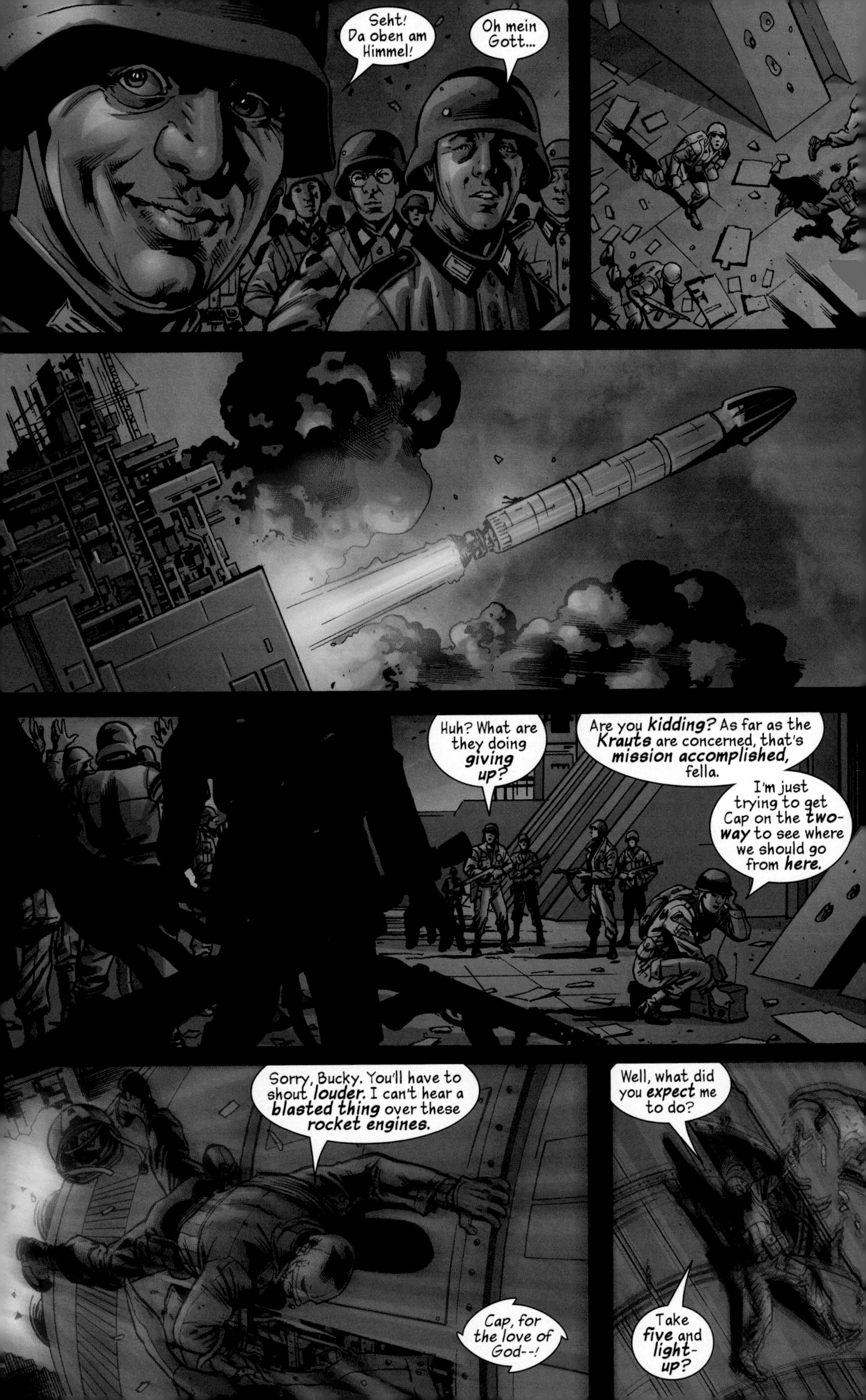
Seht! Da oben am Himmel!
Oh mein Gott...
Huh? What are they doing giving up?
Are you kidding? As far as the Krauts are concerned, that's mission accomplished, fella.
I'm just trying to get Cap on the two-way to see where we should go from here.
Sorry, Bucky. You'll have to shout louder. I can't hear a blasted thing over these rocket engines.
Cap, for the love of God--!
Well, what did you expect me to do?
Take five and light-up?

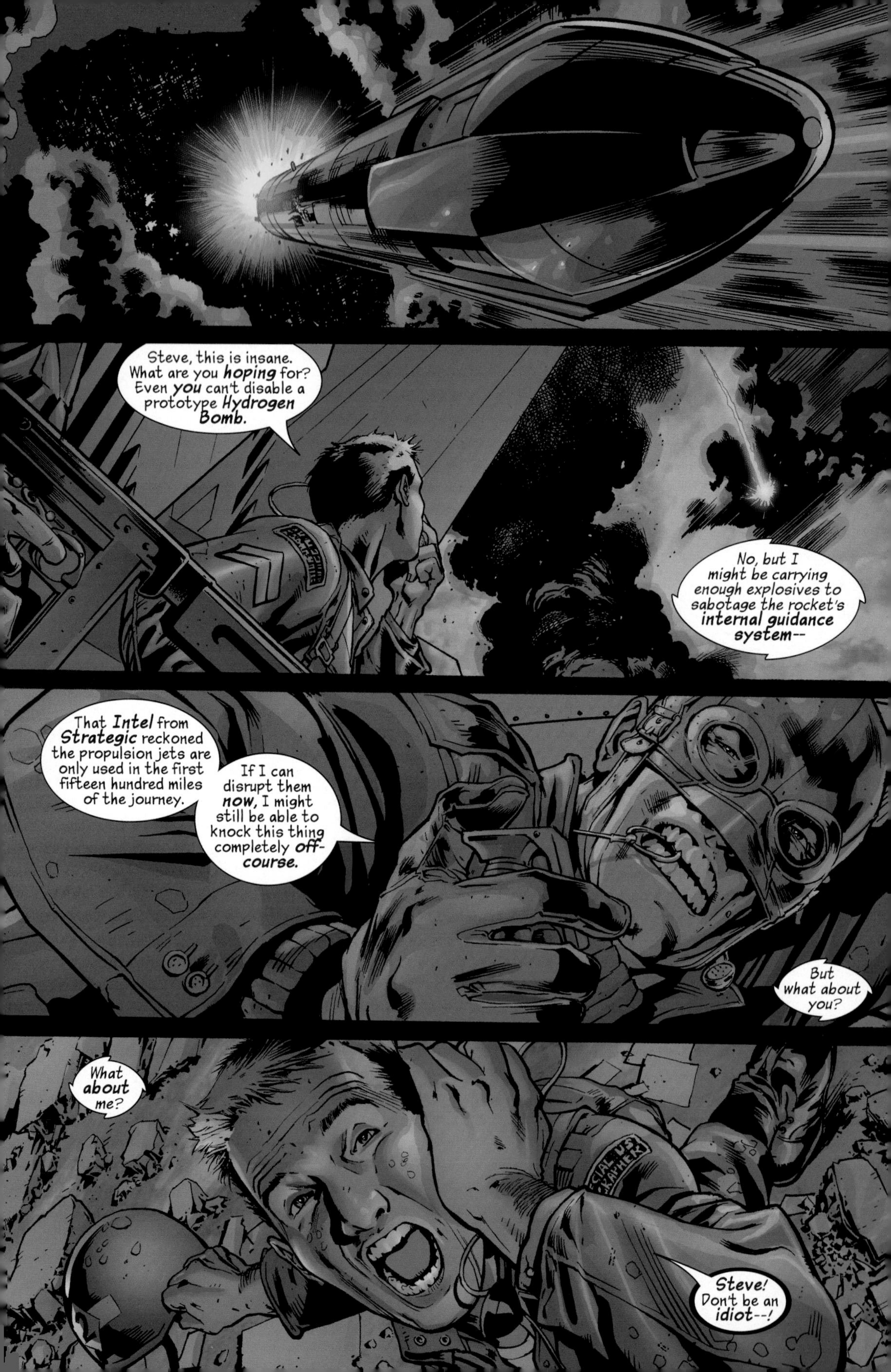

Steve, this is insane. What are you **hoping** for? Even **you** can't disable a prototype **Hydrogen Bomb.**
No, but I might be carrying enough explosives to sabotage the rocket's **internal guidance system--**
That **Intel** from **Strategic** reckoned the propulsion jets are only used in the first fifteen hundred miles of the journey.
If I can disrupt them **now,** I might still be able to knock this thing completely **off-course.**
But what about you?
What **about** me?
Steve! Don't be an **idiot--!**

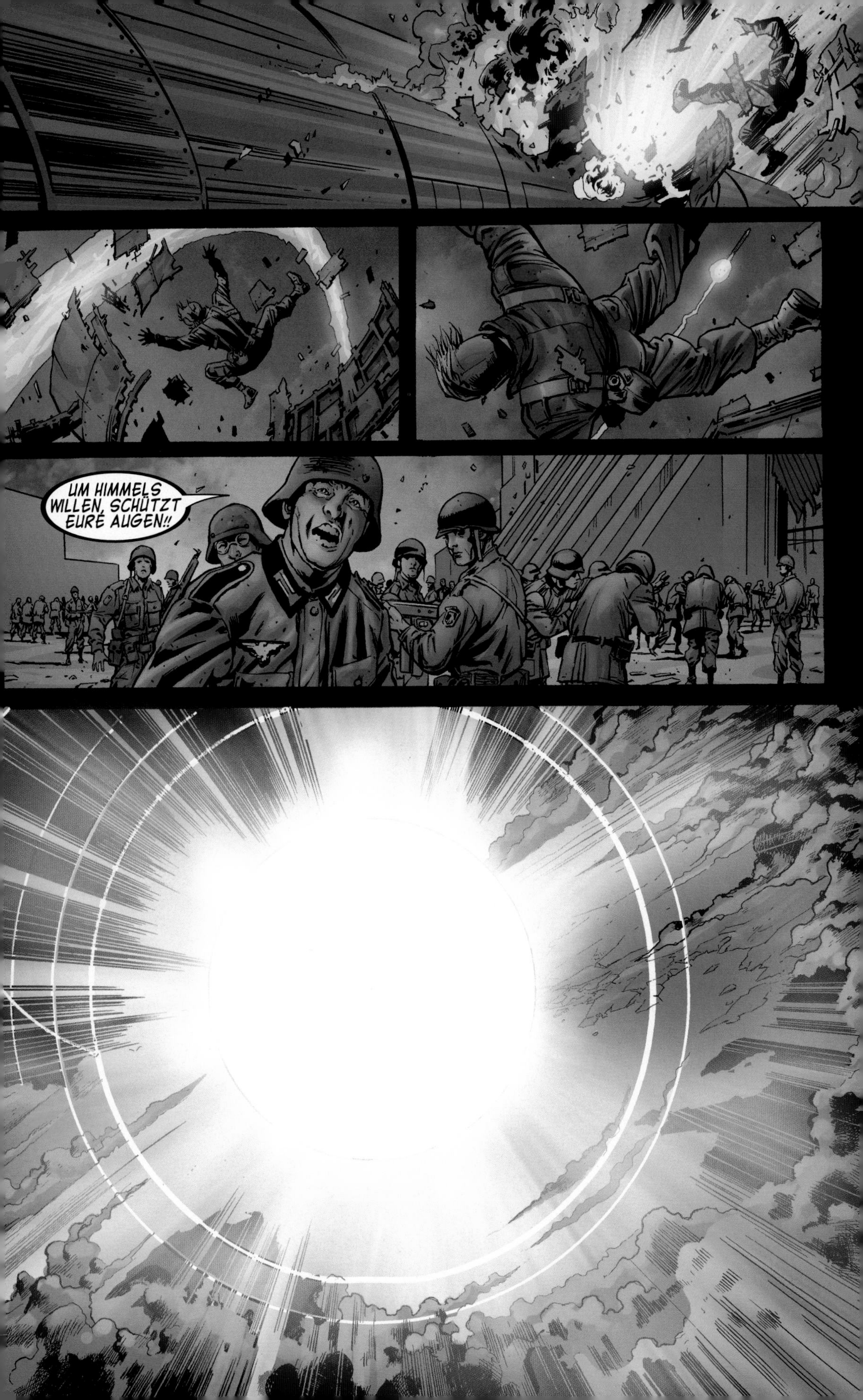
UM HIMMELS WILLEN, SCHÜTZT EURE AUGEN!!

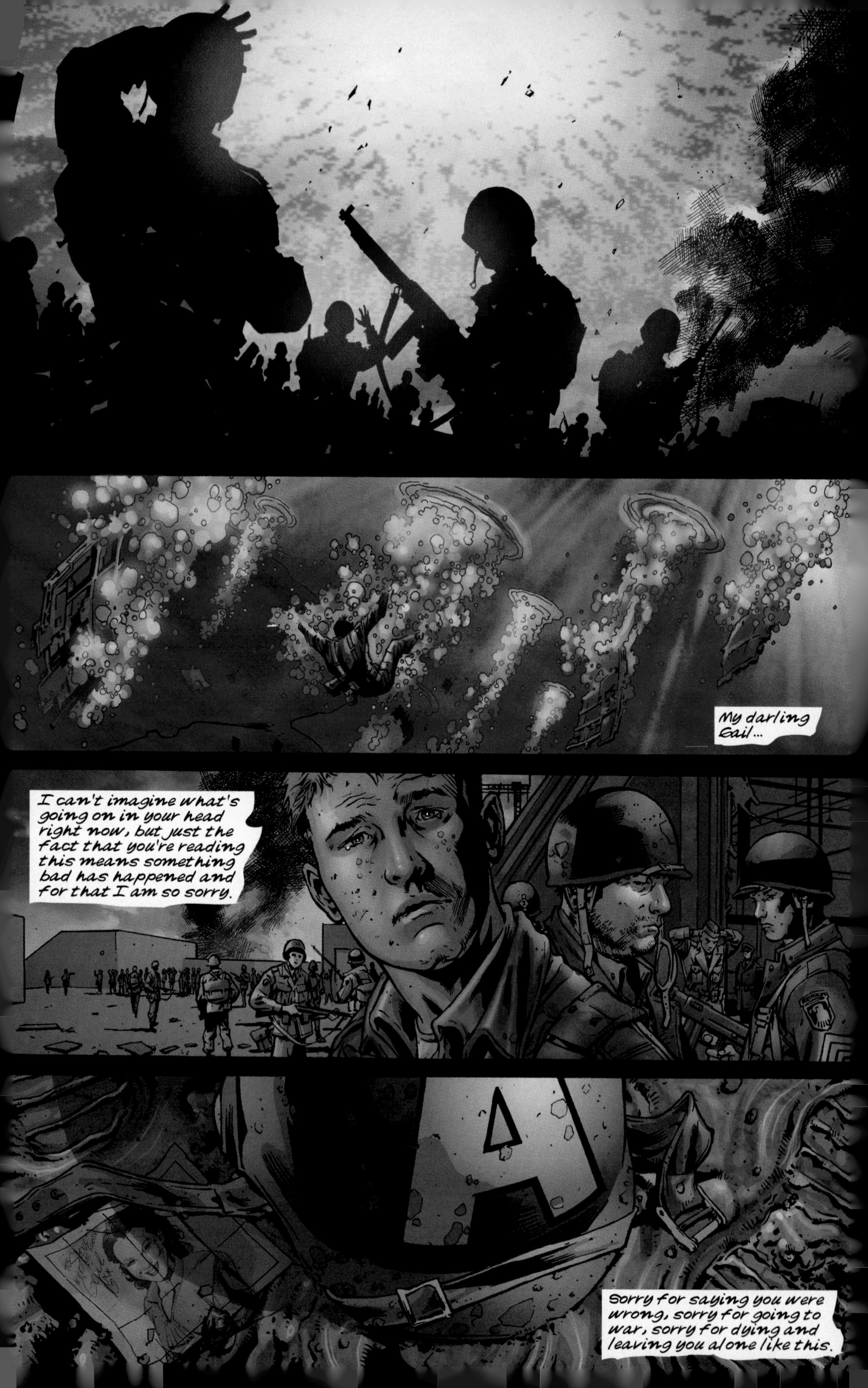
My darling Gail...
I can't imagine what's going on in your head right now, but just the fact that you're reading this means something bad has happened and for that I am so sorry.
Sorry for saying you were wrong, sorry for going to war, sorry for dying and leaving you alone like this.

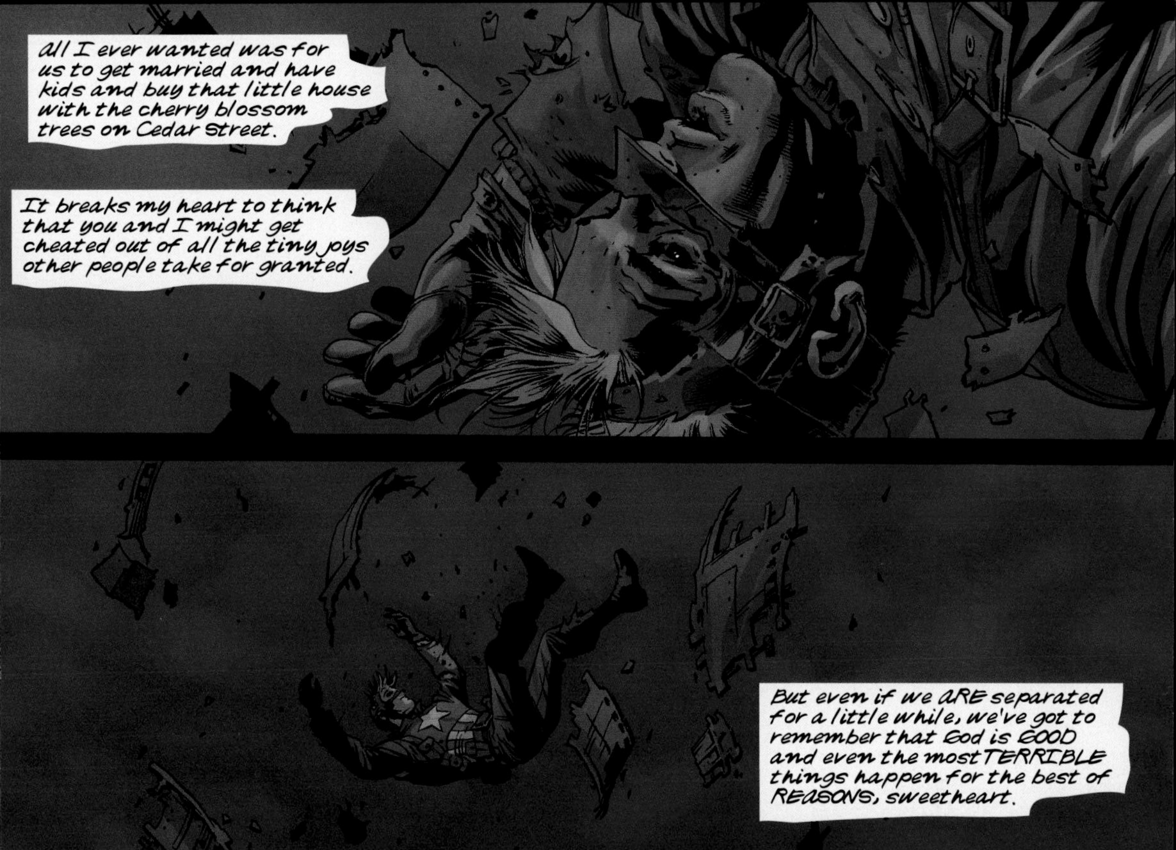
All I ever wanted was for us to get married and have kids and buy that little house with the cherry blossom trees on Cedar Street.
It breaks my heart to think that you and I might get cheated out of all the tiny joys other people take for granted.
But even if we ARE separated for a little while, we've got to remember that God is GOOD and even the most TERRIBLE things happen for the best of REASONS, sweetheart.

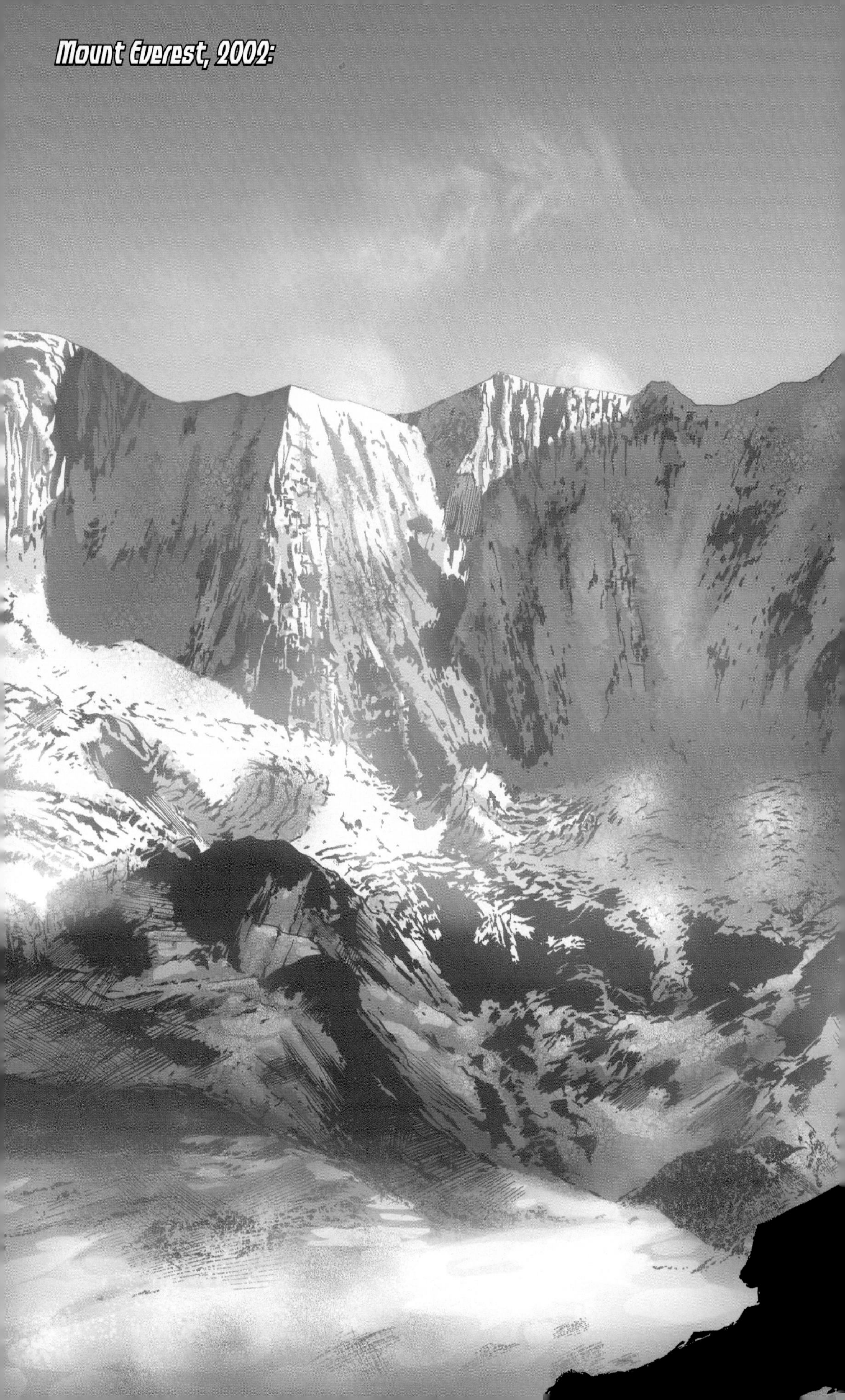
Mount Everest, 2002:

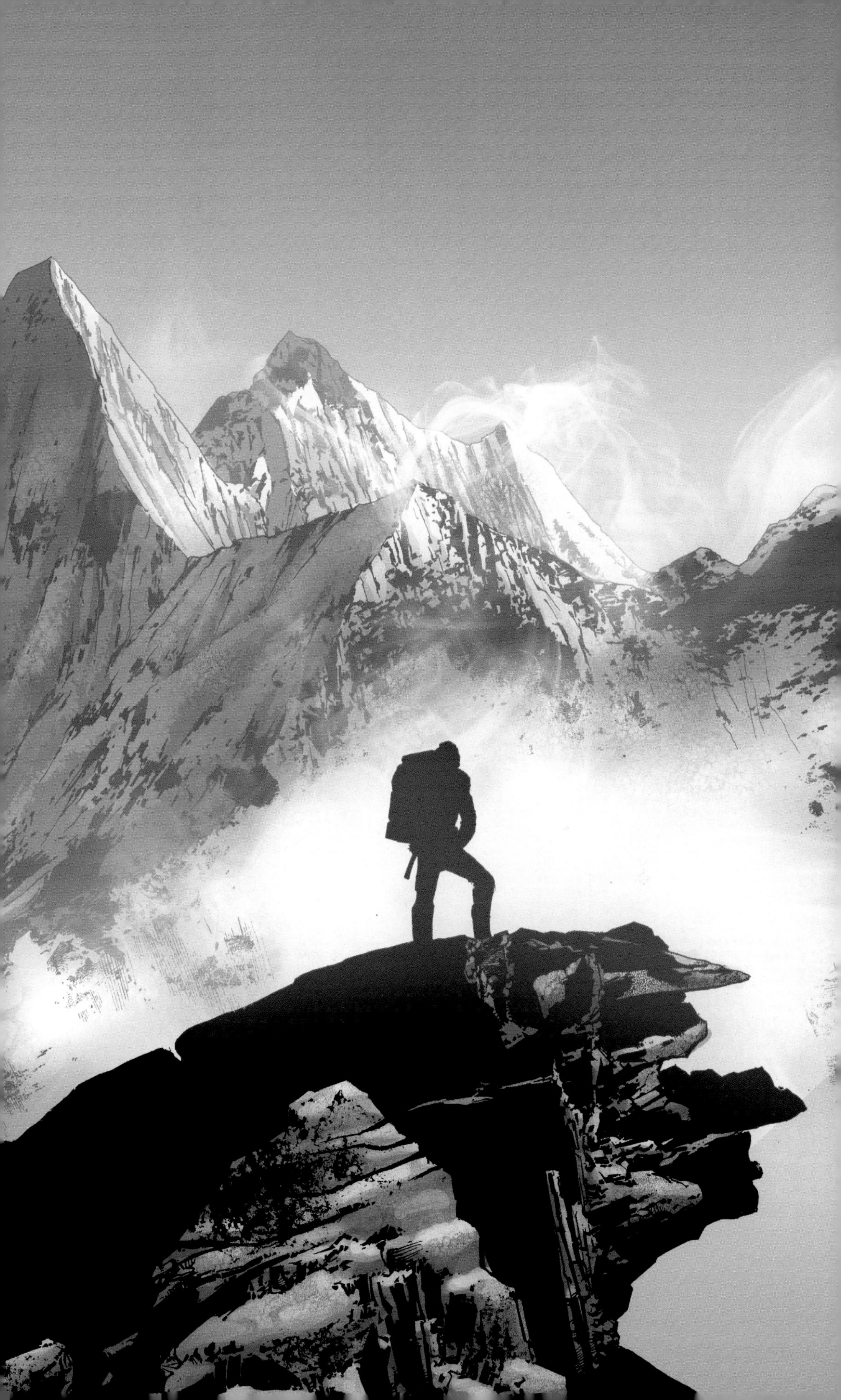

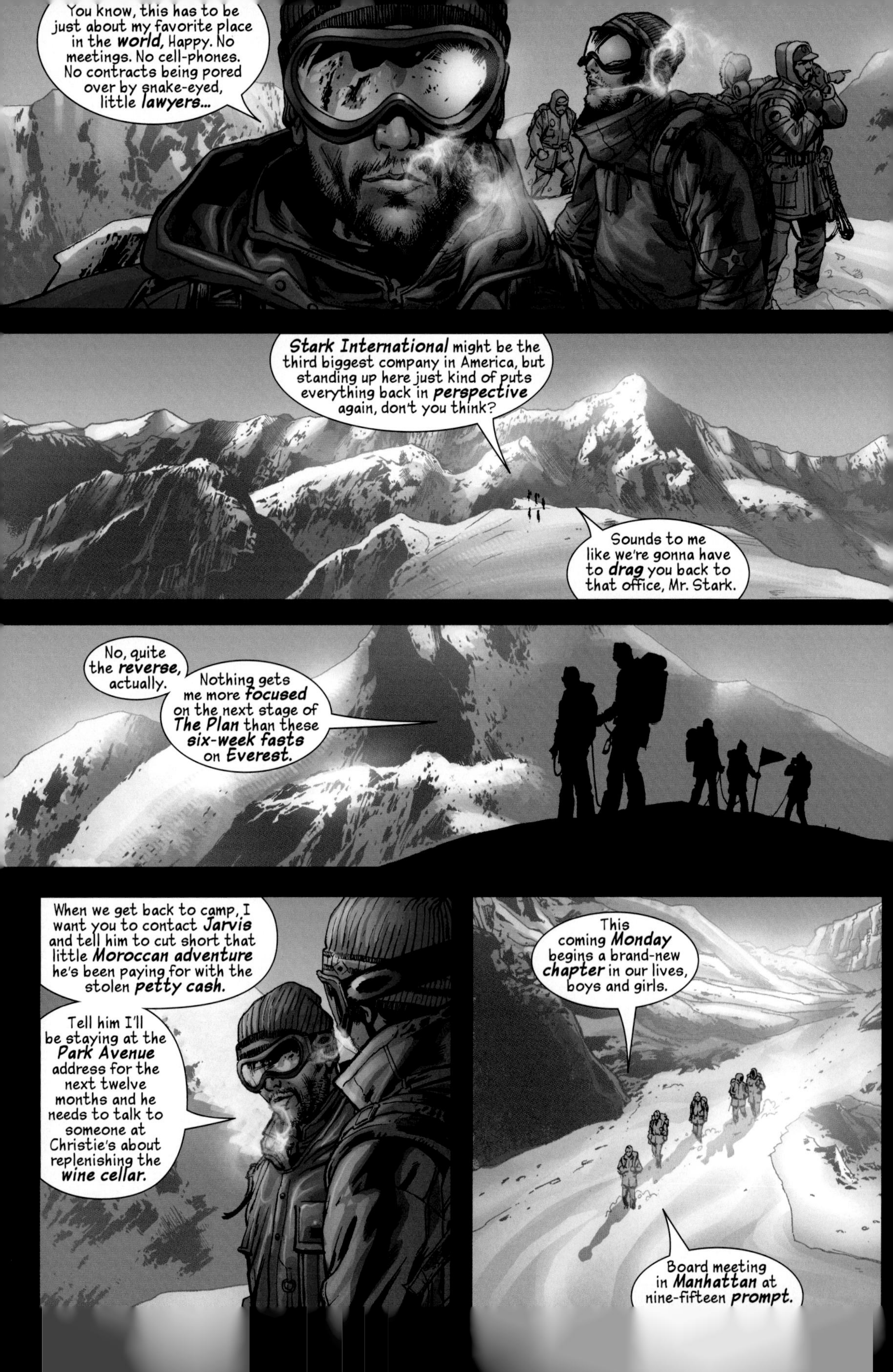
You know, this has to be just about my favorite place in the world, Happy. No meetings. No cell-phones. No contracts being pored over by snake-eyed, little lawyers...
Stark International might be the third biggest company in America, but standing up here just kind of puts everything back in perspective again, don't you think?
Sounds to me like we're gonna have to drag you back to that office, Mr. Stark.
No, quite the reverse, actually.
Nothing gets me more focused on the next stage of The Plan than these six-week fasts on Everest.
When we get back to camp, I want you to contact Jarvis and tell him to cut short that little Moroccan adventure he's been paying for with the stolen petty cash.
Tell him I'll be staying at the Park Avenue address for the next twelve months and he needs to talk to someone at Christie's about replenishing the wine cellar.
This coming Monday begins a brand-new chapter in our lives, boys and girls.
Board meeting in Manhattan at nine-fifteen prompt.

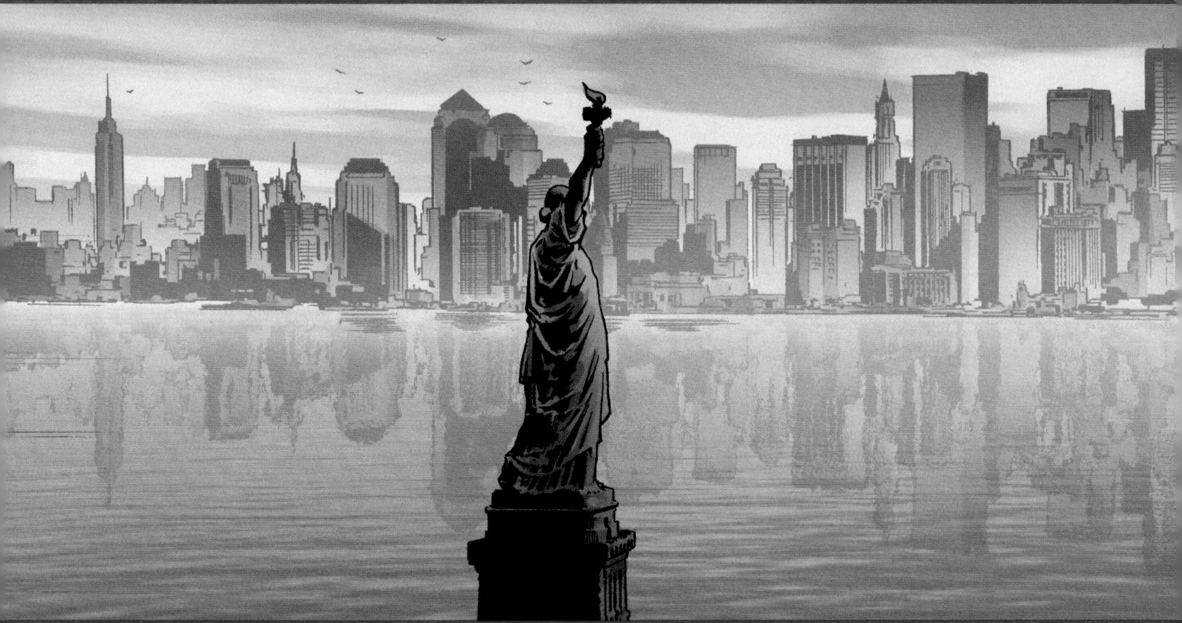

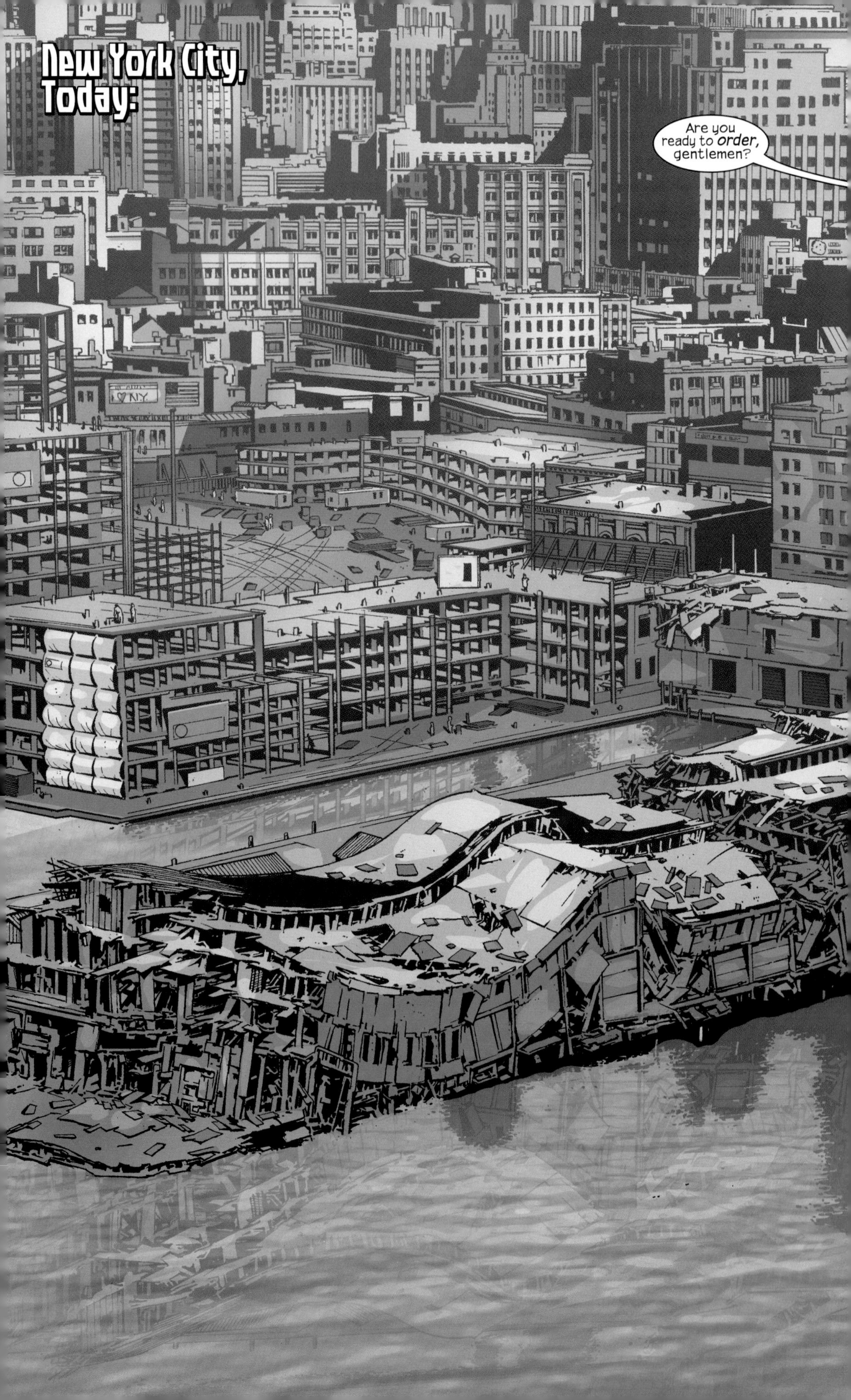
New York City, Today:
Are you ready to *order*, gentlemen?

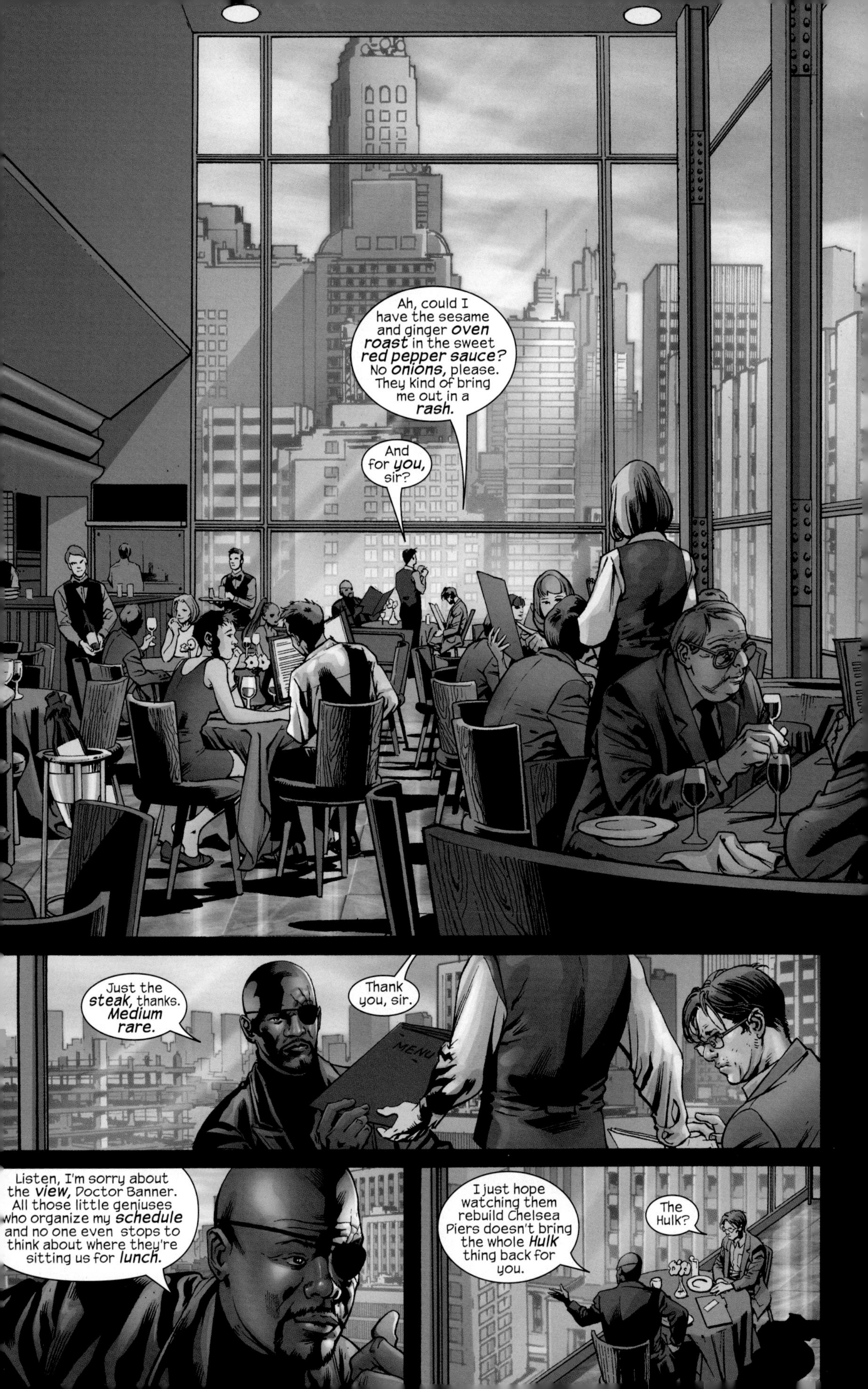
Ah, could I have the sesame and ginger oven roast in the sweet red pepper sauce? No onions, please. They kind of bring me out in a rash.
And for you, sir?
Just the steak, thanks. Medium rare.
Thank you, sir.
MENU
Listen, I'm sorry about the view, Doctor Banner. All those little geniuses who organize my schedule and no one even stops to think about where they're sitting us for lunch.
I just hope watching them rebuild Chelsea Piers doesn't bring the whole Hulk thing back for you.
The Hulk?

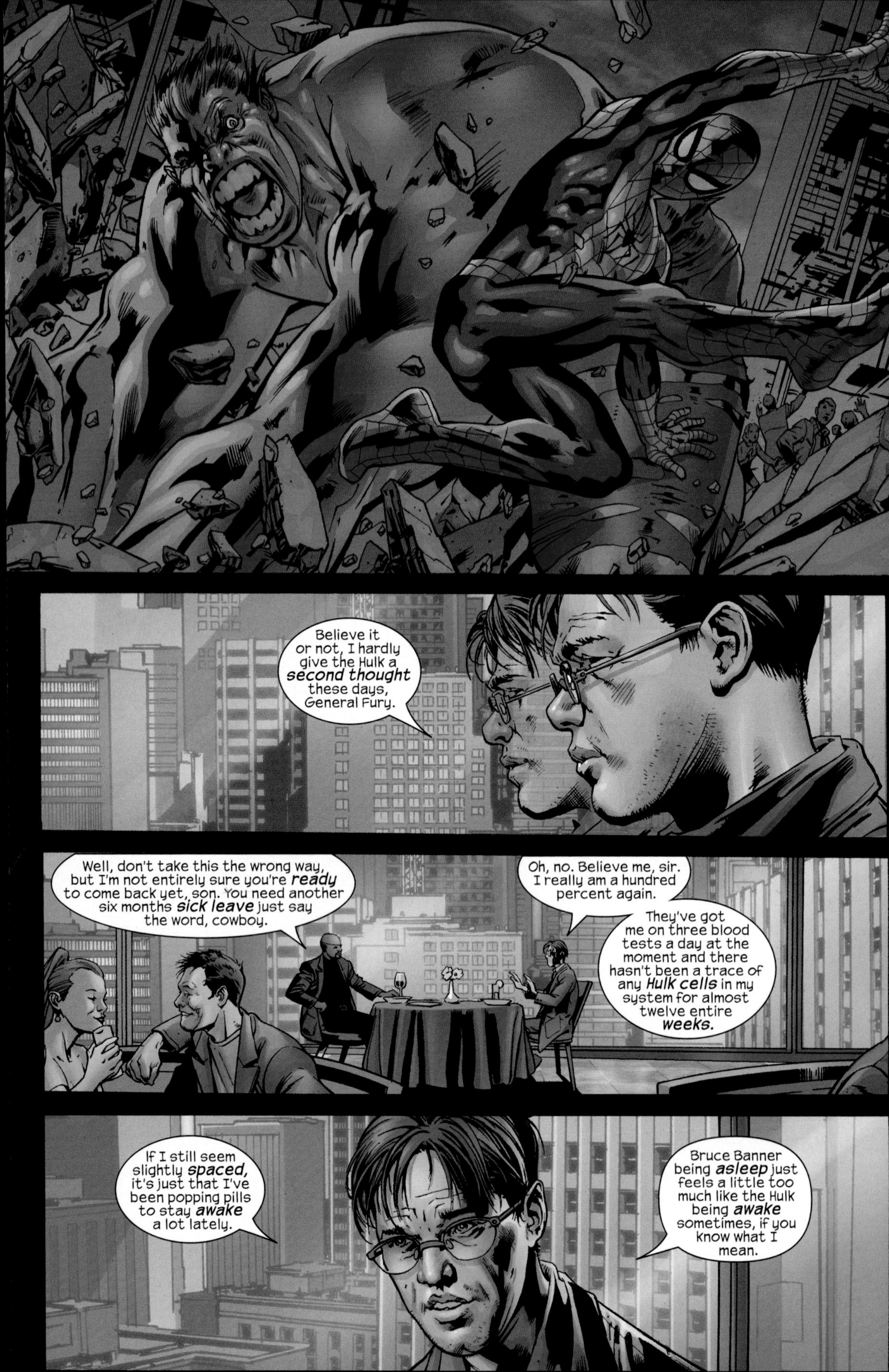
Believe it or not, I hardly give the Hulk a *second thought* these days, General Fury.
Well, don't take this the wrong way, but I'm not entirely sure you're *ready* to come back yet, son. You need another six months *sick leave* just say the word, cowboy.
Oh, no. Believe me, sir. I really am a hundred percent again.
They've got me on three blood tests a day at the moment and there hasn't been a trace of any *Hulk cells* in my system for almost twelve entire *weeks.*
If I still seem slightly *spaced,* it's just that I've been popping pills to stay *awake* a lot lately.
Bruce Banner being *asleep* just feels a little too much like the Hulk being *awake* sometimes, if you know what I mean.

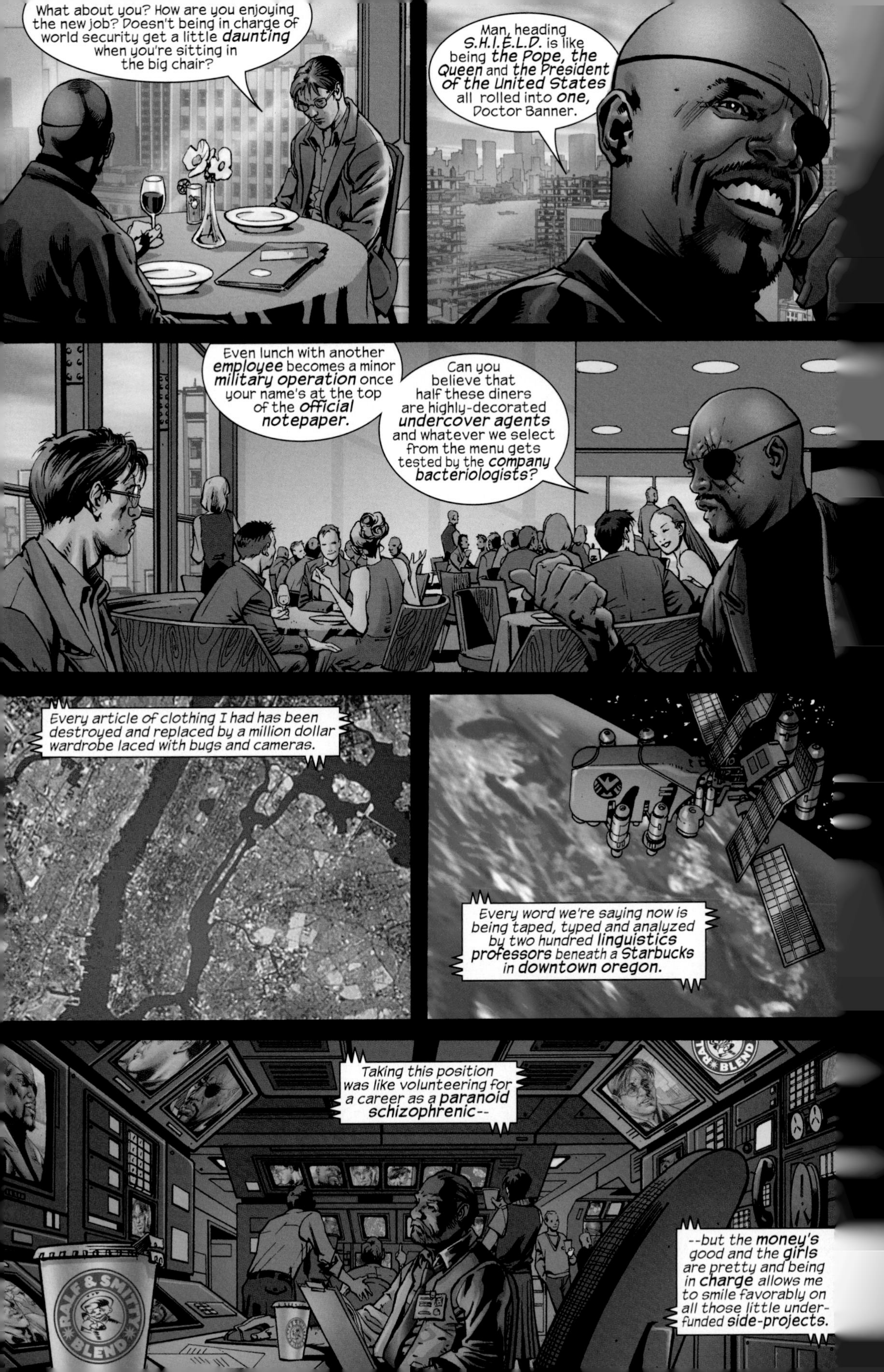
What about you? How are you enjoying the new job? Doesn't being in charge of world security get a little daunting when you're sitting in the big chair?
Man, heading S.H.I.E.L.D. is like being the Pope, the Queen and the President of the United States all rolled into one, Doctor Banner.
Even lunch with another employee becomes a minor military operation once your name's at the top of the official notepaper.
Can you believe that half these diners are highly-decorated undercover agents and whatever we select from the menu gets tested by the company bacteriologists?
Every article of clothing I had has been destroyed and replaced by a million dollar wardrobe laced with bugs and cameras.
Every word we're saying now is being taped, typed and analyzed by two hundred linguistics professors beneath a Starbucks in downtown oregon.
Taking this position was like volunteering for a career as a paranoid schizophrenic--
--but the money's good and the girls are pretty and being in charge allows me to smile favorably on all those little under-funded side-projects.

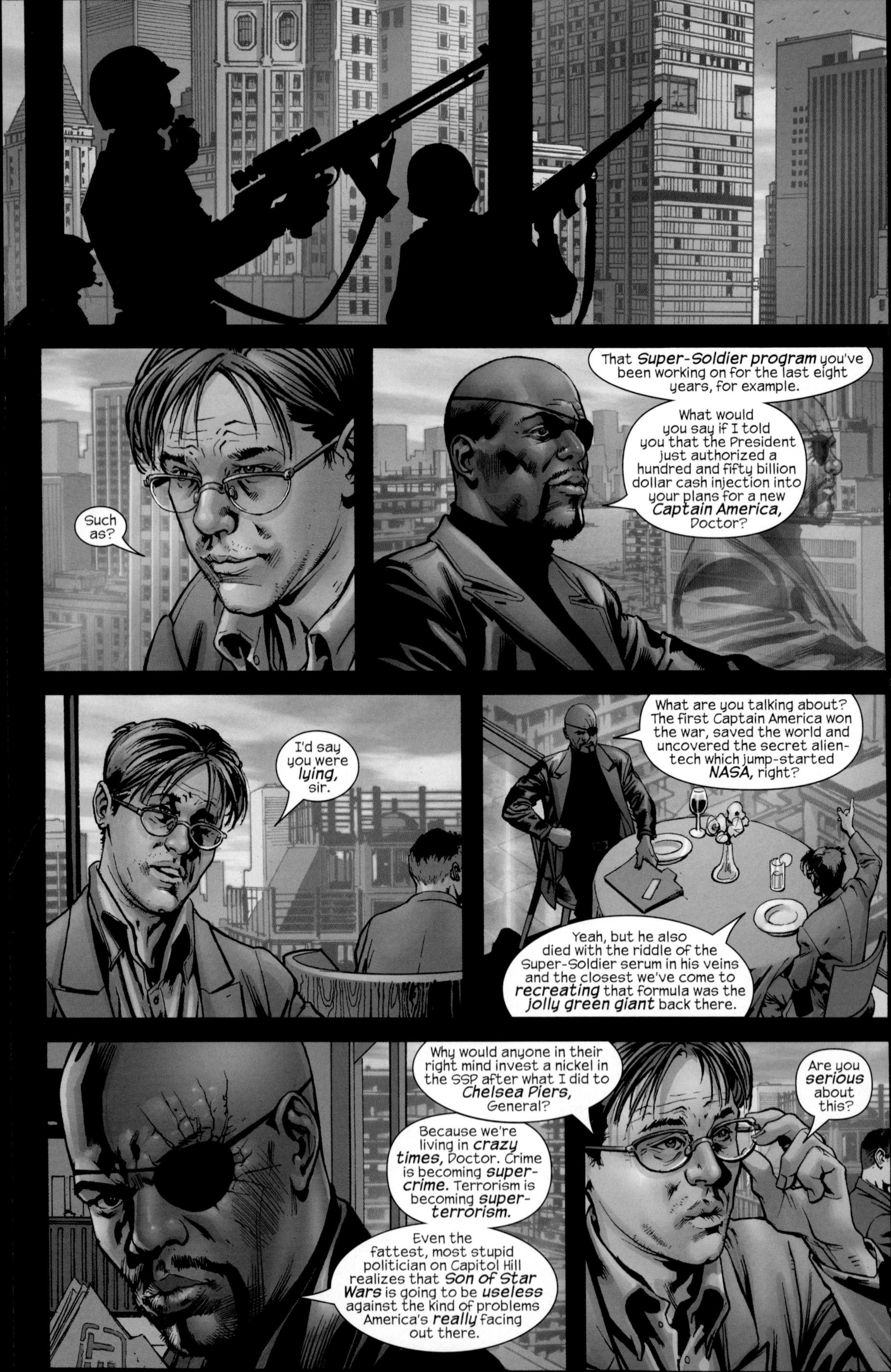
Such as?
That *Super-Soldier program* you've been working on for the last eight years, for example.
What would you say if I told you that the President just authorized a hundred and fifty billion dollar cash injection into your plans for a new *Captain America,* Doctor?
I'd say you were *lying,* sir.
What are you talking about? The first Captain America won the war, saved the world and uncovered the secret alien-tech which jump-started *NASA,* right?
Yeah, but he also died with the riddle of the Super-Soldier serum in his veins and the closest we've come to *recreating* that formula was the *jolly green giant* back there.
Why would anyone in their right mind invest a nickel in the SSP after what I did to *Chelsea Piers,* General?
Because we're living in *crazy times,* Doctor. Crime is becoming *super-crime.* Terrorism is becoming *super-terrorism.*
Even the fattest, most stupid politician on Capitol Hill realizes that *Son of Star Wars* is going to be *useless* against the kind of problems America's *really* facing out there.
Are you *serious* about this?

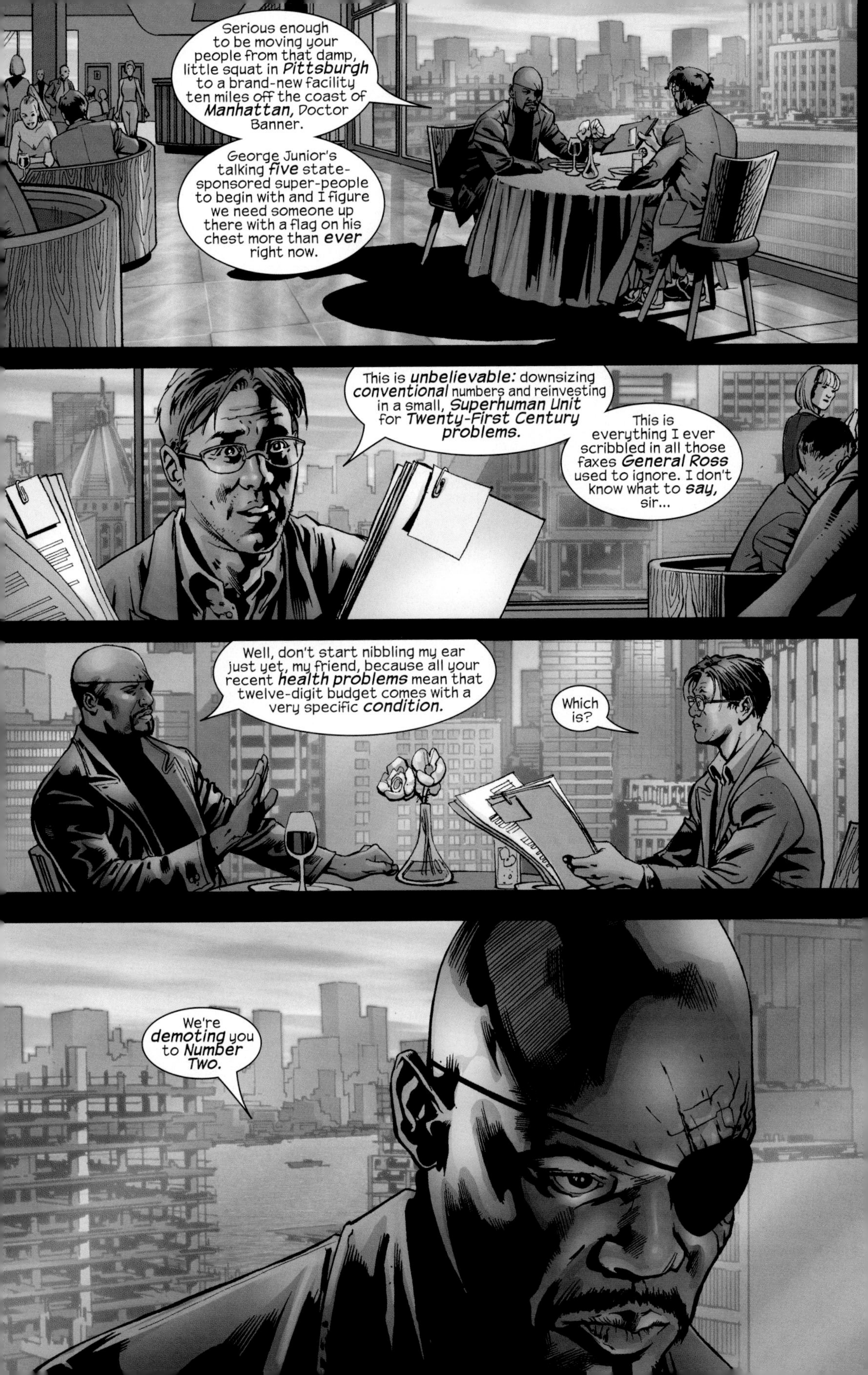
Serious enough to be moving your people from that damp, little squat in Pittsburgh to a brand-new facility ten miles off the coast of Manhattan, Doctor Banner.
George Junior's talking five state-sponsored super-people to begin with and I figure we need someone up there with a flag on his chest more than ever right now.
This is unbelievable: downsizing conventional numbers and reinvesting in a small, Superhuman Unit for Twenty-First Century problems.
This is everything I ever scribbled in all those faxes General Ross used to ignore. I don't know what to say, sir...
Well, don't start nibbling my ear just yet, my friend, because all your recent health problems mean that twelve-digit budget comes with a very specific condition.
Which is?
We're demoting you to Number Two.

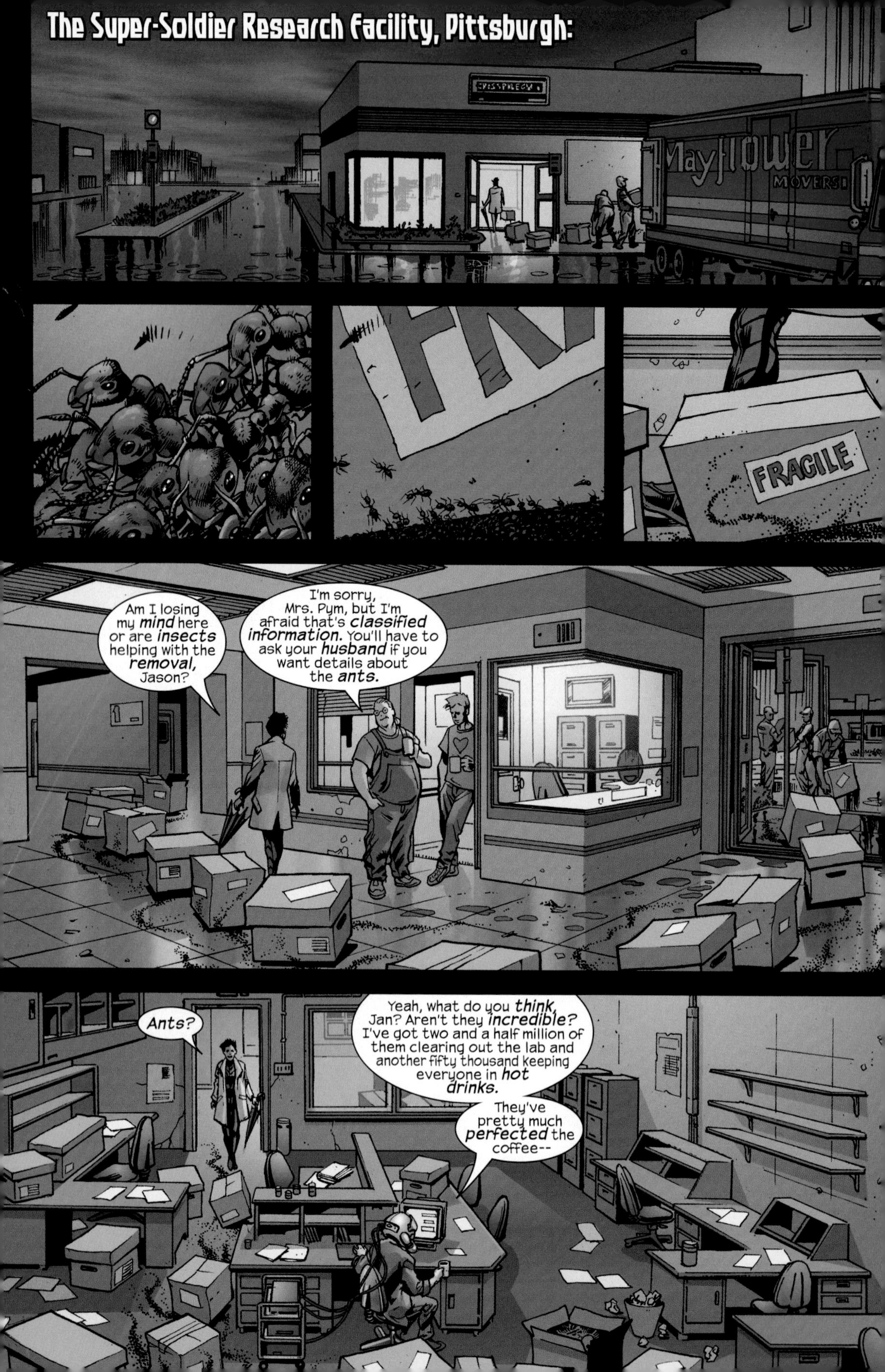
The Super-Soldier Research Facility, Pittsburgh:
Mayflower
MOVERS
FRAGILE
Am I losing my *mind* here or are *insects* helping with the *removal,* Jason?
I'm sorry, Mrs. Pym, but I'm afraid that's *classified information.* You'll have to ask your *husband* if you want details about the *ants.*
Ants?
Yeah, what do you *think,* Jan? Aren't they *incredible?* I've got two and a half million of them clearing out the lab and another fifty thousand keeping everyone in *hot drinks.*
They've pretty much *perfected* the coffee--

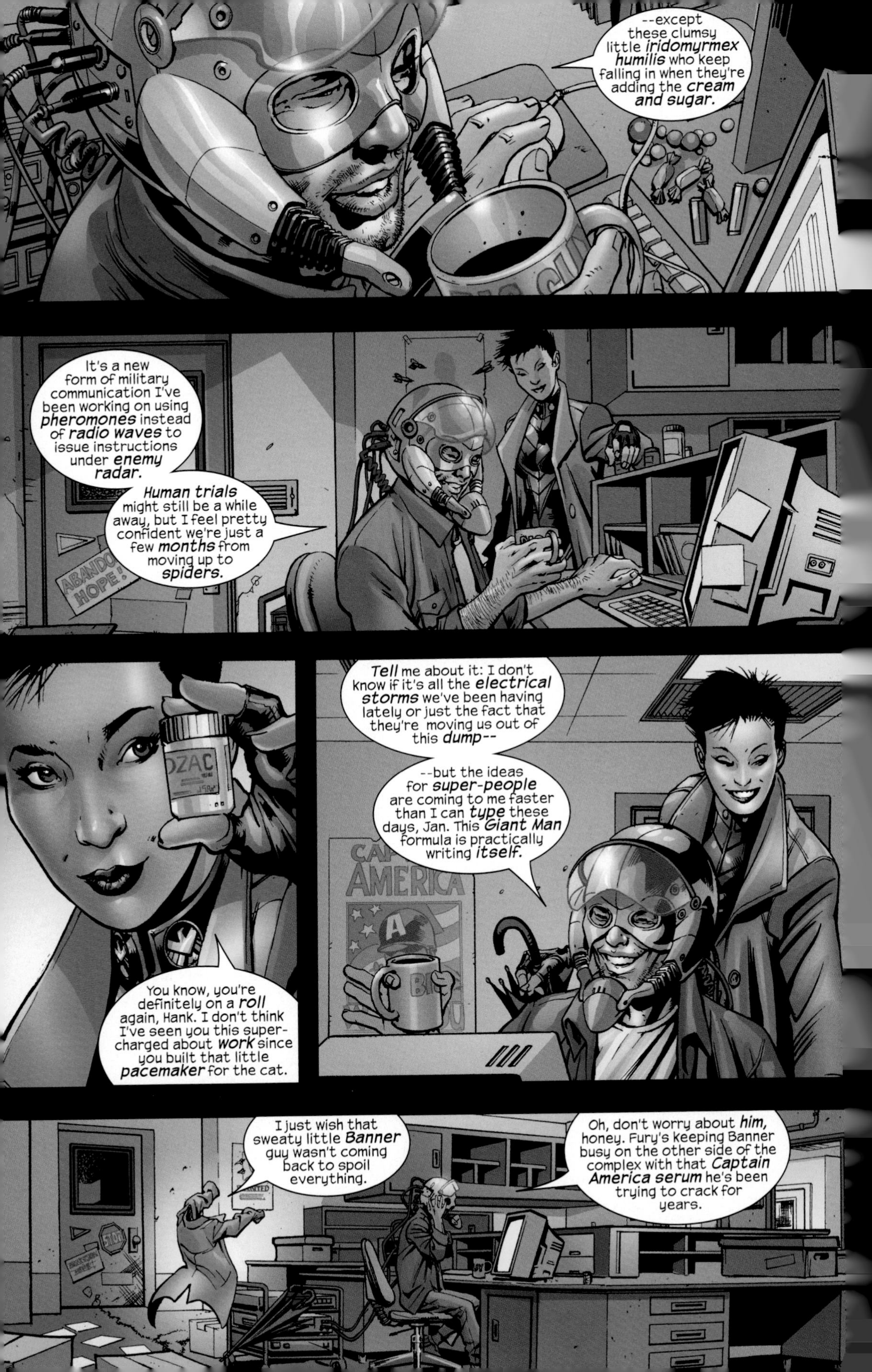
--except these clumsy little iridomyrmex humilis who keep falling in when they're adding the cream and sugar.
It's a new form of military communication I've been working on using pheromones instead of radio waves to issue instructions under enemy radar.
Human trials might still be a while away, but I feel pretty confident we're just a few months from moving up to spiders.
You know, you're definitely on a roll again, Hank. I don't think I've seen you this super-charged about work since you built that little pacemaker for the cat.
Tell me about it: I don't know if it's all the electrical storms we've been having lately or just the fact that they're moving us out of this dump--
--but the ideas for super-people are coming to me faster than I can type these days, Jan. This Giant Man formula is practically writing itself.
AMERICA
I just wish that sweaty little Banner guy wasn't coming back to spoil everything.
Oh, don't worry about him, honey. Fury's keeping Banner busy on the other side of the complex with that Captain America serum he's been trying to crack for years.

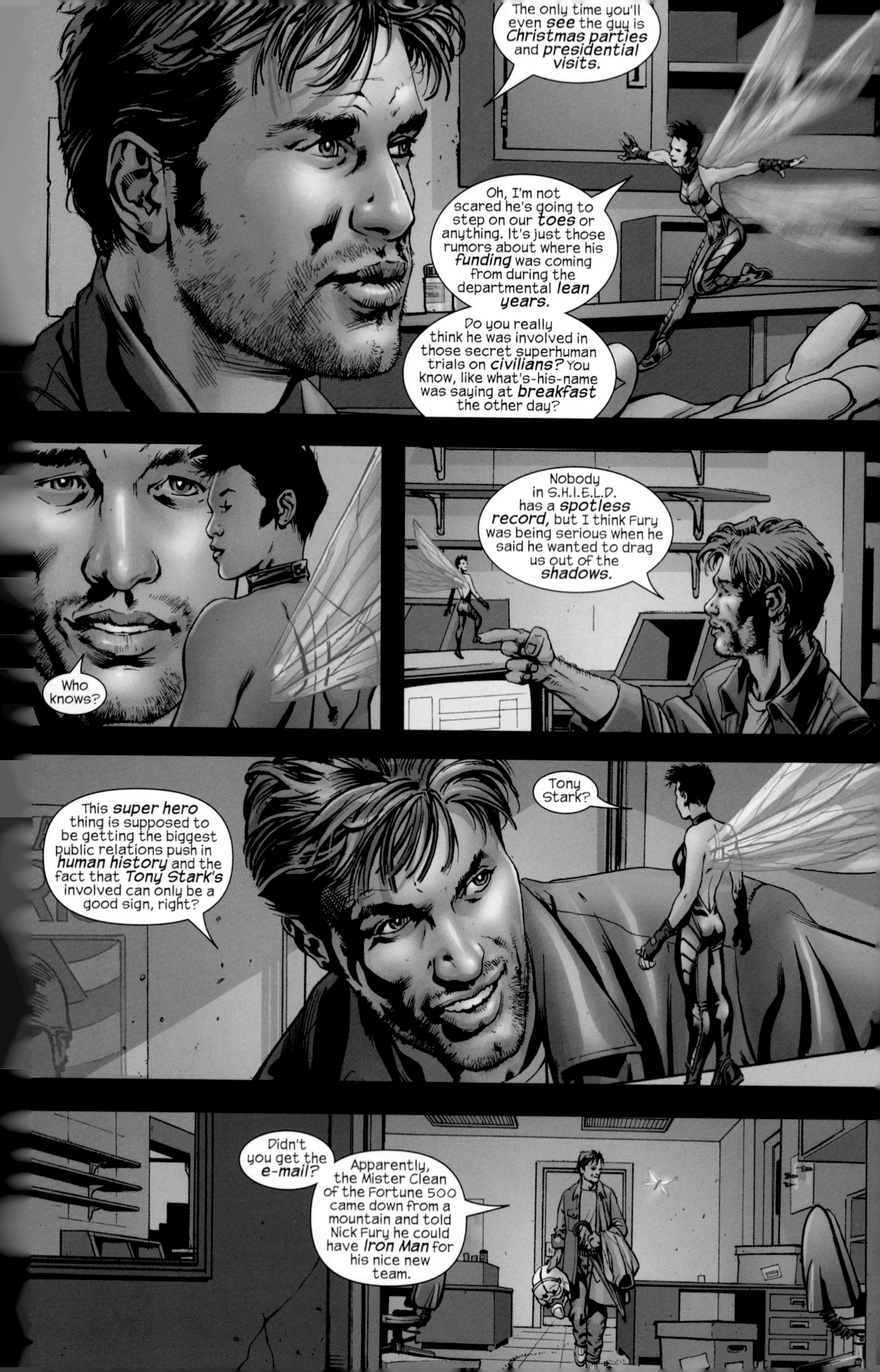

The only time you'll even see the guy is Christmas parties and presidential visits.
Oh, I'm not scared he's going to step on our toes or anything. It's just those rumors about where his funding was coming from during the departmental lean years.
Do you really think he was involved in those secret superhuman trials on civilians? You know, like what's-his-name was saying at breakfast the other day?
Who knows?
Nobody in S.H.I.E.L.D. has a spotless record, but I think Fury was being serious when he said he wanted to drag us out of the shadows.
This super hero thing is supposed to be getting the biggest public relations push in human history and the fact that Tony Stark's involved can only be a good sign, right?
Tony Stark?
Didn't you get the e-mail?
Apparently, the Mister Clean of the Fortune 500 came down from a mountain and told Nick Fury he could have Iron Man for his nice new team.

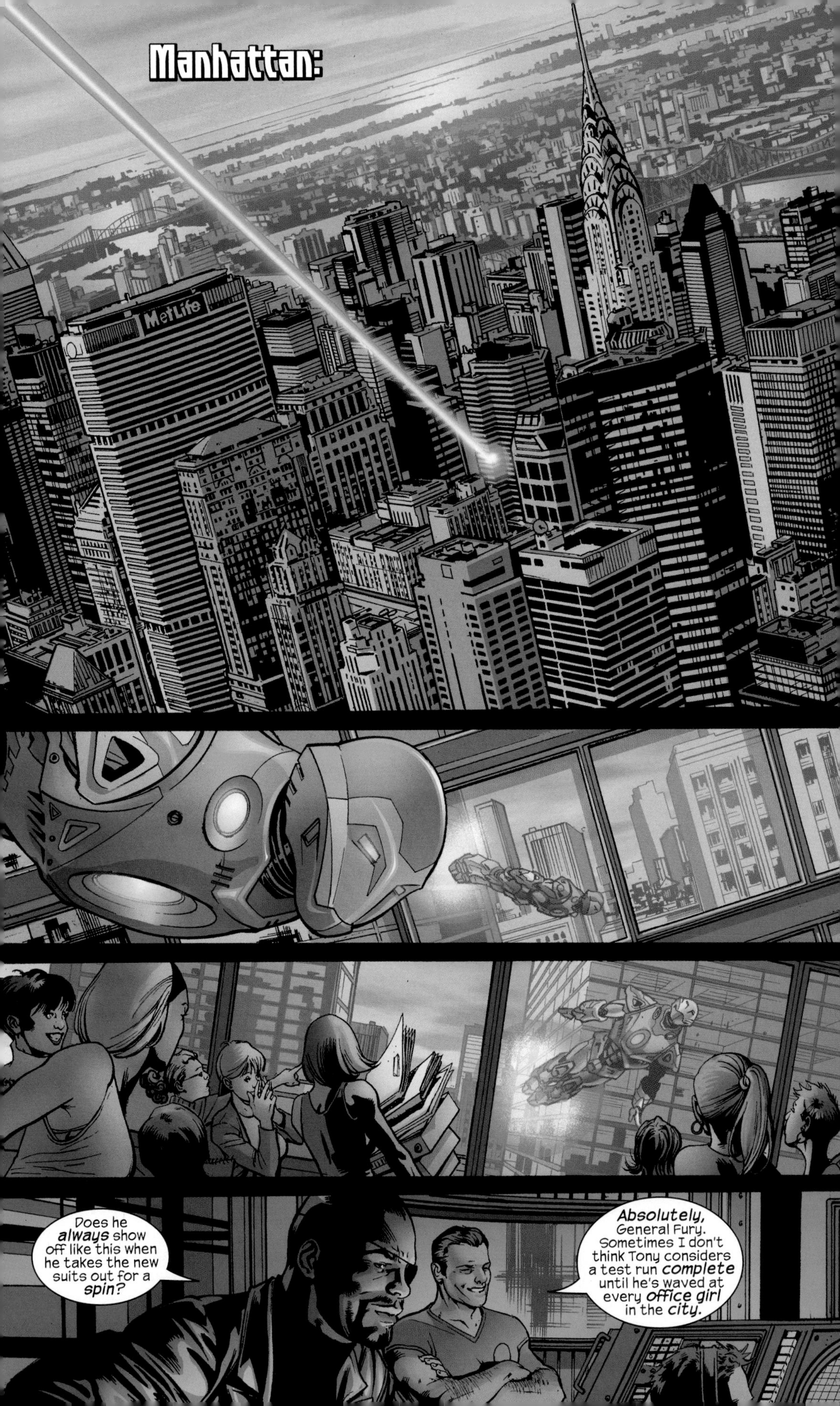
Manhattan:
MetLife
Does he *always* show off like this when he takes the new suits out for a *spin?*
Absolutely, General Fury. Sometimes I don't think Tony considers a test run *complete* until he's waved at every *office girl* in the *city.*

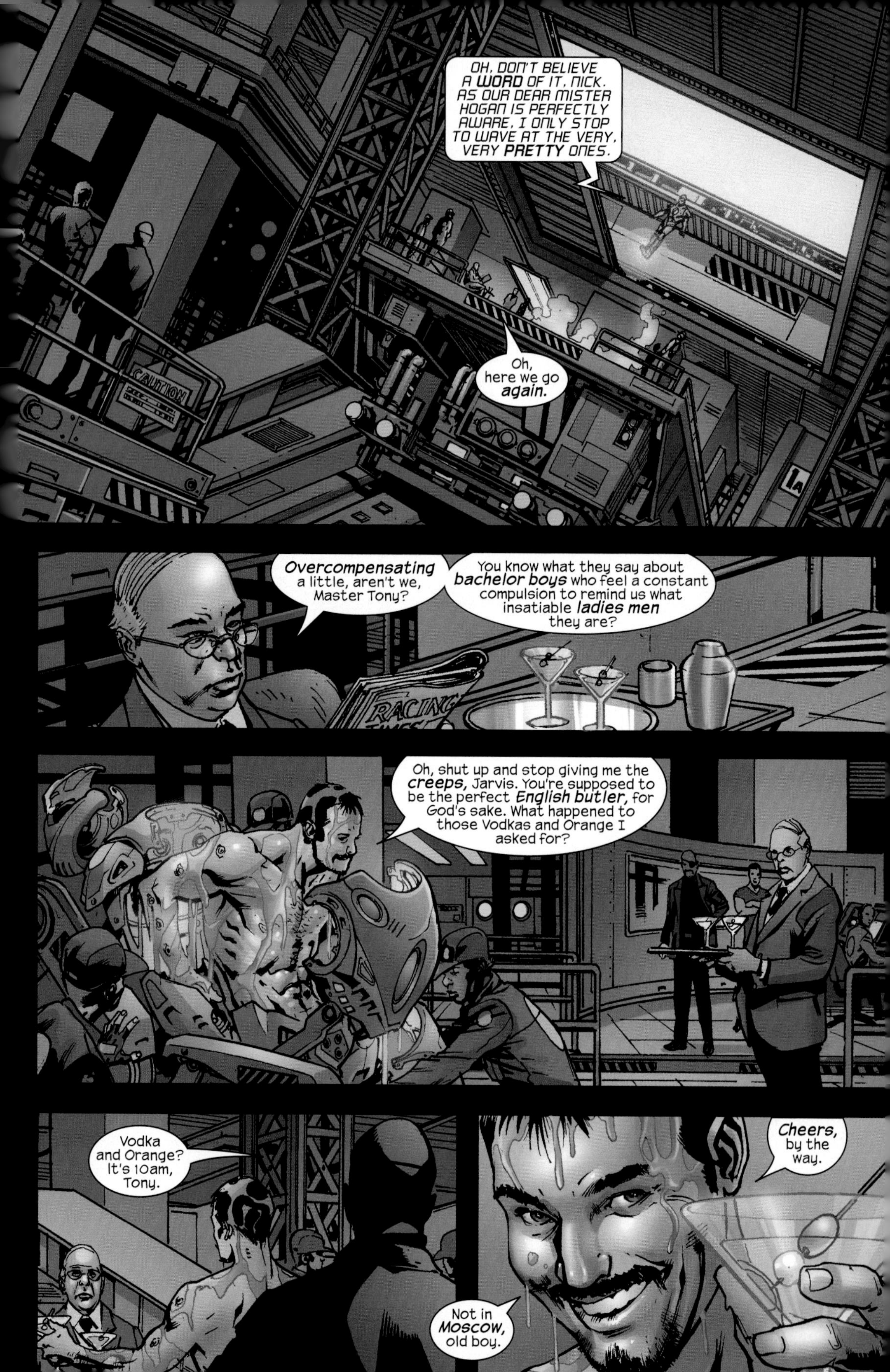
OH, DON'T BELIEVE A WORD OF IT, NICK. AS OUR DEAR MISTER HOGAN IS PERFECTLY AWARE, I ONLY STOP TO WAVE AT THE VERY, VERY PRETTY ONES.
CAUTION
Oh, here we go again.
Overcompensating a little, aren't we, Master Tony?
You know what they say about bachelor boys who feel a constant compulsion to remind us what insatiable ladies men they are?
RACING
Oh, shut up and stop giving me the creeps, Jarvis. You're supposed to be the perfect English butler, for God's sake. What happened to those Vodkas and Orange I asked for?
Vodka and Orange? It's 10am, Tony.
Cheers, by the way.
Not in Moscow, old boy.

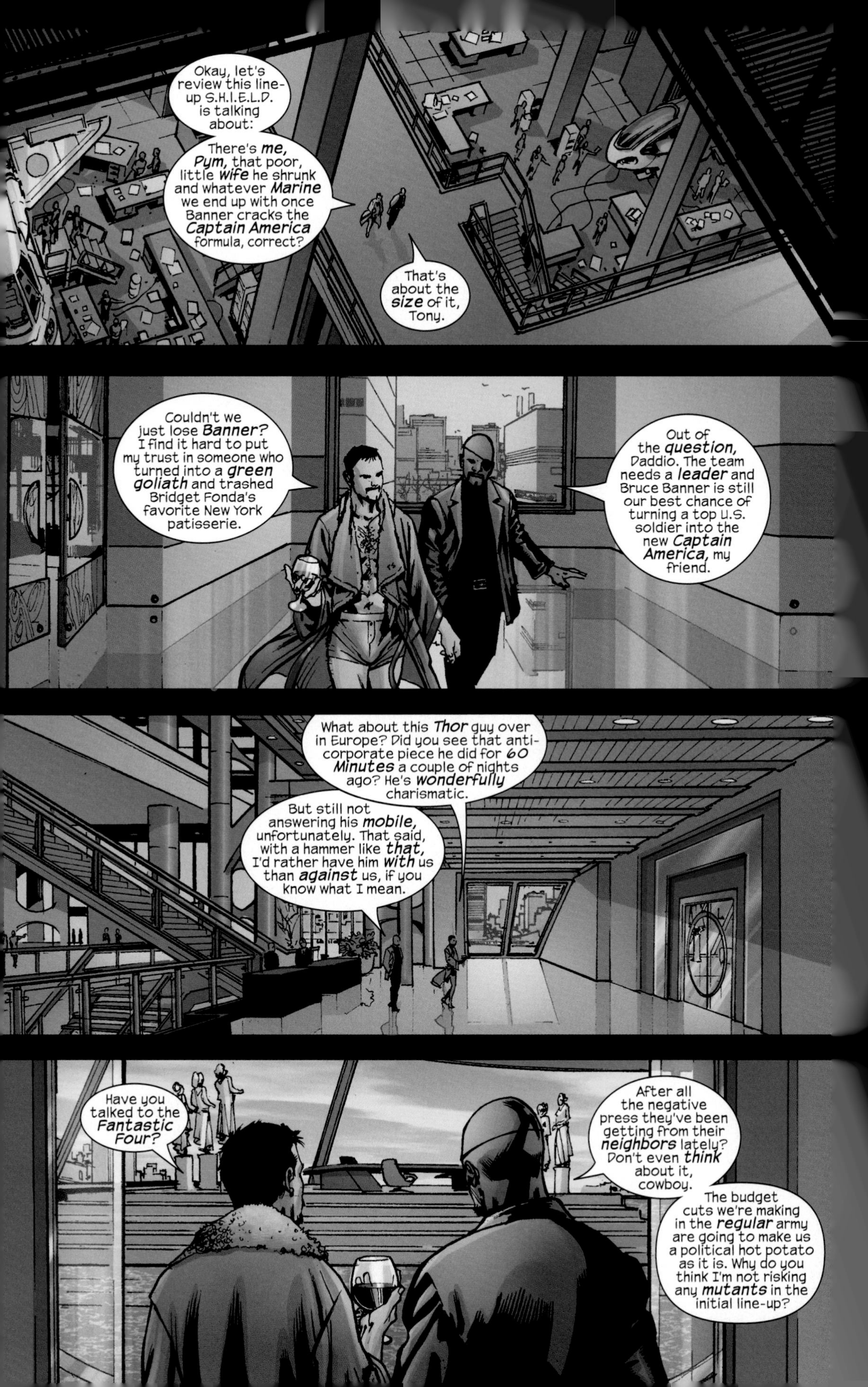
Okay, let's review this line-up S.H.I.E.L.D. is talking about:
There's me, Pym, that poor, little wife he shrunk and whatever Marine we end up with once Banner cracks the Captain America formula, correct?
That's about the size of it, Tony.
Couldn't we just lose Banner? I find it hard to put my trust in someone who turned into a green goliath and trashed Bridget Fonda's favorite New York patisserie.
Out of the question, Daddio. The team needs a leader and Bruce Banner is still our best chance of turning a top U.S. soldier into the new Captain America, my friend.
What about this Thor guy over in Europe? Did you see that anti-corporate piece he did for 60 Minutes a couple of nights ago? He's wonderfully charismatic.
But still not answering his mobile, unfortunately. That said, with a hammer like that, I'd rather have him with us than against us, if you know what I mean.
Have you talked to the Fantastic Four?
After all the negative press they've been getting from their neighbors lately? Don't even think about it, cowboy.
The budget cuts we're making in the regular army are going to make us a political hot potato as it is. Why do you think I'm not risking any mutants in the initial line-up?

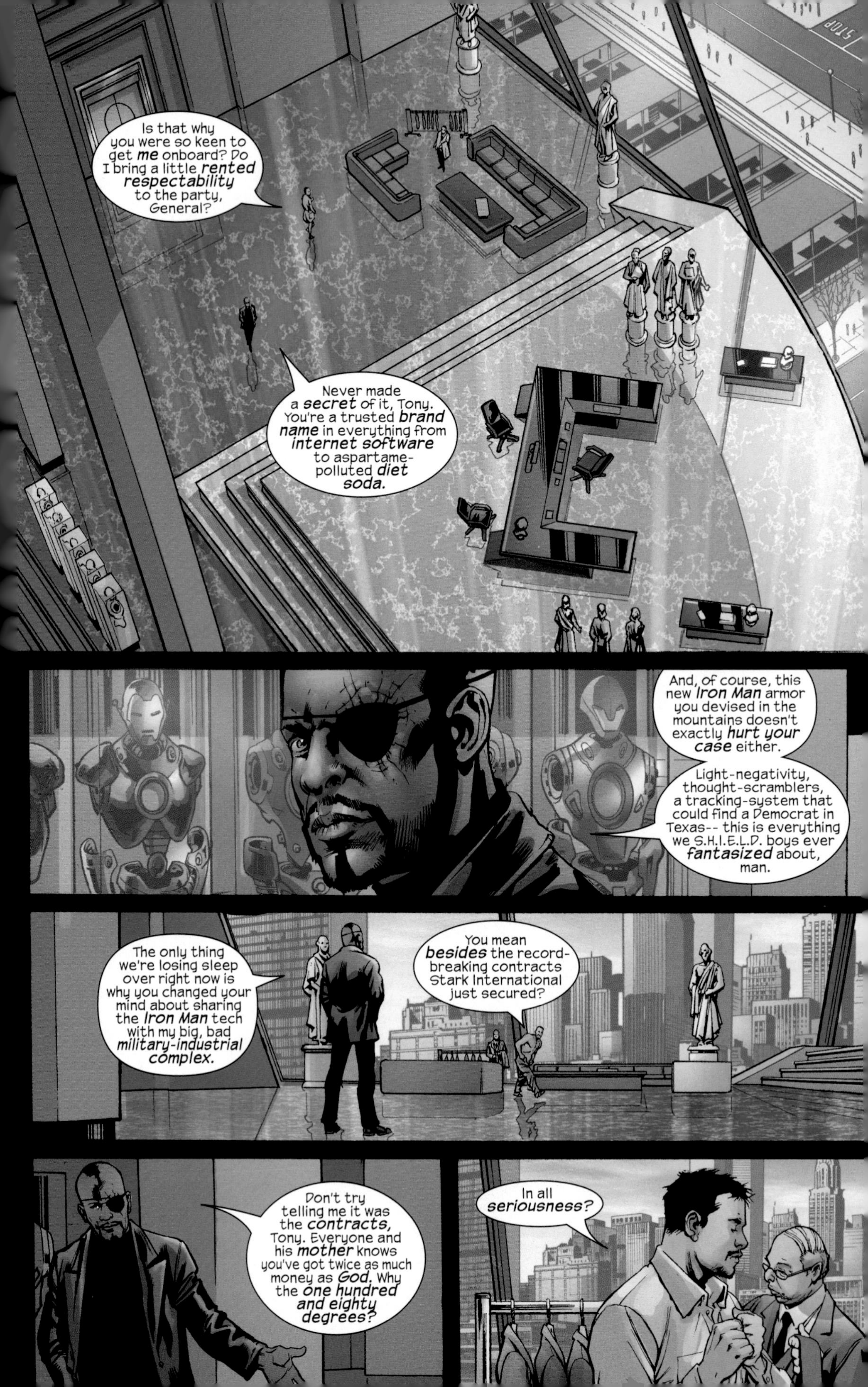
STOP
Is that why you were so keen to get me onboard? Do I bring a little rented respectability to the party, General?
Never made a secret of it, Tony. You're a trusted brand name in everything from internet software to aspartame-polluted diet soda.
And, of course, this new Iron Man armor you devised in the mountains doesn't exactly hurt your case either.
Light-negativity, thought-scramblers, a tracking-system that could find a Democrat in Texas-- this is everything we S.H.I.E.L.D. boys ever fantasized about, man.
The only thing we're losing sleep over right now is why you changed your mind about sharing the Iron Man tech with my big, bad military-industrial complex.
You mean besides the record-breaking contracts Stark International just secured?
Don't try telling me it was the contracts, Tony. Everyone and his mother knows you've got twice as much money as God. Why the one hundred and eighty degrees?
In all seriousness?

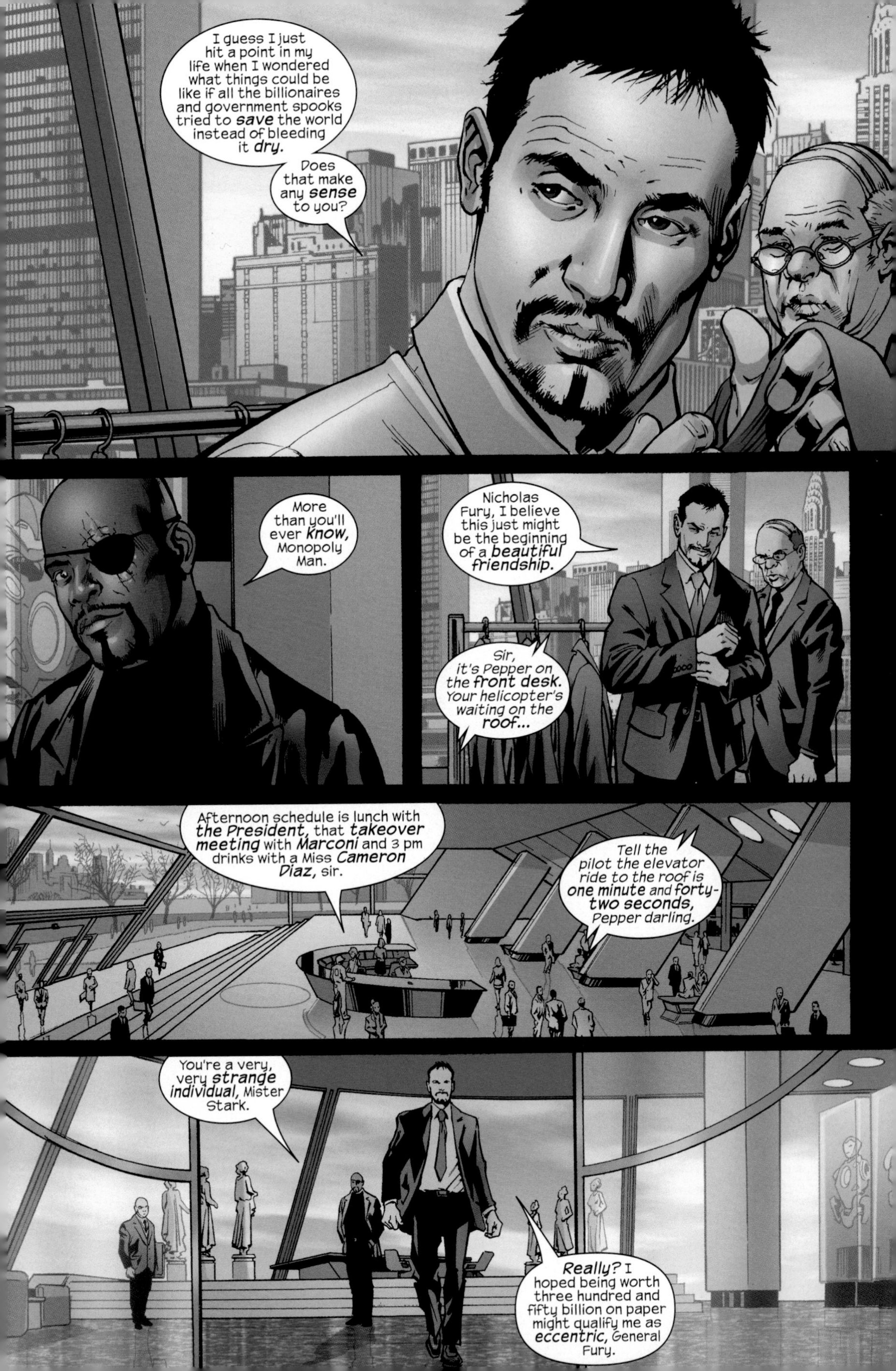
I guess I just hit a point in my life when I wondered what things could be like if all the billionaires and government spooks tried to save the world instead of bleeding it dry.
Does that make any sense to you?
More than you'll ever know, Monopoly Man.
Nicholas Fury, I believe this just might be the beginning of a beautiful friendship.
Sir, it's Pepper on the front desk. Your helicopter's waiting on the roof...
Afternoon schedule is lunch with the President, that takeover meeting with Marconi and 3 pm drinks with a Miss Cameron Diaz, sir.
Tell the pilot the elevator ride to the roof is one minute and forty-two seconds, Pepper darling.
You're a very, very strange individual, Mister Stark.
Really? I hoped being worth three hundred and fifty billion on paper might qualify me as eccentric, General Fury.

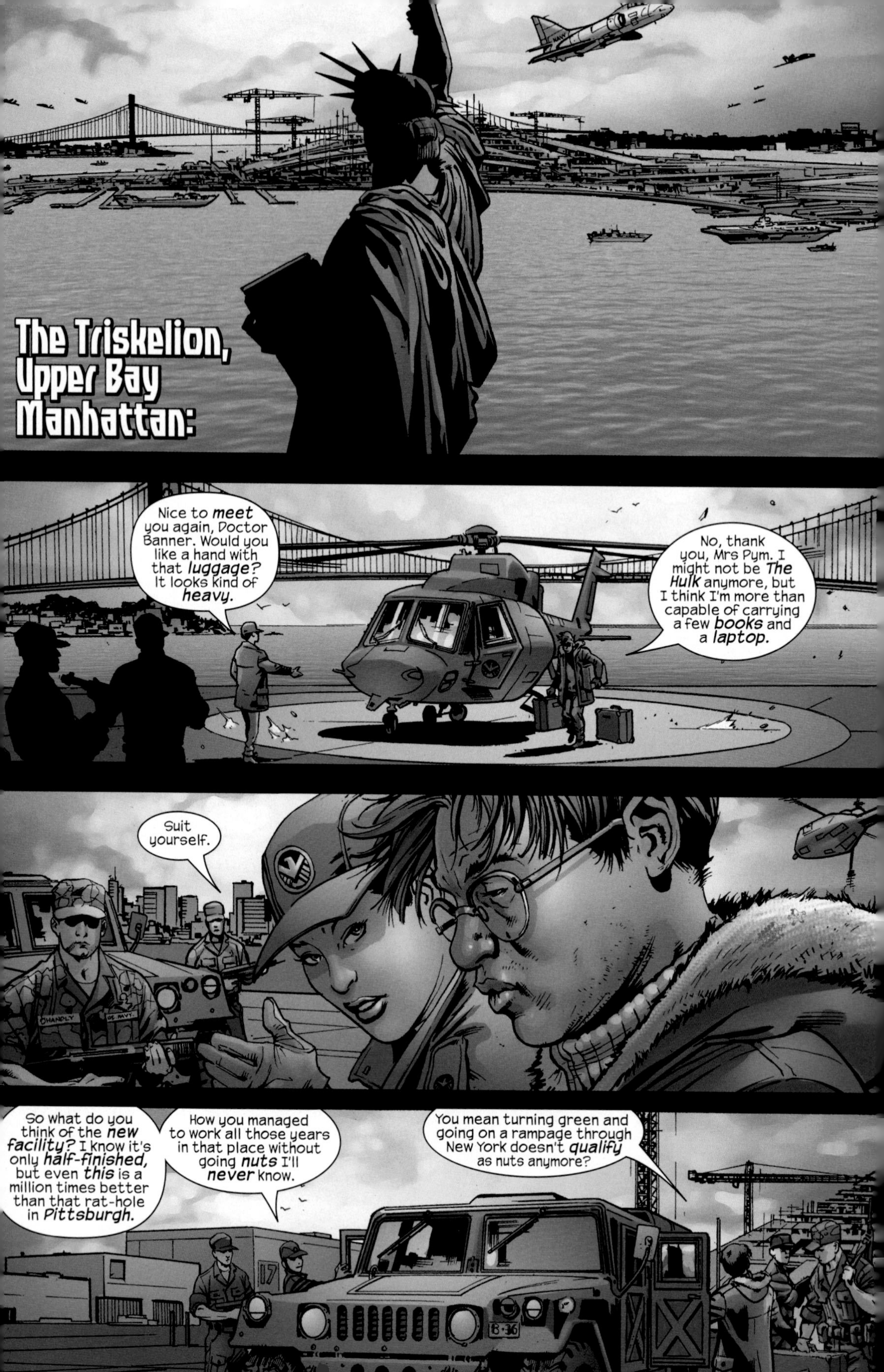
The Triskelion, Upper Bay Manhattan:
Nice to meet you again, Doctor Banner. Would you like a hand with that luggage? It looks kind of heavy.
No, thank you, Mrs Pym. I might not be The Hulk anymore, but I think I'm more than capable of carrying a few books and a laptop.
Suit yourself.
So what do you think of the new facility? I know it's only half-finished, but even this is a million times better than that rat-hole in Pittsburgh.
How you managed to work all those years in that place without going nuts I'll never know.
You mean turning green and going on a rampage through New York doesn't qualify as nuts anymore?

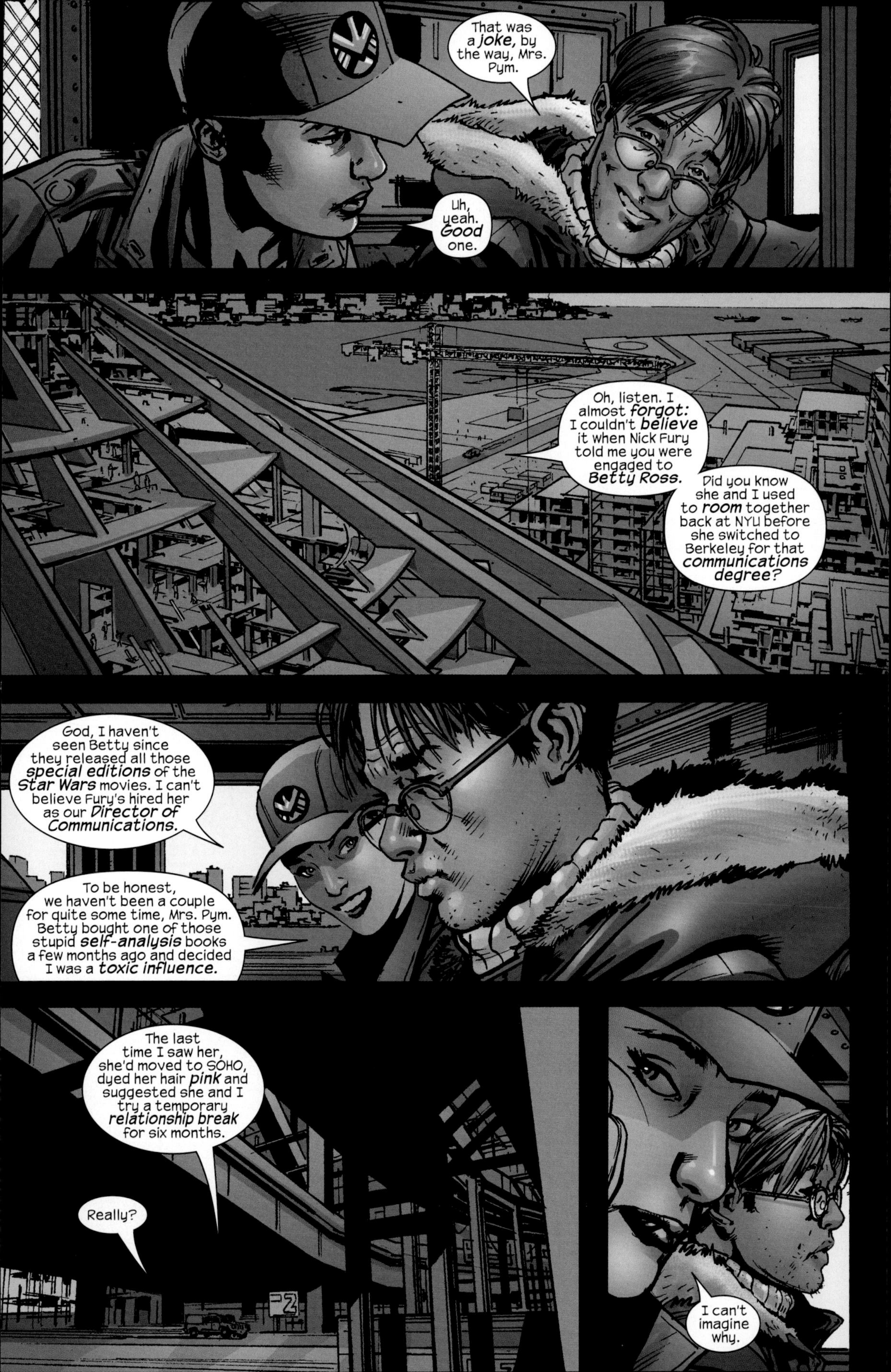
That was a joke, by the way, Mrs. Pym.
Uh, yeah. Good one.
Oh, listen. I almost forgot: I couldn't believe it when Nick Fury told me you were engaged to Betty Ross.
Did you know she and I used to room together back at NYU before she switched to Berkeley for that communications degree?
God, I haven't seen Betty since they released all those special editions of the Star Wars movies. I can't believe Fury's hired her as our Director of Communications.
To be honest, we haven't been a couple for quite some time, Mrs. Pym. Betty bought one of those stupid self-analysis books a few months ago and decided I was a toxic influence.
The last time I saw her, she'd moved to SOHO, dyed her hair pink and suggested she and I try a temporary relationship break for six months.
Really?
I can't imagine why.

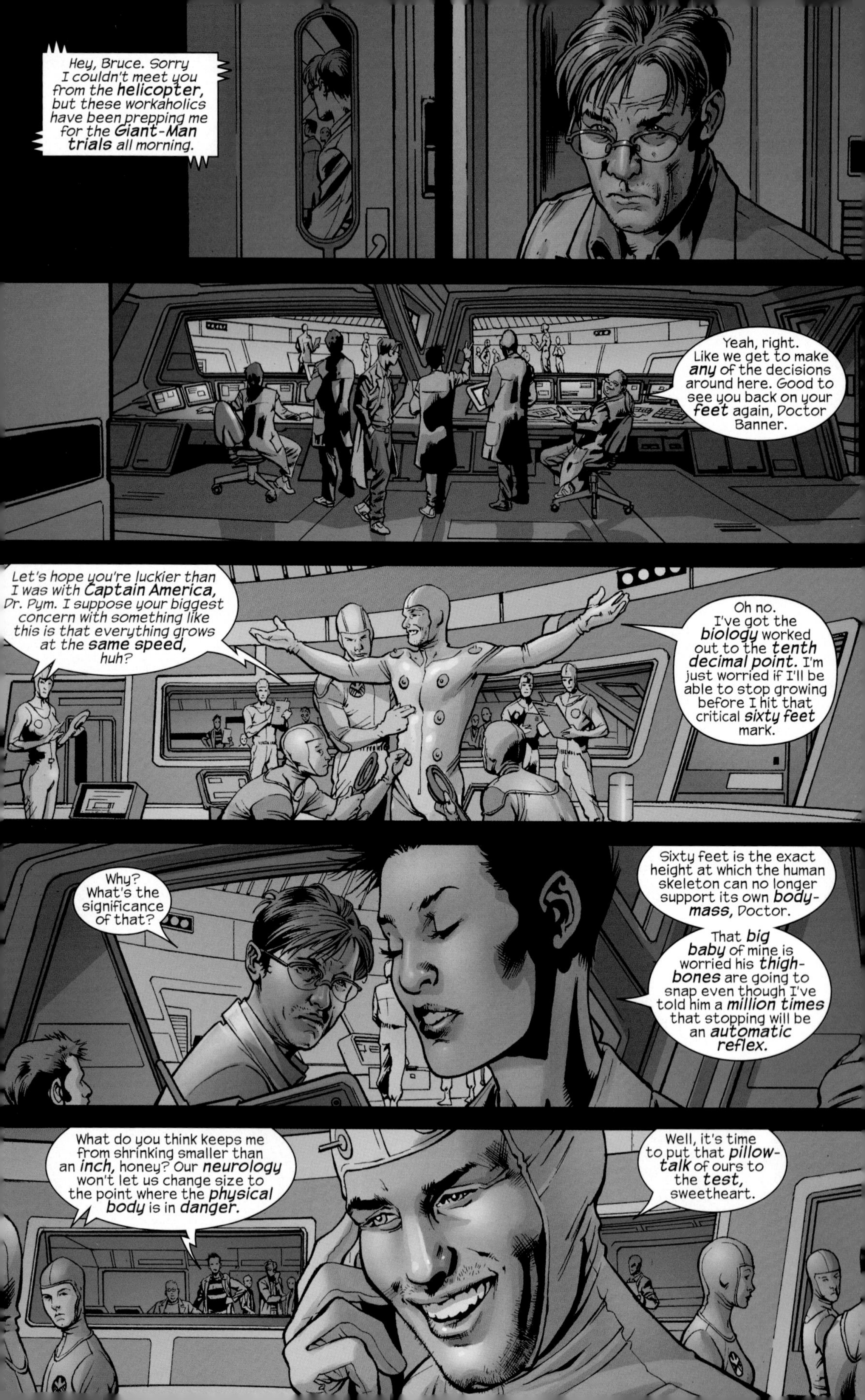
Hey, Bruce. Sorry I couldn't meet you from the helicopter, but these workaholics have been prepping me for the Giant-Man trials all morning.
Yeah, right. Like we get to make any of the decisions around here. Good to see you back on your feet again, Doctor Banner.
Let's hope you're luckier than I was with Captain America, Dr. Pym. I suppose your biggest concern with something like this is that everything grows at the same speed, huh?
Oh no. I've got the biology worked out to the tenth decimal point. I'm just worried if I'll be able to stop growing before I hit that critical sixty feet mark.
Why? What's the significance of that?
Sixty feet is the exact height at which the human skeleton can no longer support its own body-mass, Doctor.
That big baby of mine is worried his thigh-bones are going to snap even though I've told him a million times that stopping will be an automatic reflex.
What do you think keeps me from shrinking smaller than an inch, honey? Our neurology won't let us change size to the point where the physical body is in danger.
Well, it's time to put that pillow-talk of ours to the test, sweetheart.

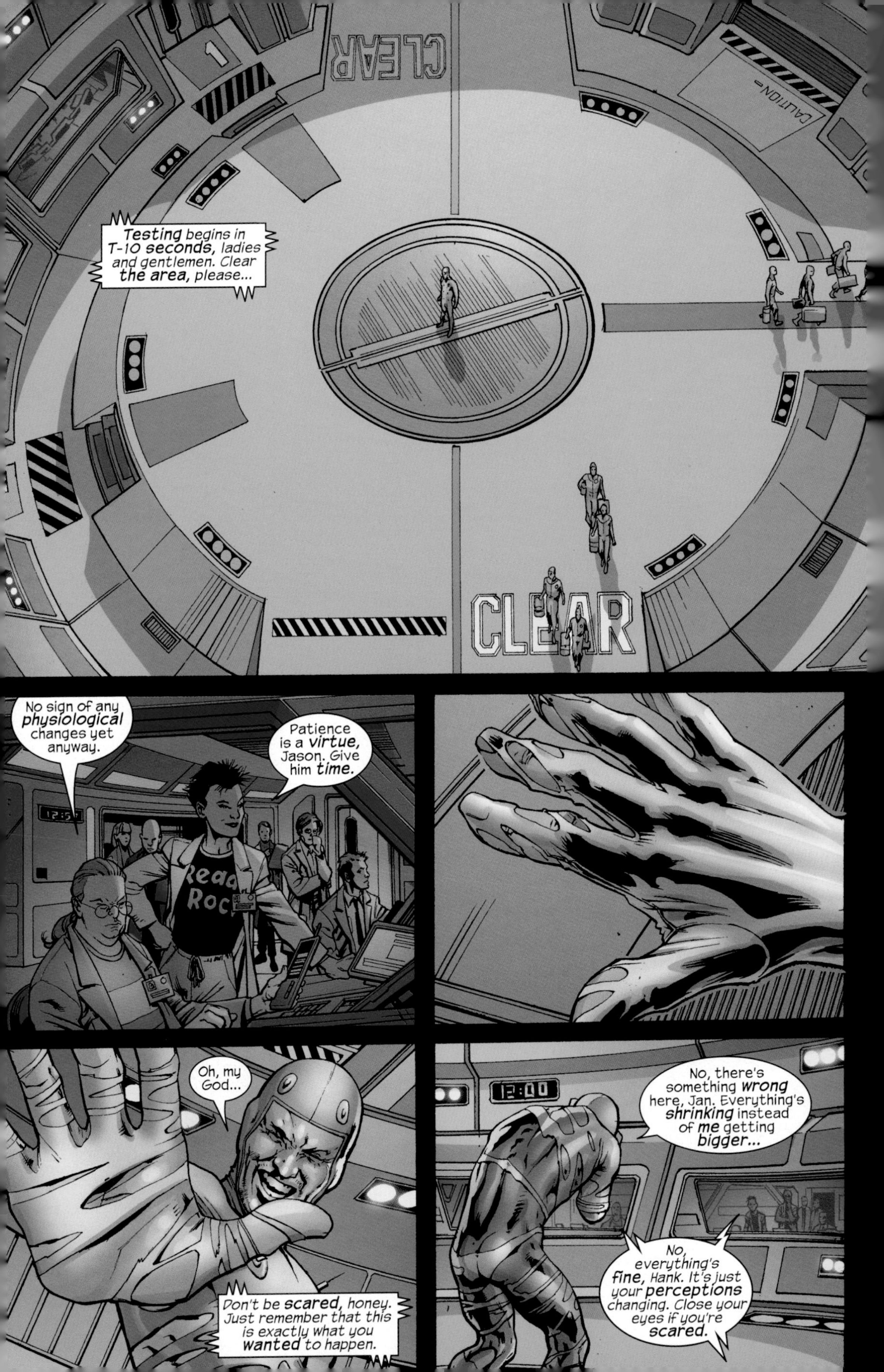

Testing begins in T-10 seconds, ladies and gentlemen. Clear the area, please...
CLEAR
No sign of any physiological changes yet anyway.
Patience is a virtue, Jason. Give him time.
Oh, my God...
Don't be scared, honey. Just remember that this is exactly what you wanted to happen.
12:00
No, there's something wrong here, Jan. Everything's shrinking instead of me getting bigger...
No, everything's fine, Hank. It's just your perceptions changing. Close your eyes if you're scared.

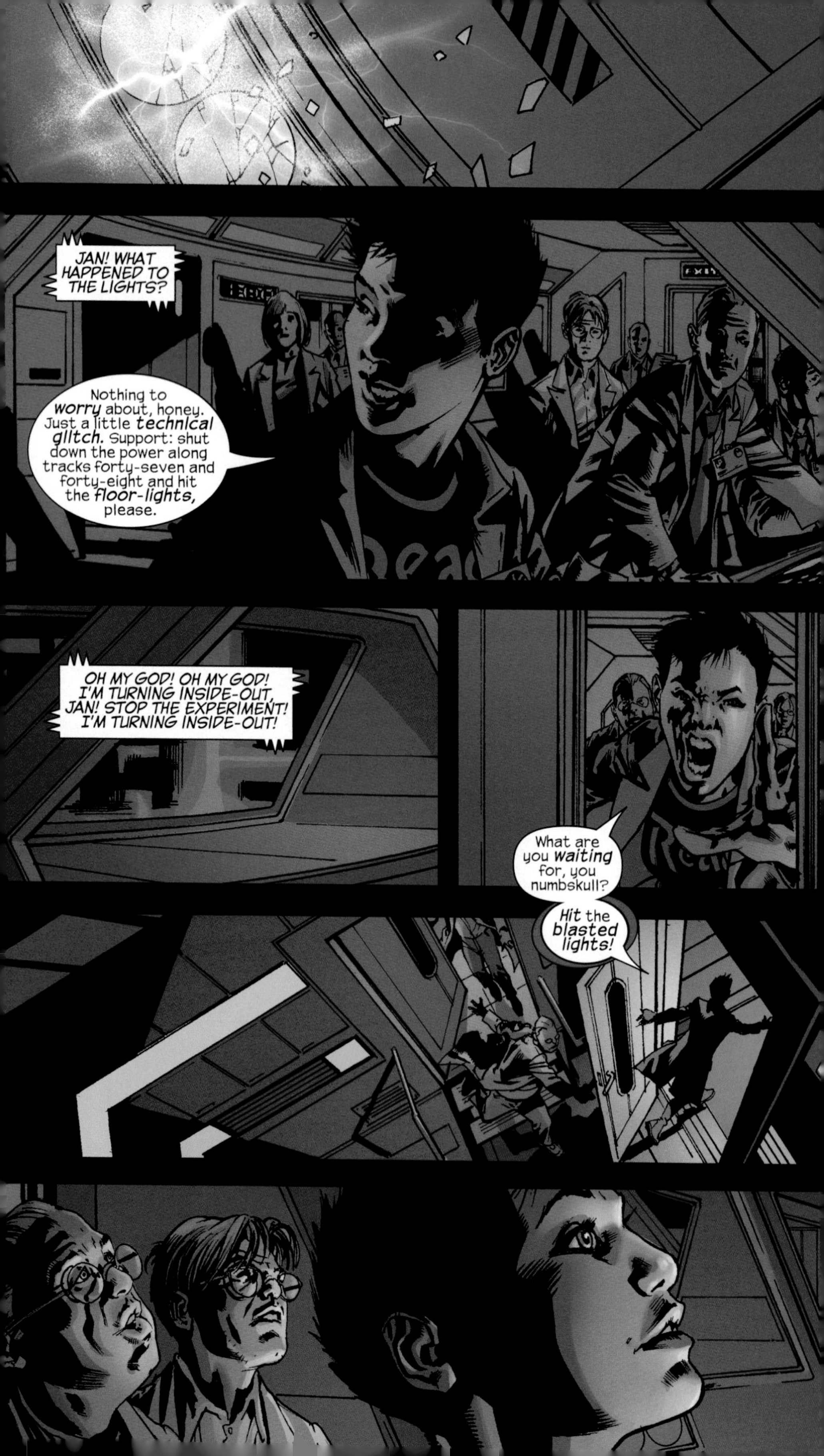
JAN! WHAT HAPPENED TO THE LIGHTS?
Nothing to worry about, honey. Just a little technical glitch. Support: shut down the power along tracks forty-seven and forty-eight and hit the floor-lights, please.
OH MY GOD! OH MY GOD! I'M TURNING INSIDE-OUT, JAN! STOP THE EXPERIMENT! I'M TURNING INSIDE-OUT!
What are you waiting for, you numbskull?
Hit the blasted lights!

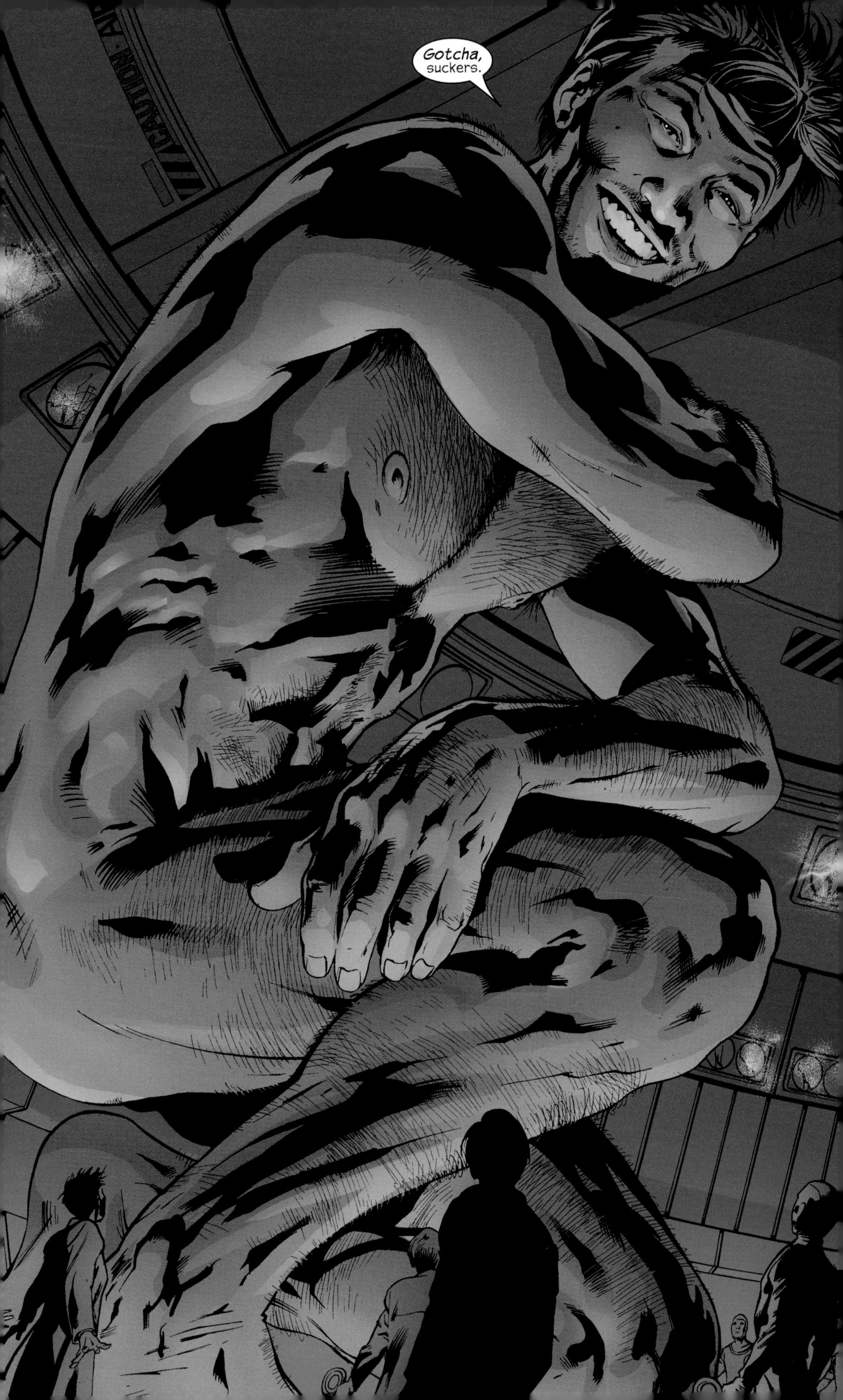
Gotcha, suckers.
CAUTION

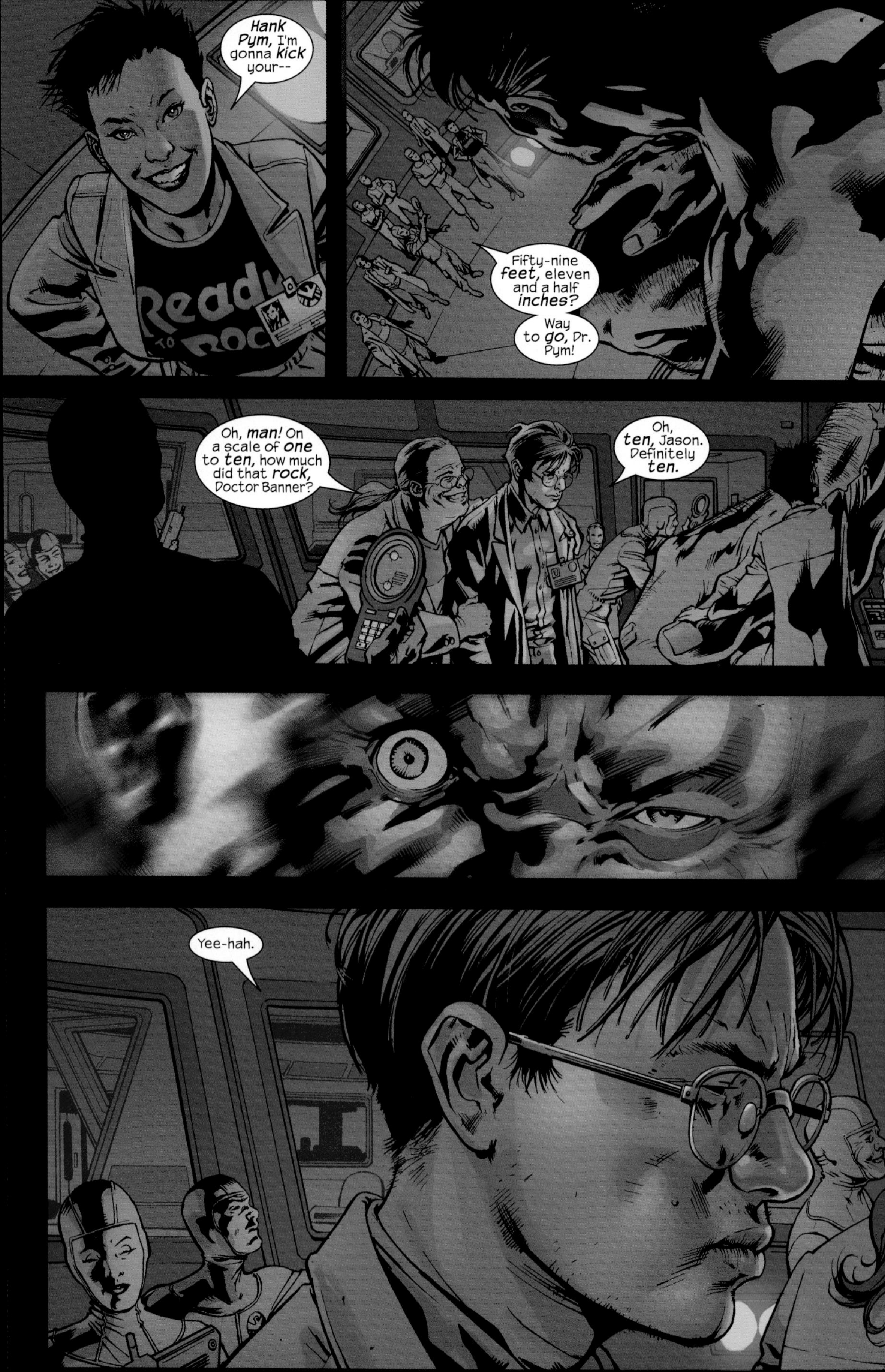
Hank Pym, I'm gonna kick your--
Ready to Rock
Fifty-nine feet, eleven and a half inches?
Way to go, Dr. Pym!
Oh, man! On a scale of one to ten, how much did that rock, Doctor Banner?
Oh, ten, Jason. Definitely ten.
Yee-hah.

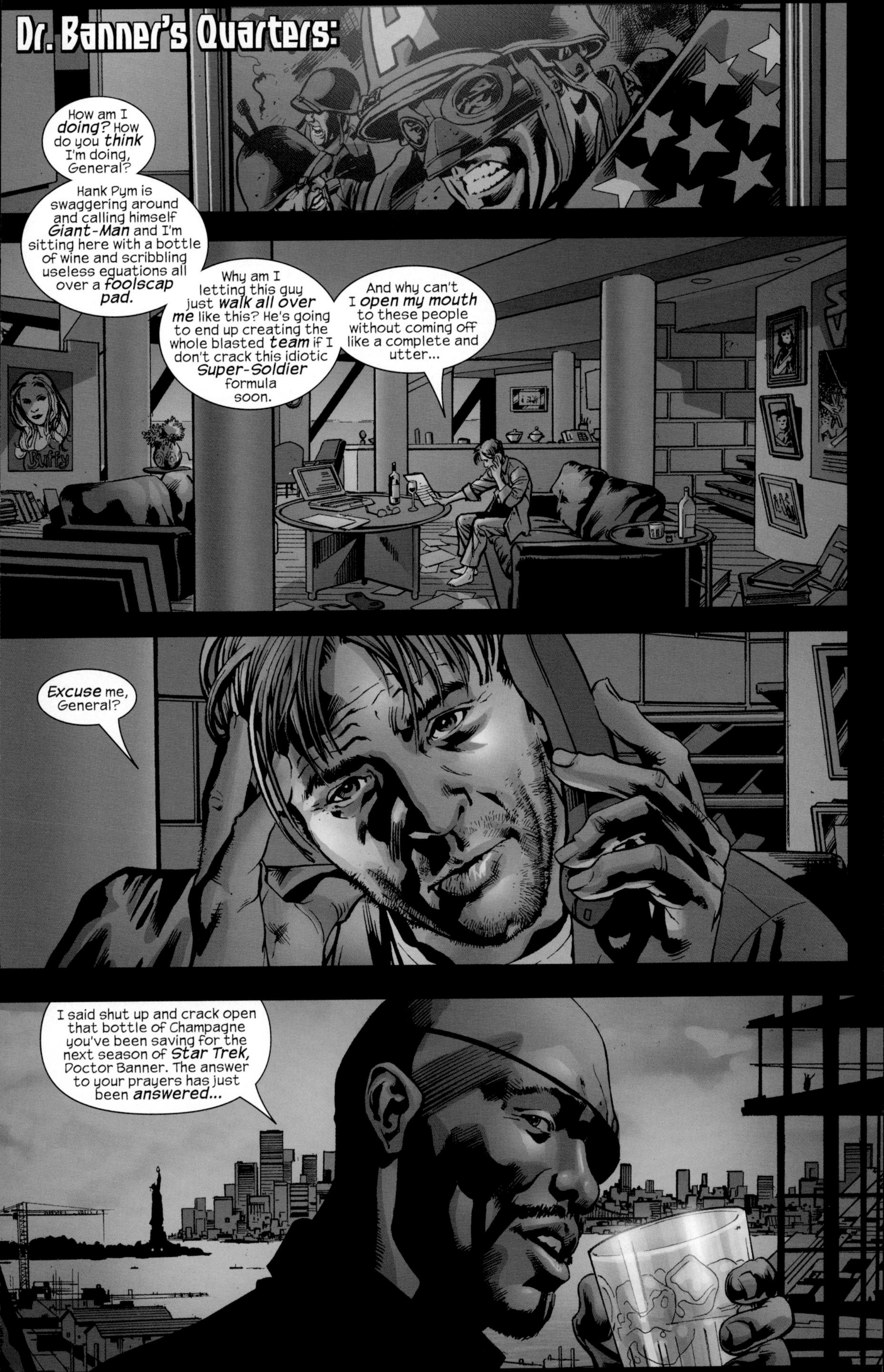

Dr. Banner's Quarters:
How am I doing? How do you think I'm doing, General?
Hank Pym is swaggering around and calling himself Giant-Man and I'm sitting here with a bottle of wine and scribbling useless equations all over a foolscap pad.
Why am I letting this guy just walk all over me like this? He's going to end up creating the whole blasted team if I don't crack this idiotic Super-Soldier formula soon.
And why can't I open my mouth to these people without coming off like a complete and utter...
Buffy
Excuse me, General?
I said shut up and crack open that bottle of Champagne you've been saving for the next season of Star Trek, Doctor Banner. The answer to your prayers has just been answered...

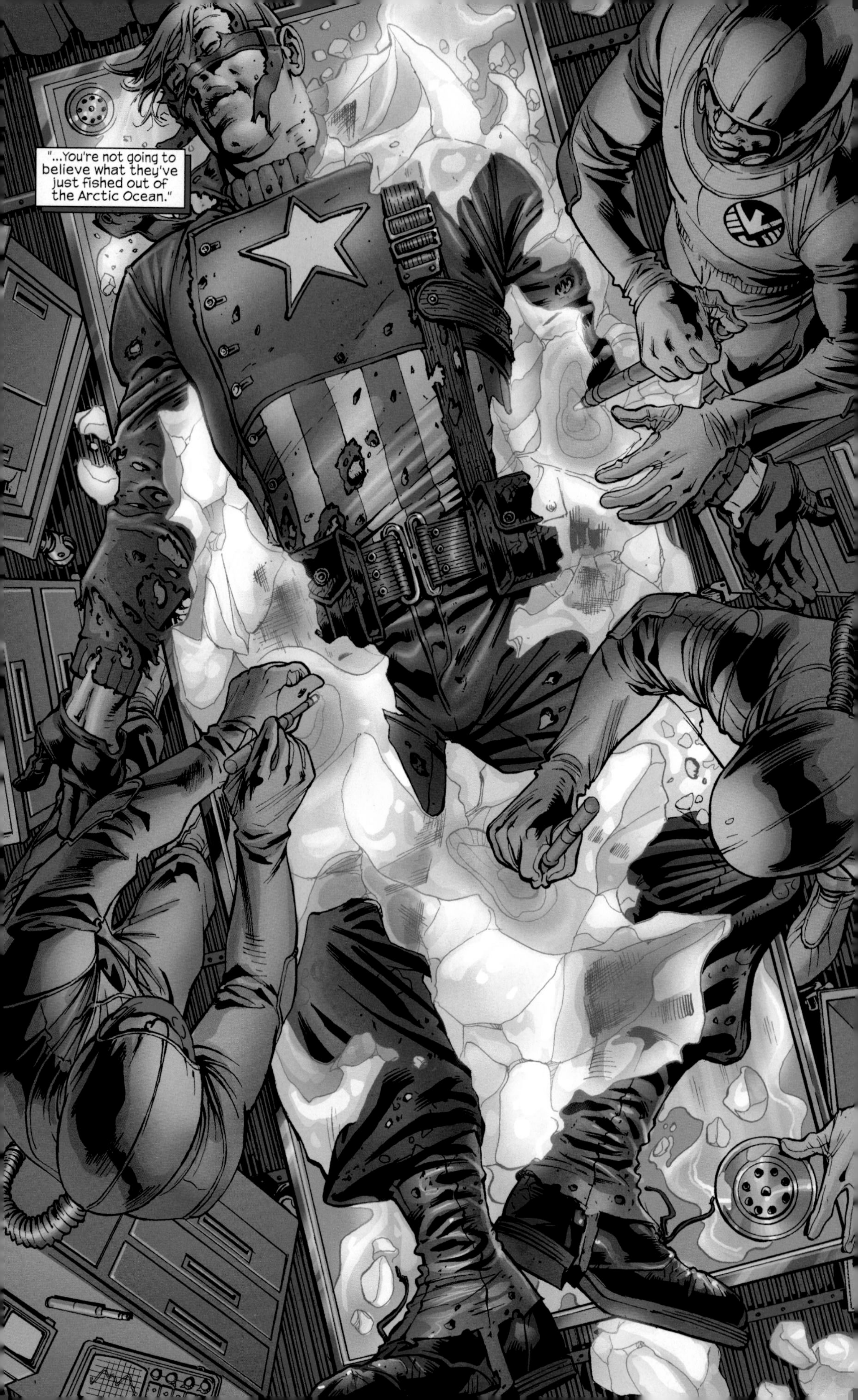
"...You're not going to believe what they've just fished out of the Arctic Ocean."

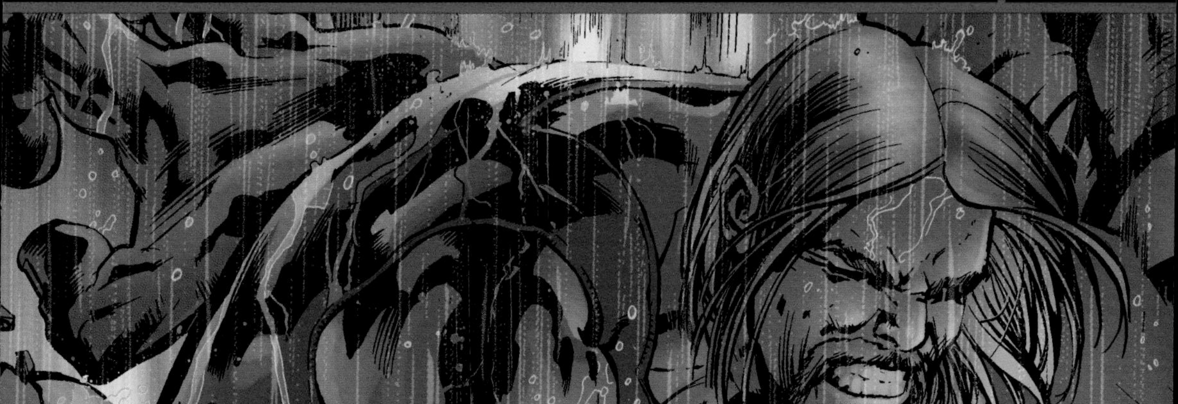
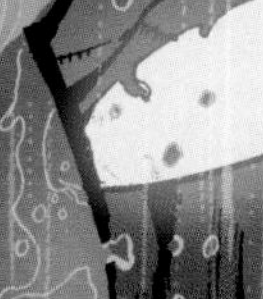
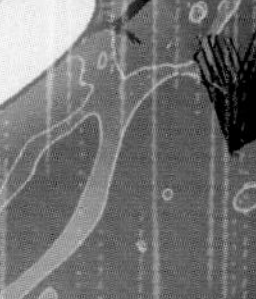
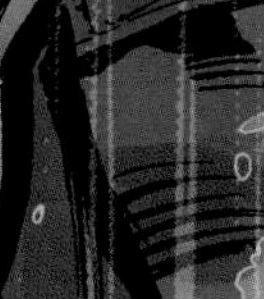

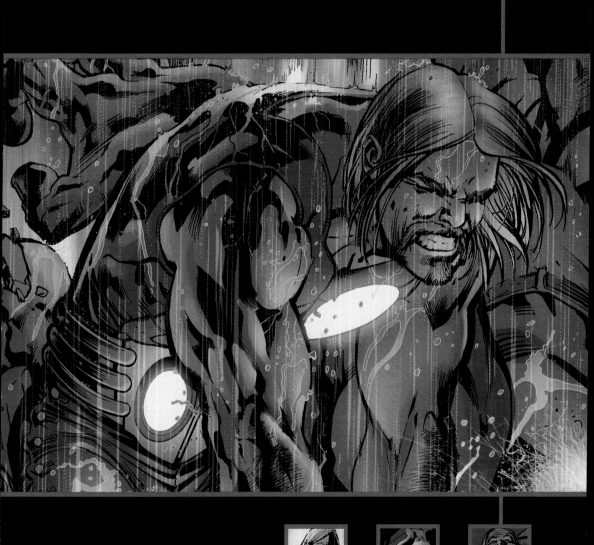

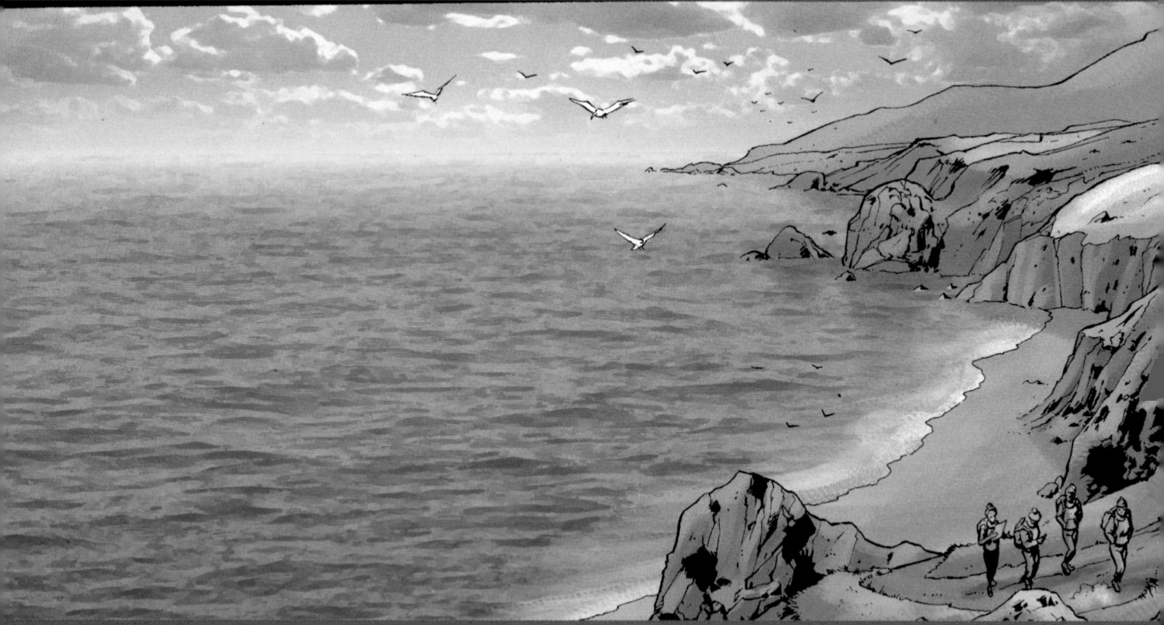

CHAPTER THREE

21st CENTURY BOY

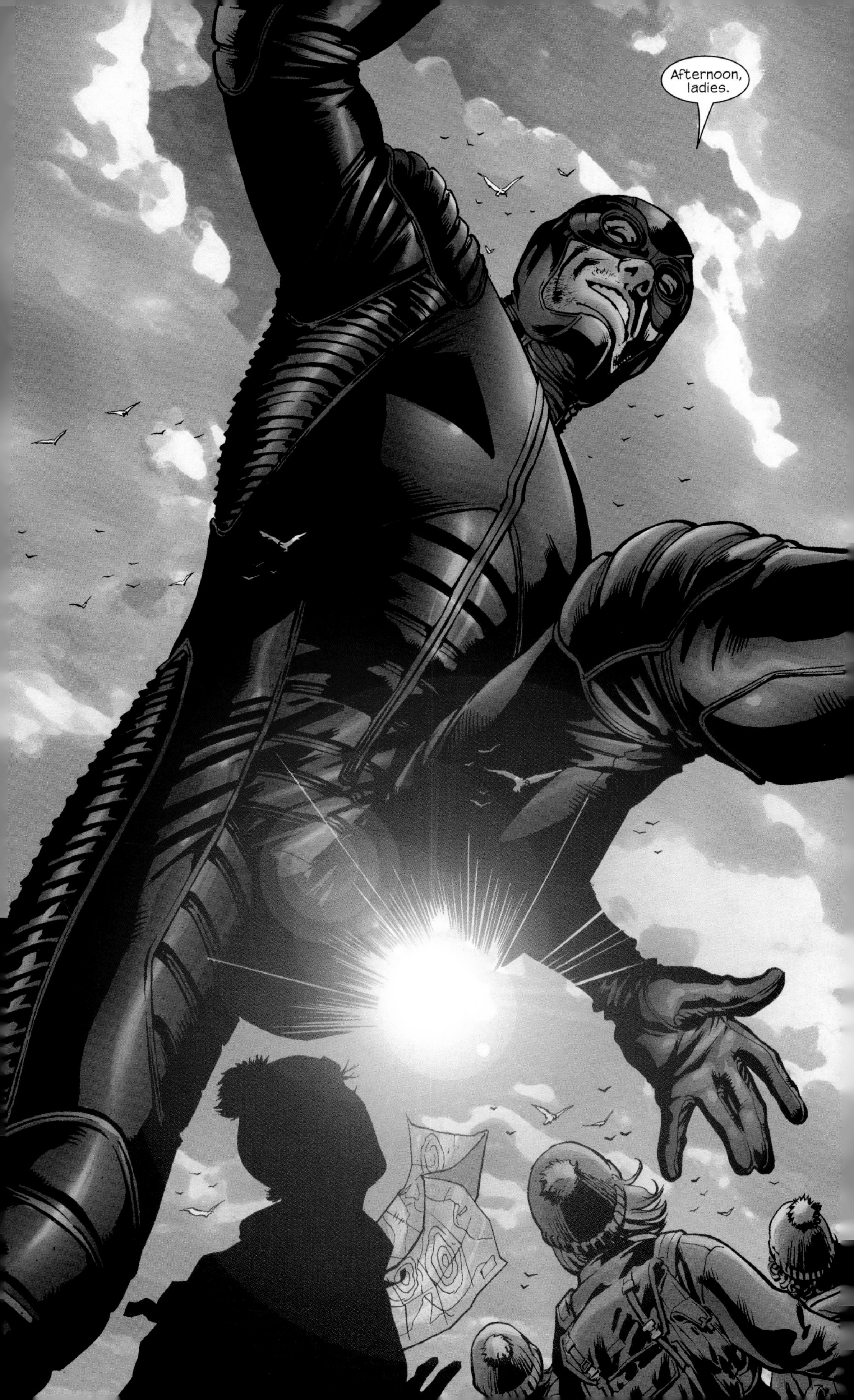
Afternoon, ladies.

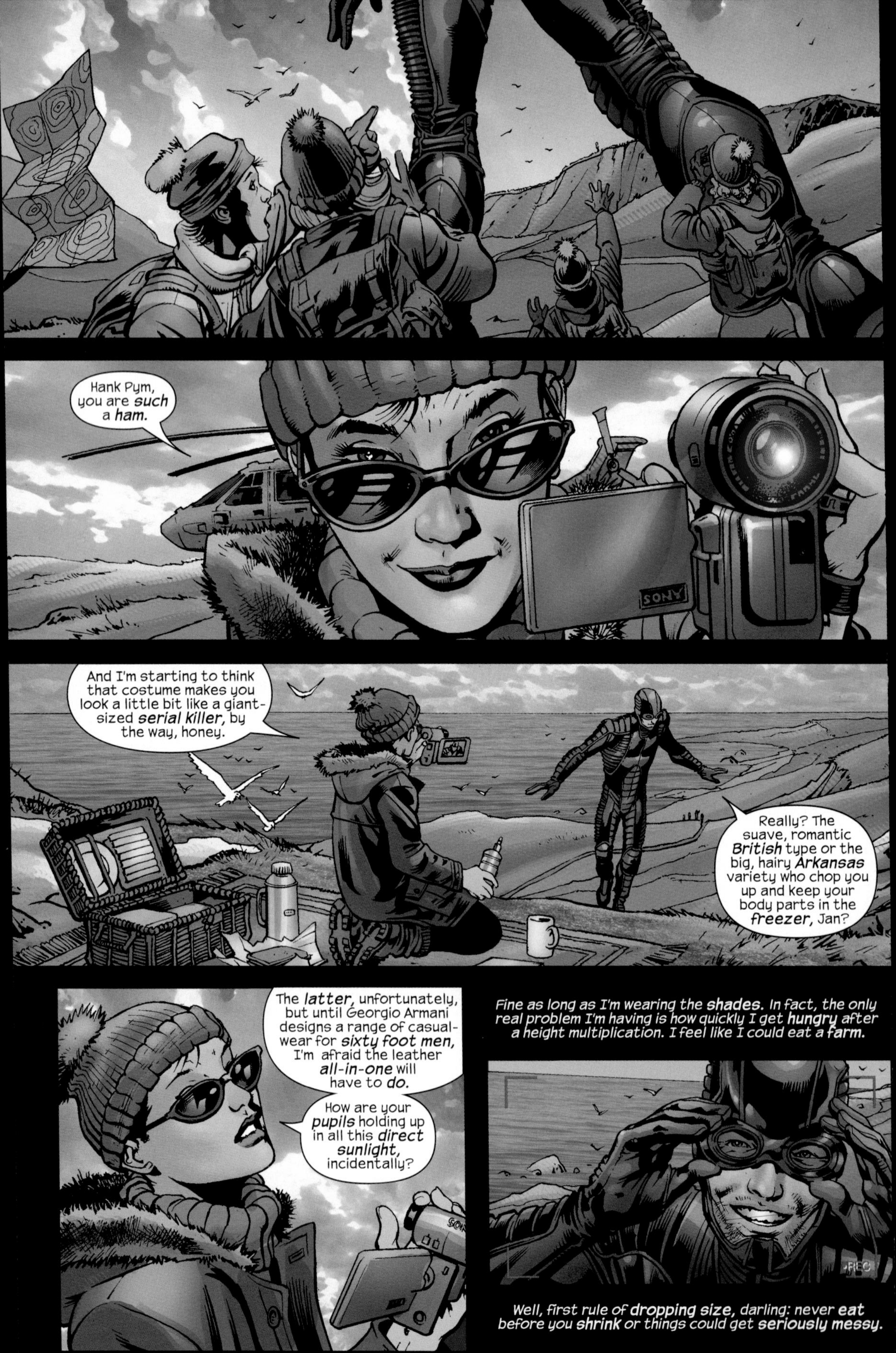
Hank Pym, you are such a ham.
And I'm starting to think that costume makes you look a little bit like a giant-sized serial killer, by the way, honey.
Really? The suave, romantic British type or the big, hairy Arkansas variety who chop you up and keep your body parts in the freezer, Jan?
The latter, unfortunately, but until Georgio Armani designs a range of casual-wear for sixty foot men, I'm afraid the leather all-in-one will have to do.
How are your pupils holding up in all this direct sunlight, incidentally?
Fine as long as I'm wearing the shades. In fact, the only real problem I'm having is how quickly I get hungry after a height multiplication. I feel like I could eat a farm.
SONY
REC
Well, first rule of dropping size, darling: never eat before you shrink or things could get seriously messy.

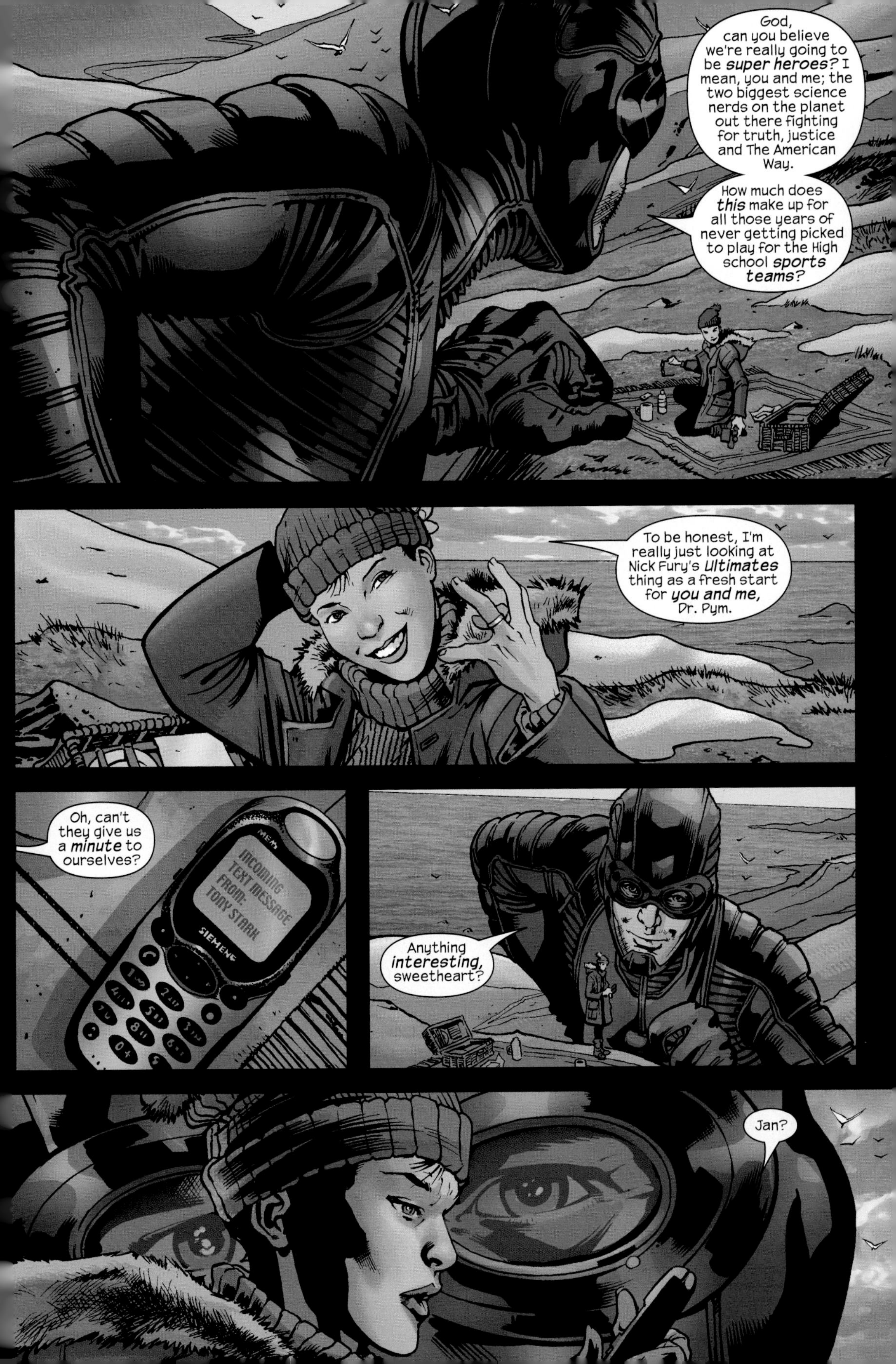
God, can you believe we're really going to be *super heroes?* I mean, you and me; the two biggest science nerds on the planet out there fighting for truth, justice and The American Way.
How much does *this* make up for all those years of never getting picked to play for the High school *sports teams?*
To be honest, I'm really just looking at Nick Fury's *Ultimates* thing as a fresh start for *you and me,* Dr. Pym.
Oh, can't they give us a *minute* to ourselves?
INCOMING TEXT MESSAGE FROM: TONY STARK
SIEMENS
Anything *interesting,* sweetheart?
Jan?

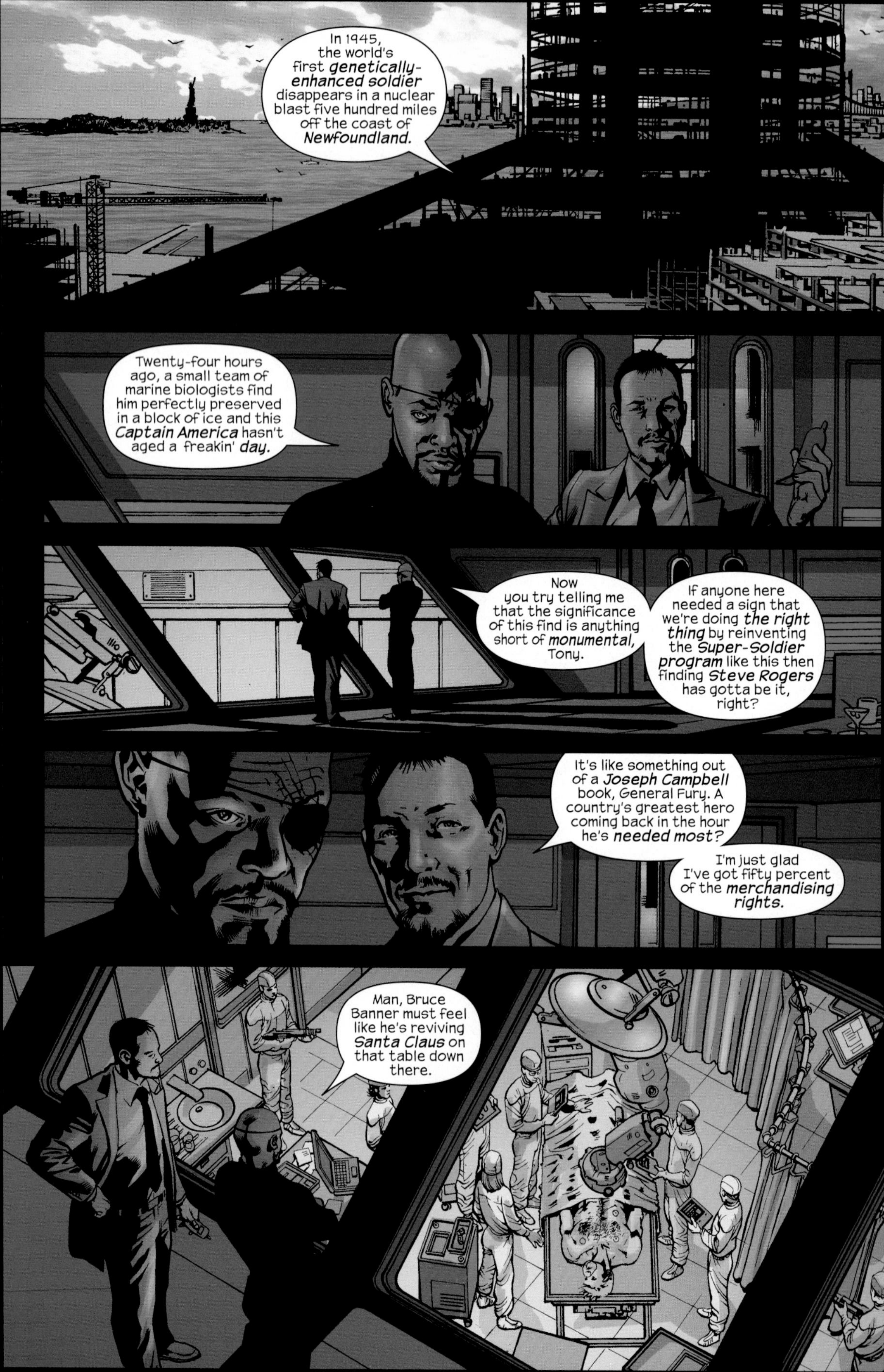
In 1945, the world's first genetically-enhanced soldier disappears in a nuclear blast five hundred miles off the coast of Newfoundland.
Twenty-four hours ago, a small team of marine biologists find him perfectly preserved in a block of ice and this Captain America hasn't aged a freakin' day.
Now you try telling me that the significance of this find is anything short of monumental, Tony.
If anyone here needed a sign that we're doing the right thing by reinventing the Super-Soldier program like this then finding Steve Rogers has gotta be it, right?
It's like something out of a Joseph Campbell book, General Fury. A country's greatest hero coming back in the hour he's needed most?
I'm just glad I've got fifty percent of the merchandising rights.
Man, Bruce Banner must feel like he's reviving Santa Claus on that table down there.

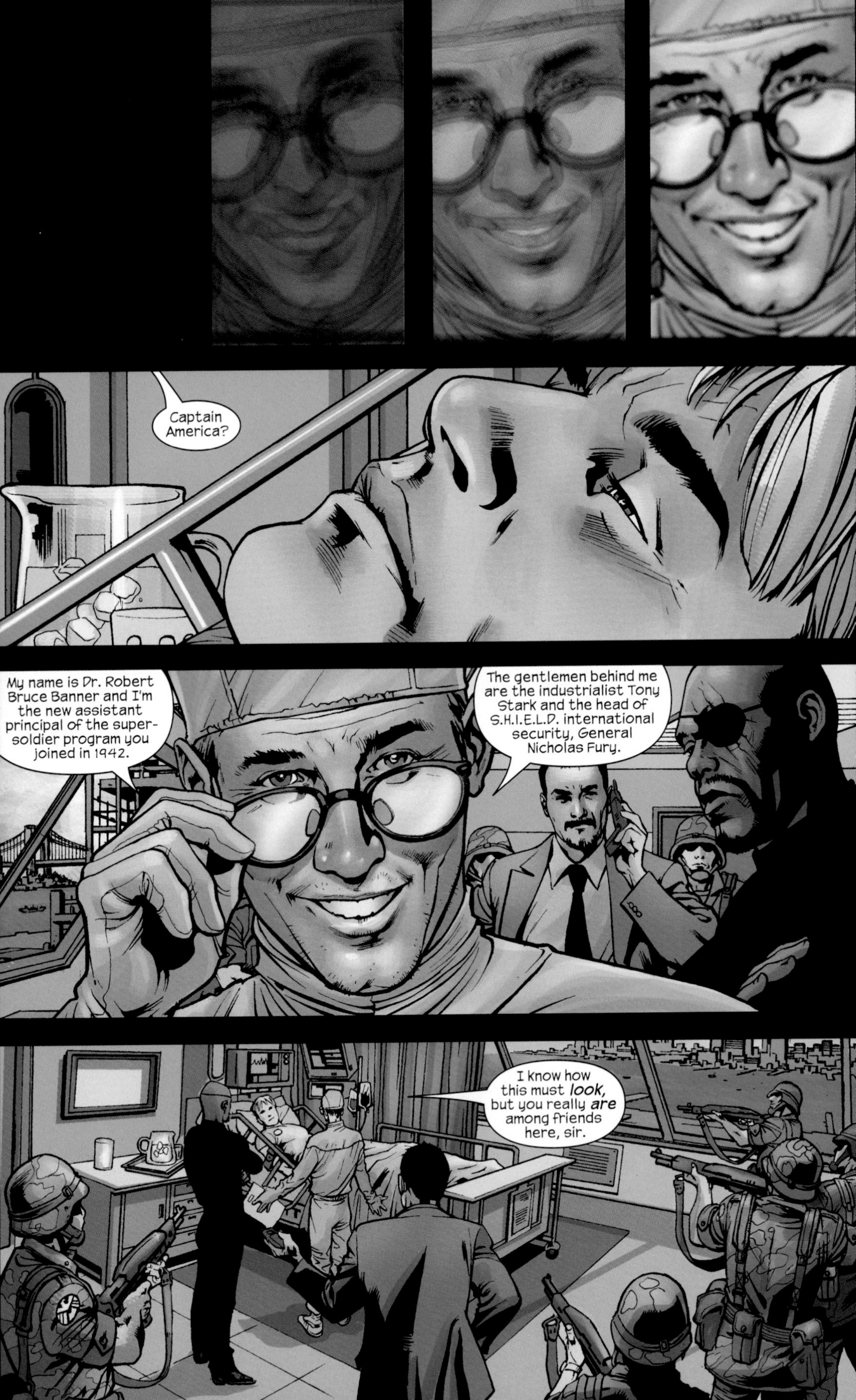
Captain America?
My name is Dr. Robert Bruce Banner and I'm the new assistant principal of the super-soldier program you joined in 1942.
The gentlemen behind me are the industrialist Tony Stark and the head of S.H.I.E.L.D. international security, General Nicholas Fury.
I know how this must *look,* but you really *are* among friends here, sir.

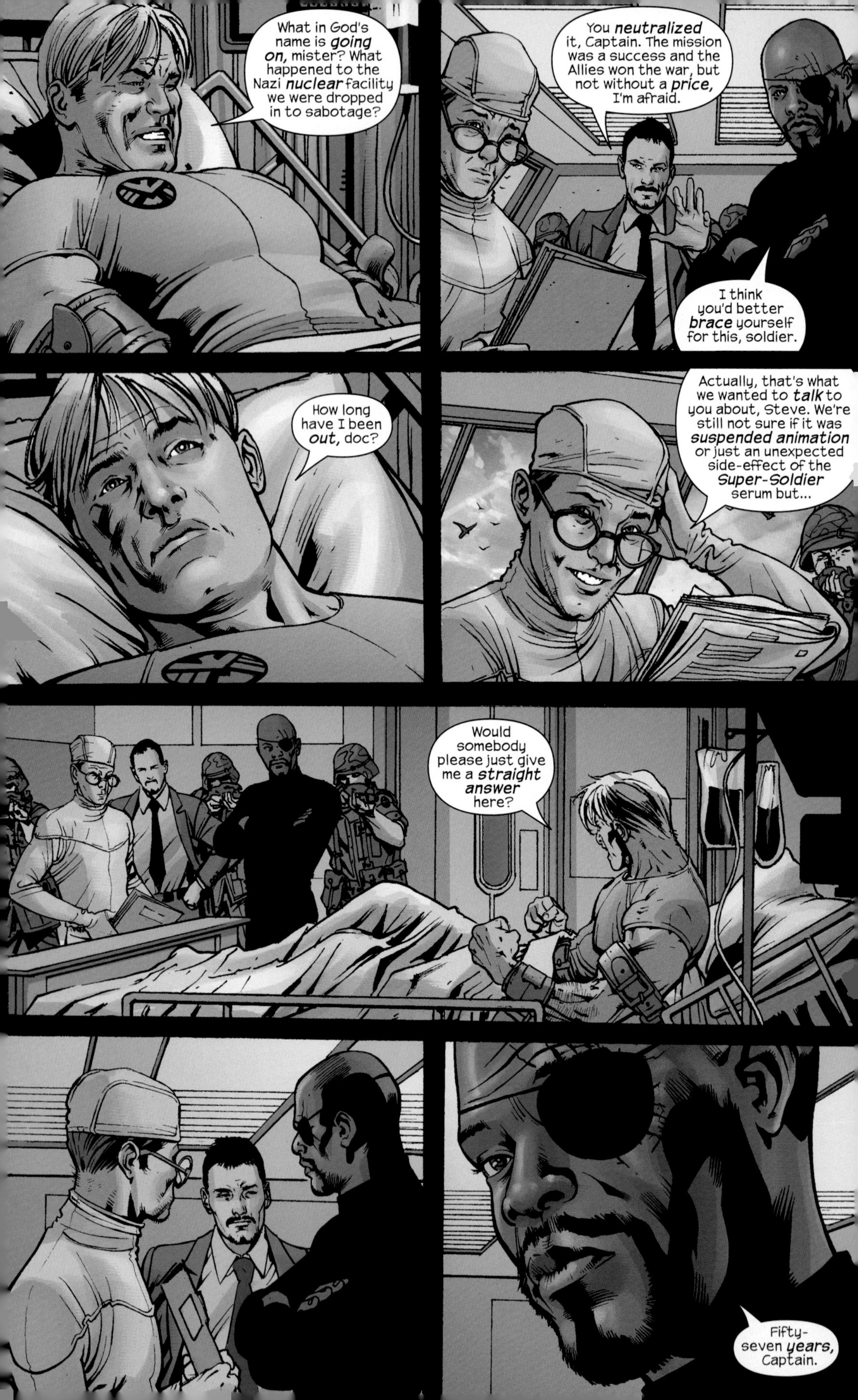
What in God's name is *going on,* mister? What happened to the Nazi *nuclear* facility we were dropped in to sabotage?
You *neutralized* it, Captain. The mission was a success and the Allies won the war, but not without a *price,* I'm afraid.
I think you'd better *brace* yourself for this, soldier.
How long have I been *out,* doc?
Actually, that's what we wanted to *talk* to you about, Steve. We're still not sure if it was *suspended animation* or just an unexpected side-effect of the *Super-Soldier* serum but...
Would somebody please just give me a *straight answer* here?
Fifty-seven *years,* Captain.

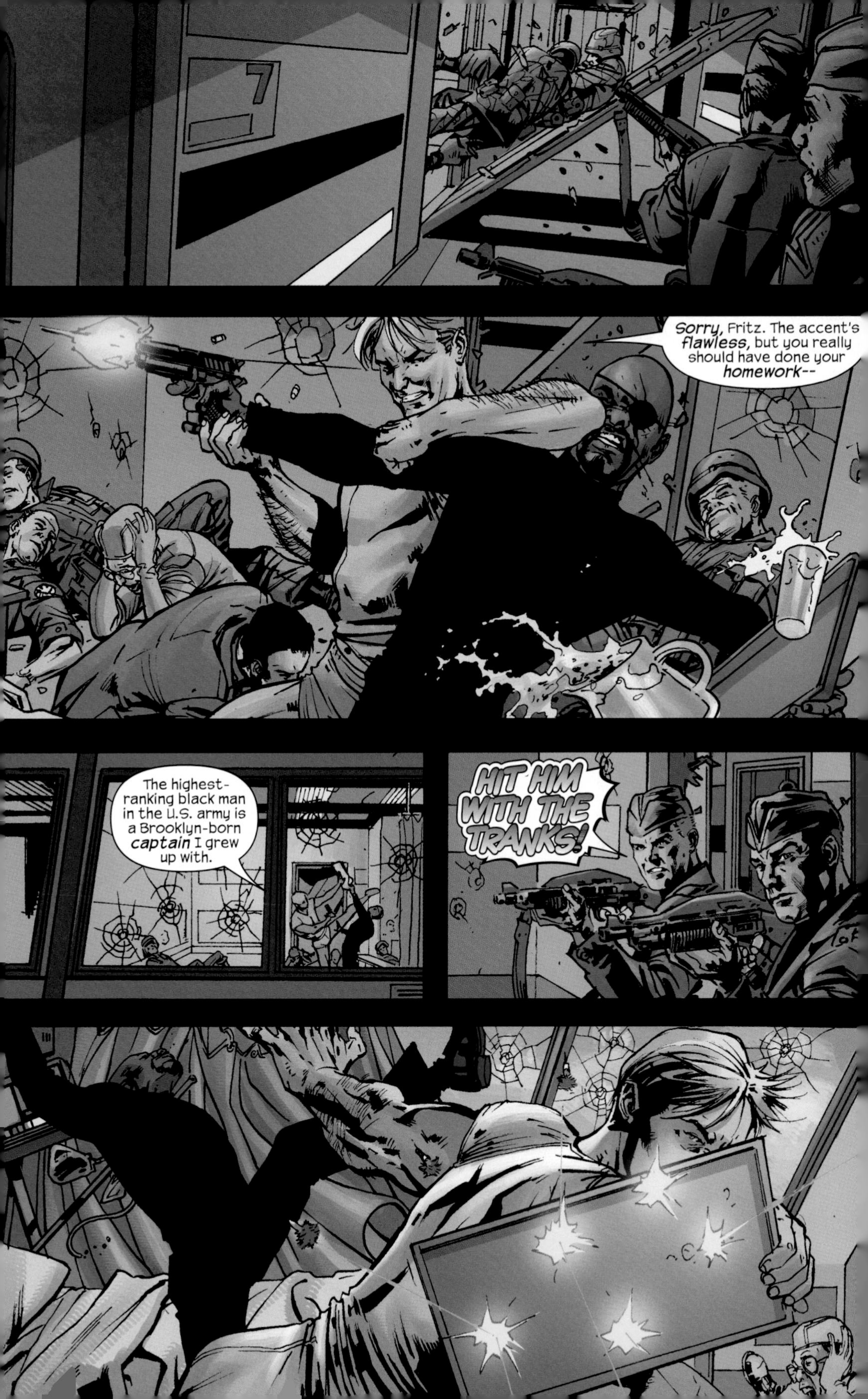
Sorry, Fritz. The accent's flawless, but you really should have done your homework--
The highest-ranking black man in the U.S. army is a Brooklyn-born captain I grew up with.
HIT HIM WITH THE TRANKS!

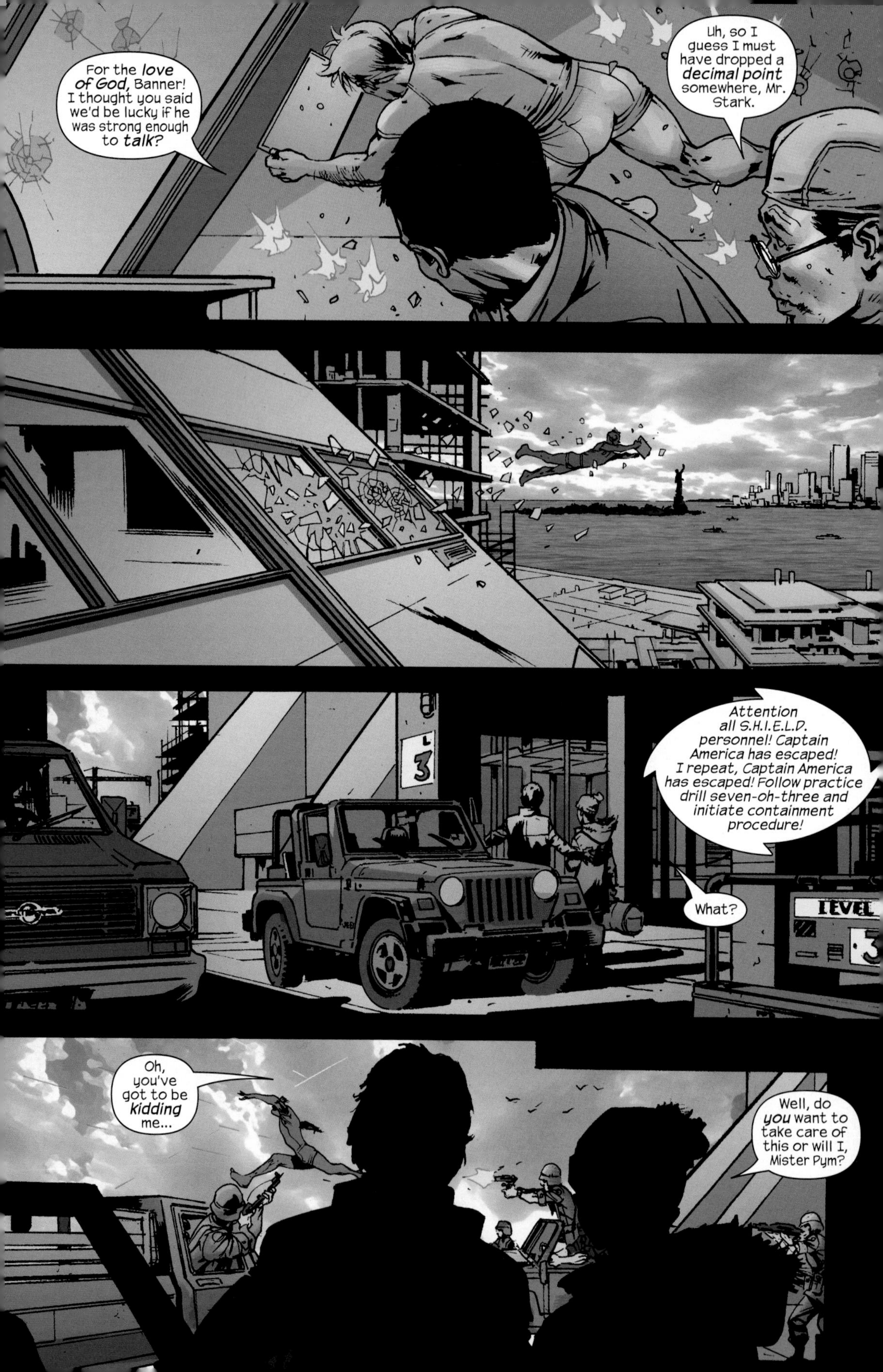
For the *love of God,* Banner! I thought you said we'd be lucky if he was strong enough to ***talk***?
Uh, so I guess I must have dropped a **decimal point** somewhere, Mr. Stark.
L 3
Attention all S.H.I.E.L.D. personnel! Captain America has escaped! I repeat, Captain America has escaped! Follow practice drill seven-oh-three and initiate containment procedure!
What?
LEVEL 3
Oh, you've got to be ***kidding*** me...
Well, do ***you*** want to take care of this or will I, Mister Pym?

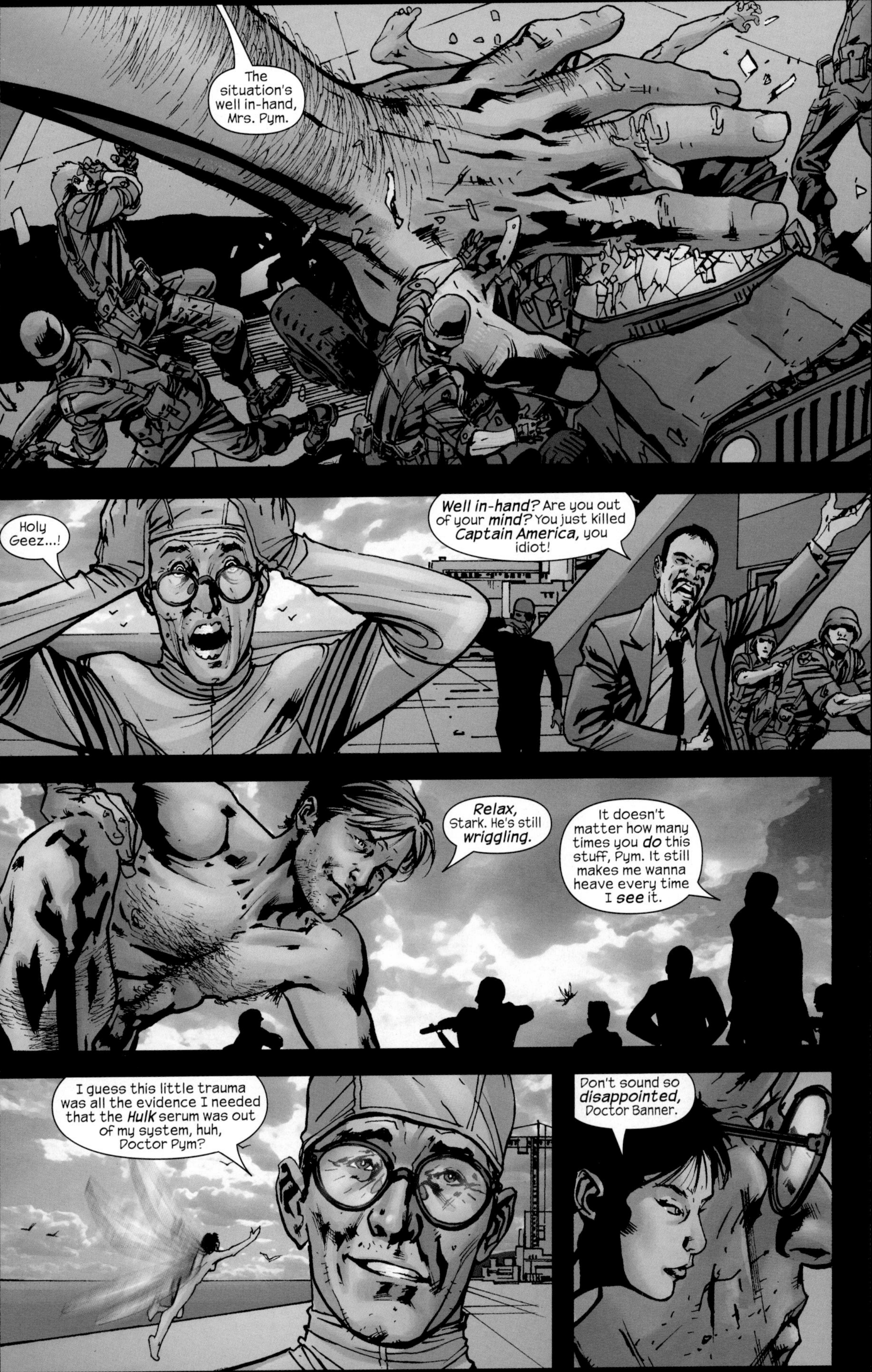
The situation's well in-hand, Mrs. Pym.
Holy Geez...!
Well in-hand? Are you out of your mind? You just killed Captain America, you idiot!
Relax, Stark. He's still wriggling.
It doesn't matter how many times you do this stuff, Pym. It still makes me wanna heave every time I see it.
I guess this little trauma was all the evidence I needed that the Hulk serum was out of my system, huh, Doctor Pym?
Don't sound so disappointed, Doctor Banner.

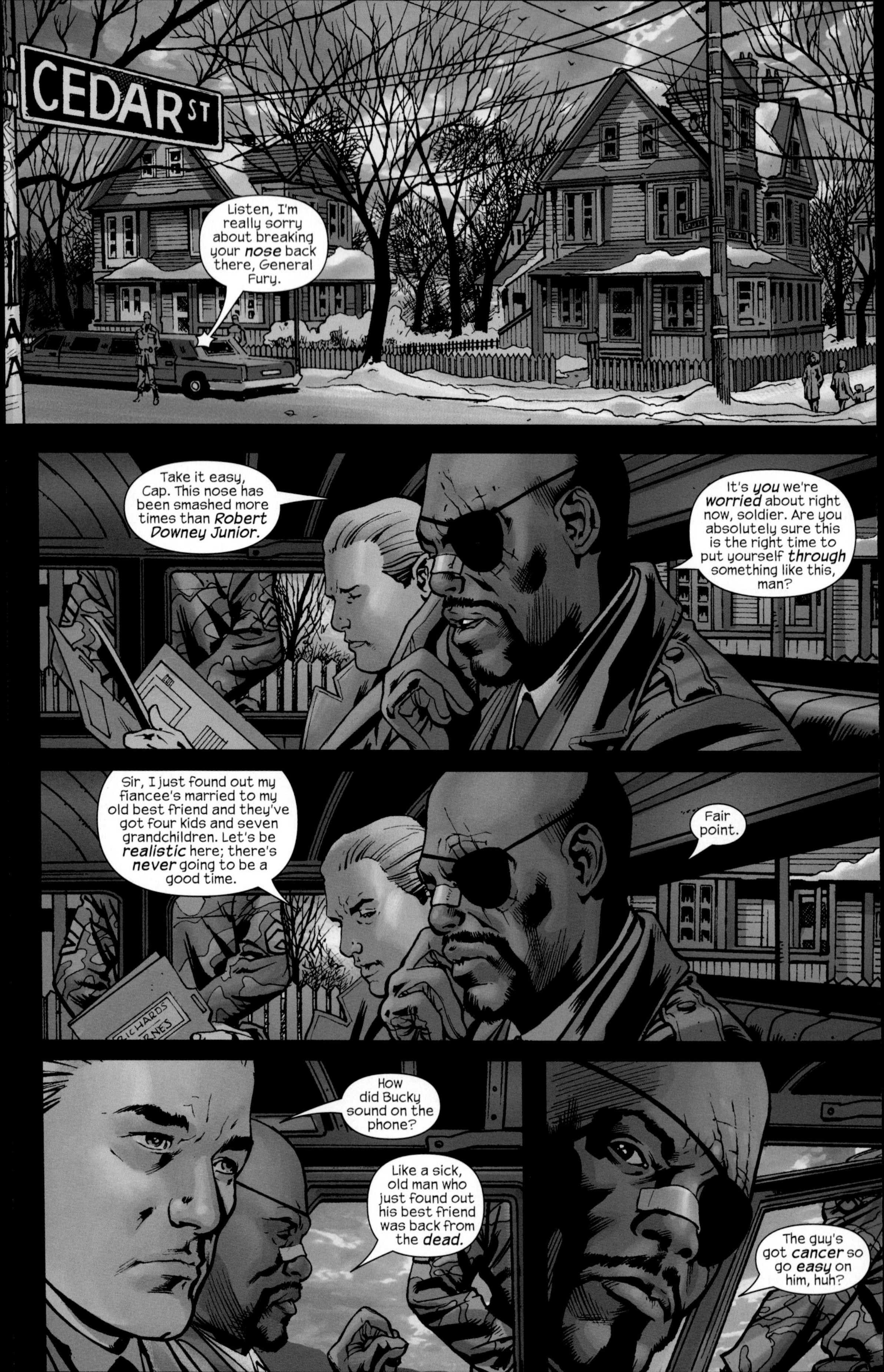
CEDAR ST
Listen, I'm really sorry about breaking your nose back there, General Fury.
Take it easy, Cap. This nose has been smashed more times than Robert Downey Junior.
It's you we're worried about right now, soldier. Are you absolutely sure this is the right time to put yourself through something like this, man?
Sir, I just found out my fiancee's married to my old best friend and they've got four kids and seven grandchildren. Let's be realistic here; there's never going to be a good time.
Fair point.
How did Bucky sound on the phone?
Like a sick, old man who just found out his best friend was back from the dead.
The guy's got cancer so go easy on him, huh?

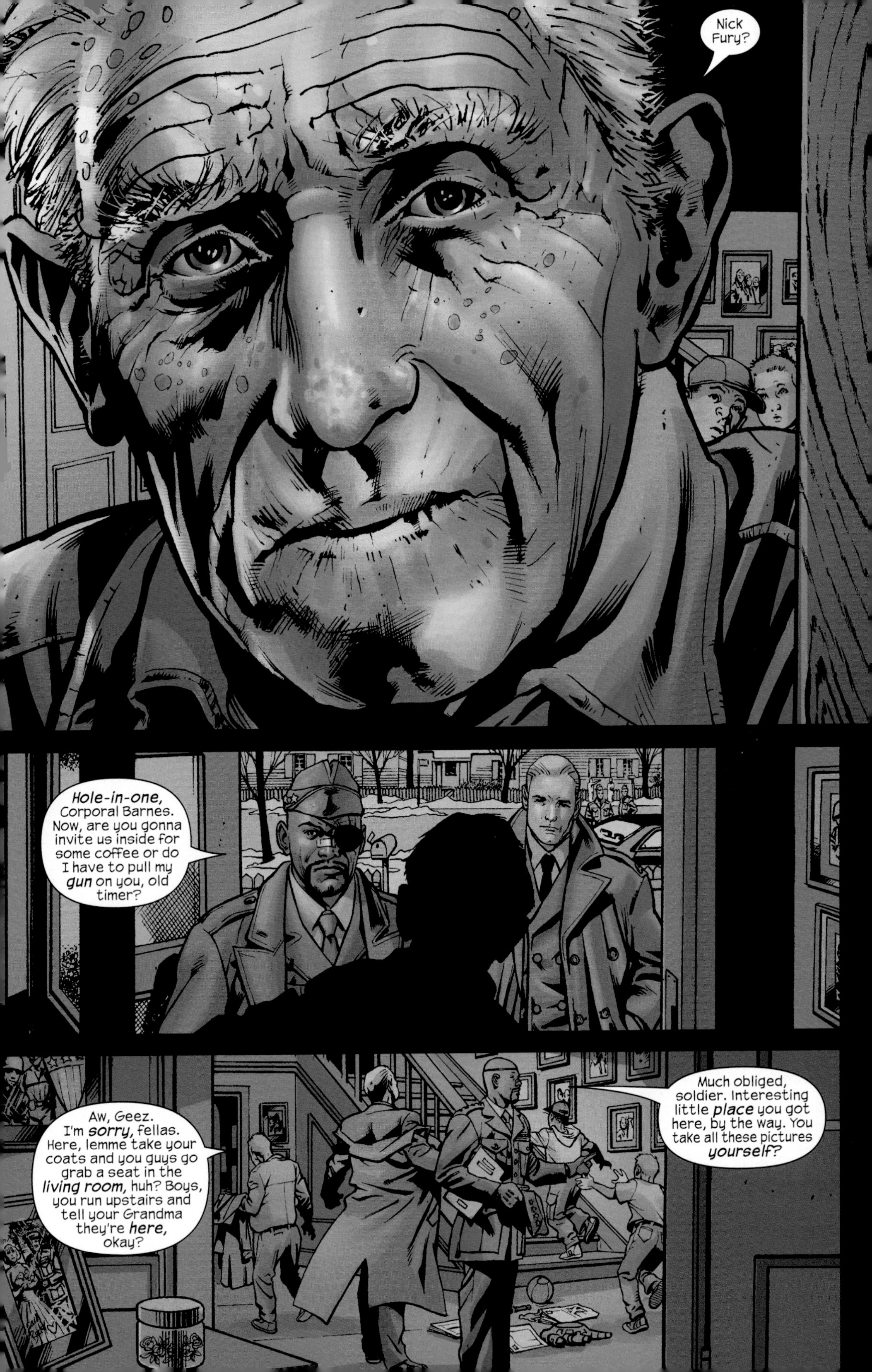
Nick Fury?
Hole-in-one, Corporal Barnes. Now, are you gonna invite us inside for some coffee or do I have to pull my gun on you, old timer?
Aw, Geez. I'm sorry, fellas. Here, lemme take your coats and you guys go grab a seat in the living room, huh? Boys, you run upstairs and tell your Grandma they're here, okay?
Much obliged, soldier. Interesting little place you got here, by the way. You take all these pictures yourself?

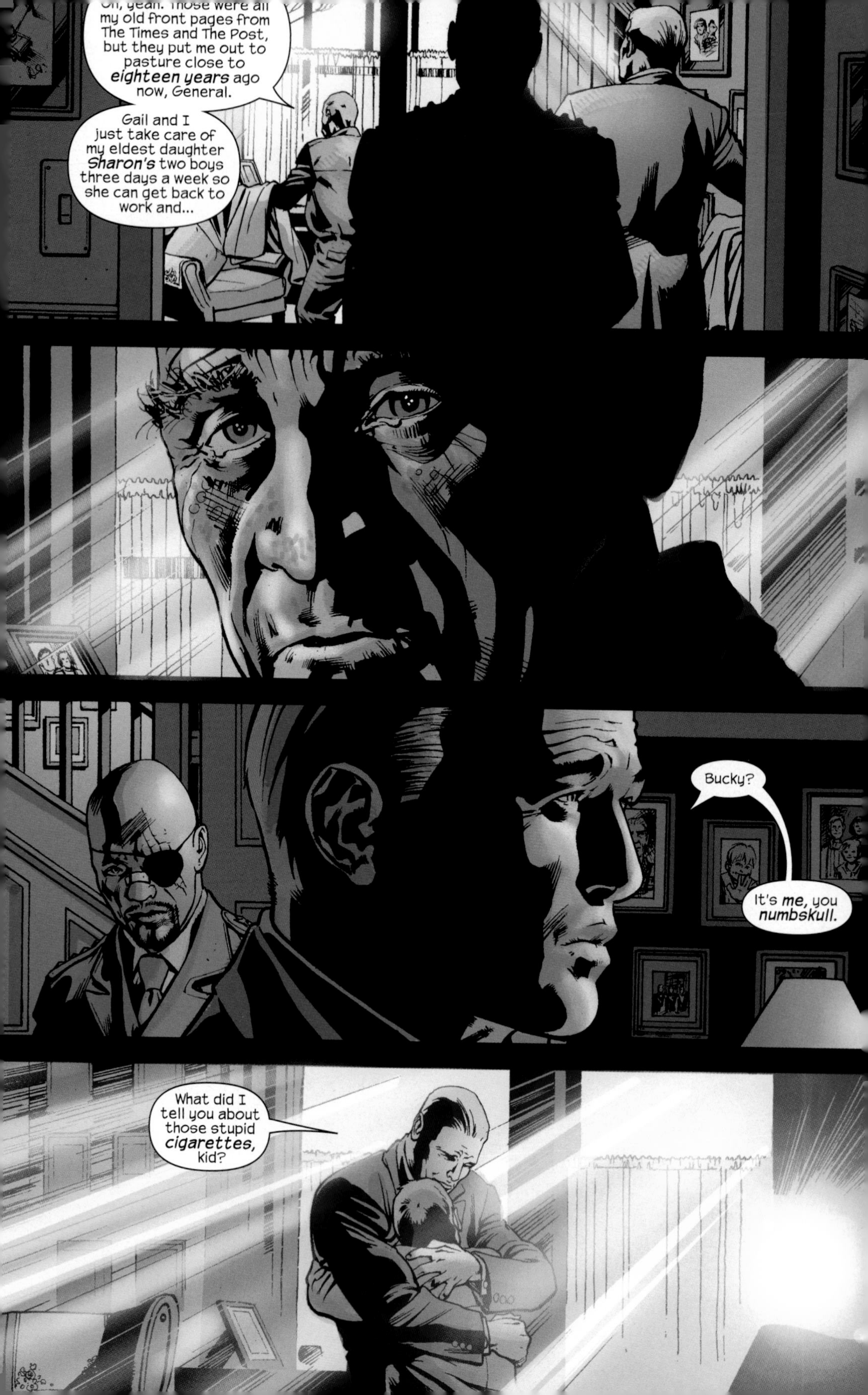
Oh, yeah. Those were all my old front pages from The Times and The Post, but they put me out to pasture close to eighteen years ago now, General.
Gail and I just take care of my eldest daughter Sharon's two boys three days a week so she can get back to work and...
Bucky?
It's me, you numbskull.
What did I tell you about those stupid cigarettes, kid?

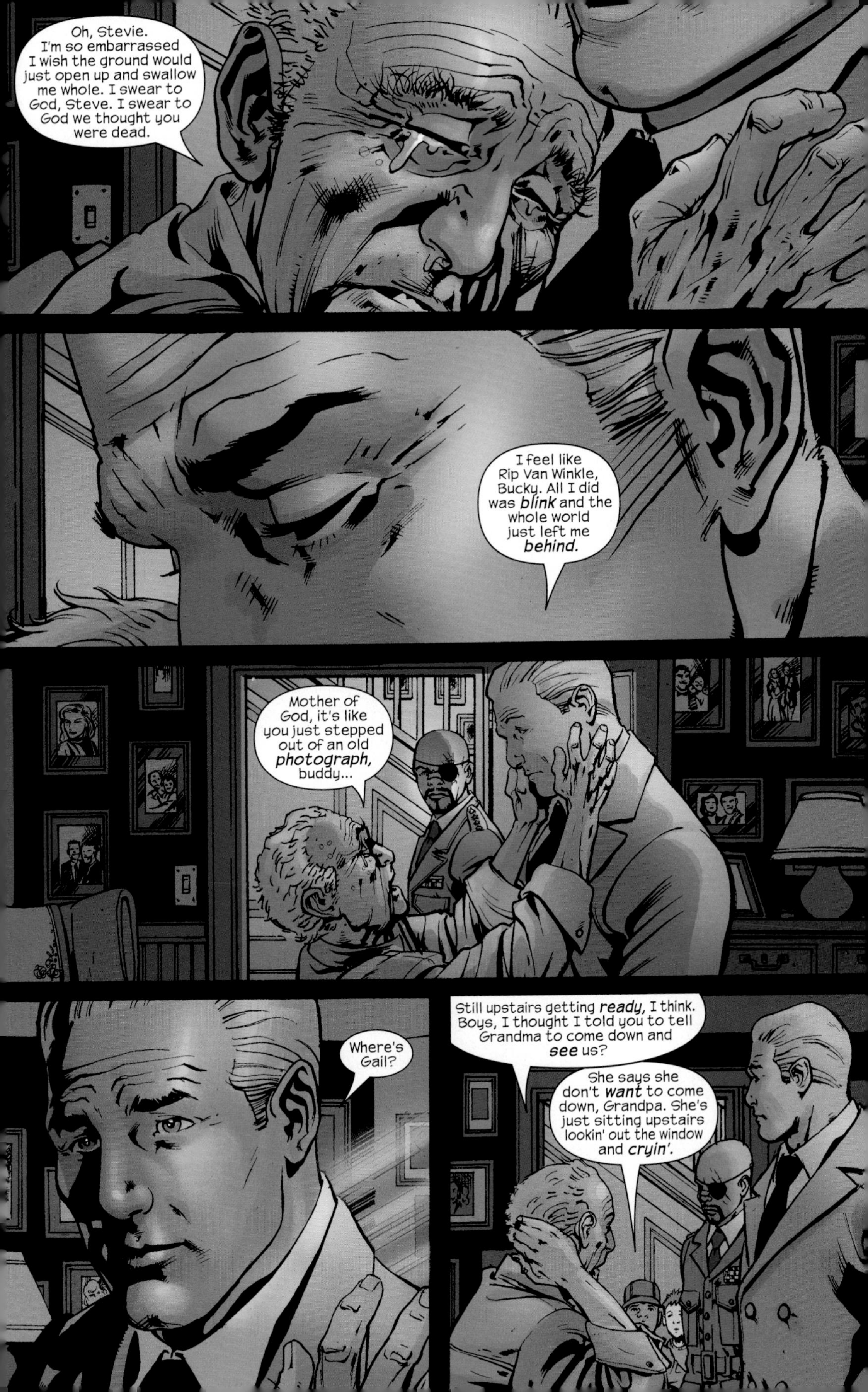
Oh, Stevie. I'm so embarrassed I wish the ground would just open up and swallow me whole. I swear to God, Steve. I swear to God we thought you were dead.
I feel like Rip Van Winkle, Bucky. All I did was *blink* and the whole world just left me *behind.*
Mother of God, it's like you just stepped out of an old *photograph,* buddy...
Where's Gail?
Still upstairs getting *ready,* I think. Boys, I thought I told you to tell Grandma to come down and *see* us?
She says she don't *want* to come down, Grandpa. She's just sitting upstairs lookin' out the window and *cryin'.*

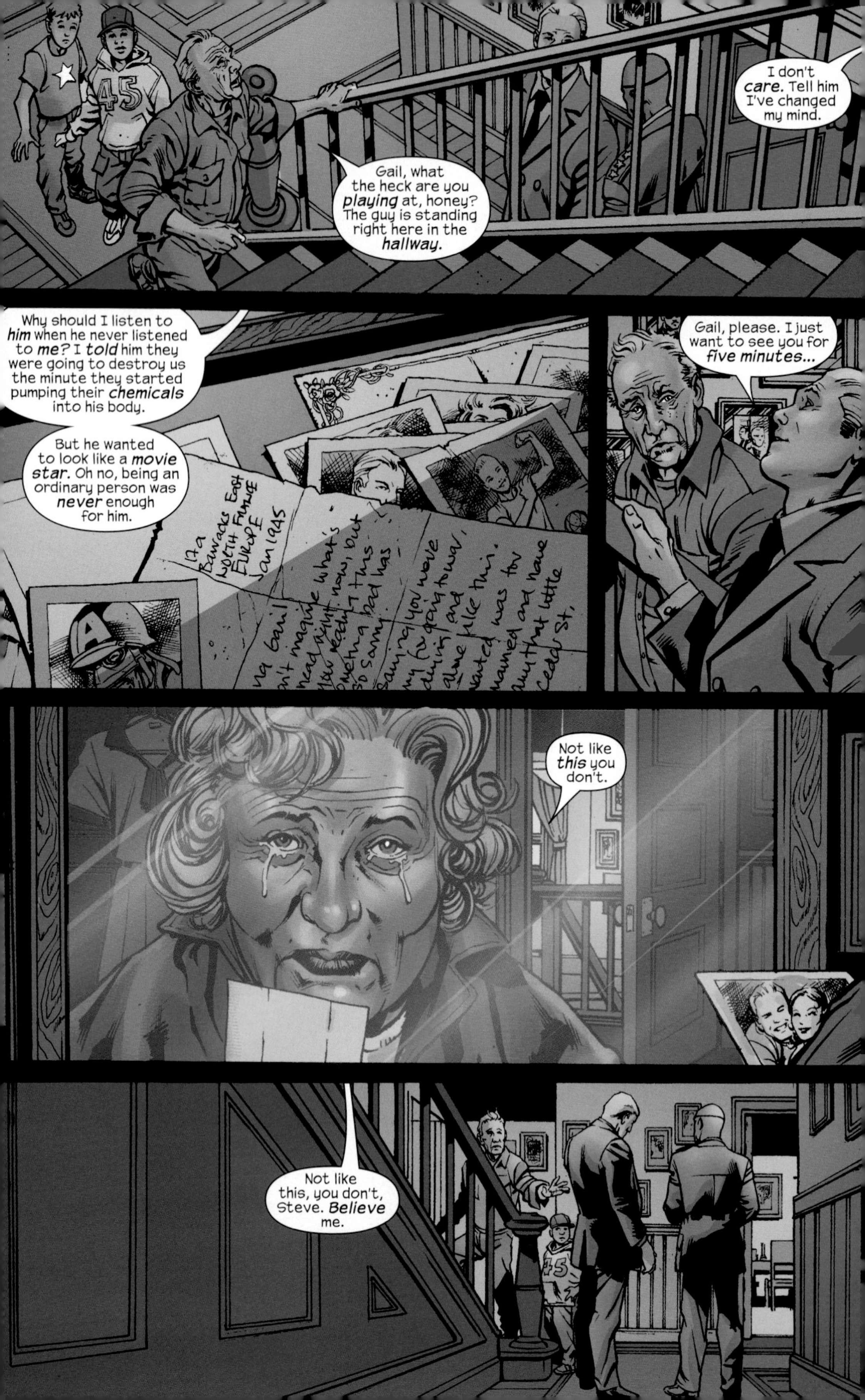
Gail, what the heck are you *playing* at, honey? The guy is standing right here in the *hallway.*
I don't *care.* Tell him I've changed my mind.
Why should I listen to *him* when he never listened to *me*? I *told* him they were going to destroy us the minute they started pumping their *chemicals* into his body.
But he wanted to look like a *movie star.* Oh no, being an ordinary person was *never* enough for him.
Gail, please. I just want to see you for *five minutes...*
Not like *this* you don't.
Not like this, you don't, Steve. *Believe* me.

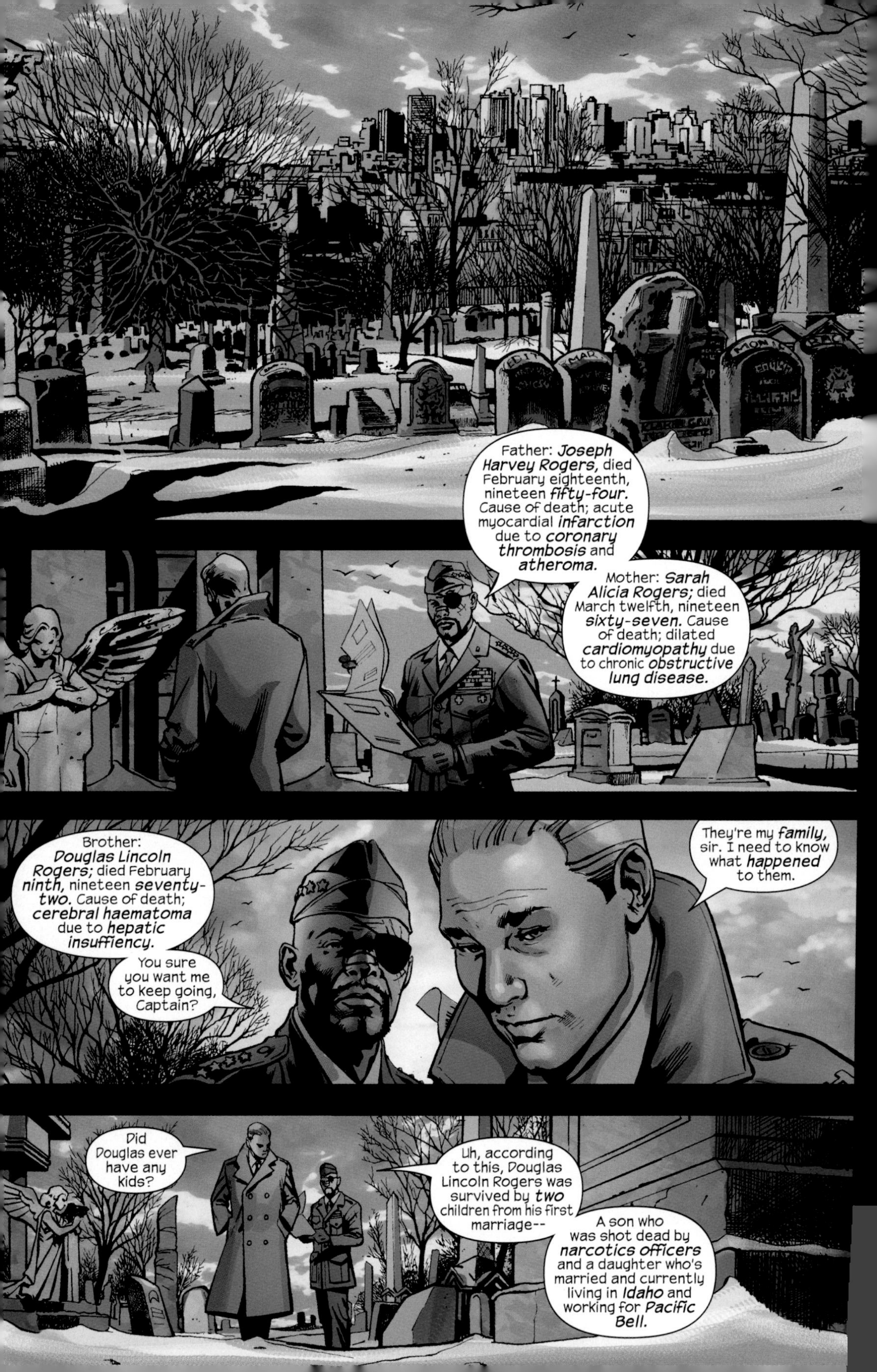

Father: *Joseph Harvey Rogers,* died February eighteenth, nineteen *fifty-four.* Cause of death; acute myocardial *infarction* due to *coronary thrombosis* and *atheroma.*
Mother: *Sarah Alicia Rogers;* died March twelfth, nineteen *sixty-seven.* Cause of death; dilated *cardiomyopathy* due to chronic *obstructive lung disease.*
Brother: *Douglas Lincoln Rogers;* died February *ninth,* nineteen *seventy-two.* Cause of death; *cerebral haematoma* due to *hepatic insuffiency.*
You sure you want me to keep going, Captain?
They're my *family,* sir. I need to know what *happened* to them.
Did Douglas ever have any kids?
Uh, according to this, Douglas Lincoln Rogers was survived by *two* children from his first marriage--
A son who was shot dead by *narcotics officers* and a daughter who's married and currently living in *Idaho* and working for *Pacific Bell.*

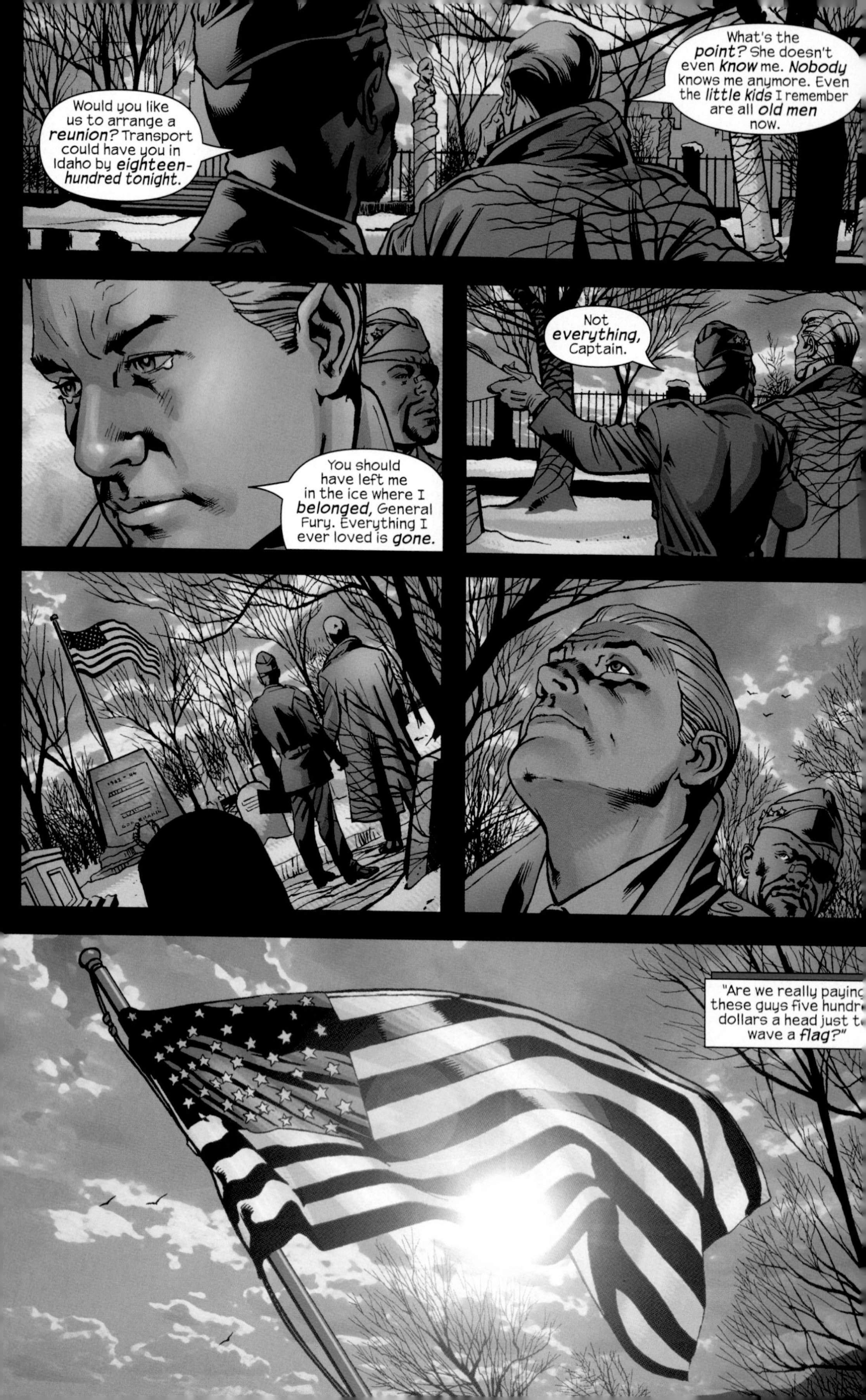
Would you like us to arrange a reunion? Transport could have you in Idaho by eighteen-hundred tonight.
What's the point? She doesn't even know me. Nobody knows me anymore. Even the little kids I remember are all old men now.
You should have left me in the ice where I belonged, General Fury. Everything I ever loved is gone.
Not everything, Captain.
"Are we really payin these guys five hundr dollars a head just t wave a flag?"

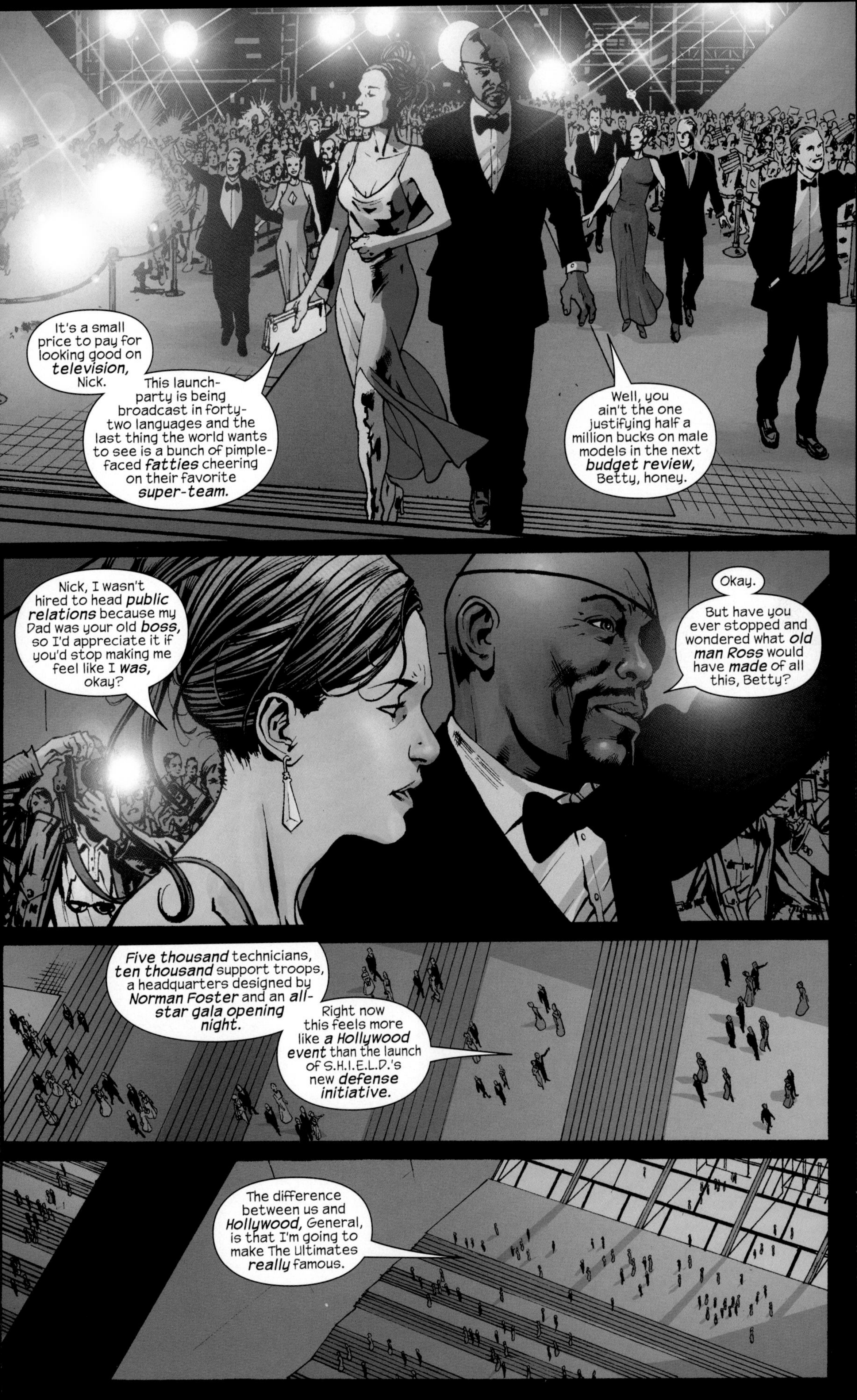
It's a small price to pay for looking good on television, Nick.
This launch-party is being broadcast in forty-two languages and the last thing the world wants to see is a bunch of pimple-faced fatties cheering on their favorite super-team.
Well, you ain't the one justifying half a million bucks on male models in the next budget review, Betty, honey.
Nick, I wasn't hired to head public relations because my Dad was your old boss, so I'd appreciate it if you'd stop making me feel like I was, okay?
Okay.
But have you ever stopped and wondered what old man Ross would have made of all this, Betty?
Five thousand technicians, ten thousand support troops, a headquarters designed by Norman Foster and an all-star gala opening night.
Right now this feels more like a Hollywood event than the launch of S.H.I.E.L.D.'s new defense initiative.
The difference between us and Hollywood, General, is that I'm going to make The Ultimates really famous.

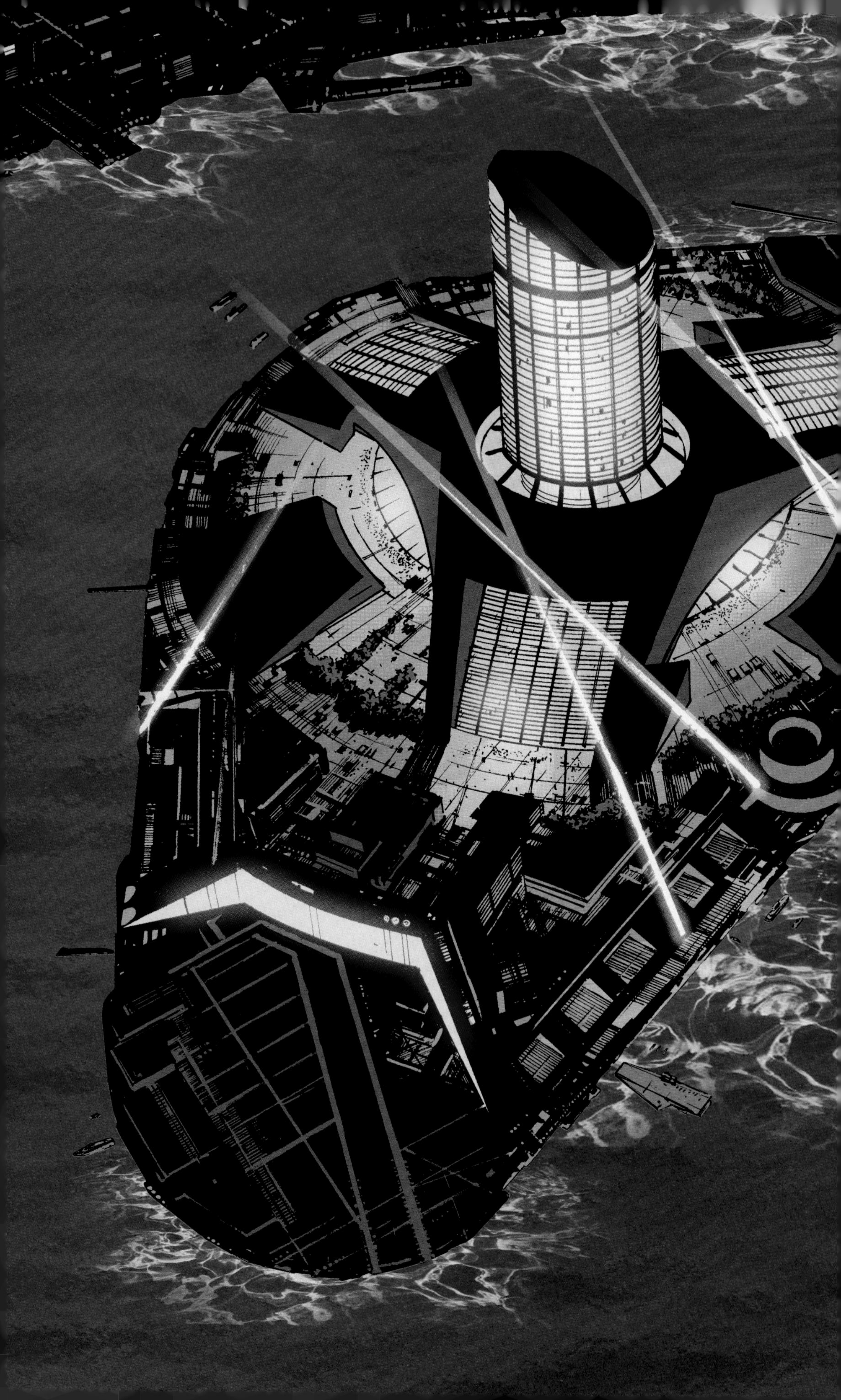

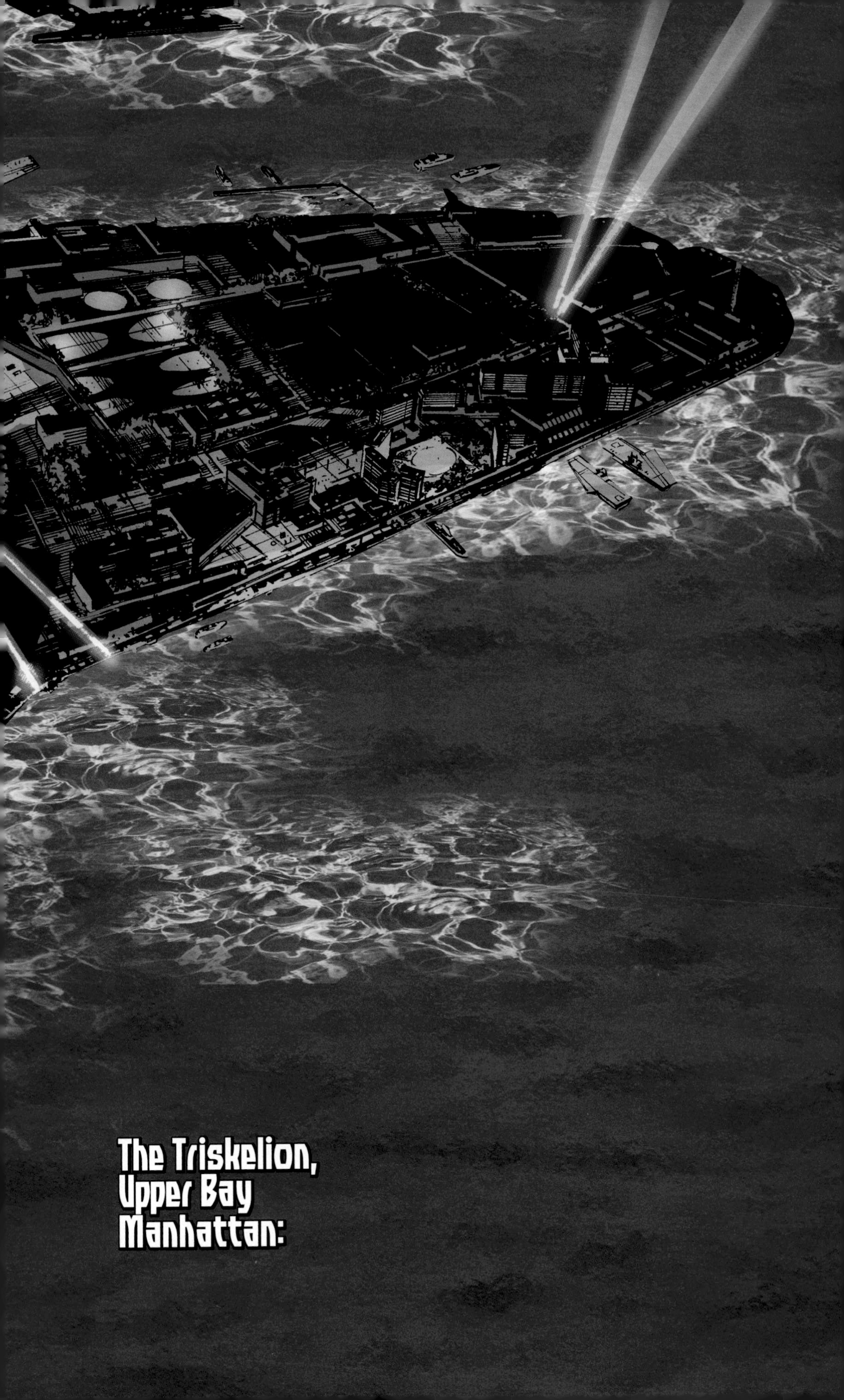
The Triskelion, Upper Bay Manhattan:

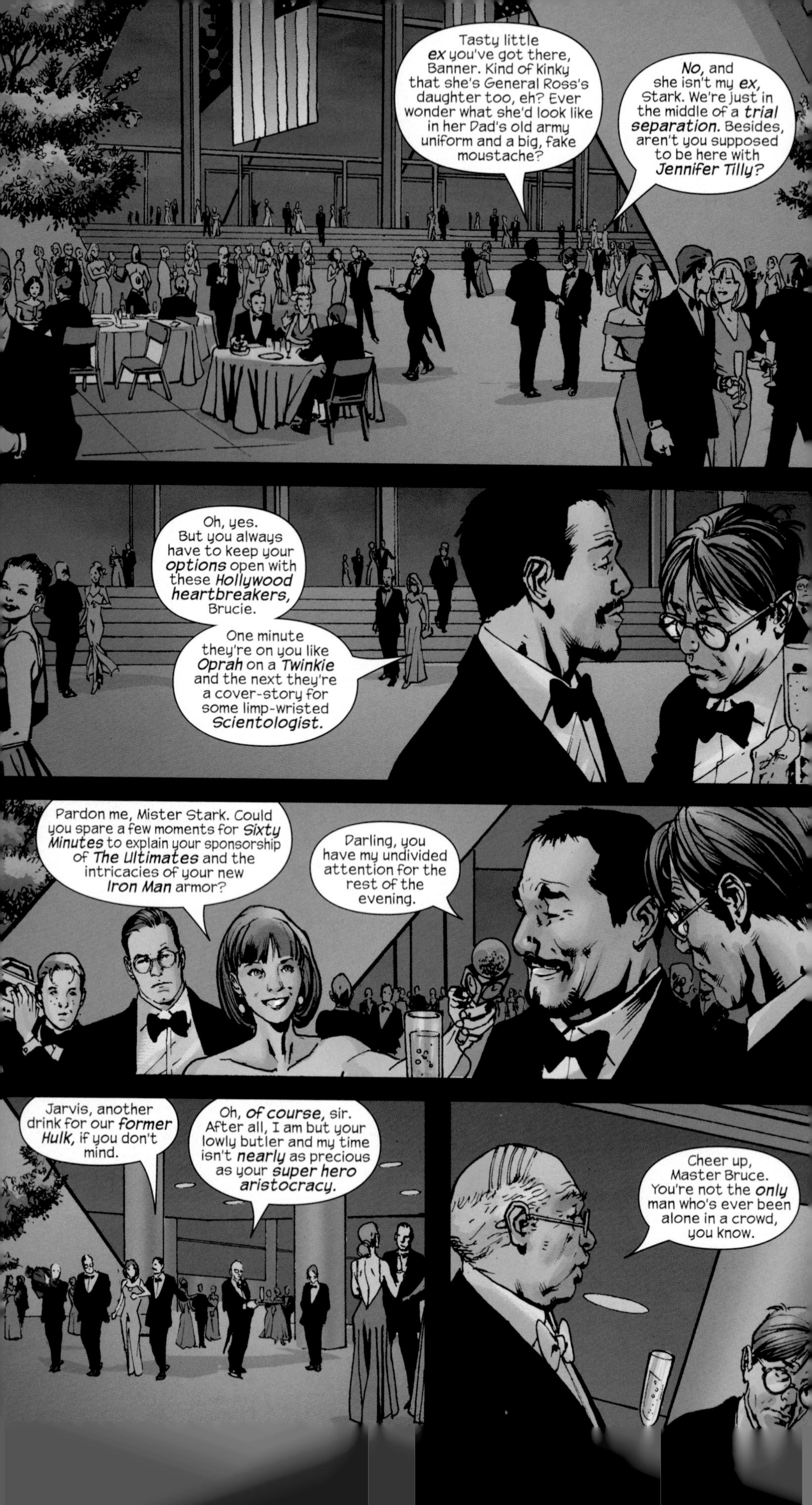

Tasty little ex you've got there, Banner. Kind of kinky that she's General Ross's daughter too, eh? Ever wonder what she'd look like in her Dad's old army uniform and a big, fake moustache?
No, and she isn't my ex, Stark. We're just in the middle of a trial separation. Besides, aren't you supposed to be here with Jennifer Tilly?
Oh, yes. But you always have to keep your options open with these Hollywood heartbreakers, Brucie.
One minute they're on you like Oprah on a Twinkie and the next they're a cover-story for some limp-wristed Scientologist.
Pardon me, Mister Stark. Could you spare a few moments for Sixty Minutes to explain your sponsorship of The Ultimates and the intricacies of your new Iron Man armor?
Darling, you have my undivided attention for the rest of the evening.
Jarvis, another drink for our former Hulk, if you don't mind.
Oh, of course, sir. After all, I am but your lowly butler and my time isn't nearly as precious as your super hero aristocracy.
Cheer up, Master Bruce. You're not the only man who's ever been alone in a crowd, you know.

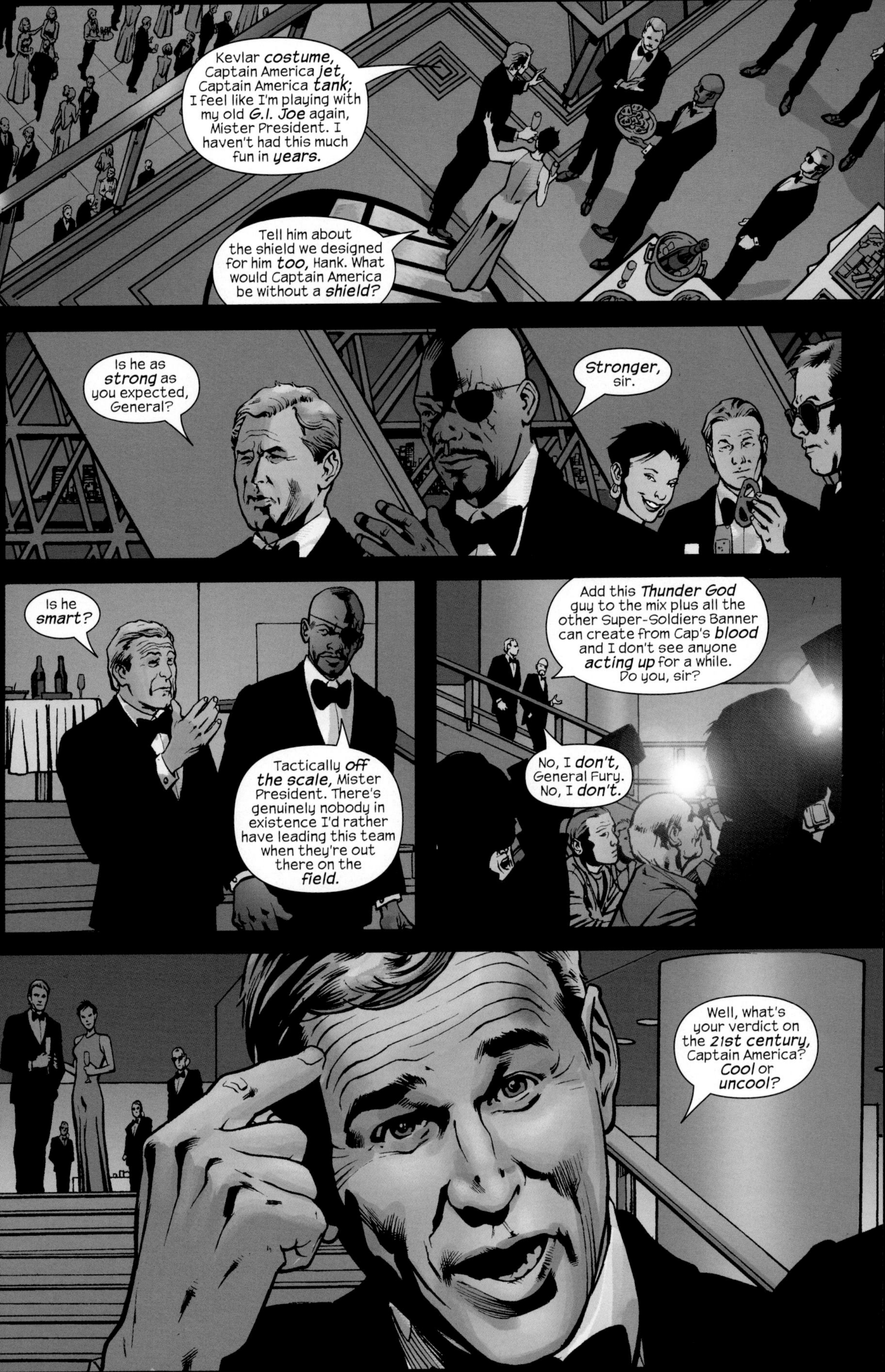

Kevlar *costume,* Captain America *jet,* Captain America *tank;* I feel like I'm playing with my old *G.I. Joe* again, Mister President. I haven't had this much fun in *years.*
Tell him about the shield we designed for him *too,* Hank. What would Captain America be without a *shield?*
Is he as *strong* as you expected, General?
Stronger, sir.
Is he *smart?*
Tactically *off the scale,* Mister President. There's genuinely nobody in existence I'd rather have leading this team when they're out there on the *field.*
Add this *Thunder God* guy to the mix plus all the other Super-Soldiers Banner can create from Cap's *blood* and I don't see anyone *acting up* for a while. Do you, sir?
No, I *don't,* General Fury. No, I *don't.*
Well, what's your verdict on the *21st century,* Captain America? *Cool* or *uncool?*

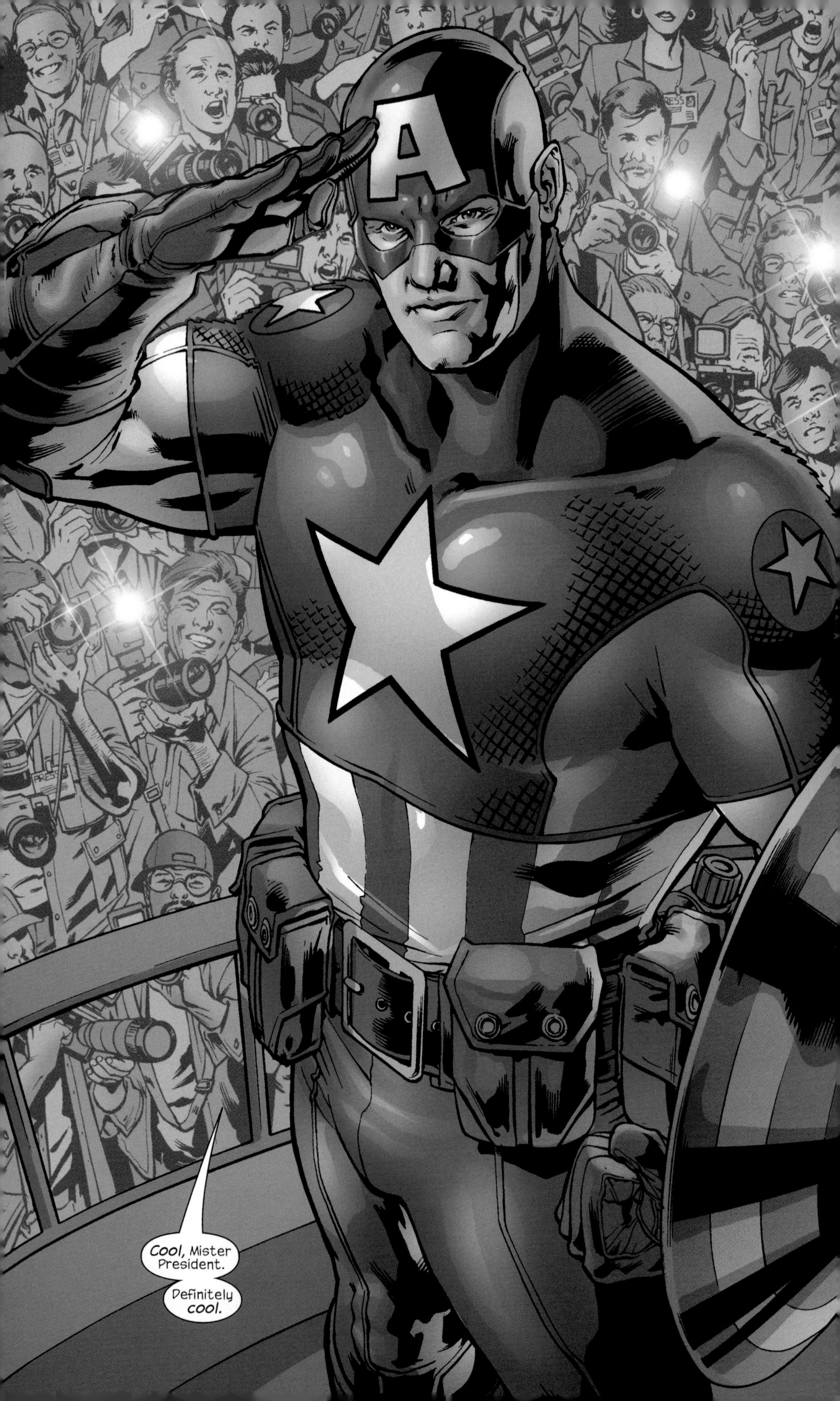
Cool, Mister President.
Definitely cool.

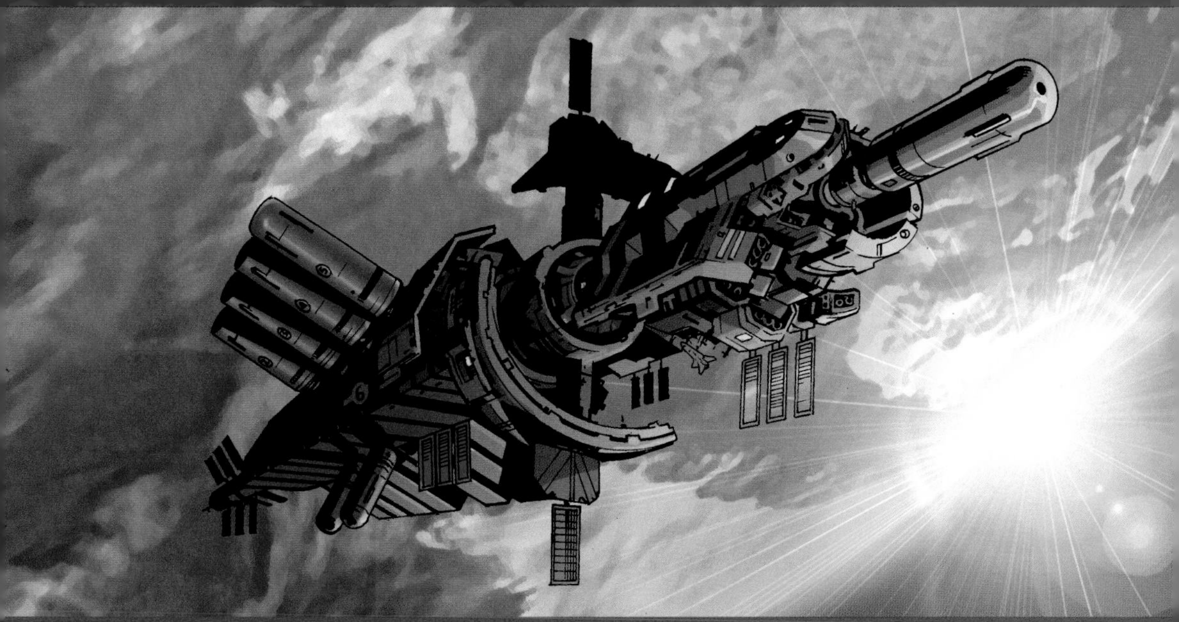

CHAPTER FOUR
THUNDER

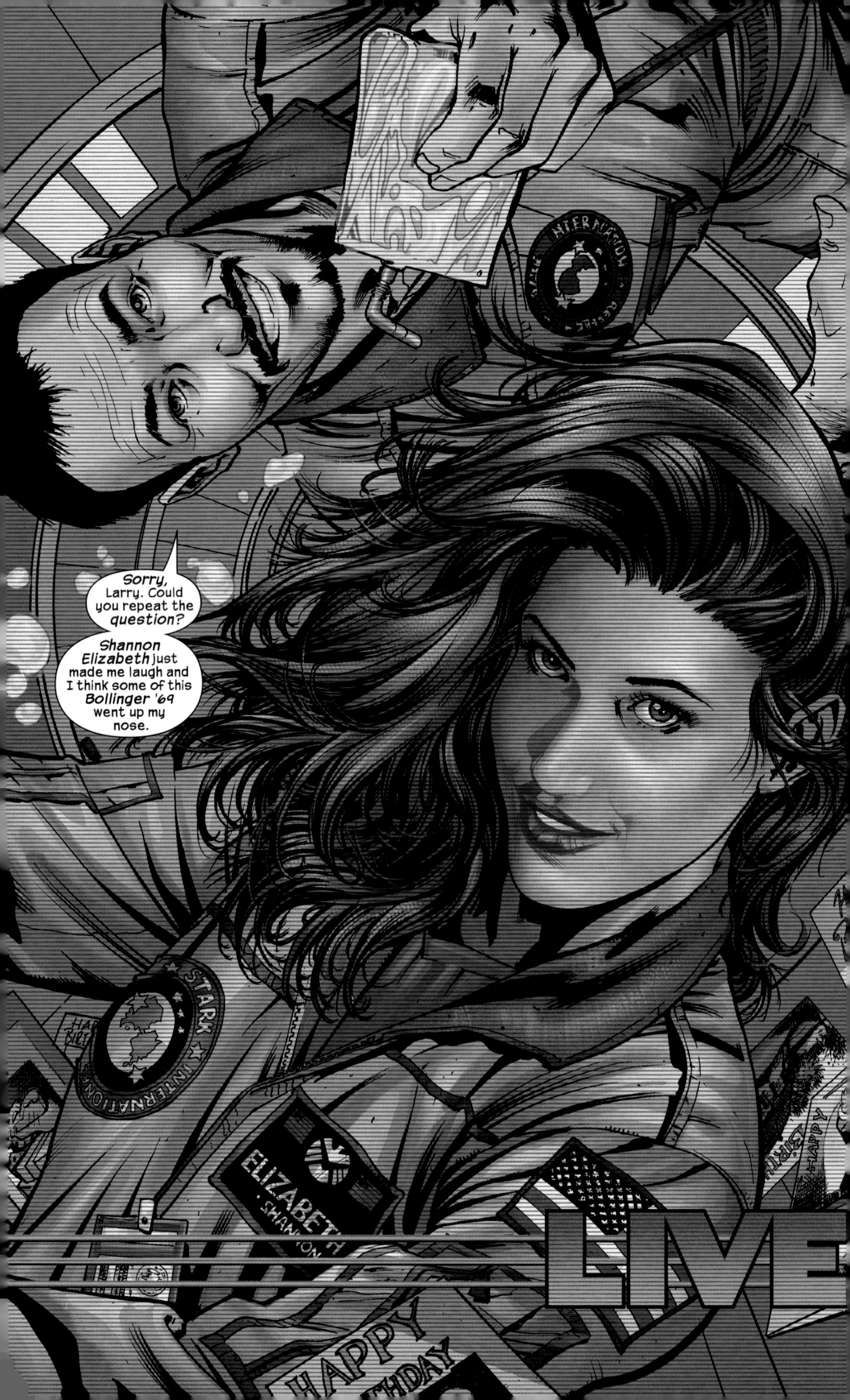
Sorry, Larry. Could you repeat the question?
Shannon Elizabeth just made me laugh and I think some of this Bollinger '69 went up my nose.
LIVE

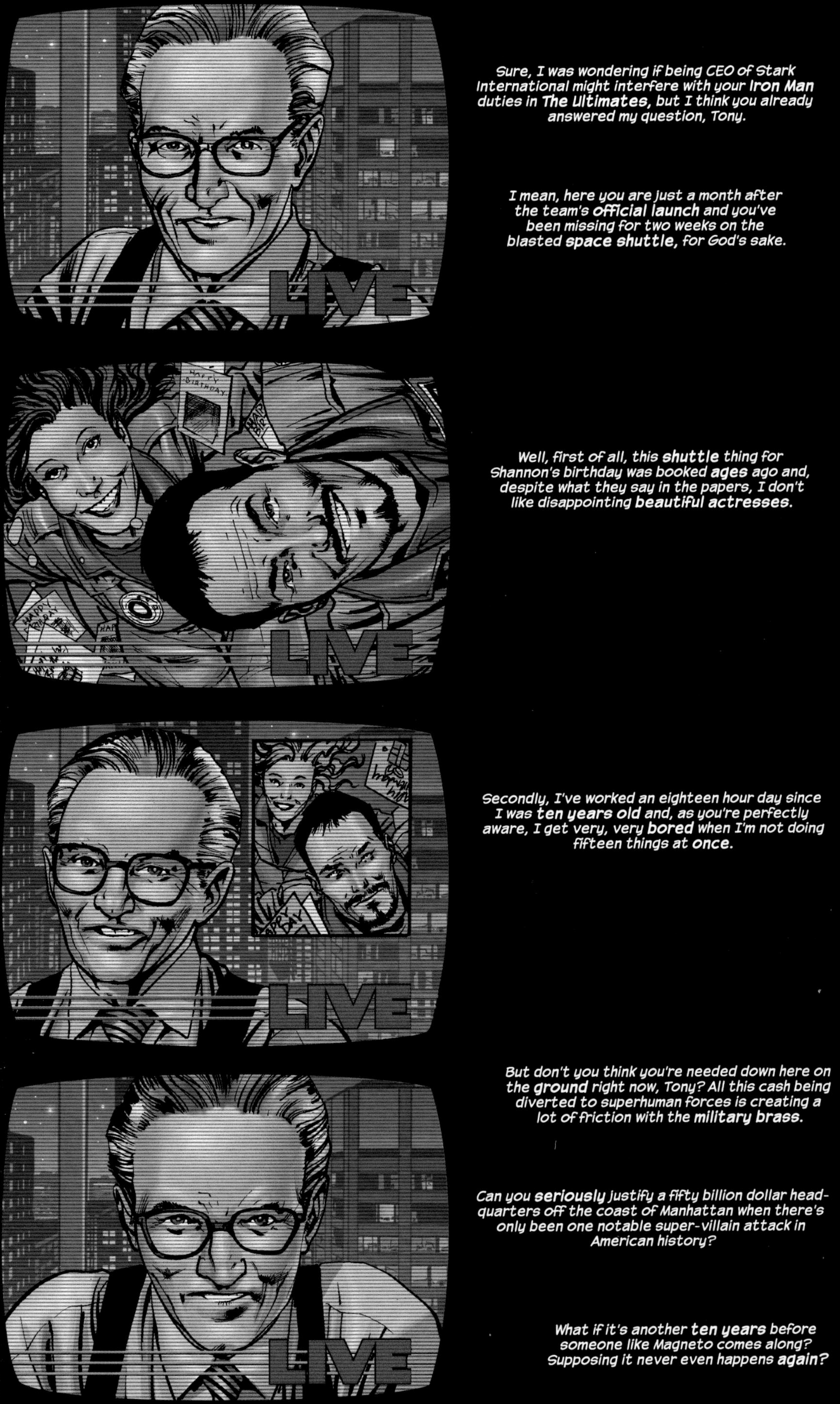
LIVE
Sure, I was wondering if being CEO of Stark International might interfere with your Iron Man duties in The Ultimates, but I think you already answered my question, Tony.
I mean, here you are just a month after the team's official launch and you've been missing for two weeks on the blasted space shuttle, for God's sake.
HAPPY BIRTHDAY
LIVE
Well, first of all, this shuttle thing for Shannon's birthday was booked ages ago and, despite what they say in the papers, I don't like disappointing beautiful actresses.
LIVE
Secondly, I've worked an eighteen hour day since I was ten years old and, as you're perfectly aware, I get very, very bored when I'm not doing fifteen things at once.
LIVE
But don't you think you're needed down here on the ground right now, Tony? All this cash being diverted to superhuman forces is creating a lot of friction with the military brass.
Can you seriously justify a fifty billion dollar head-quarters off the coast of Manhattan when there's only been one notable super-villain attack in American history?
What if it's another ten years before someone like Magneto comes along? Supposing it never even happens again?

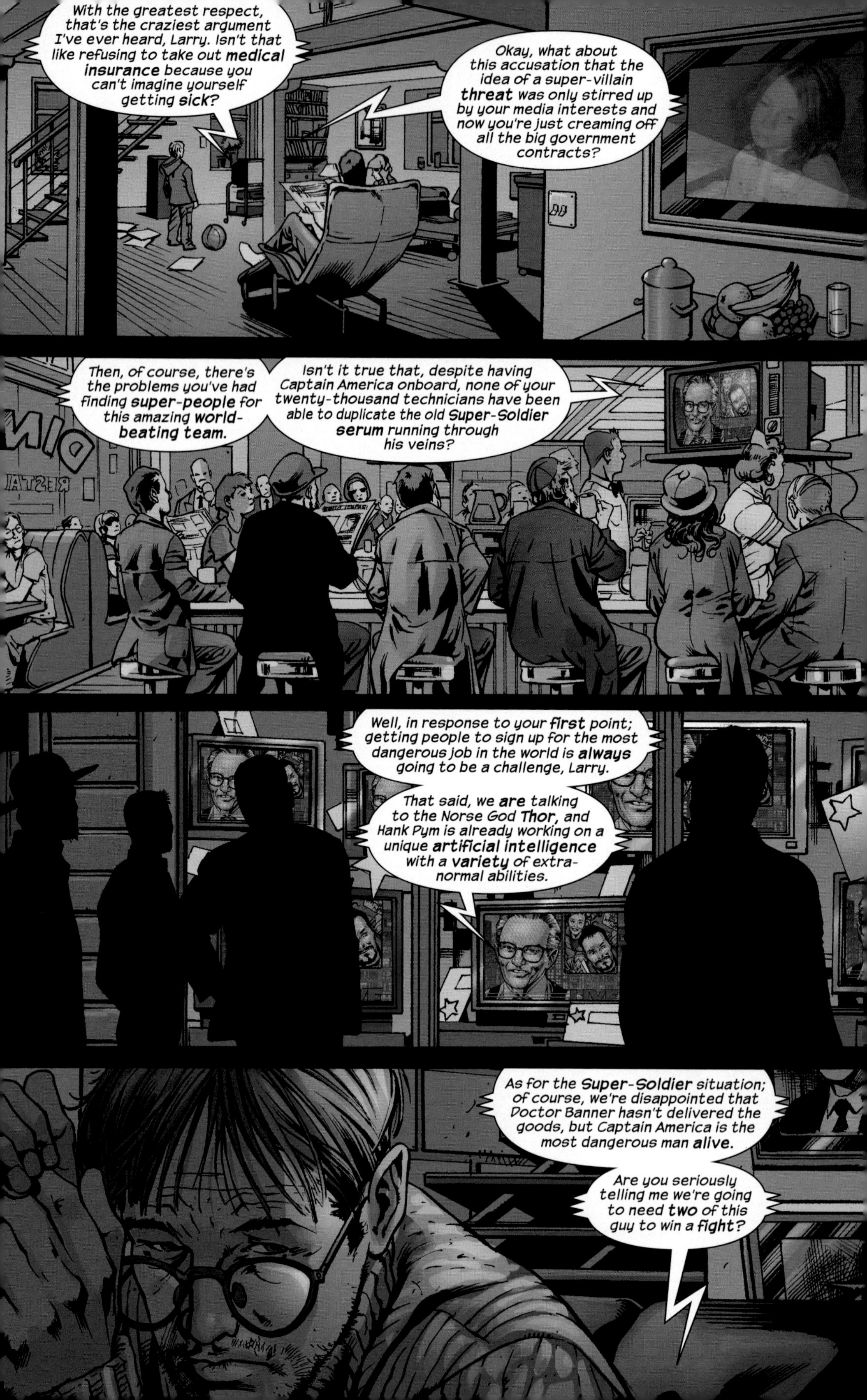
With the greatest respect, that's the craziest argument I've ever heard, Larry. Isn't that like refusing to take out medical insurance because you can't imagine yourself getting sick?
Okay, what about this accusation that the idea of a super-villain threat was only stirred up by your media interests and now you're just creaming off all the big government contracts?
Then, of course, there's the problems you've had finding super-people for this amazing world-beating team.
Isn't it true that, despite having Captain America onboard, none of your twenty-thousand technicians have been able to duplicate the old Super-Soldier serum running through his veins?
Well, in response to your first point; getting people to sign up for the most dangerous job in the world is always going to be a challenge, Larry.
That said, we are talking to the Norse God Thor, and Hank Pym is already working on a unique artificial intelligence with a variety of extra-normal abilities.
As for the Super-Soldier situation; of course, we're disappointed that Doctor Banner hasn't delivered the goods, but Captain America is the most dangerous man alive.
Are you seriously telling me we're going to need two of this guy to win a fight?

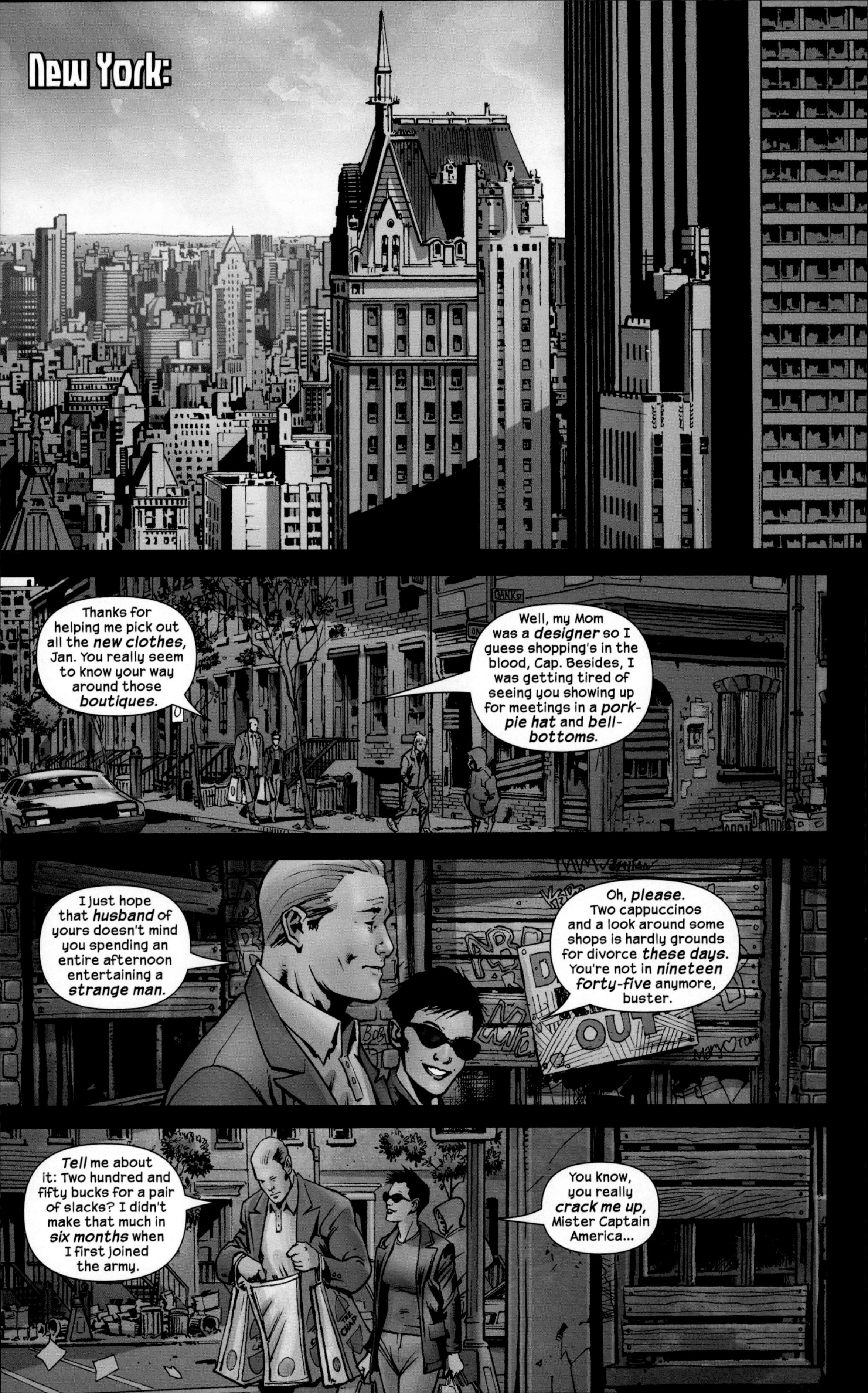

New York:
Thanks for helping me pick out all the new clothes, Jan. You really seem to know your way around those boutiques.
Well, my Mom was a designer so I guess shopping's in the blood, Cap. Besides, I was getting tired of seeing you showing up for meetings in a pork-pie hat and bell-bottoms.
I just hope that husband of yours doesn't mind you spending an entire afternoon entertaining a strange man.
Oh, please. Two cappuccinos and a look around some shops is hardly grounds for divorce these days. You're not in nineteen forty-five anymore, buster.
OUT
Tell me about it: Two hundred and fifty bucks for a pair of slacks? I didn't make that much in six months when I first joined the army.
You know, you really crack me up, Mister Captain America...

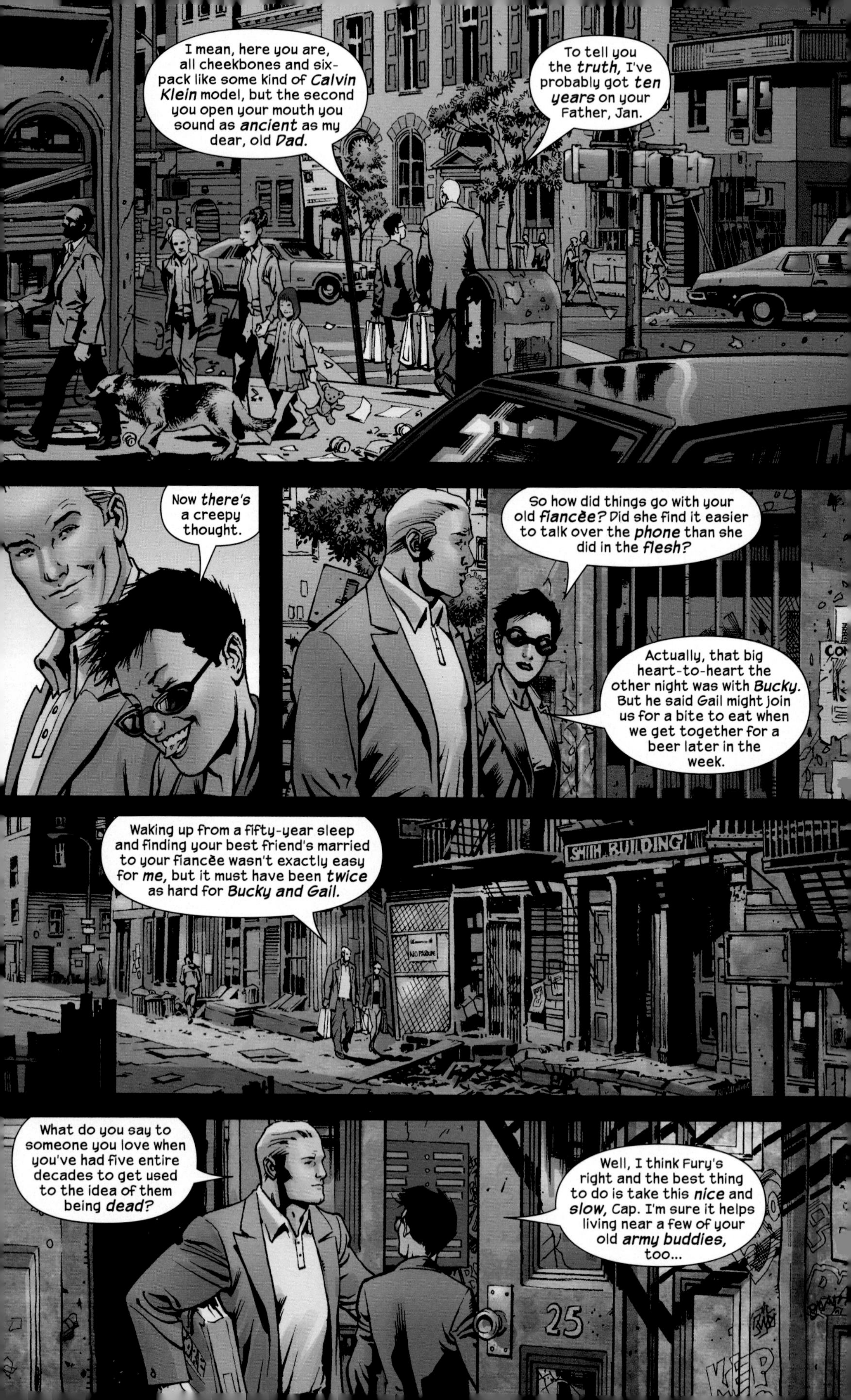
I mean, here you are, all cheekbones and six-pack like some kind of *Calvin Klein* model, but the second you open your mouth you sound as *ancient* as my dear, old *Dad.*
To tell you the *truth,* I've probably got *ten years* on your Father, Jan.
Now *there's* a creepy thought.
So how did things go with your old *fiancée?* Did she find it easier to talk over the *phone* than she did in the *flesh?*
Actually, that big heart-to-heart the other night was with *Bucky.* But he said Gail might join us for a bite to eat when we get together for a beer later in the week.
Waking up from a fifty-year sleep and finding your best friend's married to your fiancée wasn't exactly easy for *me,* but it must have been *twice* as hard for *Bucky and Gail.*
SMITH BUILDING
NO PARKING
What do you say to someone you love when you've had five entire decades to get used to the idea of them being *dead?*
Well, I think Fury's right and the best thing to do is take this *nice* and *slow,* Cap. I'm sure it helps living near a few of your old *army buddies,* too...
25

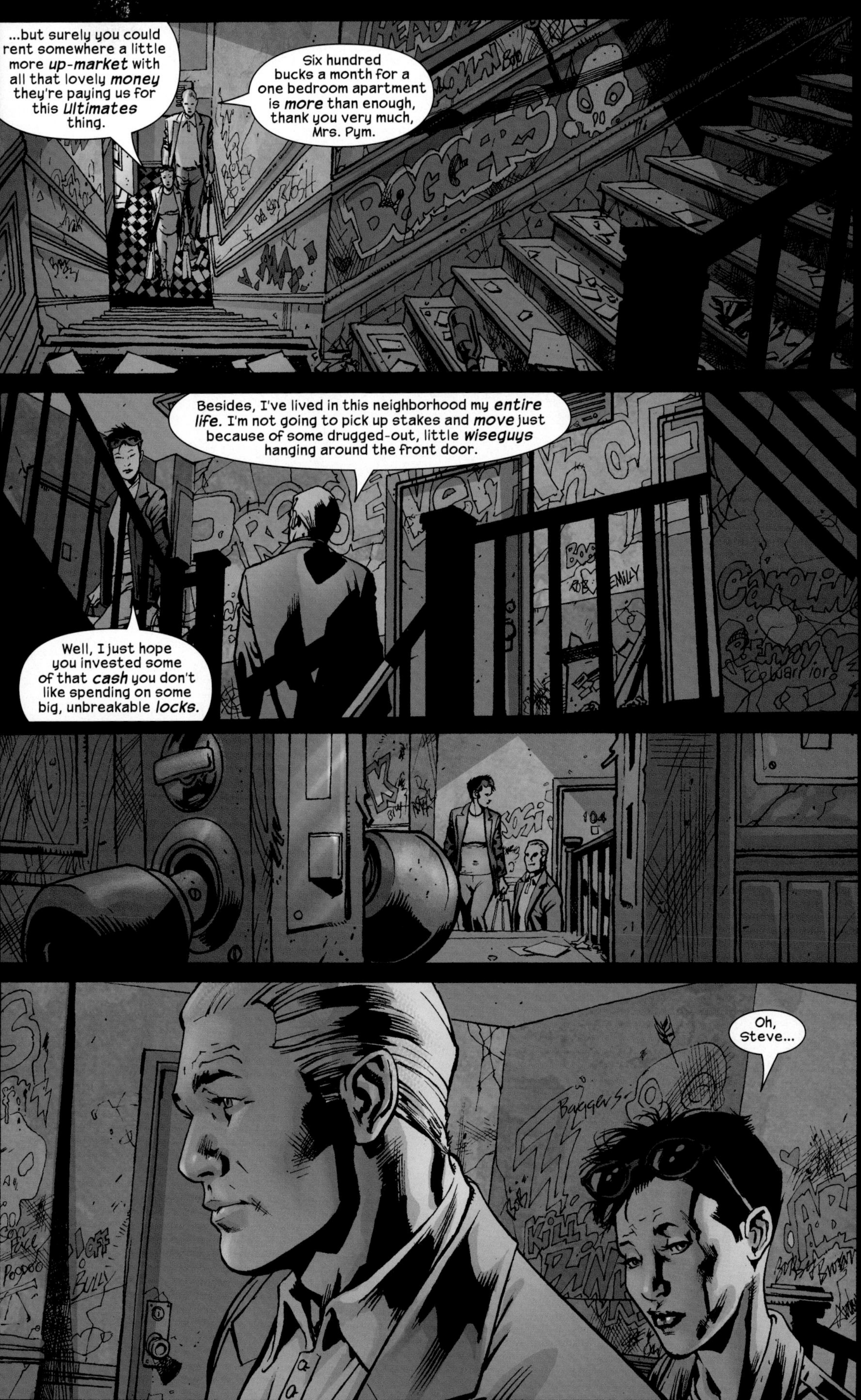
...but surely you could rent somewhere a little more up-market with all that lovely money they're paying us for this Ultimates thing.
Six hundred bucks a month for a one bedroom apartment is more than enough, thank you very much, Mrs. Pym.
Besides, I've lived in this neighborhood my entire life. I'm not going to pick up stakes and move just because of some drugged-out, little wiseguys hanging around the front door.
Well, I just hope you invested some of that cash you don't like spending on some big, unbreakable locks.
Oh, Steve...

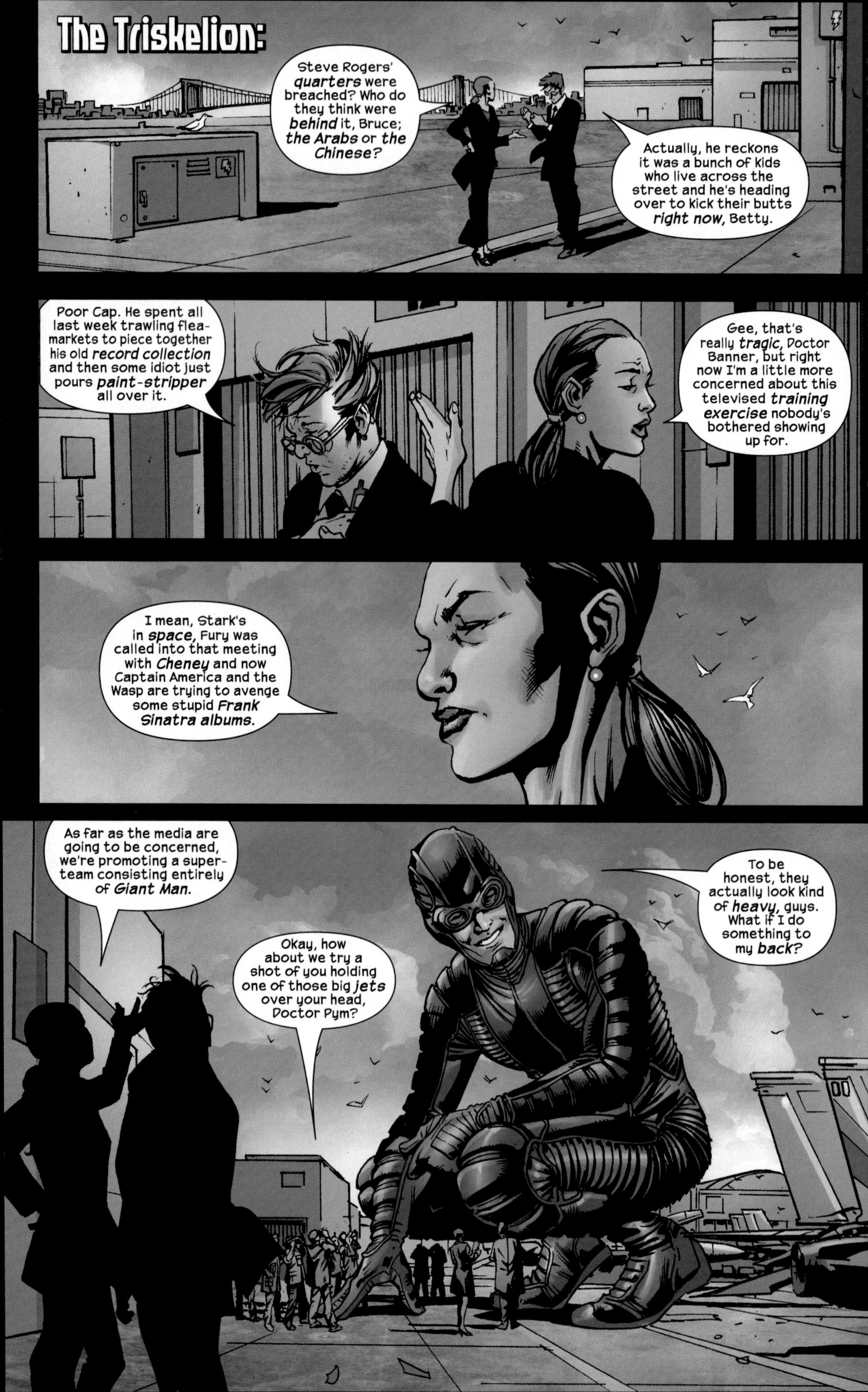

The Triskelion:
Steve Rogers' quarters were breached? Who do they think were behind it, Bruce; the Arabs or the Chinese?
Actually, he reckons it was a bunch of kids who live across the street and he's heading over to kick their butts right now, Betty.
Poor Cap. He spent all last week trawling flea-markets to piece together his old record collection and then some idiot just pours paint-stripper all over it.
Gee, that's really tragic, Doctor Banner, but right now I'm a little more concerned about this televised training exercise nobody's bothered showing up for.
I mean, Stark's in space, Fury was called into that meeting with Cheney and now Captain America and the Wasp are trying to avenge some stupid Frank Sinatra albums.
As far as the media are going to be concerned, we're promoting a super-team consisting entirely of Giant Man.
Okay, how about we try a shot of you holding one of those big jets over your head, Doctor Pym?
To be honest, they actually look kind of heavy, guys. What if I do something to my back?

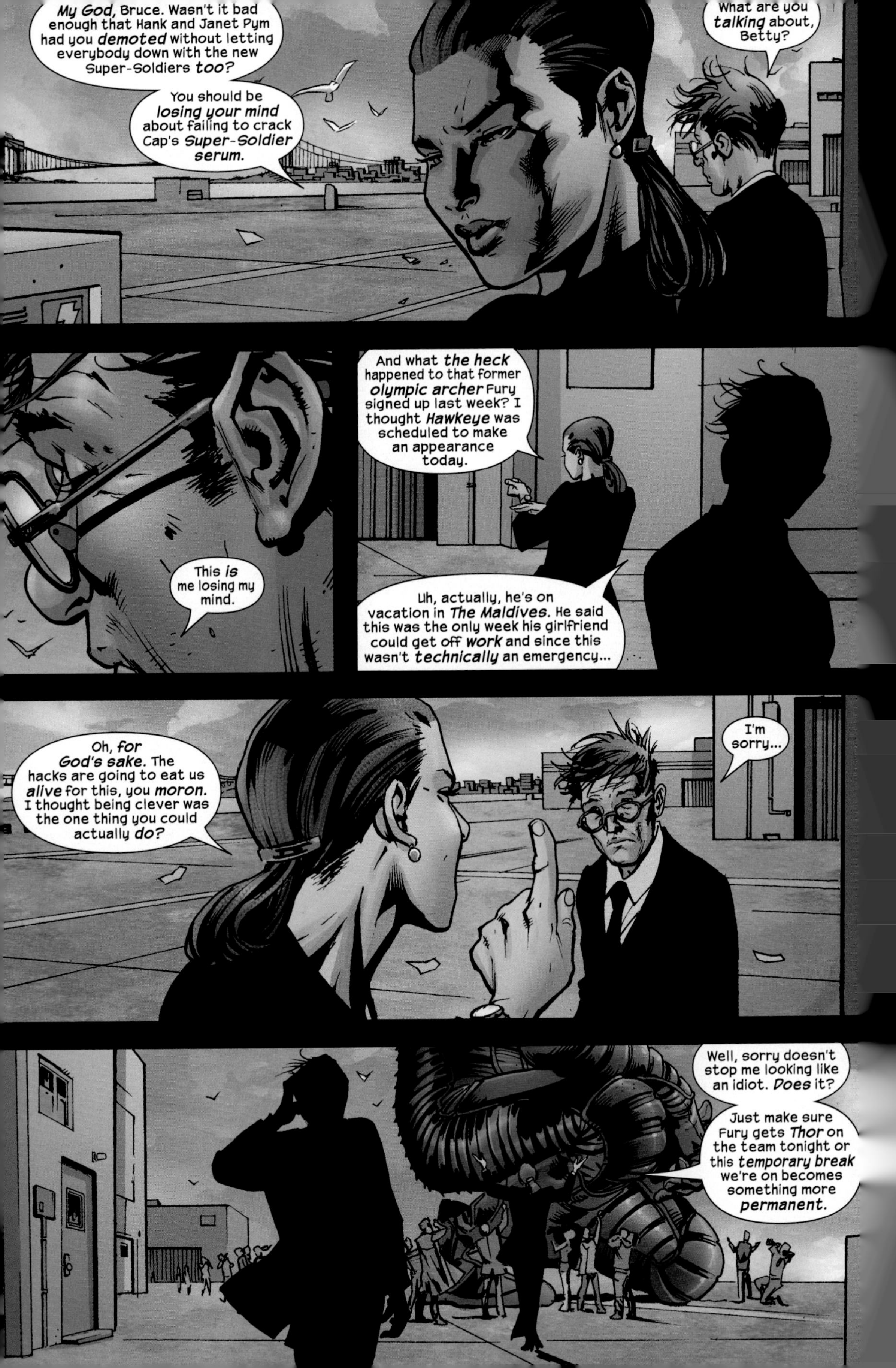
My God, Bruce. Wasn't it bad enough that Hank and Janet Pym had you demoted without letting everybody down with the new Super-Soldiers too?
You should be losing your mind about failing to crack Cap's Super-Soldier serum.
What are you talking about, Betty?
This is me losing my mind.
And what the heck happened to that former olympic archer Fury signed up last week? I thought Hawkeye was scheduled to make an appearance today.
Uh, actually, he's on vacation in The Maldives. He said this was the only week his girlfriend could get off work and since this wasn't technically an emergency...
Oh, for God's sake. The hacks are going to eat us alive for this, you moron. I thought being clever was the one thing you could actually do?
I'm sorry...
Well, sorry doesn't stop me looking like an idiot. Does it?
Just make sure Fury gets Thor on the team tonight or this temporary break we're on becomes something more permanent.

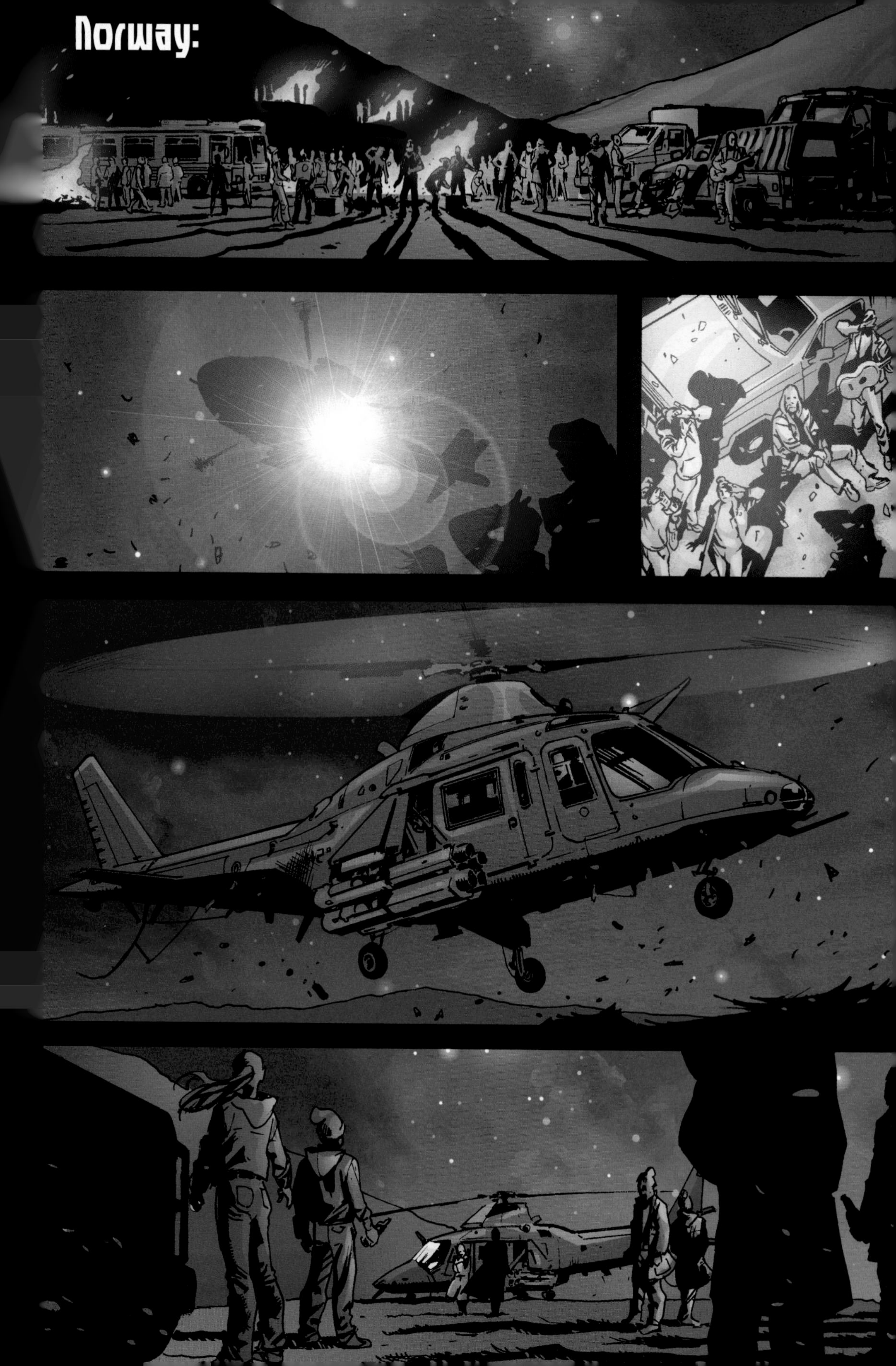
Norway:

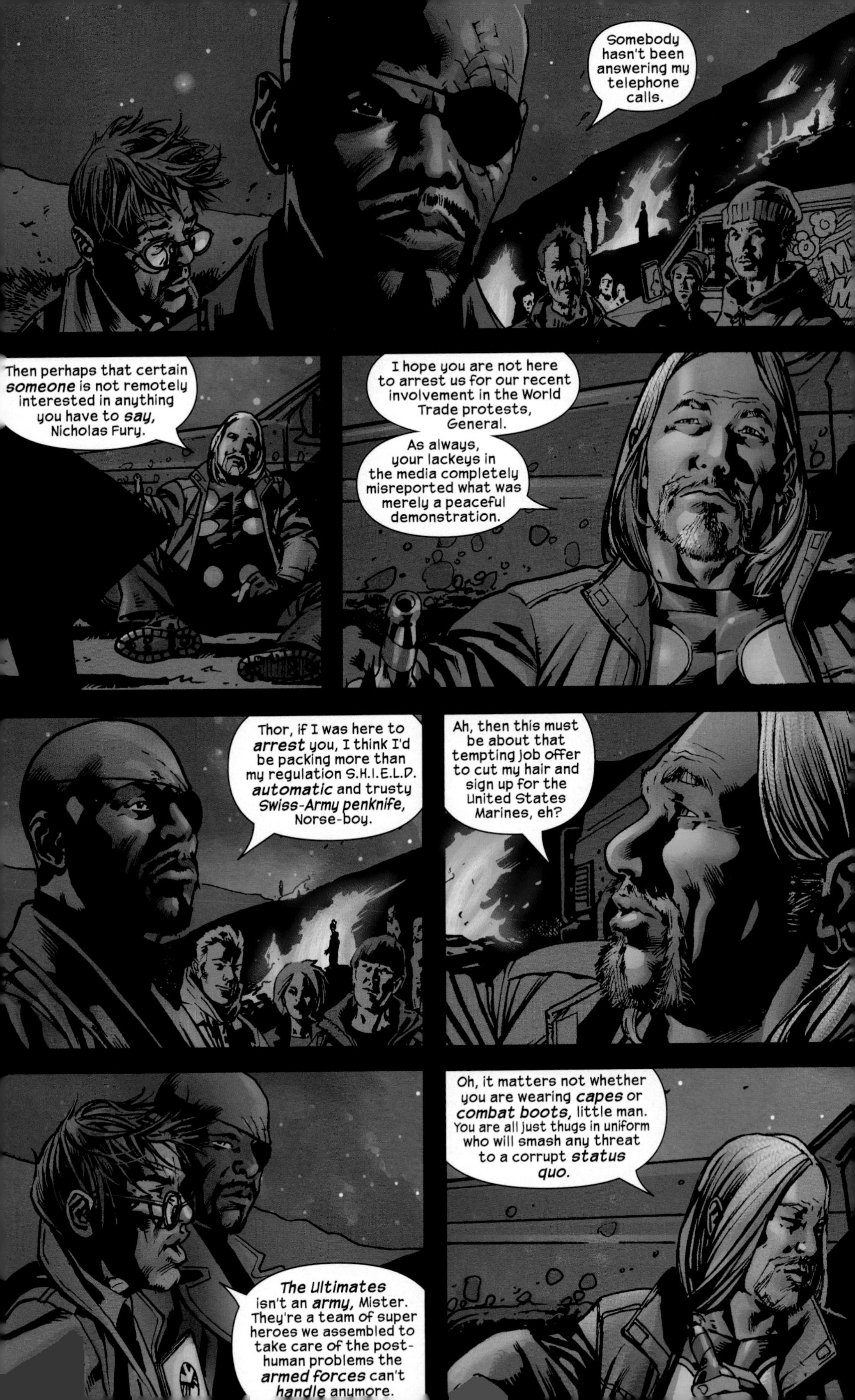
Somebody hasn't been answering my telephone calls.
Then perhaps that certain *someone* is not remotely interested in anything you have to *say*, Nicholas Fury.
I hope you are not here to arrest us for our recent involvement in the World Trade protests, General.
As always, your lackeys in the media completely misreported what was merely a peaceful demonstration.
Thor, if I was here to *arrest* you, I think I'd be packing more than my regulation S.H.I.E.L.D. *automatic* and trusty *Swiss-Army penknife*, Norse-boy.
Ah, then this must be about that tempting job offer to cut my hair and sign up for the United States Marines, eh?
The Ultimates isn't an *army*, Mister. They're a team of super heroes we assembled to take care of the post-human problems the *armed forces* can't *handle* anymore.
Oh, it matters not whether you are wearing *capes* or *combat boots*, little man. You are all just thugs in uniform who will smash any threat to a corrupt *status quo*.

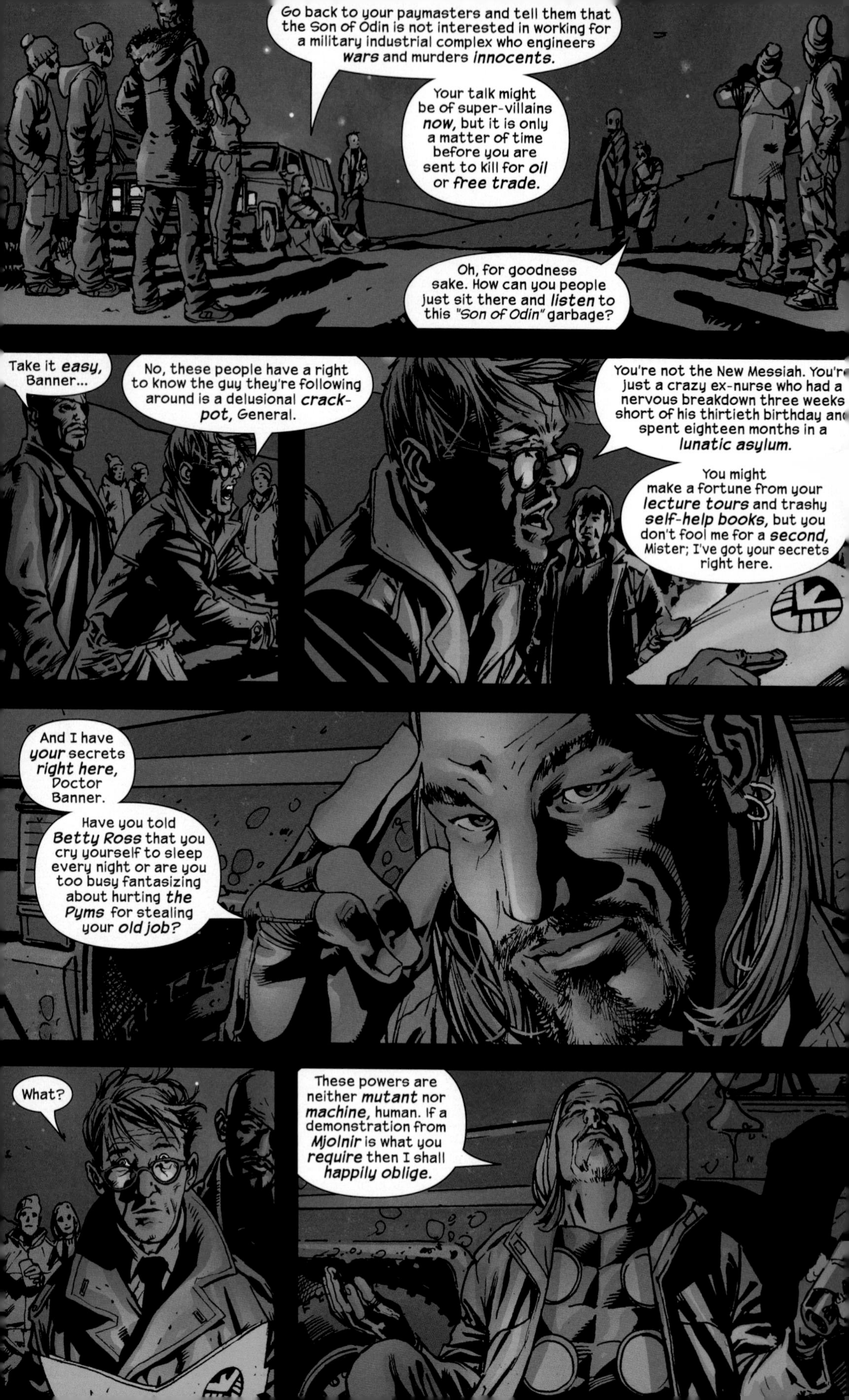

Go back to your paymasters and tell them that the Son of Odin is not interested in working for a military industrial complex who engineers *wars* and murders *innocents.*
Your talk might be of super-villains *now,* but it is only a matter of time before you are sent to kill for *oil* or *free trade.*
Oh, for goodness sake. How can you people just sit there and *listen* to this *"Son of Odin"* garbage?
Take it *easy,* Banner...
No, these people have a right to know the guy they're following around is a delusional *crack-pot,* General.
You're not the New Messiah. You're just a crazy ex-nurse who had a nervous breakdown three weeks short of his thirtieth birthday and spent eighteen months in a *lunatic asylum.*
You might make a fortune from your *lecture tours* and trashy *self-help books,* but you don't fool me for a *second,* Mister; I've got your secrets right here.
And I have *your* secrets *right here,* Doctor Banner.
Have you told *Betty Ross* that you cry yourself to sleep every night or are you too busy fantasizing about hurting *the Pyms* for stealing your *old job?*
What?
These powers are neither *mutant* nor *machine,* human. If a demonstration from *Mjolnir* is what you *require* then I shall *happily oblige.*

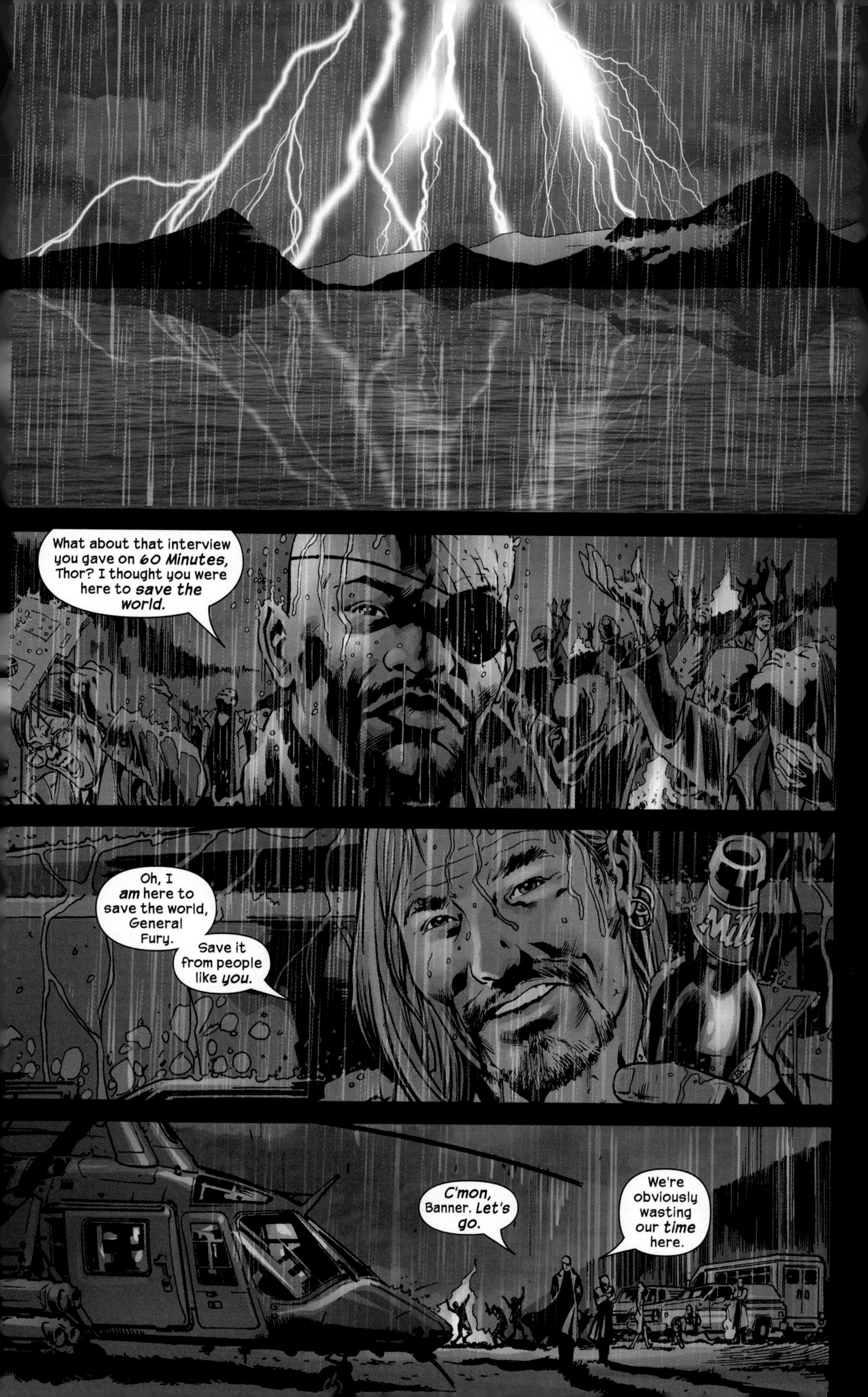
What about that interview you gave on *60 Minutes*, Thor? I thought you were here to ***save the world.***
Oh, I ***am*** here to save the world, General Fury.
Save it from people like ***you.***
C'mon, Banner. Let's ***go.***
We're obviously wasting our ***time*** here.

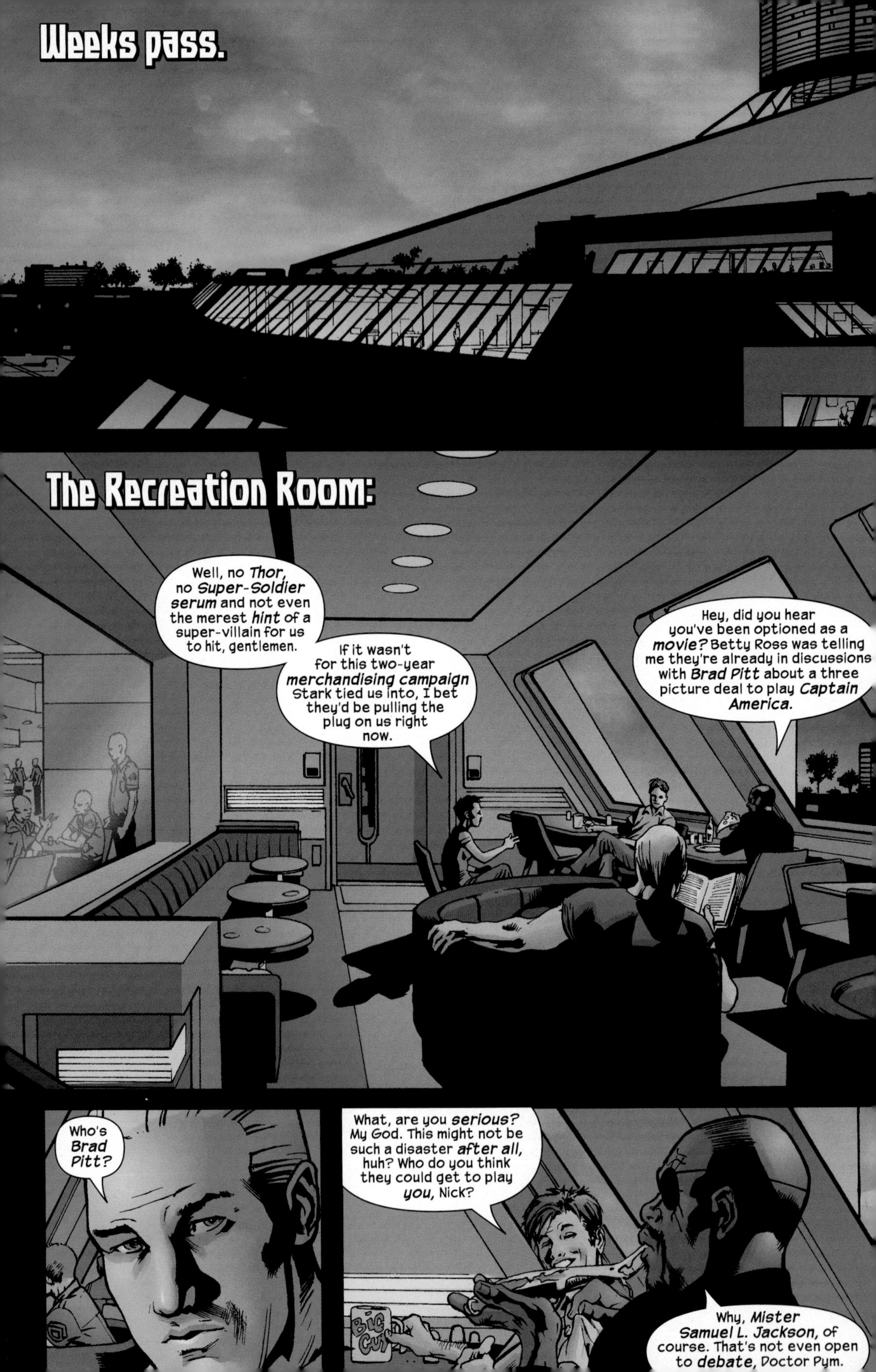
Weeks pass.
The Recreation Room:
Well, no Thor, no Super-Soldier serum and not even the merest hint of a super-villain for us to hit, gentlemen.
If it wasn't for this two-year merchandising campaign Stark tied us into, I bet they'd be pulling the plug on us right now.
Hey, did you hear you've been optioned as a movie? Betty Ross was telling me they're already in discussions with Brad Pitt about a three picture deal to play Captain America.
Who's Brad Pitt?
What, are you serious? My God. This might not be such a disaster after all, huh? Who do you think they could get to play you, Nick?
BIG CUP
Why, Mister Samuel L. Jackson, of course. That's not even open to debate, Doctor Pym.

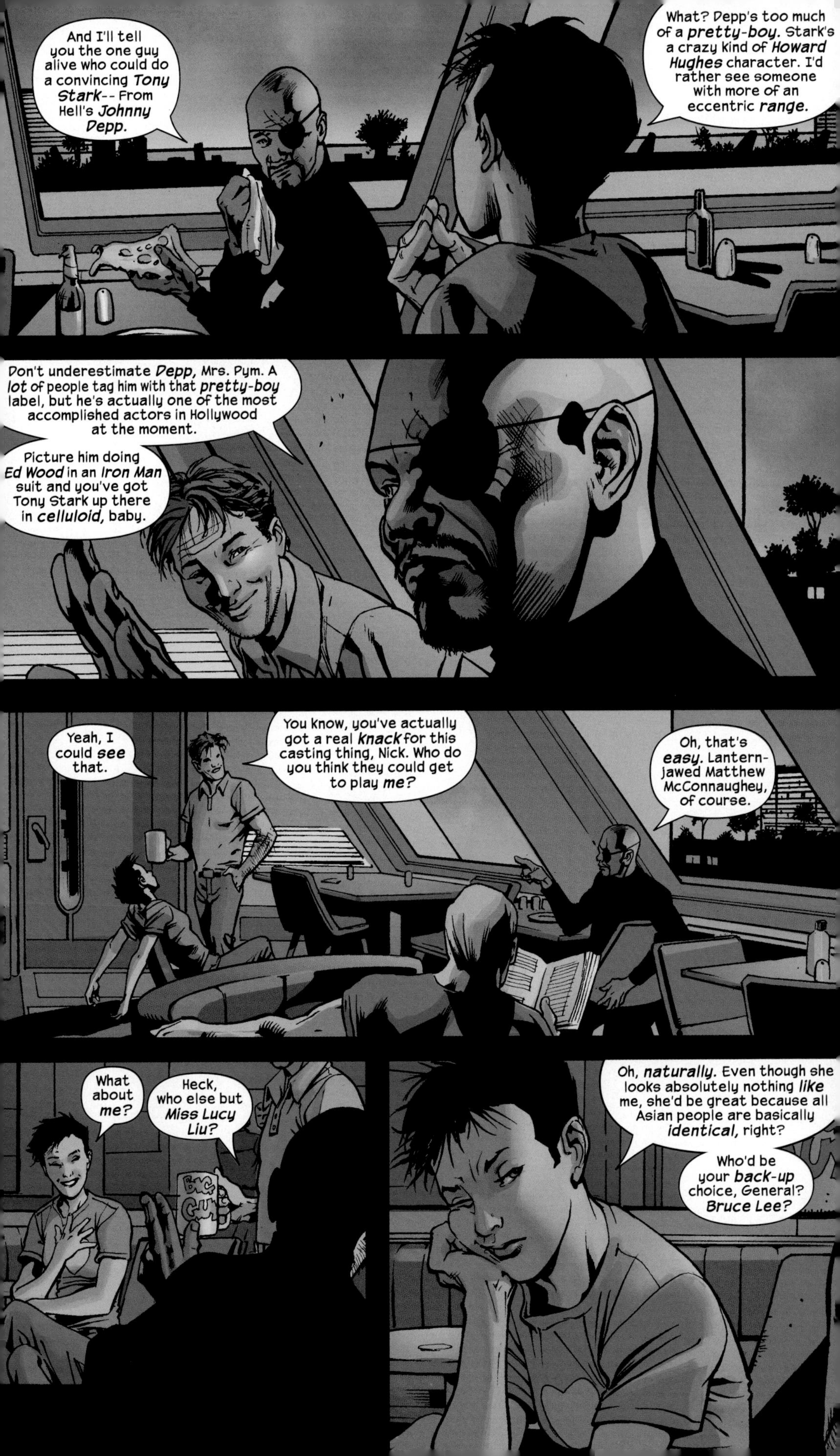
And I'll tell you the one guy alive who could do a convincing Tony Stark-- From Hell's Johnny Depp.
What? Depp's too much of a pretty-boy. Stark's a crazy kind of Howard Hughes character. I'd rather see someone with more of an eccentric range.
Don't underestimate Depp, Mrs. Pym. A lot of people tag him with that pretty-boy label, but he's actually one of the most accomplished actors in Hollywood at the moment.
Picture him doing Ed Wood in an Iron Man suit and you've got Tony Stark up there in celluloid, baby.
Yeah, I could see that.
You know, you've actually got a real knack for this casting thing, Nick. Who do you think they could get to play me?
Oh, that's easy. Lantern-jawed Matthew McConnaughey, of course.
What about me?
Heck, who else but Miss Lucy Liu?
BIG GUY
Oh, naturally. Even though she looks absolutely nothing like me, she'd be great because all Asian people are basically identical, right?
Who'd be your back-up choice, General? Bruce Lee?

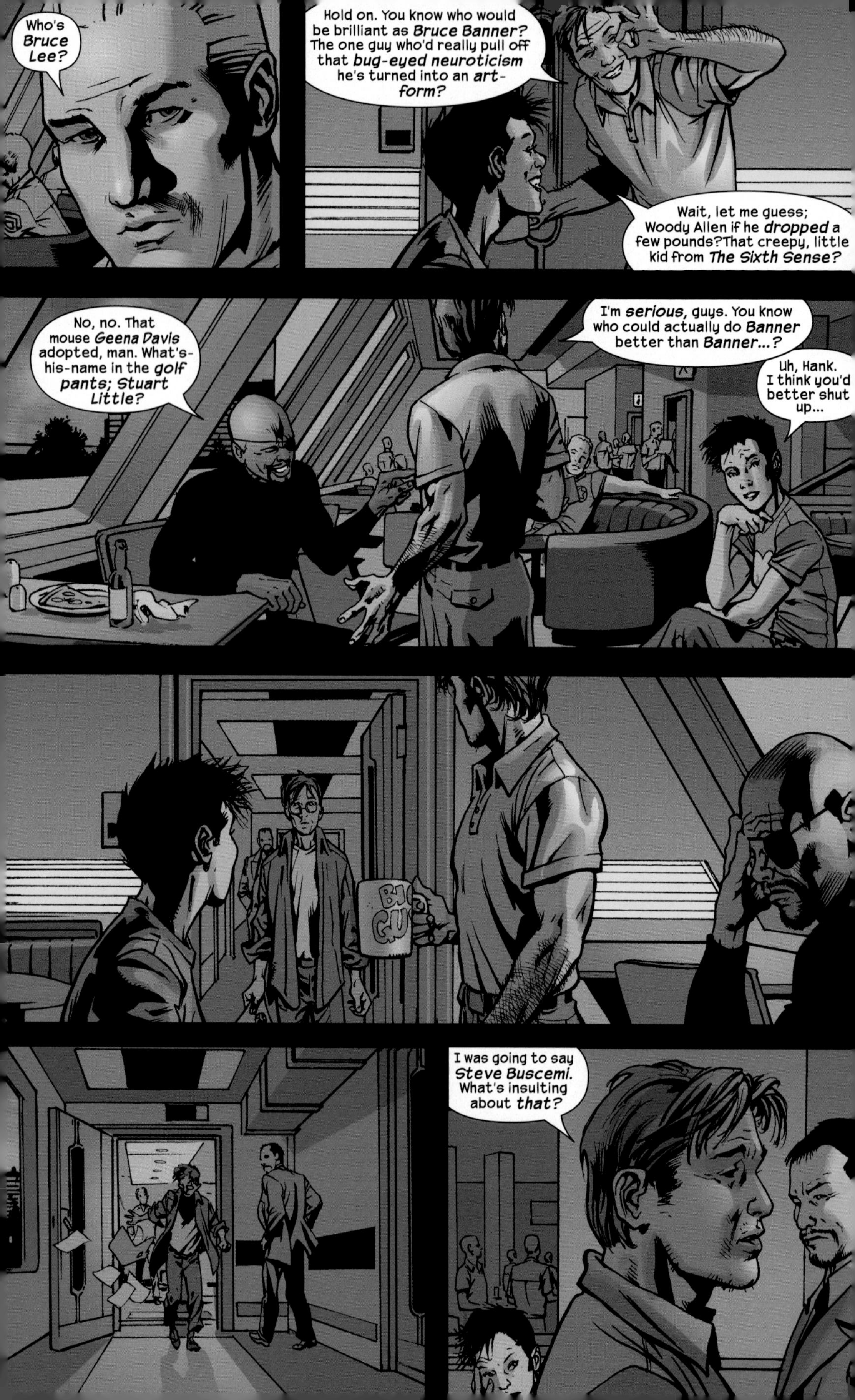
Who's Bruce Lee?
Hold on. You know who would be brilliant as Bruce Banner? The one guy who'd really pull off that bug-eyed neuroticism he's turned into an art-form?
Wait, let me guess; Woody Allen if he dropped a few pounds? That creepy, little kid from The Sixth Sense?
No, no. That mouse Geena Davis adopted, man. What's-his-name in the golf pants; Stuart Little?
I'm serious, guys. You know who could actually do Banner better than Banner...?
Uh, Hank. I think you'd better shut up...
I was going to say Steve Buscemi. What's insulting about that?

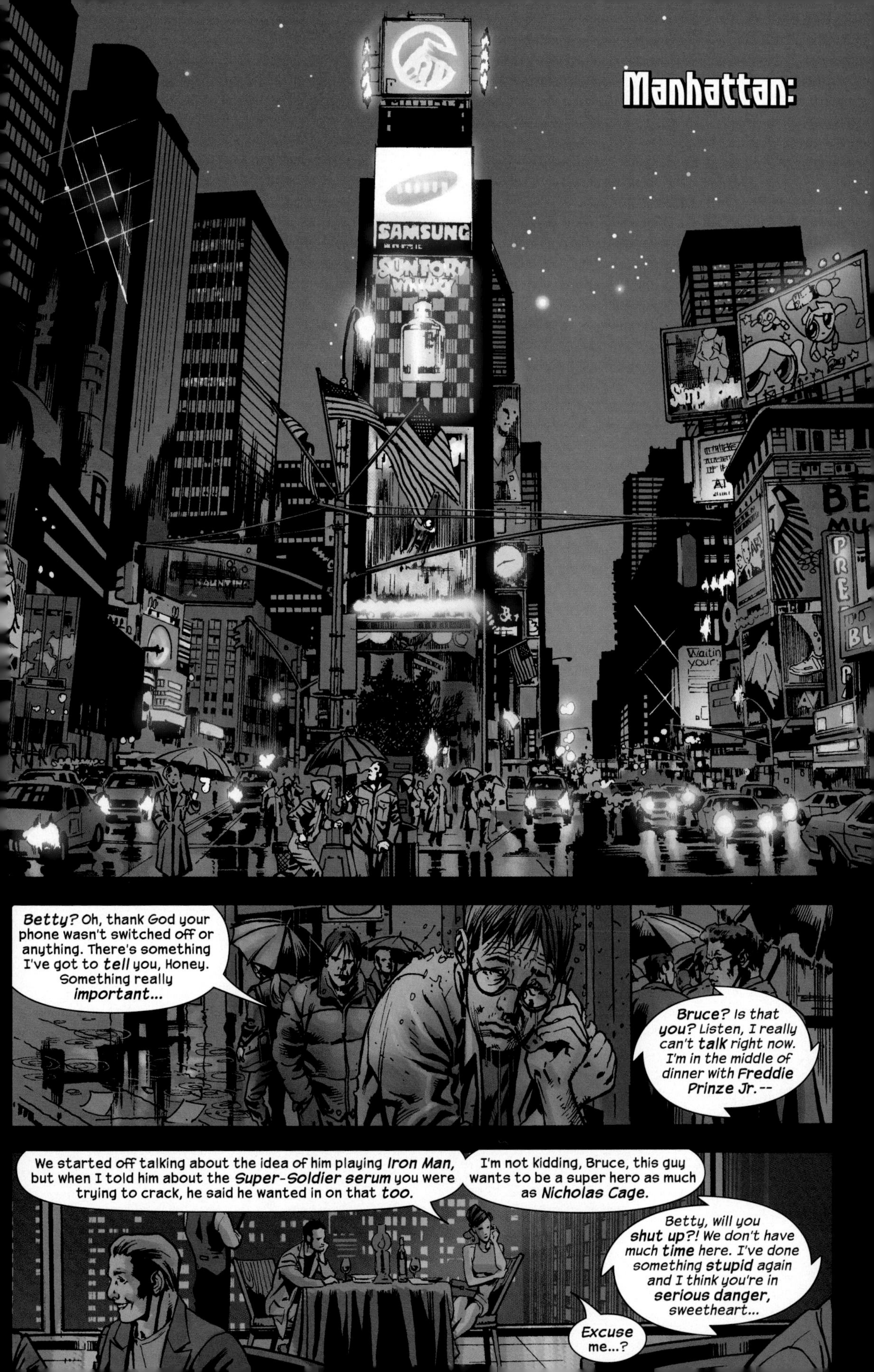

Manhattan:
SAMSUNG
Betty? Oh, thank God your phone wasn't switched off or anything. There's something I've got to tell you, Honey. Something really important...
Bruce? Is that you? Listen, I really can't talk right now. I'm in the middle of dinner with Freddie Prinze Jr.--
We started off talking about the idea of him playing Iron Man, but when I told him about the Super-Soldier serum you were trying to crack, he said he wanted in on that too.
I'm not kidding, Bruce, this guy wants to be a super hero as much as Nicholas Cage.
Betty, will you shut up?! We don't have much time here. I've done something stupid again and I think you're in serious danger, sweetheart...
Excuse me...?

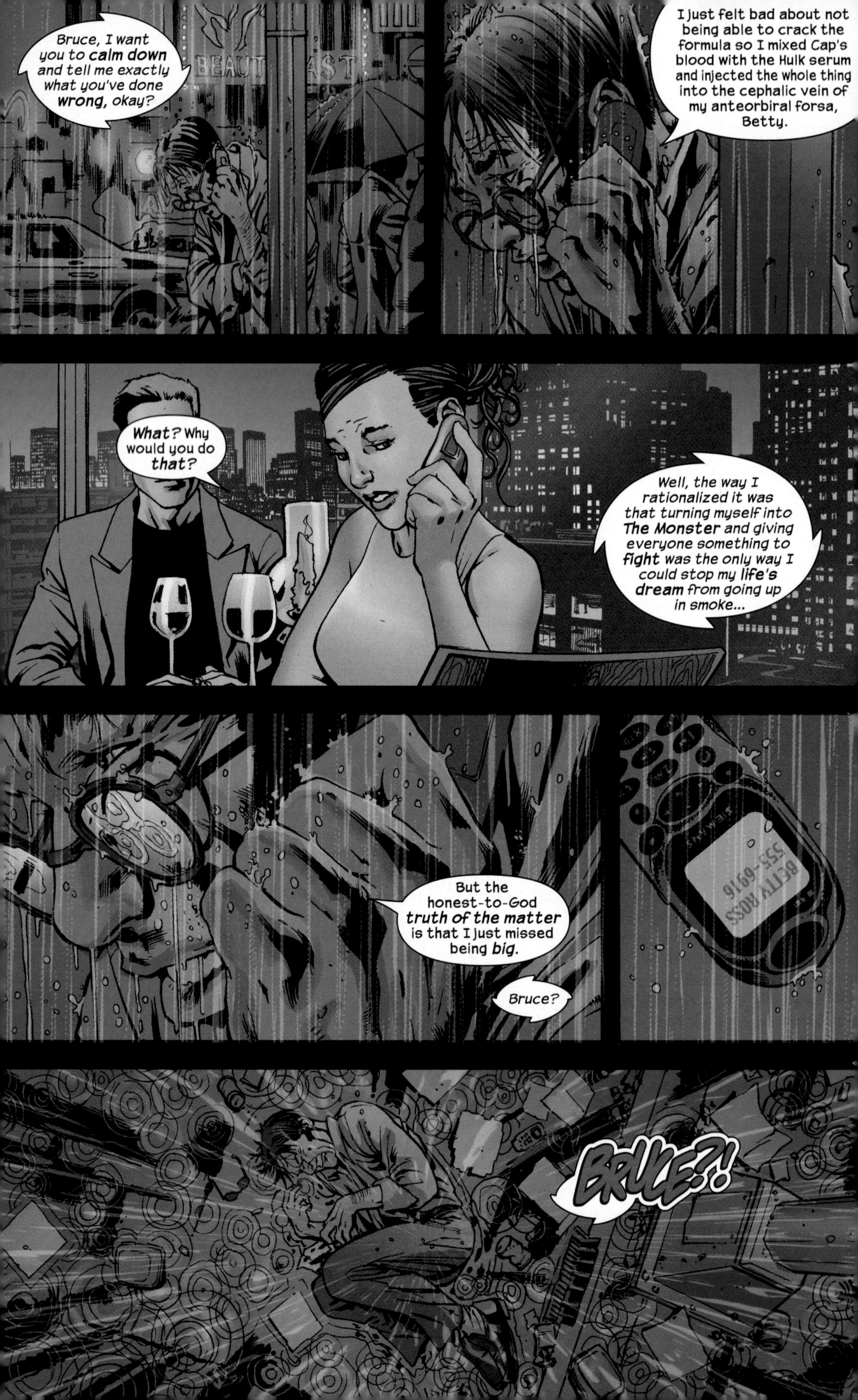
Bruce, I want you to calm down and tell me exactly what you've done wrong, okay?
BEAUTY AND THE BEAST
I just felt bad about not being able to crack the formula so I mixed Cap's blood with the Hulk serum and injected the whole thing into the cephalic vein of my anteorbiral forsa, Betty.
What? Why would you do that?
Well, the way I rationalized it was that turning myself into The Monster and giving everyone something to fight was the only way I could stop my life's dream from going up in smoke...
But the honest-to-God truth of the matter is that I just missed being big.
Bruce?
BETTY ROSS 555-6916
BRUCE?!

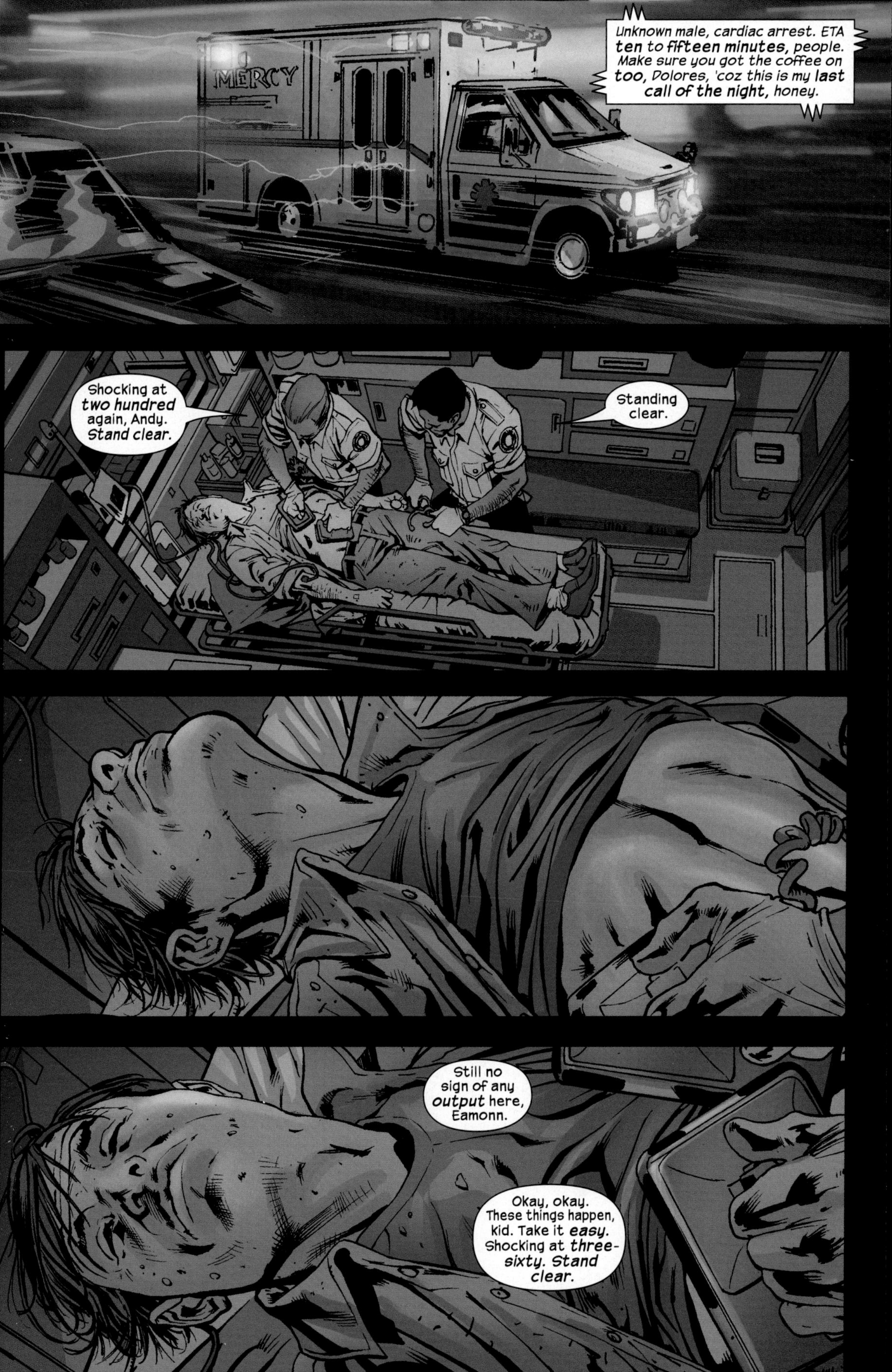
MERCY
Unknown male, cardiac arrest. ETA ten to fifteen minutes, people. Make sure you got the coffee on too, Dolores, 'coz this is my last call of the night, honey.
Shocking at two hundred again, Andy. Stand clear.
Standing clear.
Still no sign of any output here, Eamonn.
Okay, okay. These things happen, kid. Take it easy. Shocking at three-sixty. Stand clear.

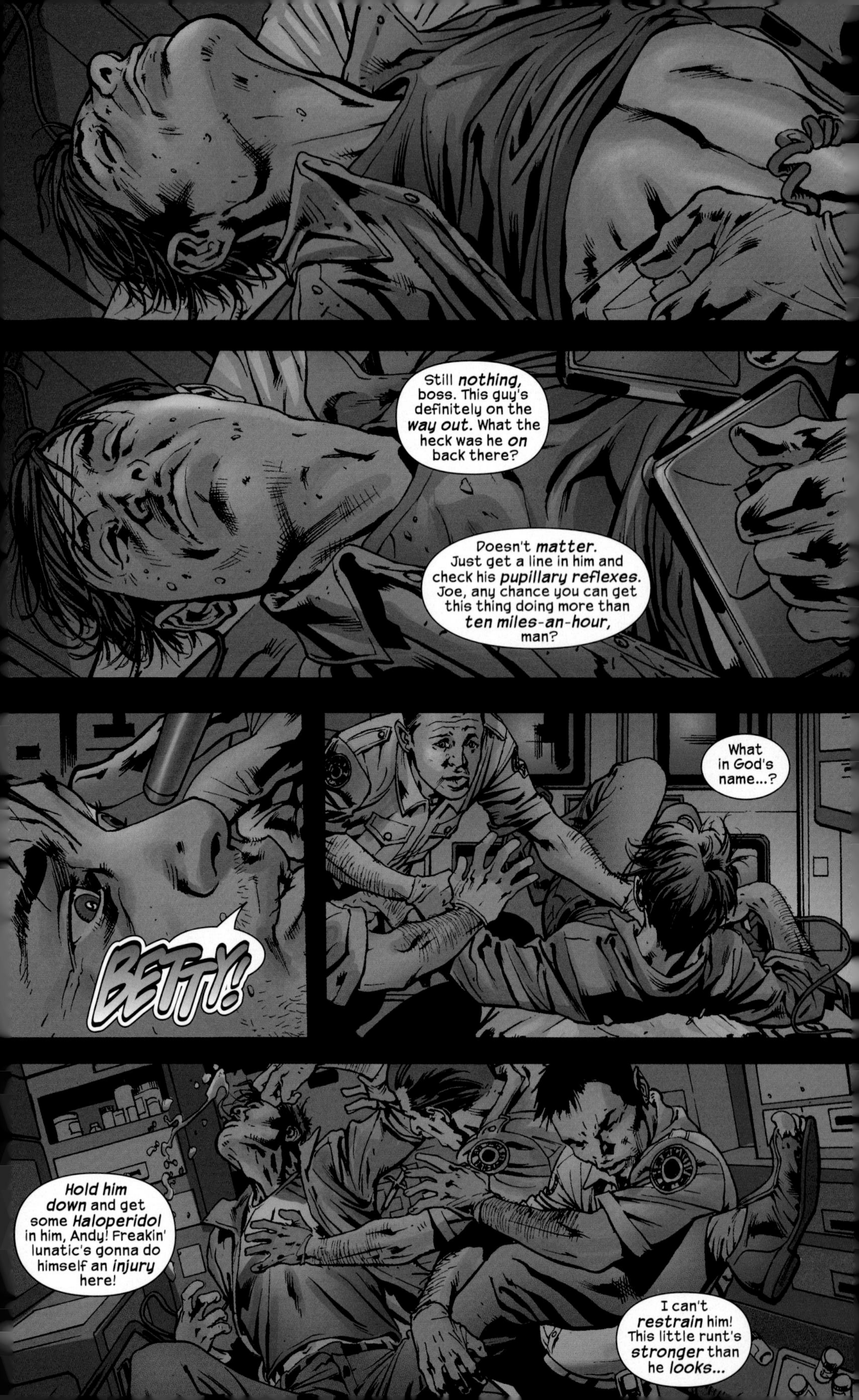
Still nothing, boss. This guy's definitely on the way out. What the heck was he on back there?
Doesn't matter. Just get a line in him and check his pupillary reflexes. Joe, any chance you can get this thing doing more than ten miles-an-hour, man?
BETTY!
What in God's name...?
Hold him down and get some Haloperidol in him, Andy! Freakin' lunatic's gonna do himself an injury here!
I can't restrain him! This little runt's stronger than he looks...

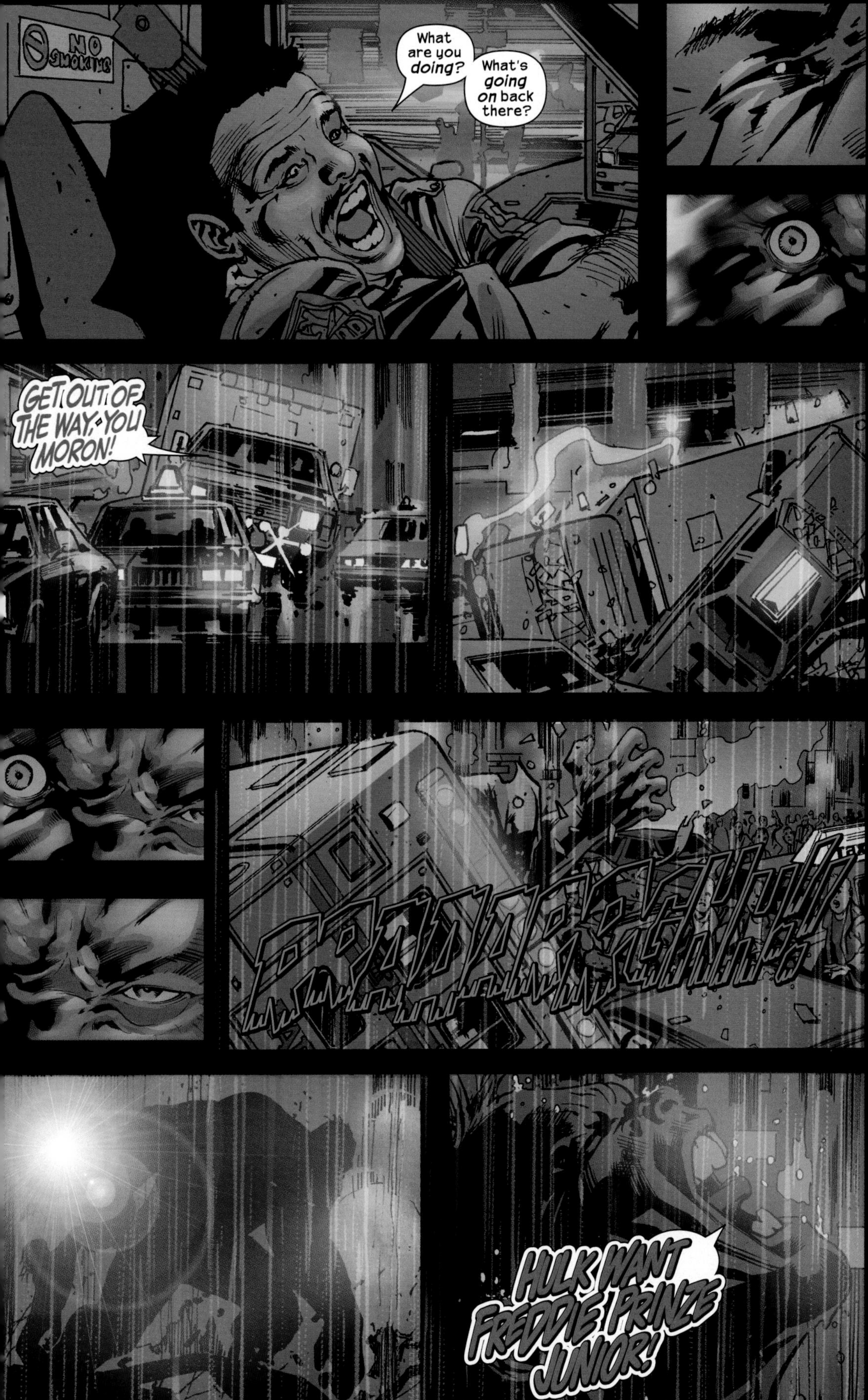
NO SMOKING
What are you doing?
What's going on back there?
GET OUT OF THE WAY, YOU MORON!
HULK WANT FREDDIE PRINZE JUNIOR!

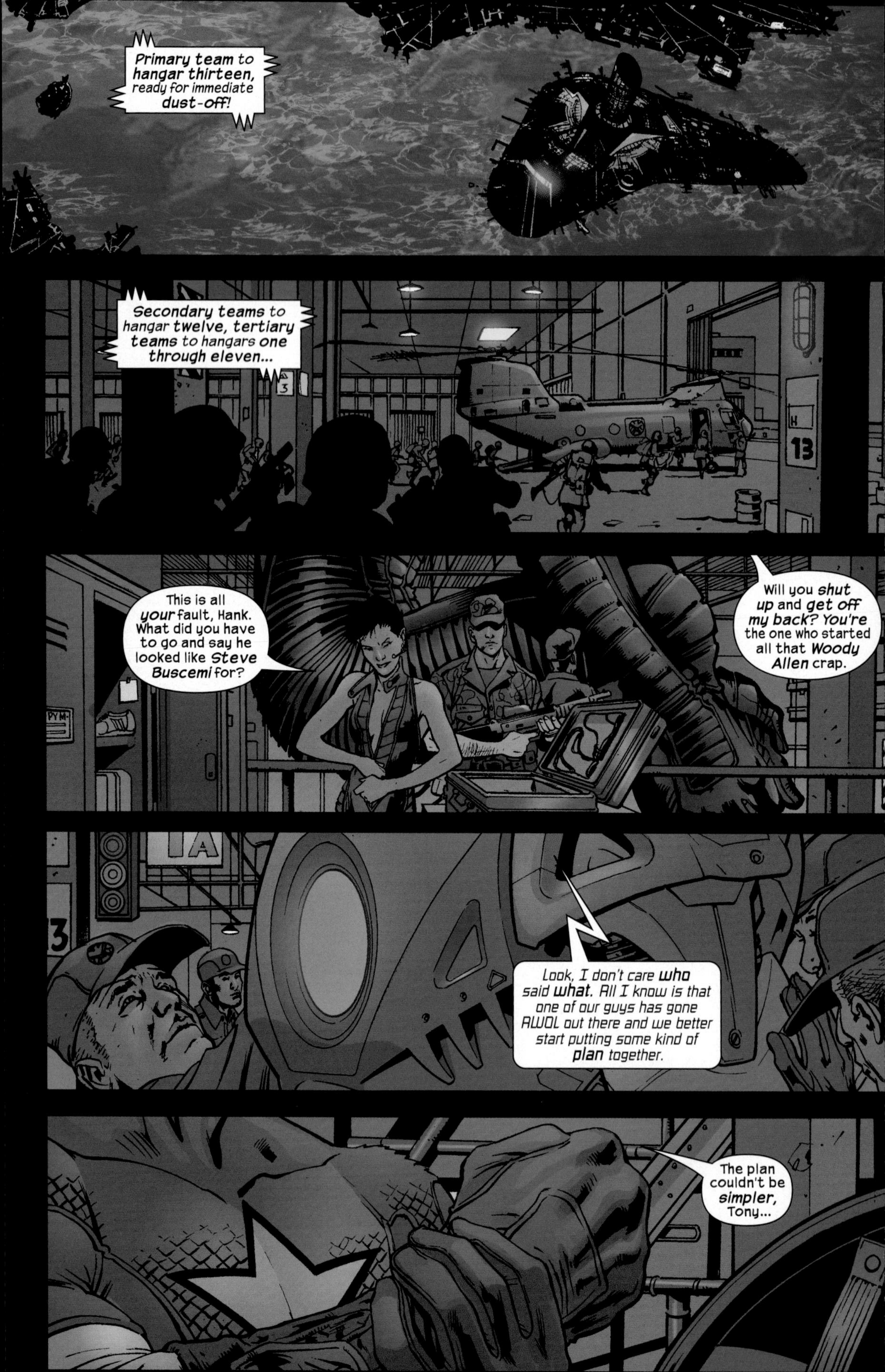
Primary team to hangar thirteen, ready for immediate dust-off!
Secondary teams to hangar twelve, tertiary teams to hangars one through eleven...
3
13
H
13
This is all your fault, Hank. What did you have to go and say he looked like Steve Buscemi for?
Will you shut up and get off my back? You're the one who started all that Woody Allen crap.
PYM
A
13
Look, I don't care who said what. All I know is that one of our guys has gone AWOL out there and we better start putting some kind of plan together.
The plan couldn't be simpler, Tony...

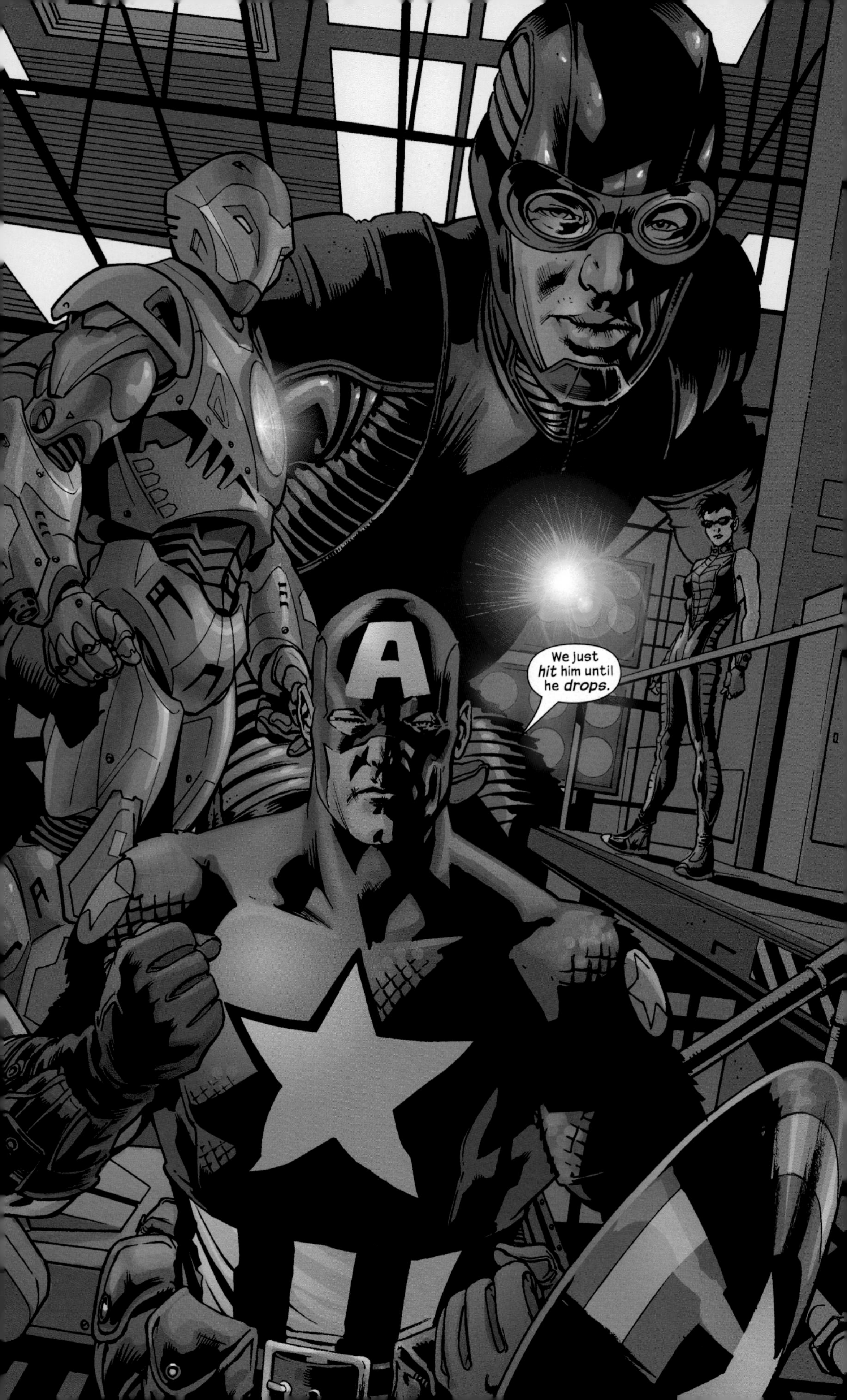
We just *hit* him until he *drops*.

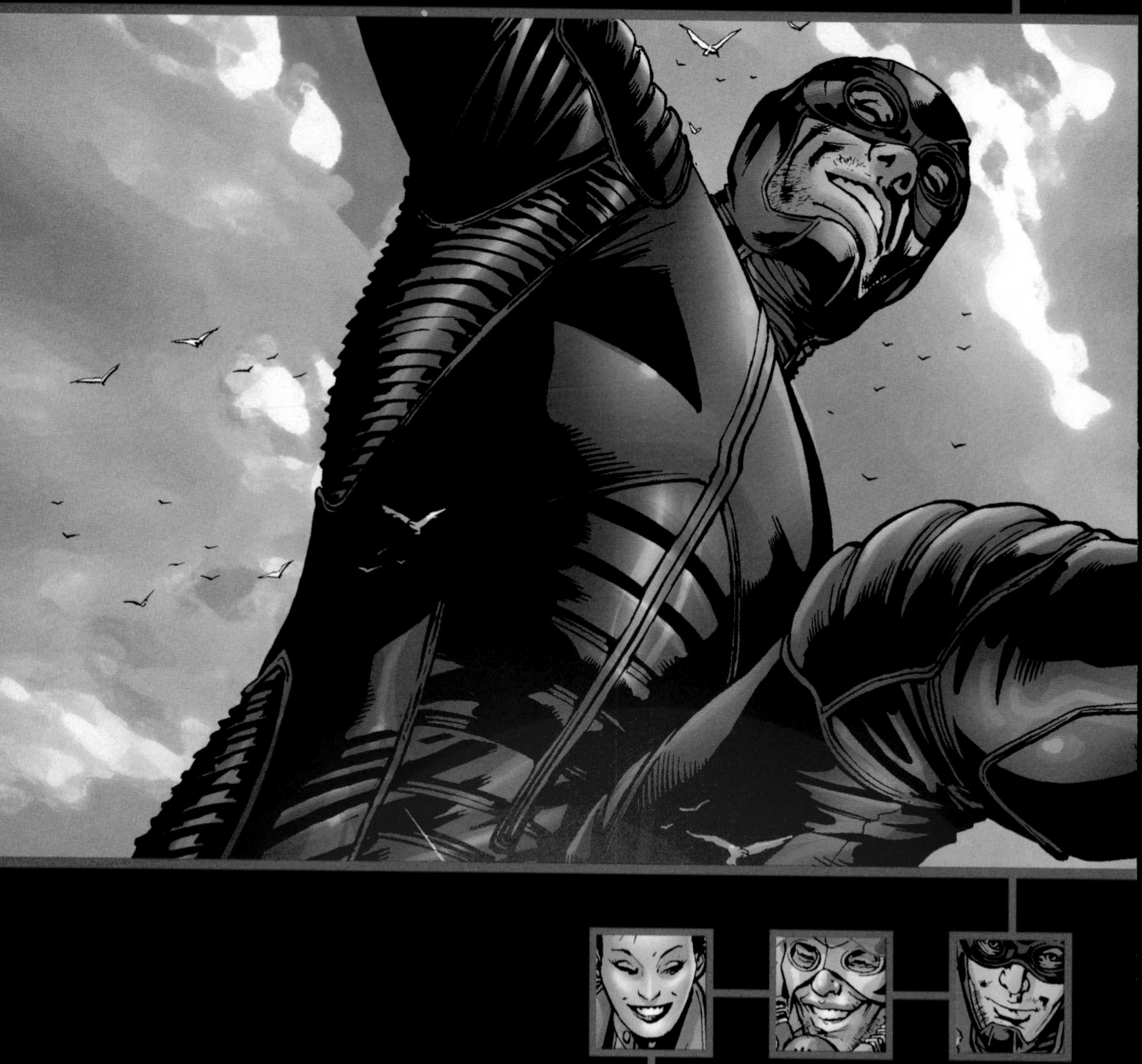

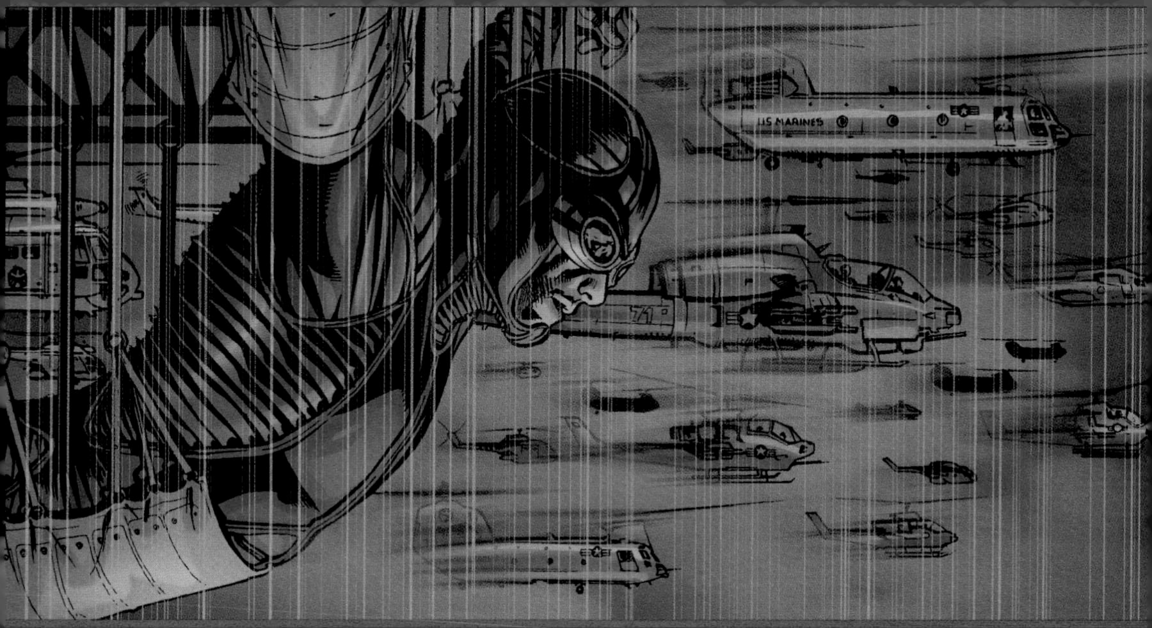
US MARINES

CHAPTER FIVE

HULK DOES MANHATTAN

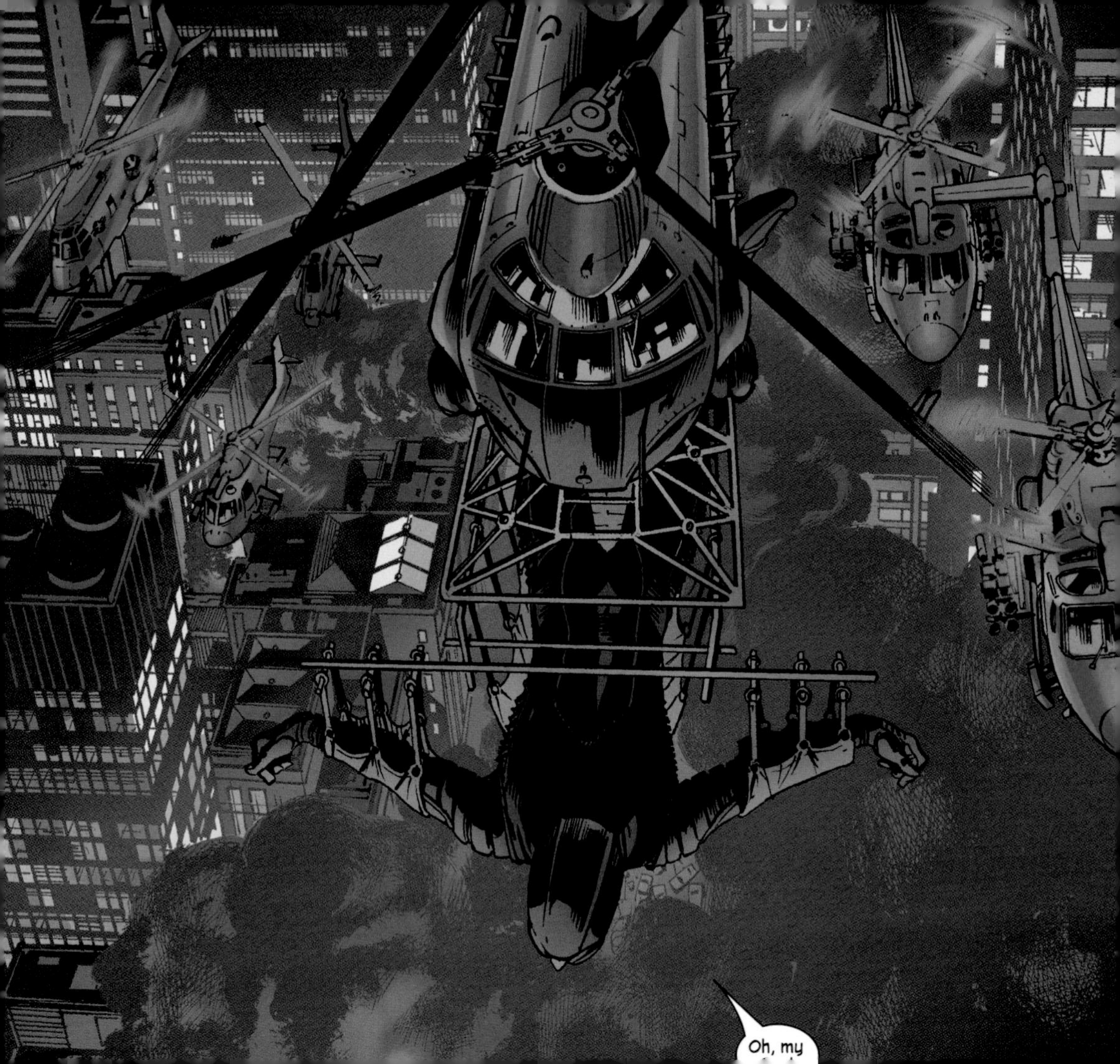
Oh, my

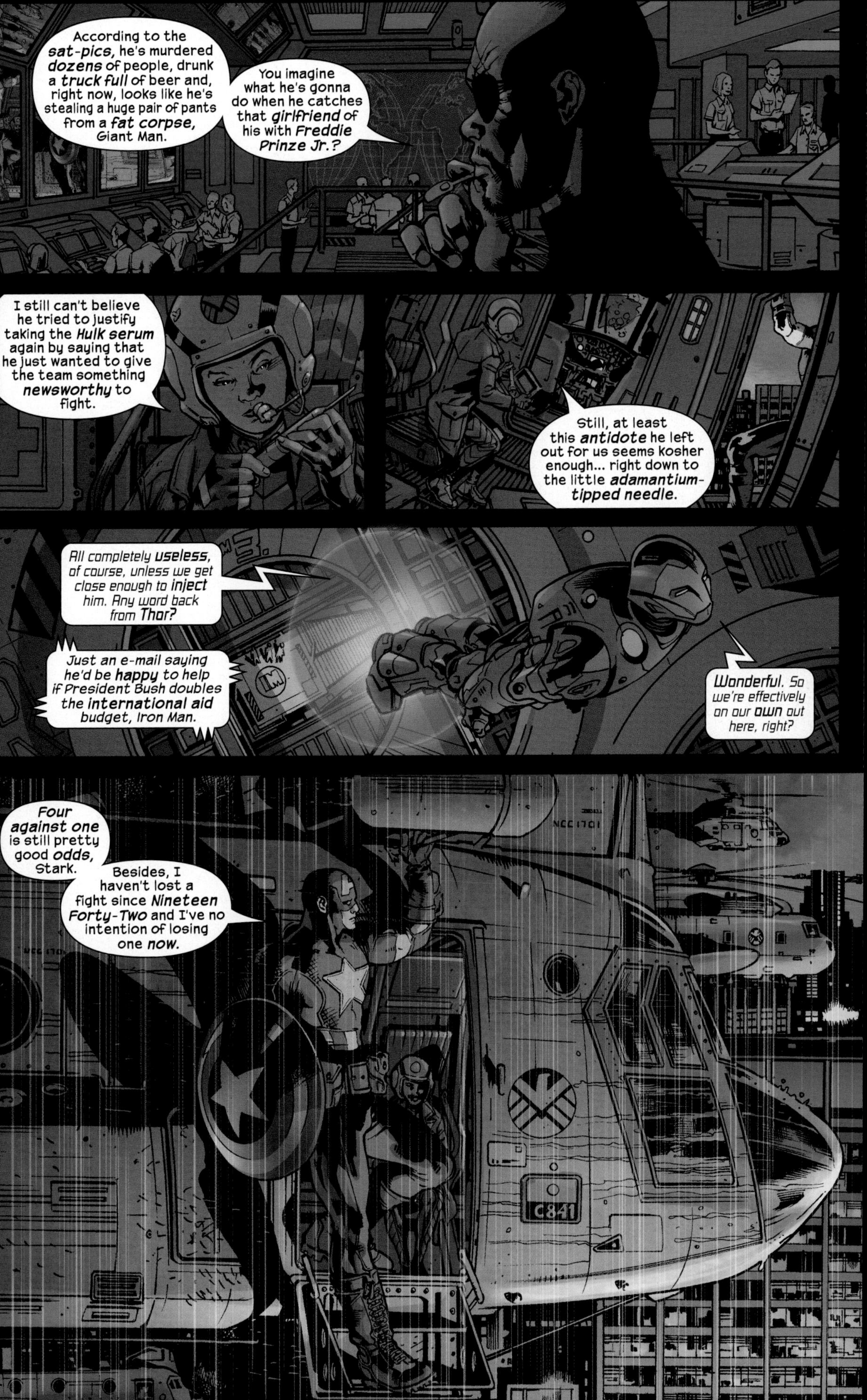

According to the sat-pics, he's murdered dozens of people, drunk a truck full of beer and, right now, looks like he's stealing a huge pair of pants from a fat corpse, Giant Man.
You imagine what he's gonna do when he catches that girlfriend of his with Freddie Prinze Jr.?
I still can't believe he tried to justify taking the Hulk serum again by saying that he just wanted to give the team something newsworthy to fight.
Still, at least this antidote he left out for us seems kosher enough... right down to the little adamantium-tipped needle.
All completely useless, of course, unless we get close enough to inject him. Any word back from Thor?
Just an e-mail saying he'd be happy to help if President Bush doubles the international aid budget, Iron Man.
Wonderful. So we're effectively on our own out here, right?
Four against one is still pretty good odds, Stark.
Besides, I haven't lost a fight since Nineteen Forty-Two and I've no intention of losing one now.

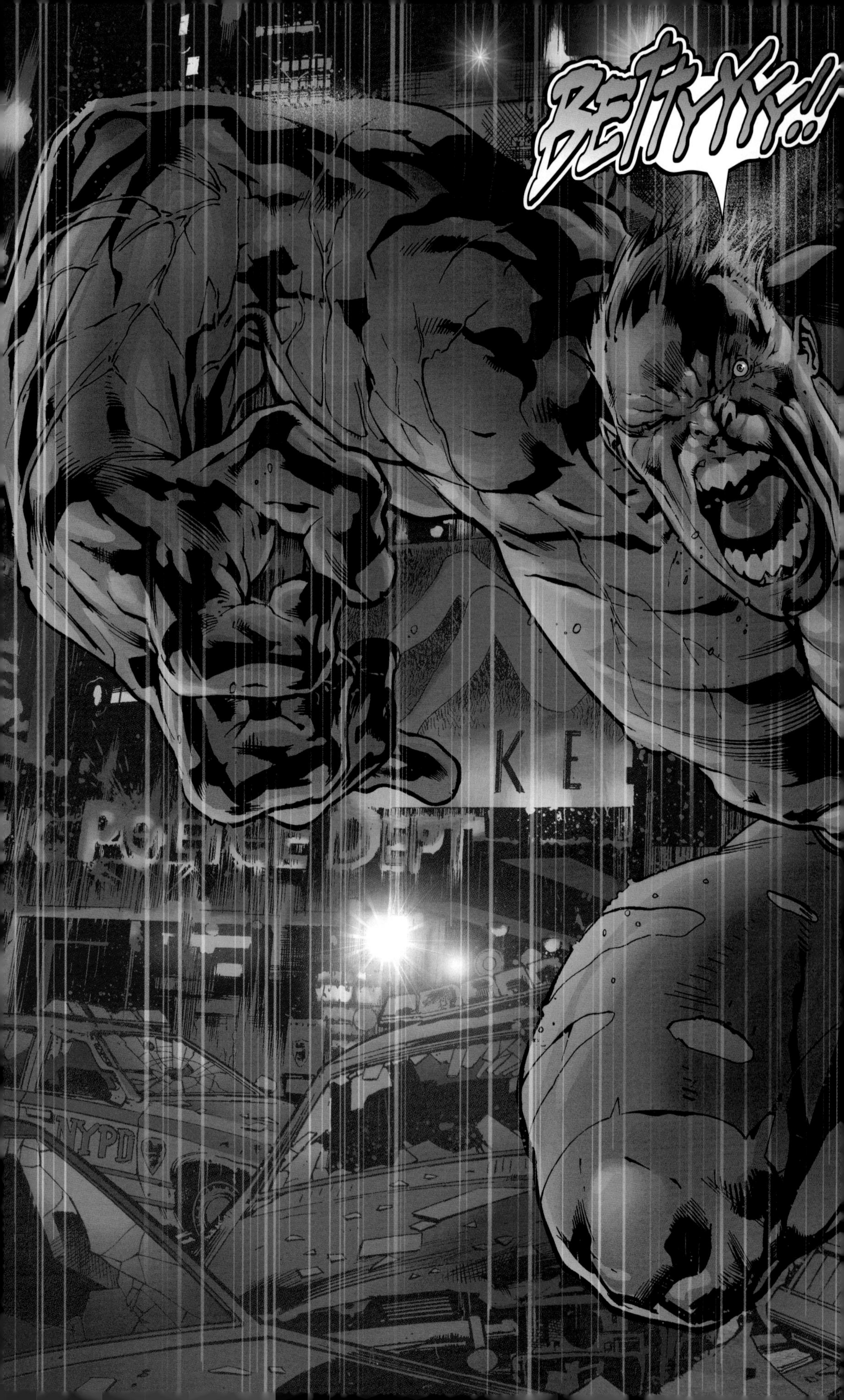
BETTYYY..!!
KE
POLICE DEPT
NYPD

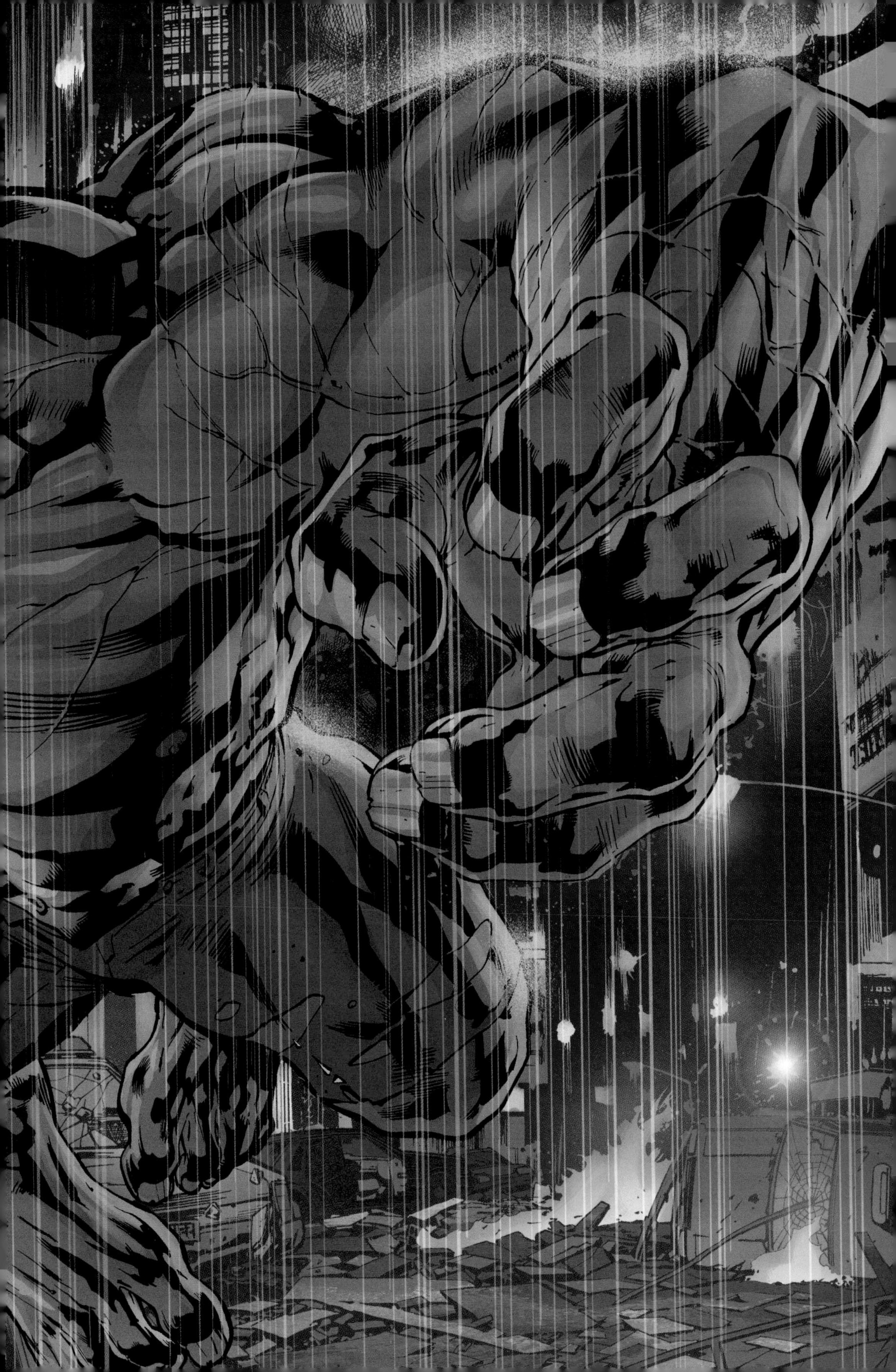

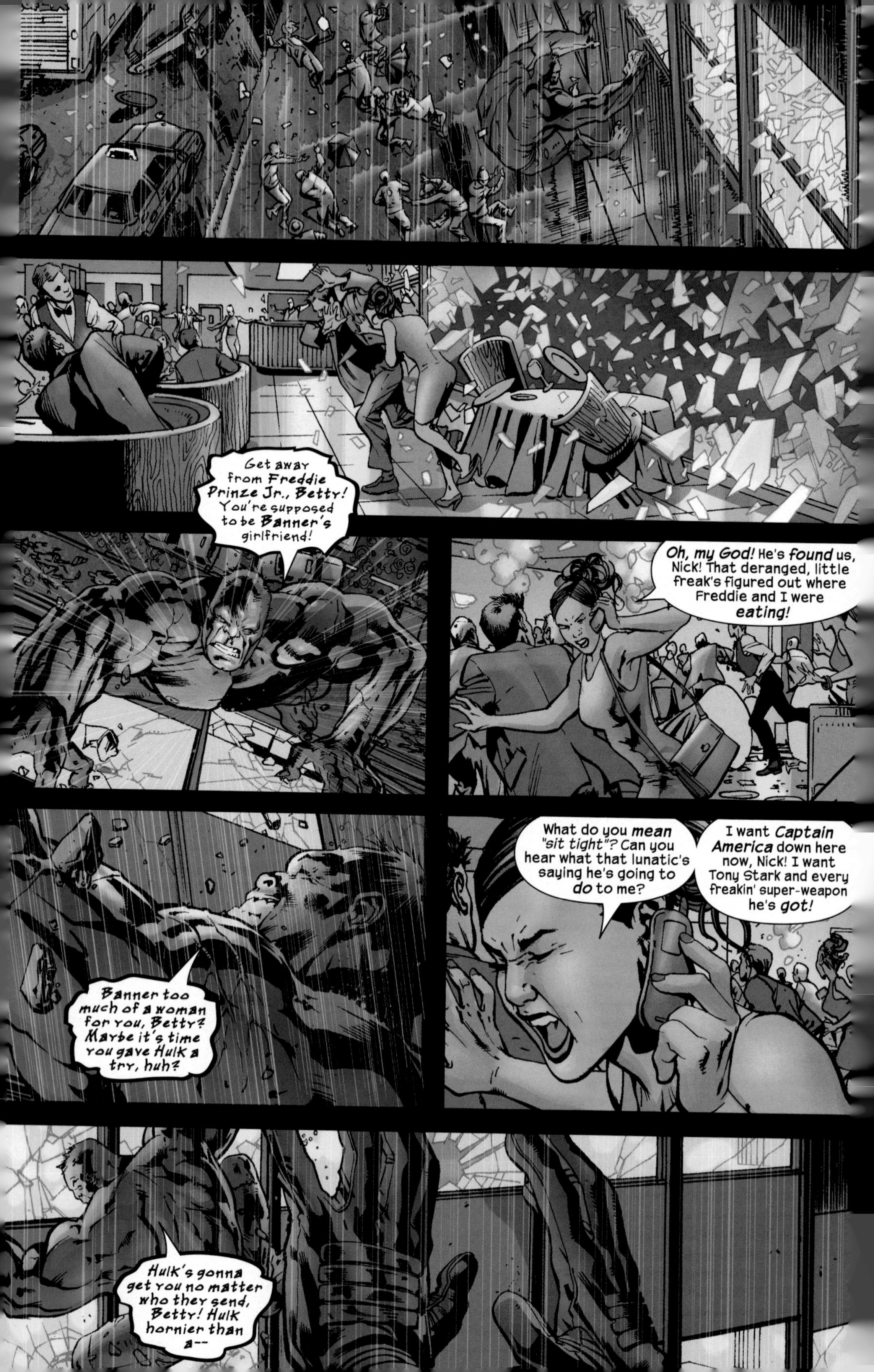

Get away from Freddie Prinze Jr., Betty! You're supposed to be Banner's girlfriend!
Oh, my God! He's found us, Nick! That deranged, little freak's figured out where Freddie and I were eating!
Banner too much of a woman for you, Betty? Maybe it's time you gave Hulk a try, huh?
What do you mean "sit tight"? Can you hear what that lunatic's saying he's going to do to me?
I want Captain America down here now, Nick! I want Tony Stark and every freakin' super-weapon he's got!
Hulk's gonna get you no matter who they send, Betty! Hulk hornier than a--

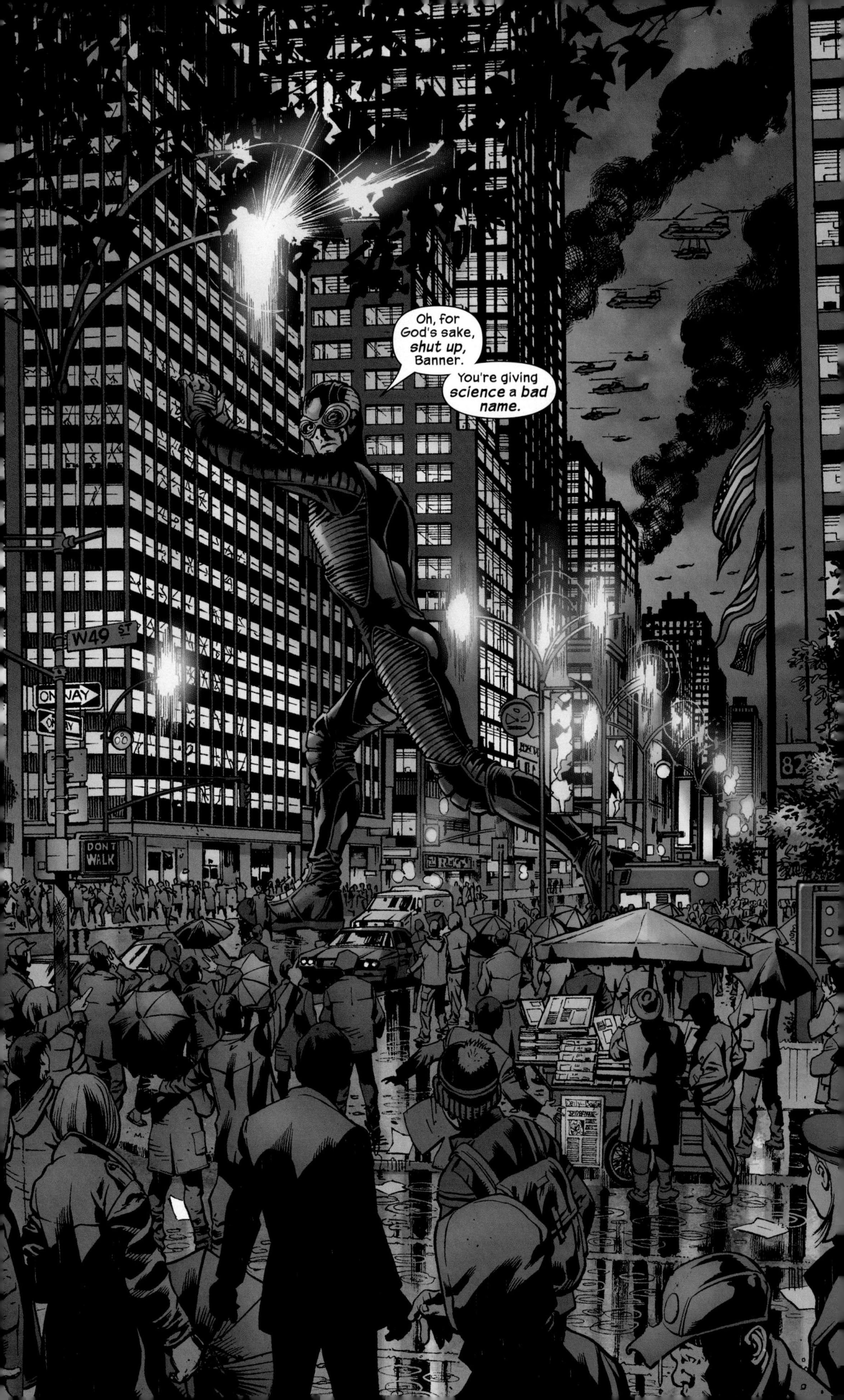
Oh, for God's sake, *shut up*, Banner.
You're giving *science* a *bad name.*
W49 ST
DON'T WALK

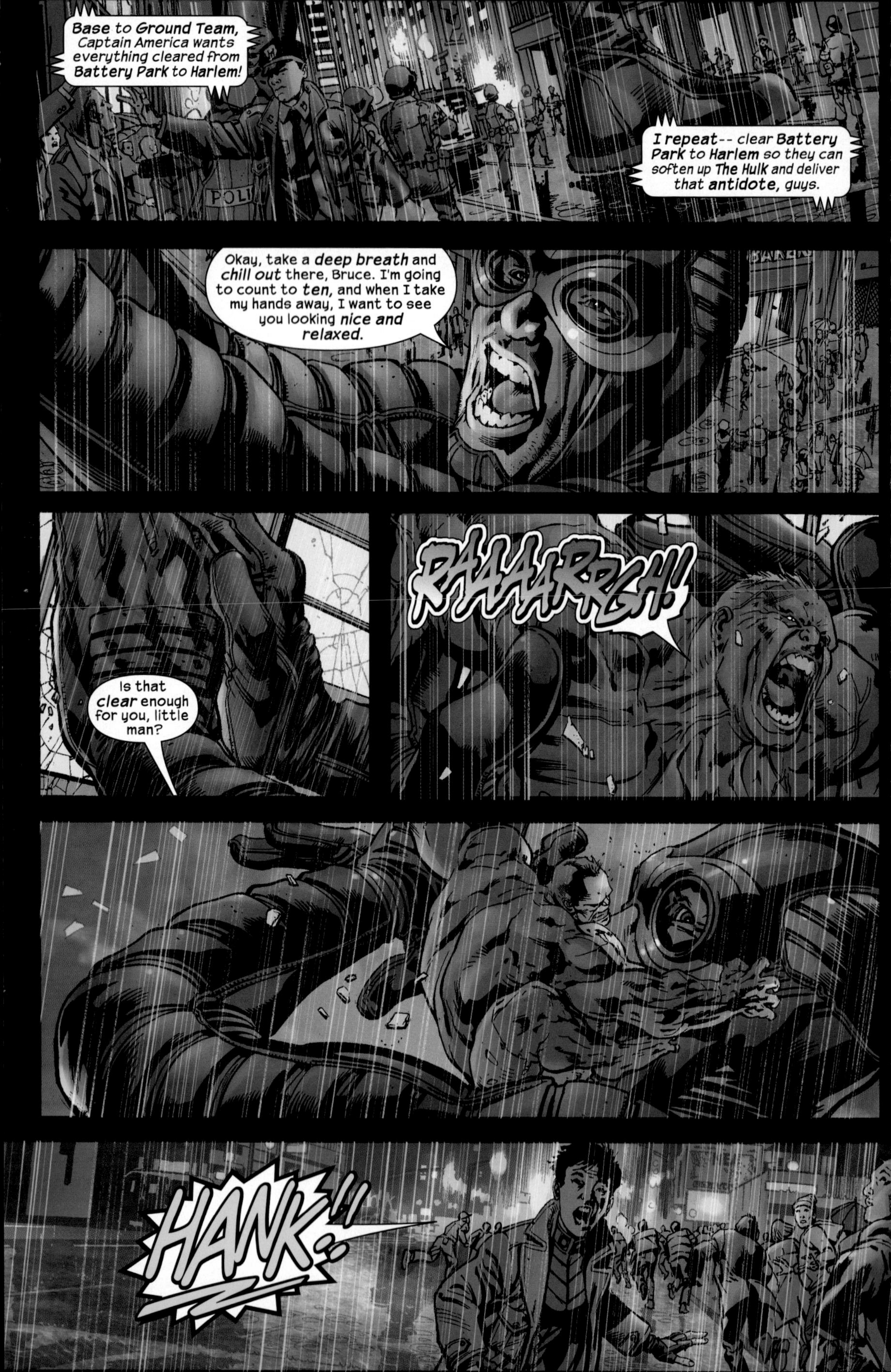
Base to Ground Team, Captain America wants everything cleared from Battery Park to Harlem!
I repeat-- clear Battery Park to Harlem so they can soften up The Hulk and deliver that antidote, guys.
Okay, take a deep breath and chill out there, Bruce. I'm going to count to ten, and when I take my hands away, I want to see you looking nice and relaxed.
Is that clear enough for you, little man?
RAAAARRGH!
HANK!!

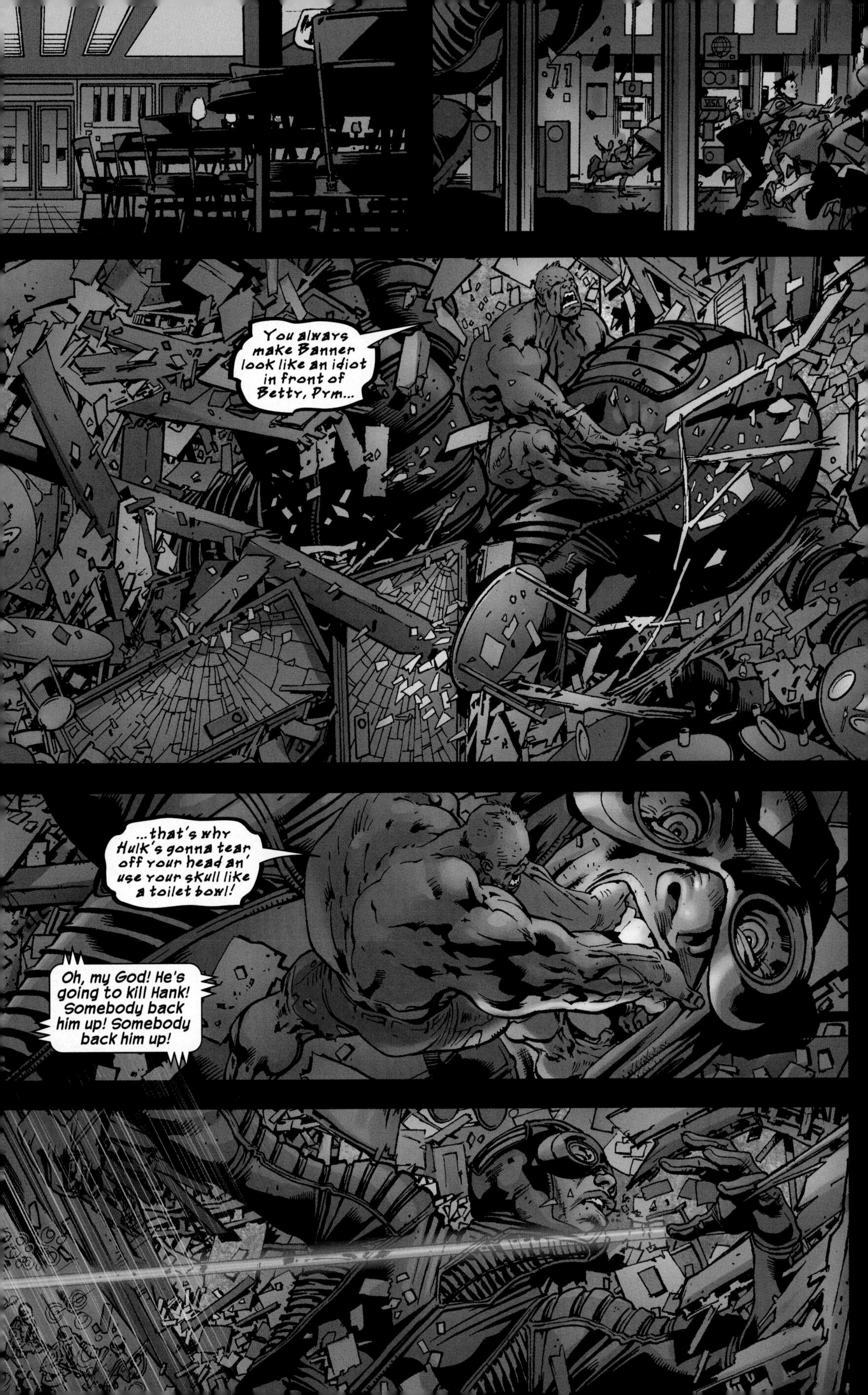
You always make Banner look like an idiot in front of Betty, Pym...
...that's why Hulk's gonna tear off your head an' use your skull like a toilet bowl!
Oh, my God! He's going to kill Hank! Somebody back him up! Somebody back him up!

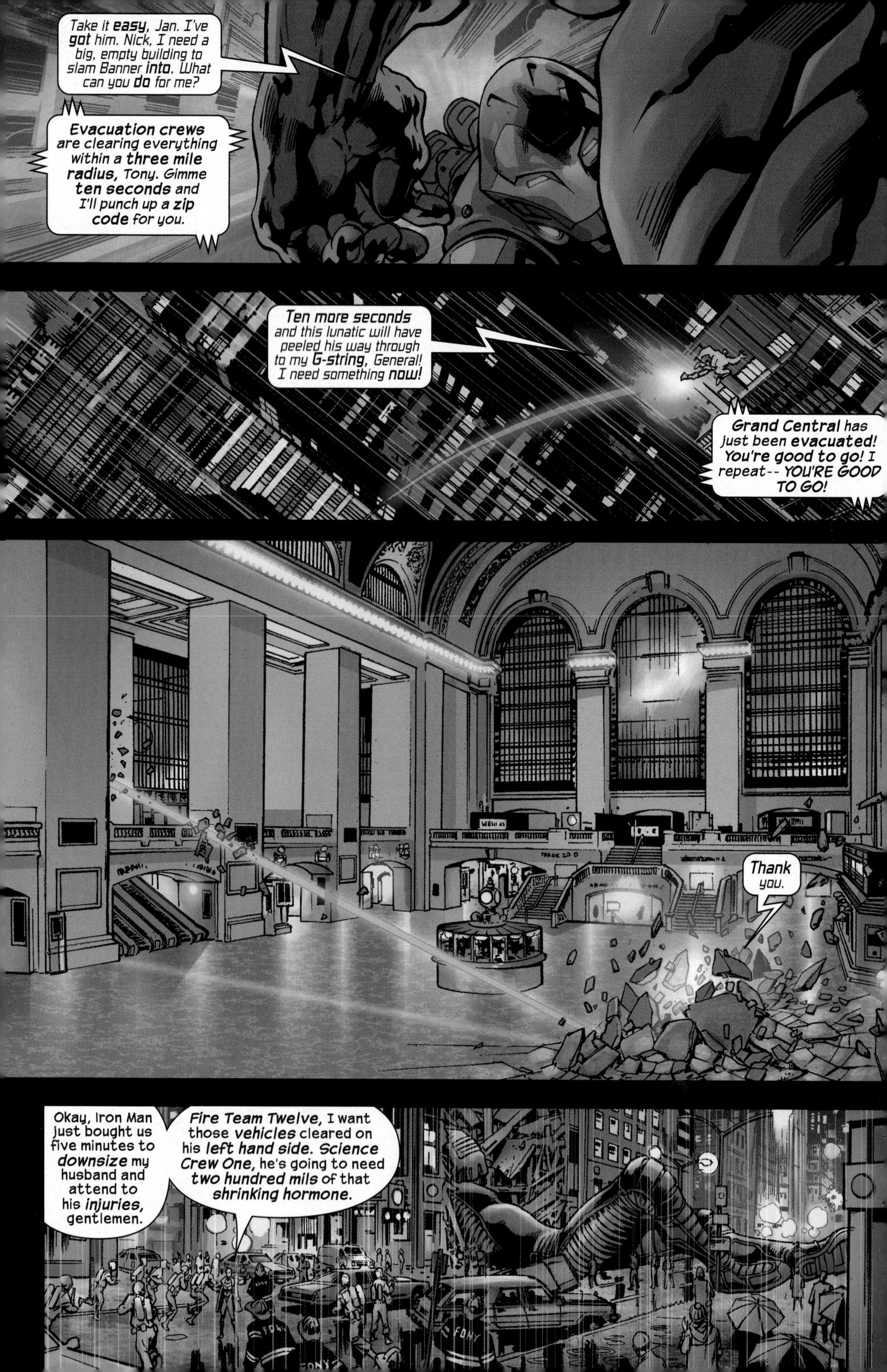
Take it easy, Jan. I've got him. Nick, I need a big, empty building to slam Banner into. What can you do for me?
Evacuation crews are clearing everything within a three mile radius, Tony. Gimme ten seconds and I'll punch up a zip code for you.
Ten more seconds and this lunatic will have peeled his way through to my G-string, General! I need something now!
Grand Central has just been evacuated! You're good to go! I repeat-- YOU'RE GOOD TO GO!
Thank you.
Okay, Iron Man just bought us five minutes to downsize my husband and attend to his injuries, gentlemen.
Fire Team Twelve, I want those vehicles cleared on his left hand side. Science Crew One, he's going to need two hundred mils of that shrinking hormone.

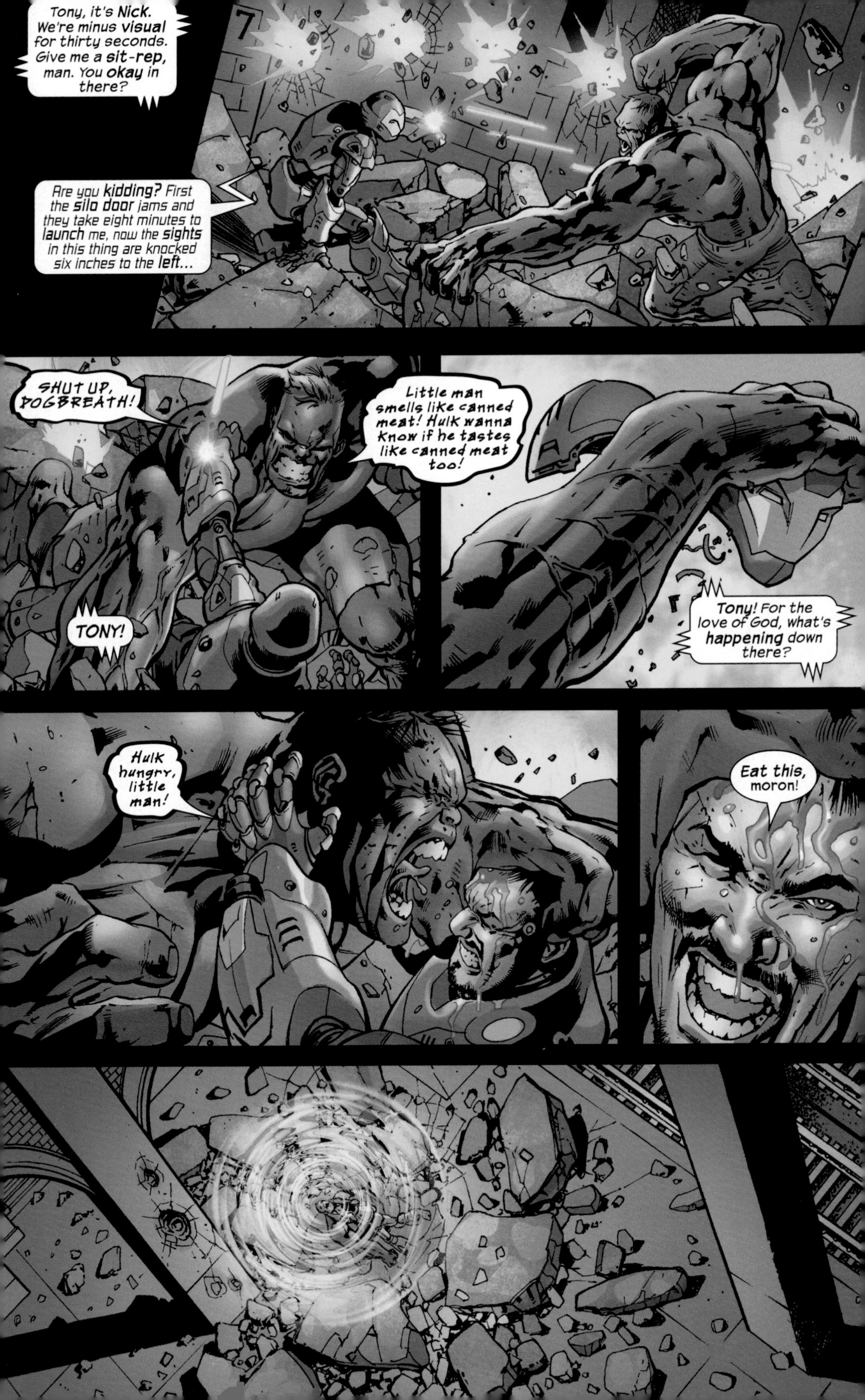
Tony, it's Nick. We're minus visual for thirty seconds. Give me a sit-rep, man. You okay in there?
Are you kidding? First the silo door jams and they take eight minutes to launch me, now the sights in this thing are knocked six inches to the left...
SHUT UP, DOGBREATH!
TONY!
Little man smells like canned meat! Hulk wanna know if he tastes like canned meat too!
Tony! For the love of God, what's happening down there?
Hulk hungry, little man!
Eat this, moron!

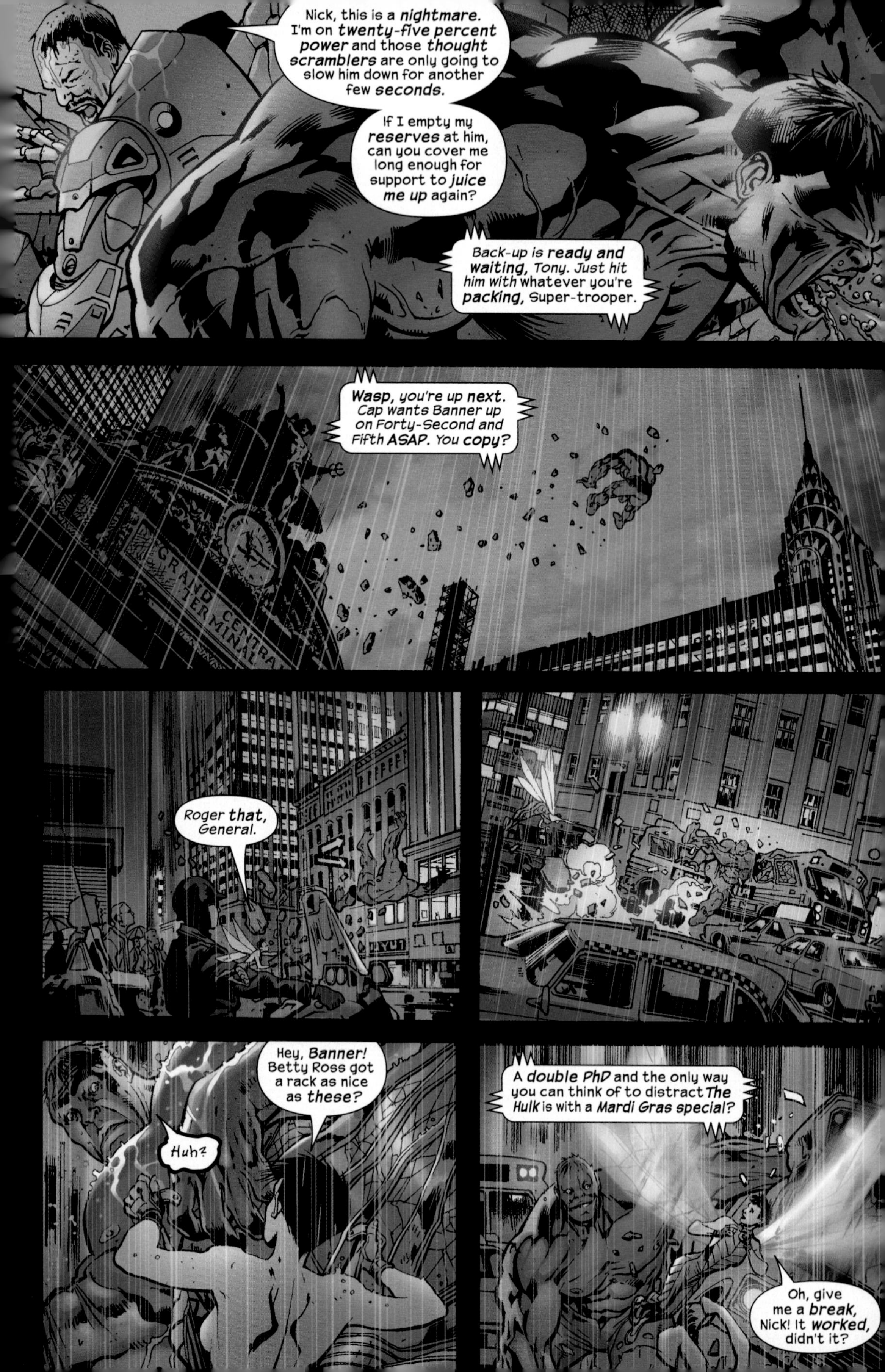
Nick, this is a nightmare. I'm on twenty-five percent power and those thought scramblers are only going to slow him down for another few seconds.
If I empty my reserves at him, can you cover me long enough for support to juice me up again?
Back-up is ready and waiting, Tony. Just hit him with whatever you're packing, Super-trooper.
Wasp, you're up next. Cap wants Banner up on Forty-Second and Fifth ASAP. You copy?
GRAND CENTRAL TERMINAL
Roger that, General.
Hey, Banner! Betty Ross got a rack as nice as these?
Huh?
A double PhD and the only way you can think of to distract The Hulk is with a Mardi Gras special?
Oh, give me a break, Nick! It worked, didn't it?

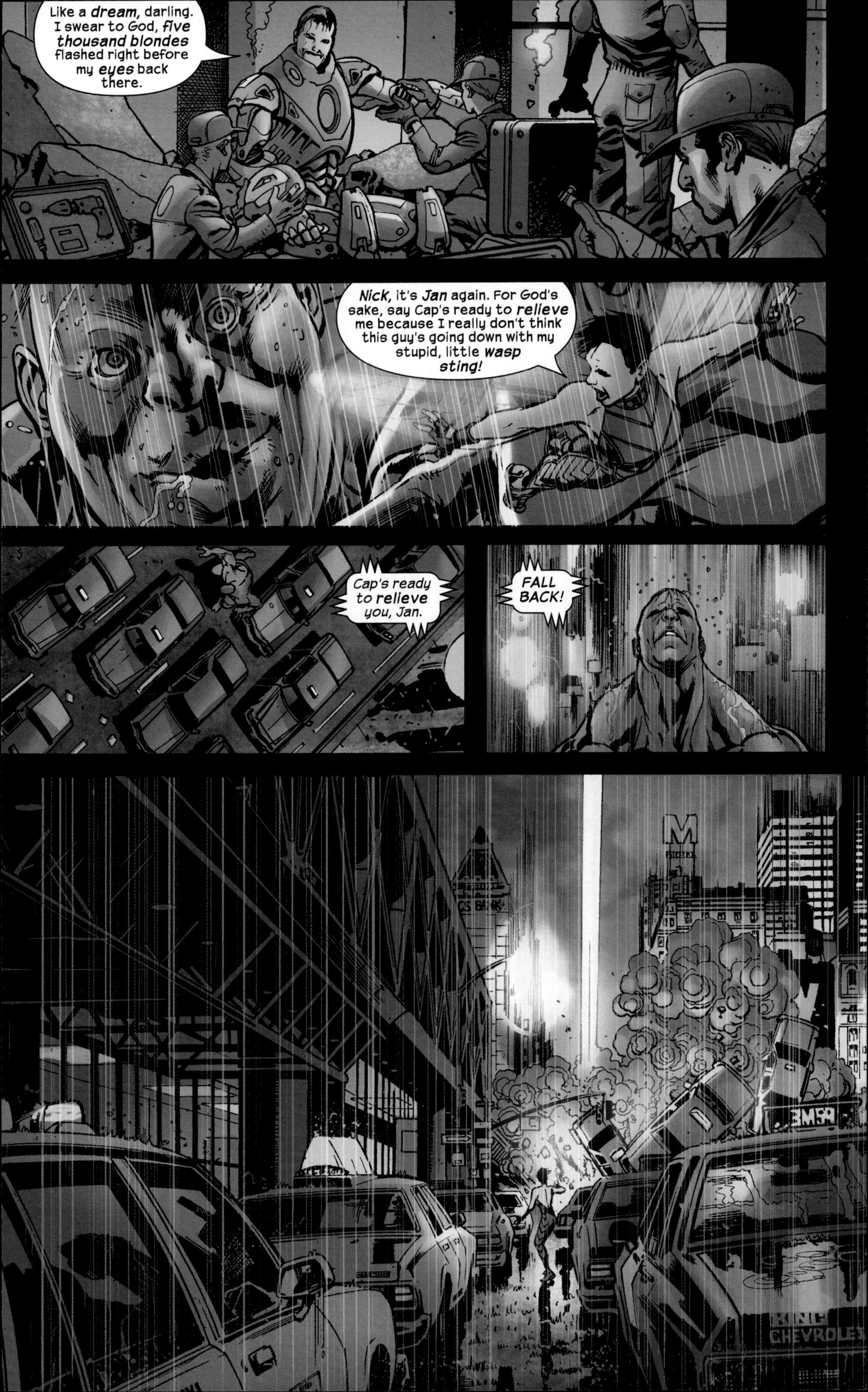

Like a *dream,* darling. I swear to God, *five thousand blondes* flashed right before my *eyes* back there.
Nick, it's *Jan* again. For God's sake, say Cap's ready to *relieve* me because I really don't think this guy's going down with my stupid, little *wasp sting!*
*Cap's ready to **relieve** you, Jan.*
FALL BACK!

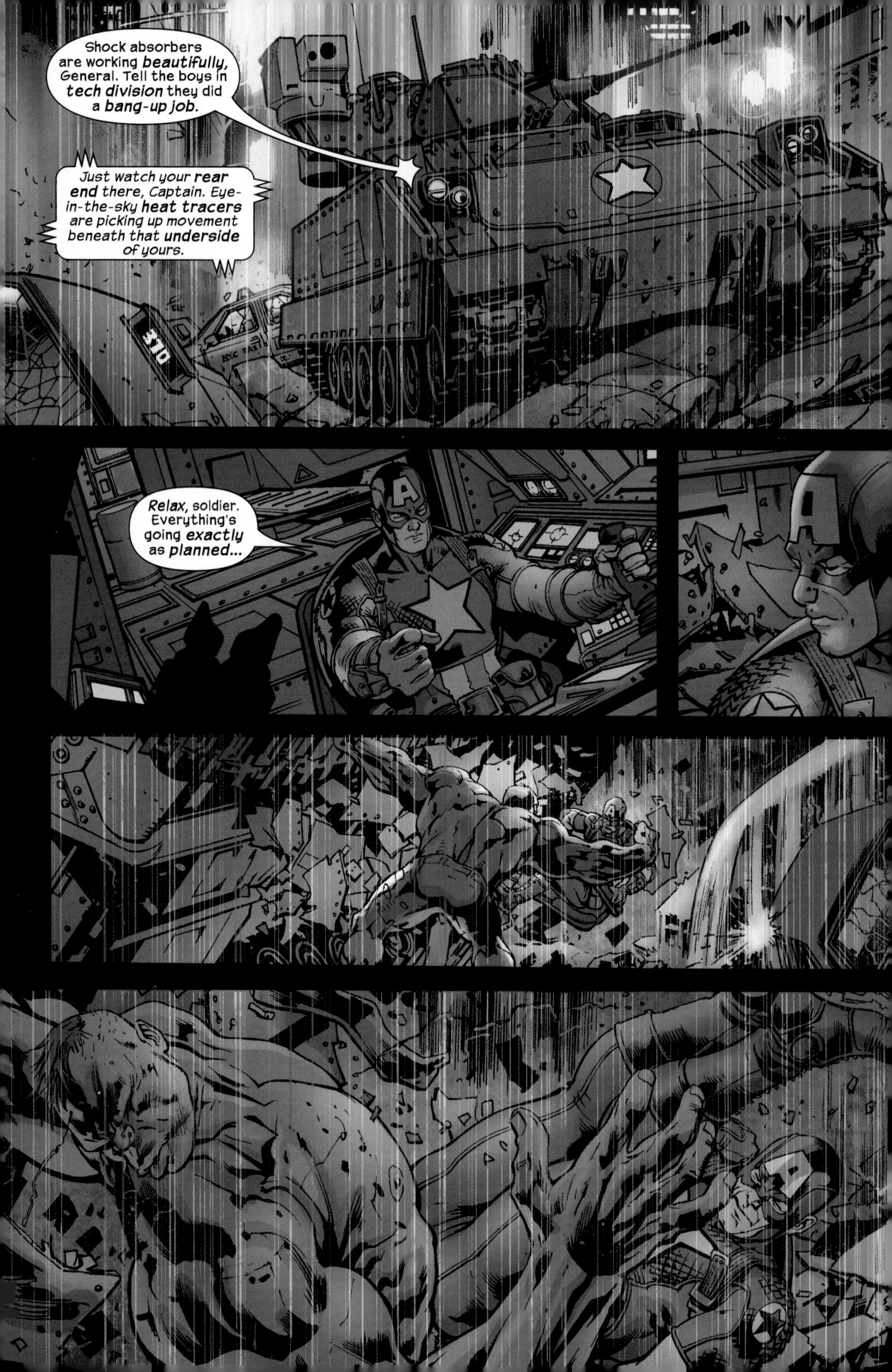
Shock absorbers are working beautifully, General. Tell the boys in tech division they did a bang-up job.
Just watch your rear end there, Captain. Eye-in-the-sky heat tracers are picking up movement beneath that underside of yours.
310
Relax, soldier. Everything's going exactly as planned...

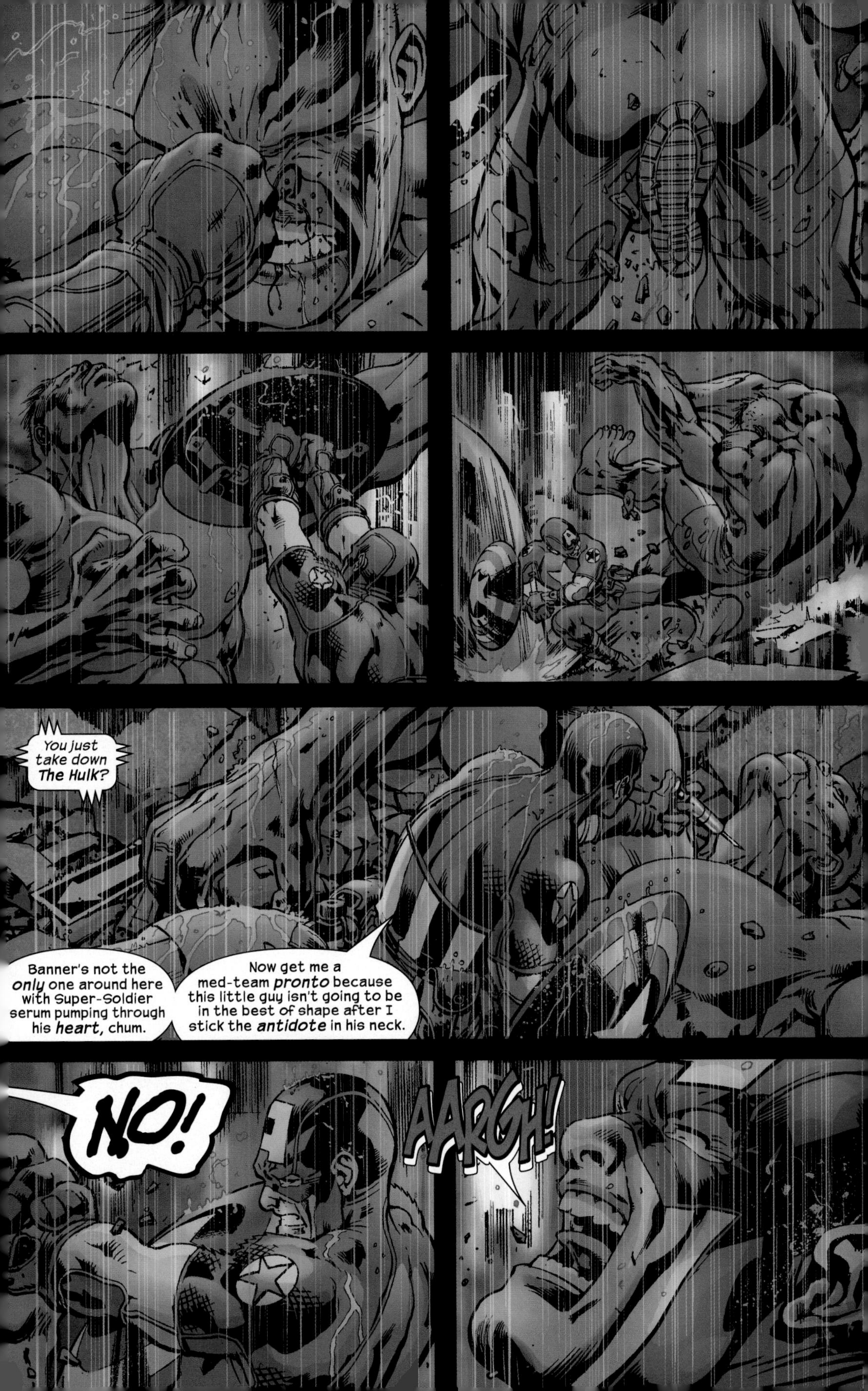
You just take down The Hulk?
Banner's not the only one around here with Super-Soldier serum pumping through his heart, chum.
Now get me a med-team pronto because this little guy isn't going to be in the best of shape after I stick the antidote in his neck.
NO!
AARGH!

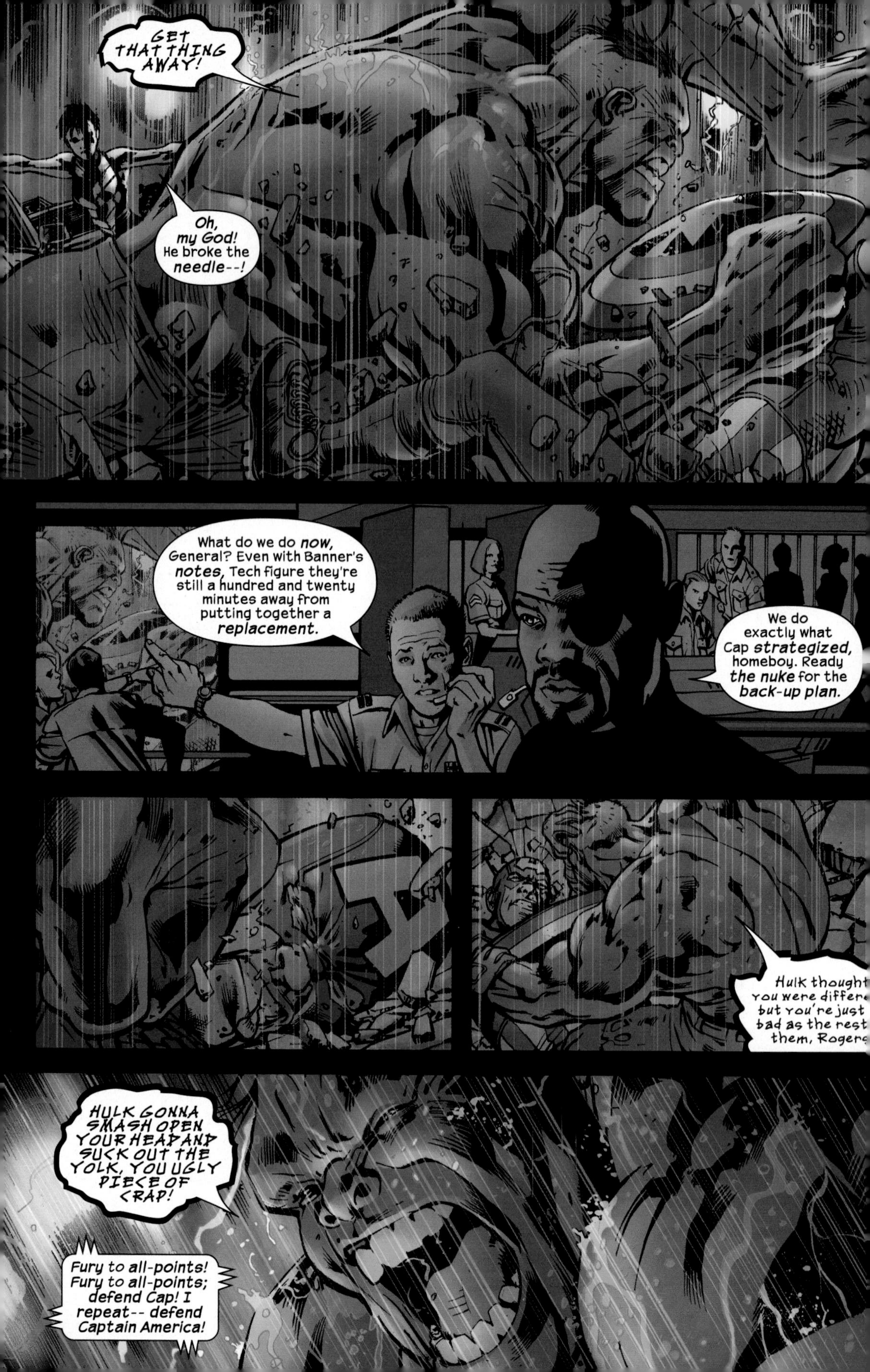
GET THAT THING AWAY!
Oh, my God! He broke the needle--!
What do we do now, General? Even with Banner's notes, Tech figure they're still a hundred and twenty minutes away from putting together a replacement.
We do exactly what Cap strategized, homeboy. Ready the nuke for the back-up plan.
Hulk thought you were differe but you're just bad as the rest them, Rogers
HULK GONNA SMASH OPEN YOUR HEAD AND SUCK OUT THE YOLK, YOU UGLY PIECE OF CRAP!
Fury to all-points! Fury to all-points; defend Cap! I repeat-- defend Captain America!

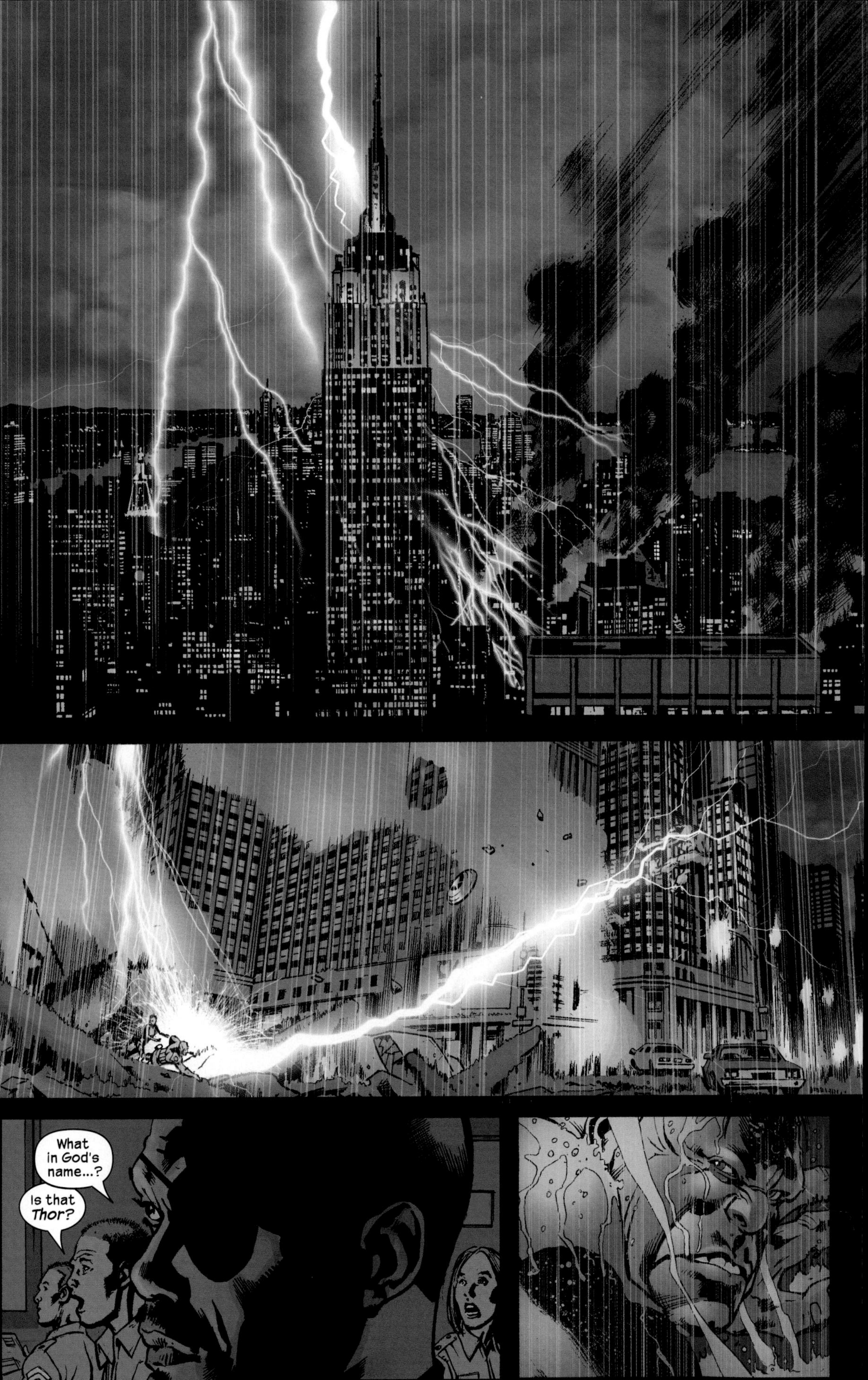
What in God's name...?
Is that *Thor?*

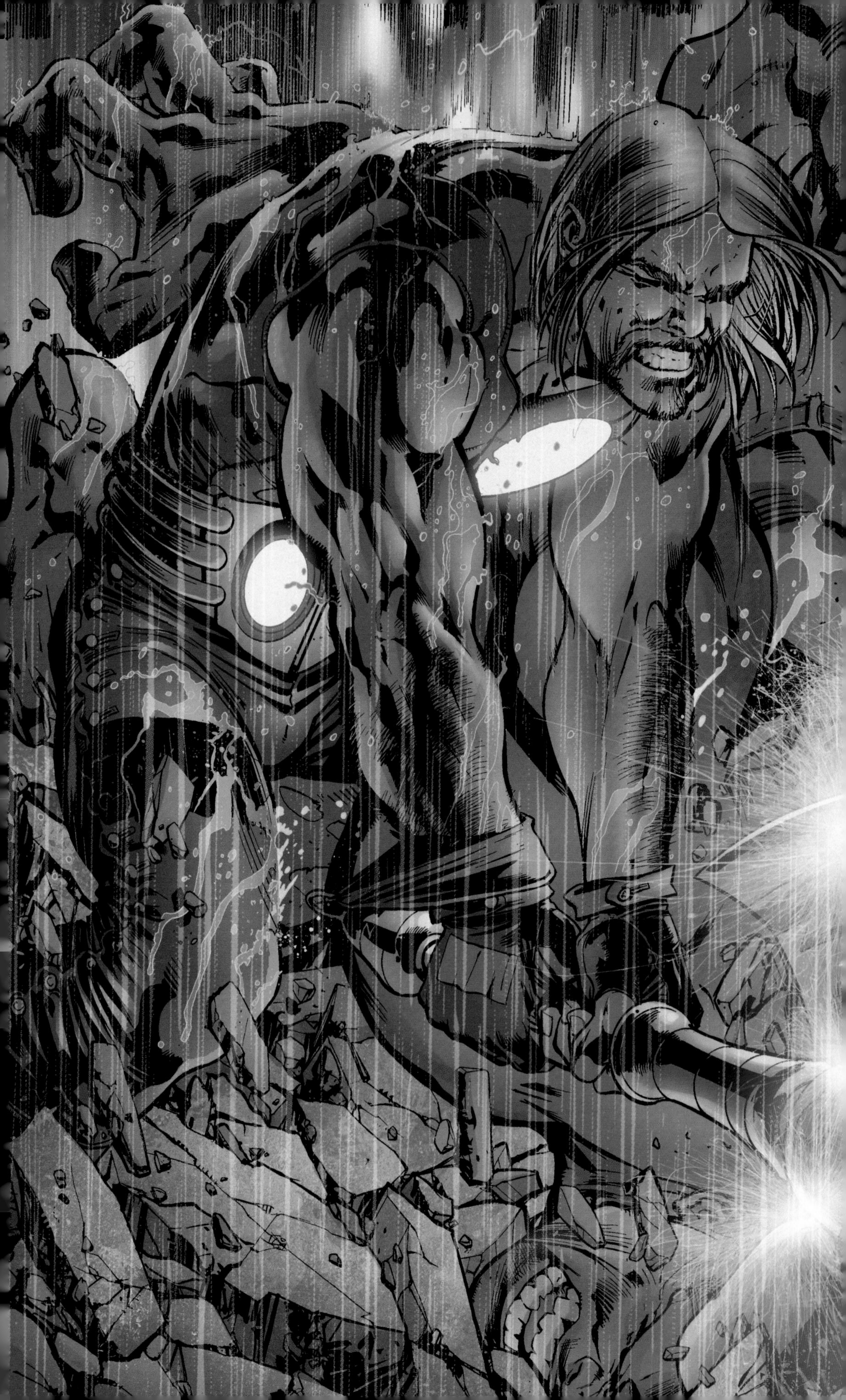

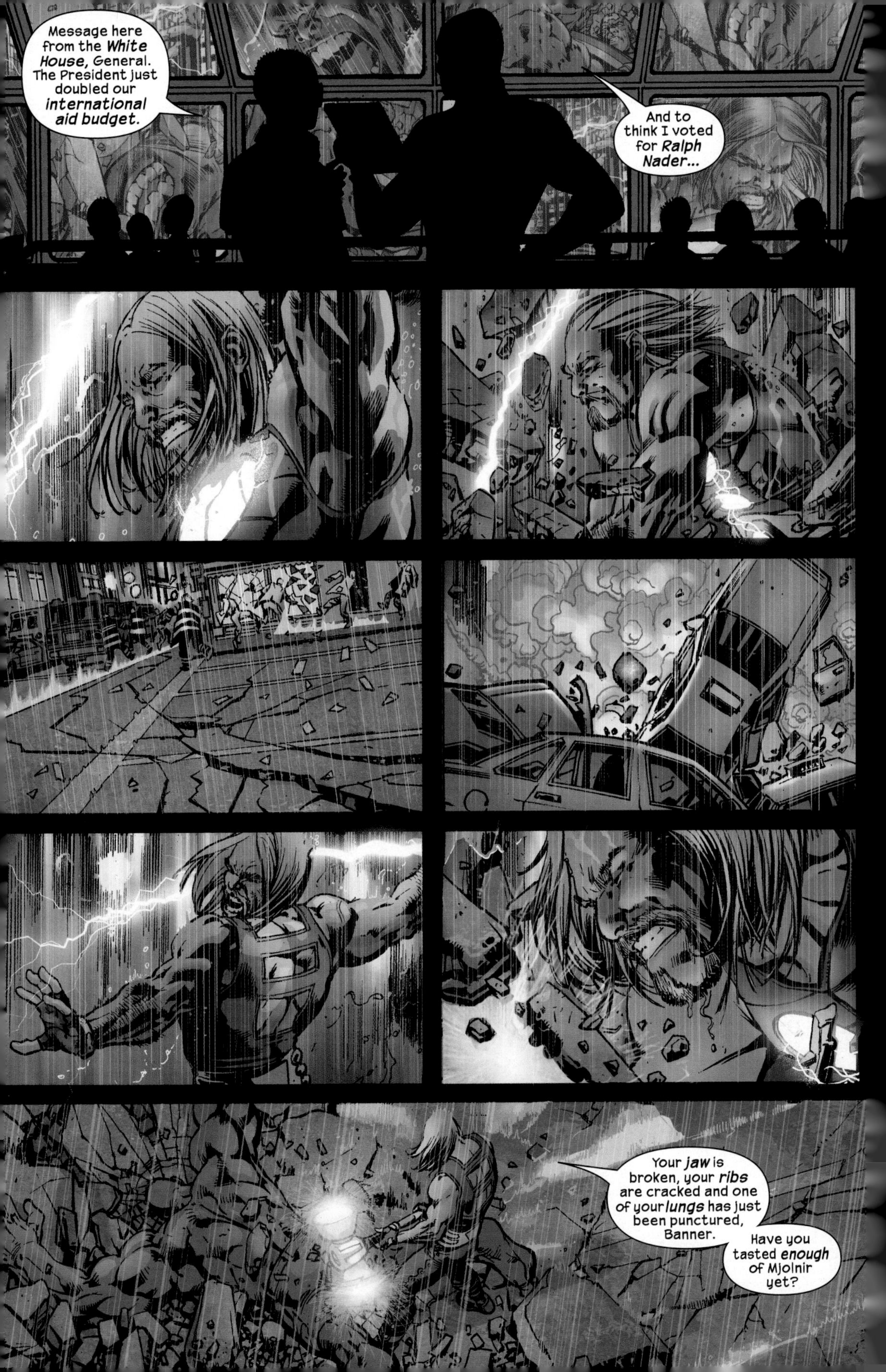
Message here from the *White House,* General. The President just doubled our ***international aid budget.***
And to think I voted for ***Ralph Nader...***
Your ***jaw*** is broken, your ***ribs*** are cracked and one of your ***lungs*** has just been punctured, Banner.
Have you tasted ***enough*** of Mjolnir yet?

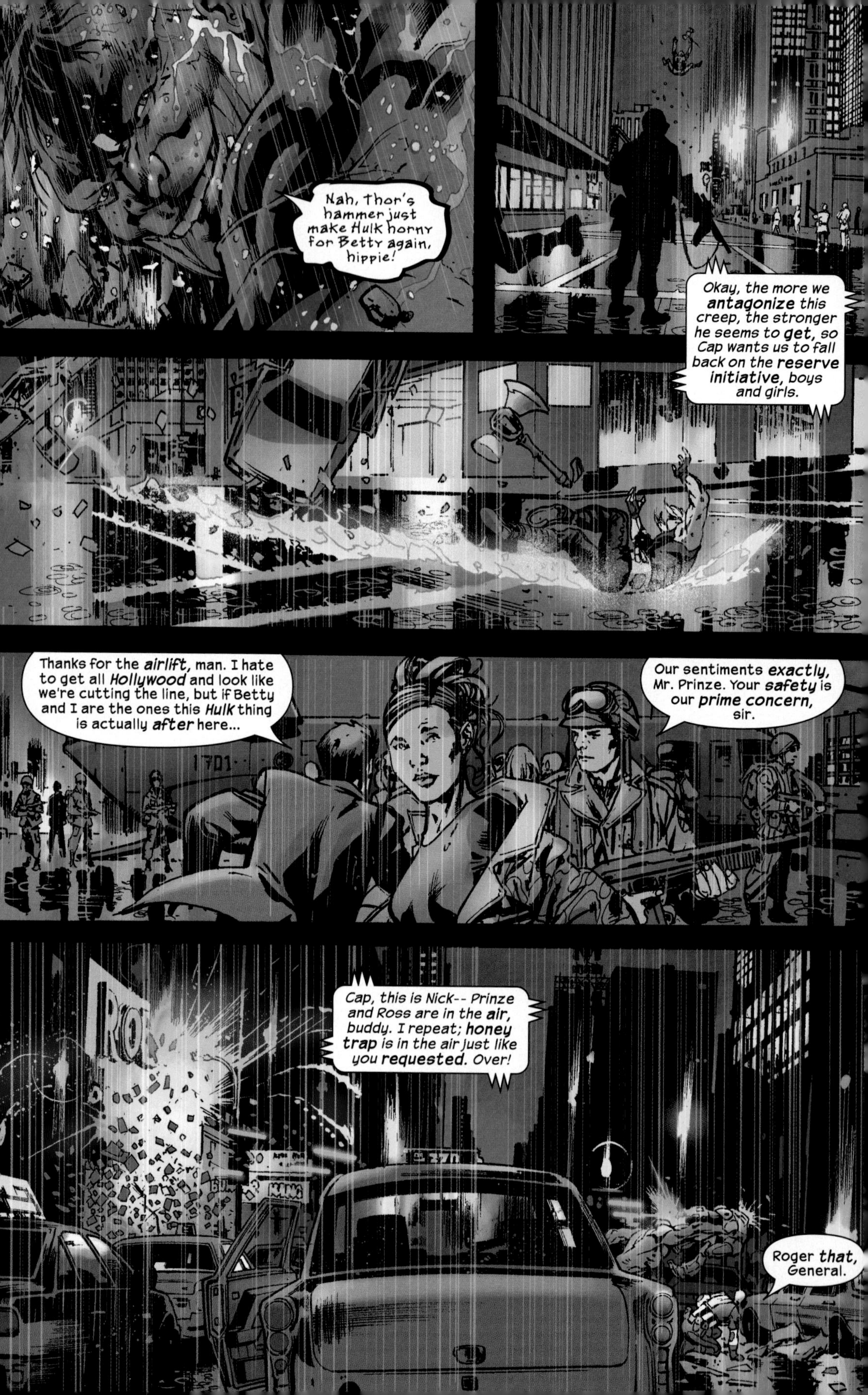
Nah, Thor's hammer just make Hulk horny for Betty again, hippie!
Okay, the more we antagonize this creep, the stronger he seems to get, so Cap wants us to fall back on the reserve initiative, boys and girls.
Thanks for the airlift, man. I hate to get all Hollywood and look like we're cutting the line, but if Betty and I are the ones this Hulk thing is actually after here...
Our sentiments exactly, Mr. Prinze. Your safety is our prime concern, sir.
Cap, this is Nick-- Prinze and Ross are in the air, buddy. I repeat; honey trap is in the air just like you requested. Over!
Roger that, General.

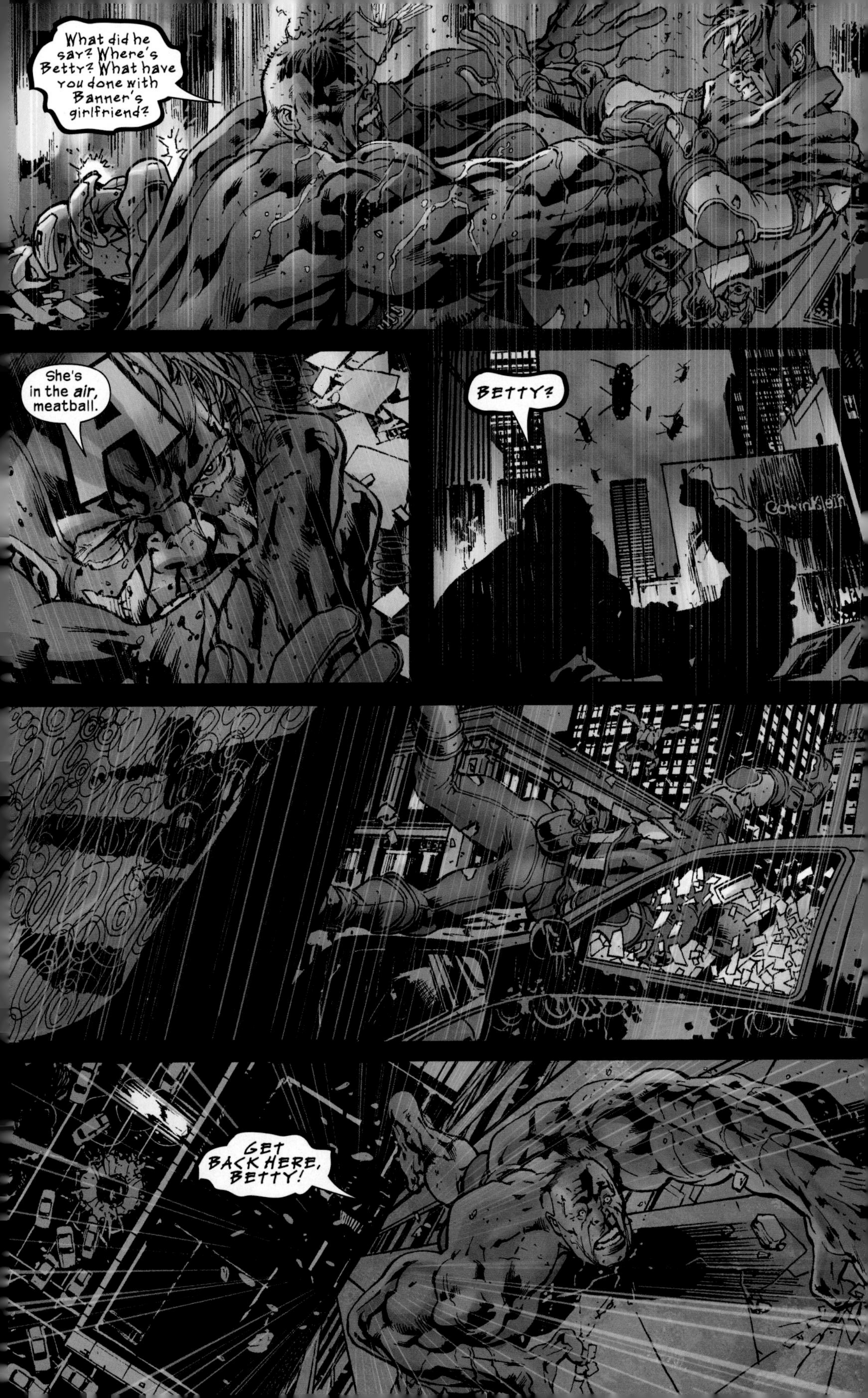
What did he say? Where's Betty? What have you done with Banner's girlfriend?
She's in the *air*, meatball.
BETTY?
Calvin Klein
GET BACK HERE, BETTY!

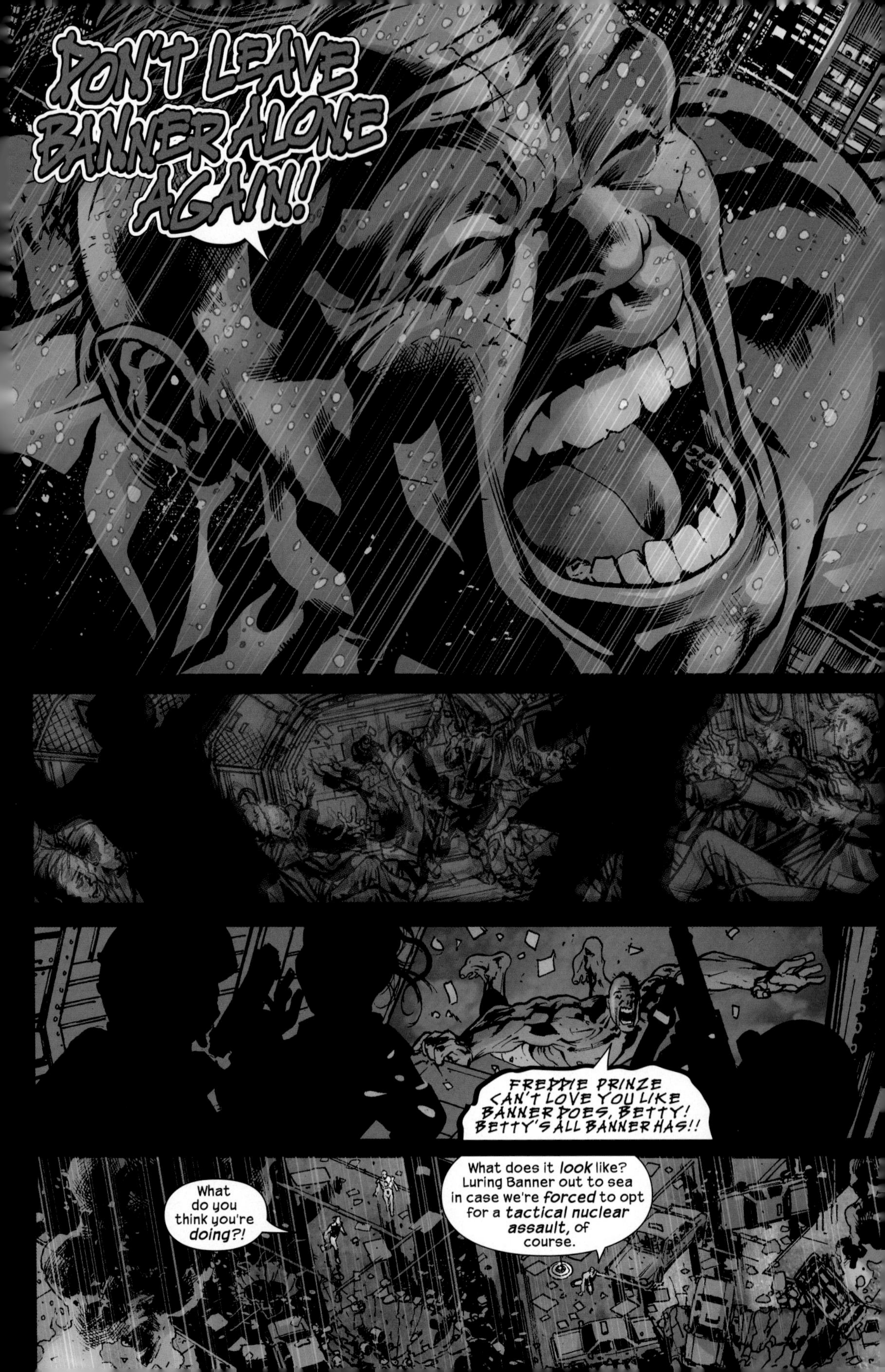
DON'T LEAVE BANNER ALONE AGAIN!
FREDDIE PRINZE CAN'T LOVE YOU LIKE BANNER DOES, BETTY! BETTY'S ALL BANNER HAS!!
What do you think you're doing?!
What does it look like? Luring Banner out to sea in case we're forced to opt for a tactical nuclear assault, of course.

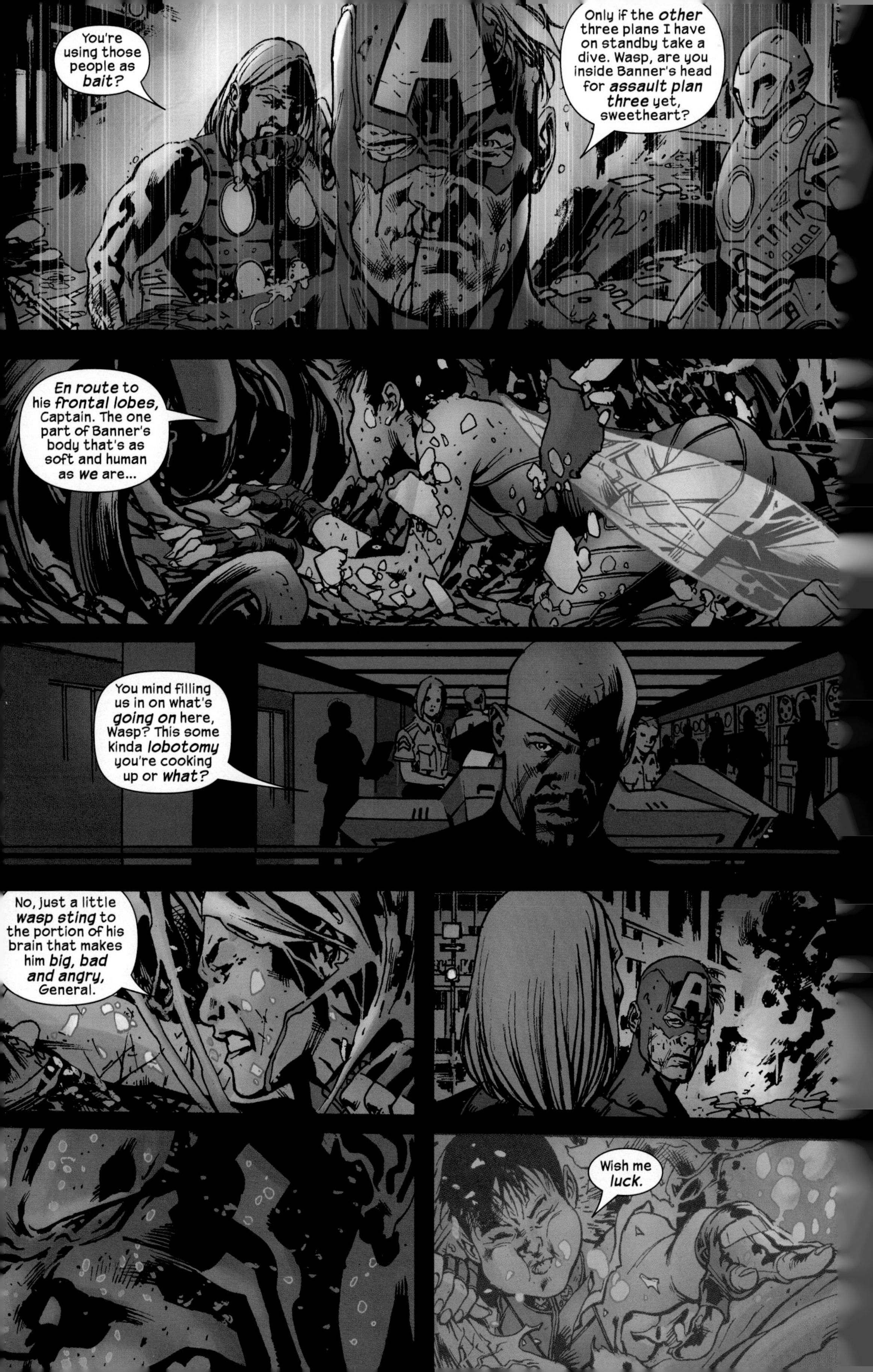
You're using those people as bait?
Only if the other three plans I have on standby take a dive. Wasp, are you inside Banner's head for assault plan three yet, sweetheart?
En route to his frontal lobes, Captain. The one part of Banner's body that's as soft and human as we are...
You mind filling us in on what's going on here, Wasp? This some kinda lobotomy you're cooking up or what?
No, just a little wasp sting to the portion of his brain that makes him big, bad and angry, General.
Wish me luck.

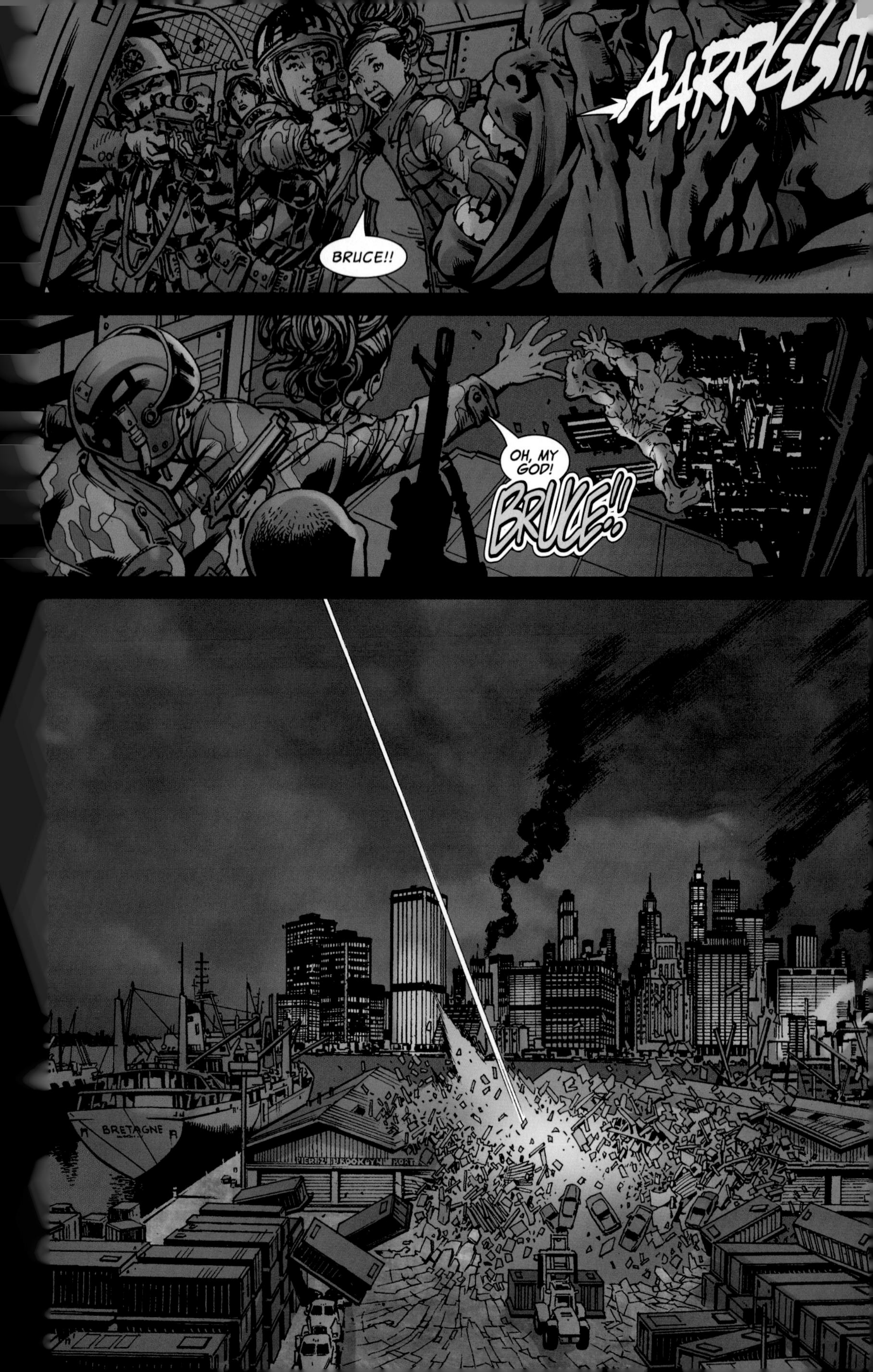
BRUCE!!
AARRGGH
OH, MY GOD!
BRUCE!!
BRETAGNE

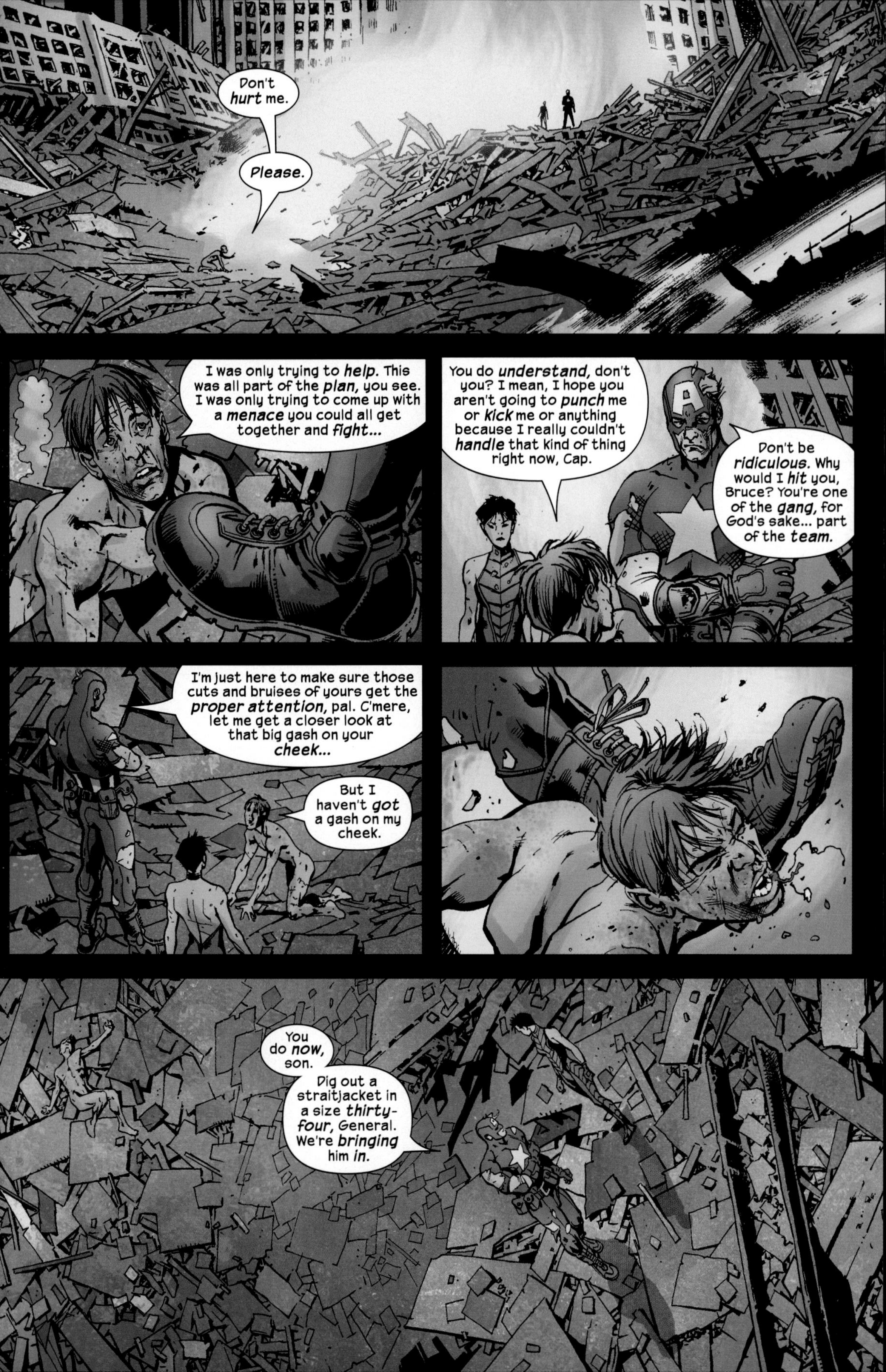
Don't *hurt* me.
Please.
I was only trying to *help.* This was all part of the *plan,* you see. I was only trying to come up with a *menace* you could all get together and *fight...*
You do *understand,* don't you? I mean, I hope you aren't going to *punch* me or *kick* me or anything because I really couldn't *handle* that kind of thing right now, Cap.
Don't be *ridiculous.* Why would I *hit* you, Bruce? You're one of the *gang,* for God's sake... part of the *team.*
I'm just here to make sure those cuts and bruises of yours get the *proper attention,* pal. C'mere, let me get a closer look at that big gash on your *cheek...*
But I haven't *got* a gash on my cheek.
You do *now,* son.
Dig out a straitjacket in a size *thirty-four,* General. We're *bringing* him *in.*

CHAPTER SIX
GIANT MAN vs THE WASP

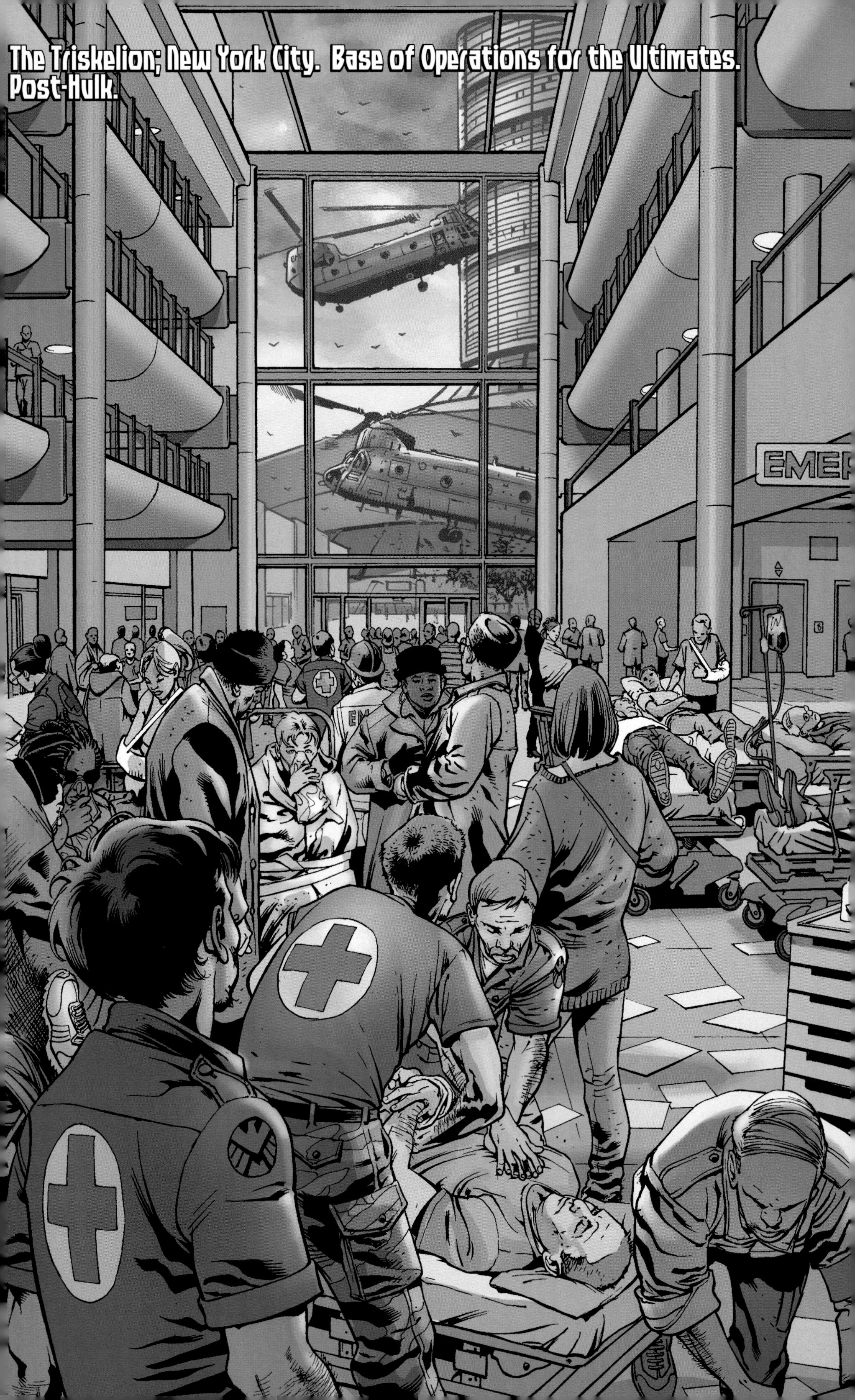
The Triskelion; New York City. Base of Operations for the Ultimates.
Post-Hulk.
EMER

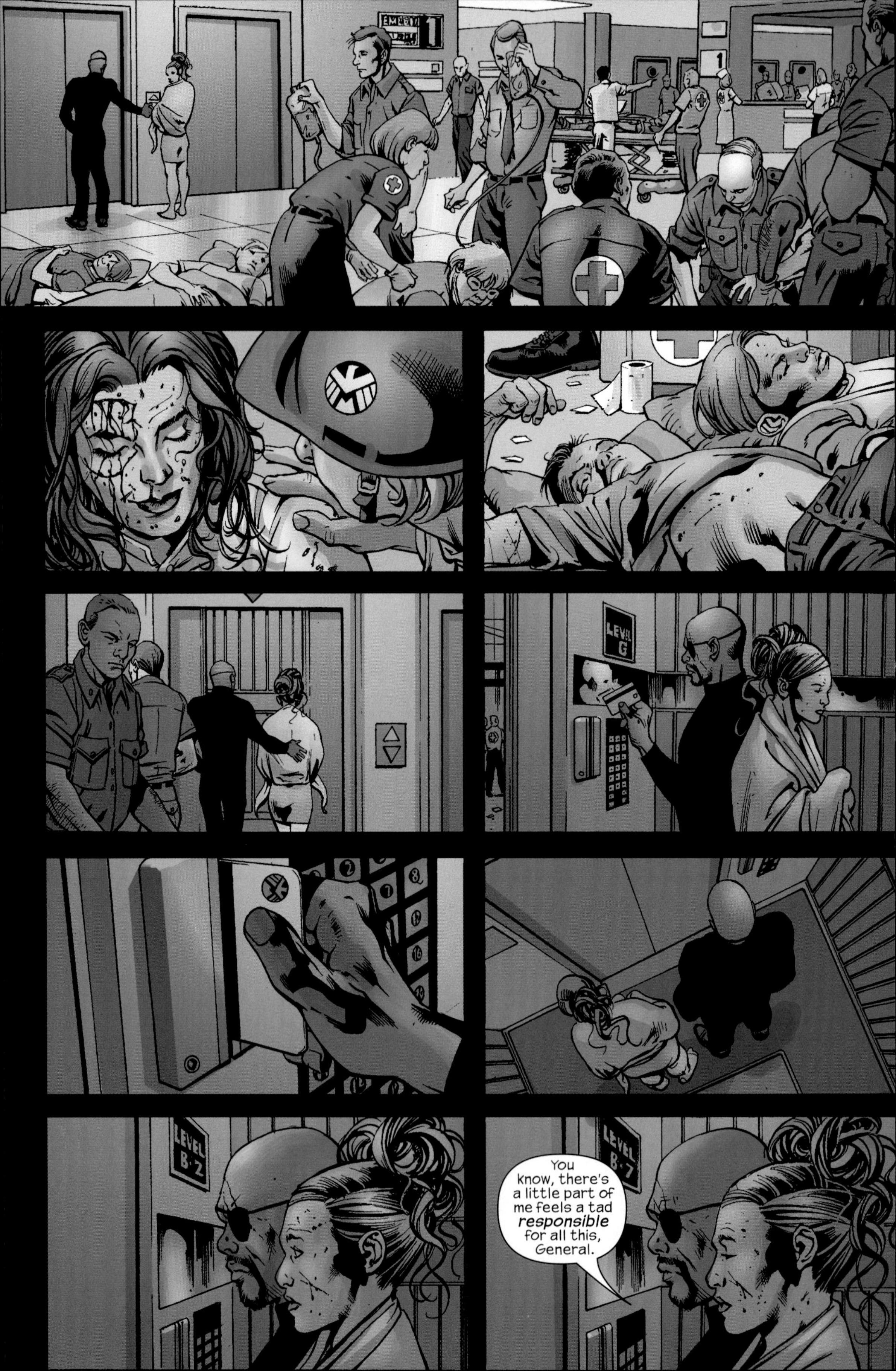

LEVEL G
LEVEL B·2
LEVEL B·7
You know, there's a little part of me feels a tad *responsible* for all this, General.

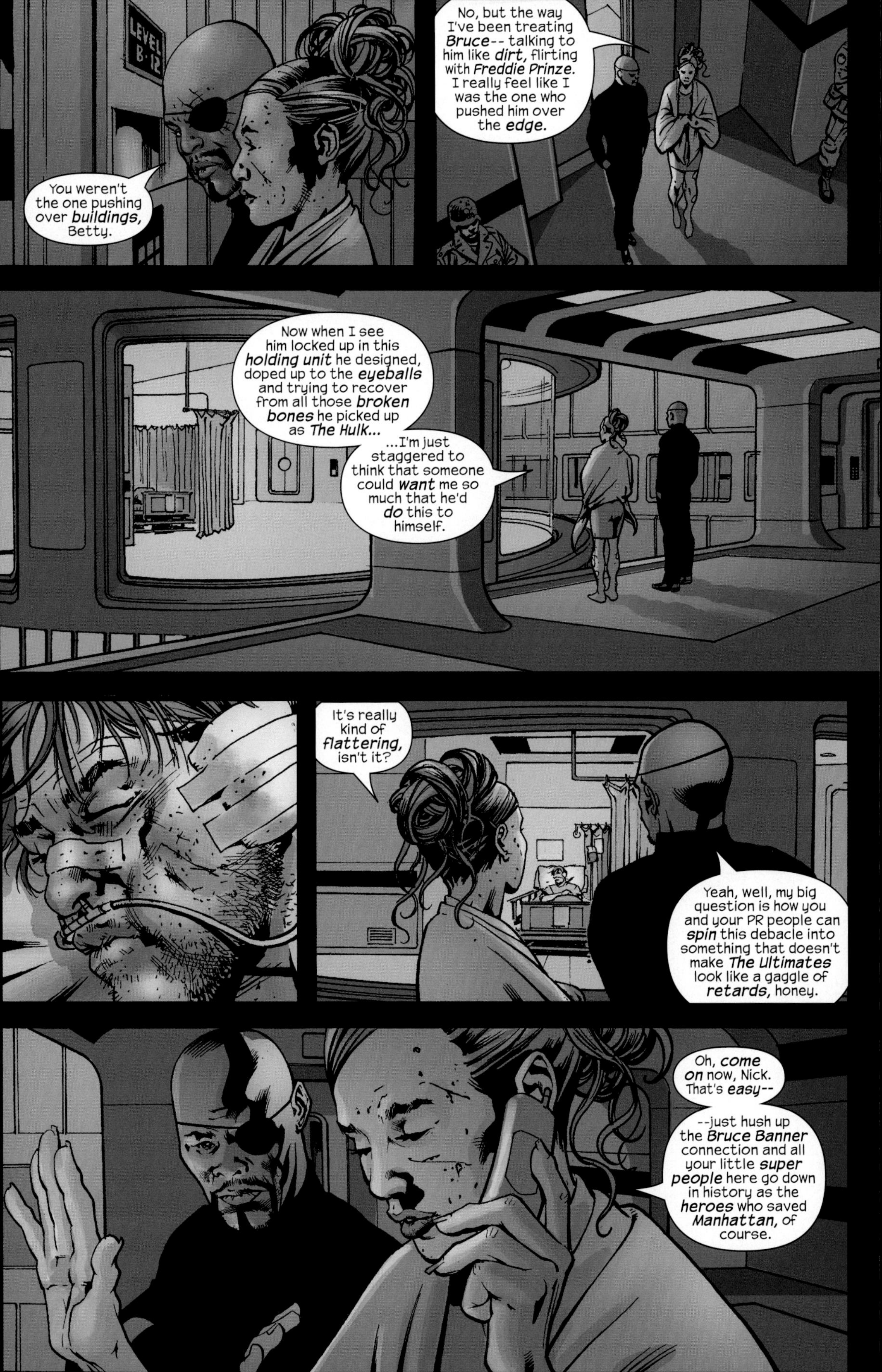
LEVEL B-12
You weren't the one pushing over buildings, Betty.
No, but the way I've been treating Bruce-- talking to him like dirt, flirting with Freddie Prinze. I really feel like I was the one who pushed him over the edge.
Now when I see him locked up in this holding unit he designed, doped up to the eyeballs and trying to recover from all those broken bones he picked up as The Hulk...
...I'm just staggered to think that someone could want me so much that he'd do this to himself.
It's really kind of flattering, isn't it?
Yeah, well, my big question is how you and your PR people can spin this debacle into something that doesn't make The Ultimates look like a gaggle of retards, honey.
Oh, come on now, Nick. That's easy--
--just hush up the Bruce Banner connection and all your little super people here go down in history as the heroes who saved Manhattan, of course.

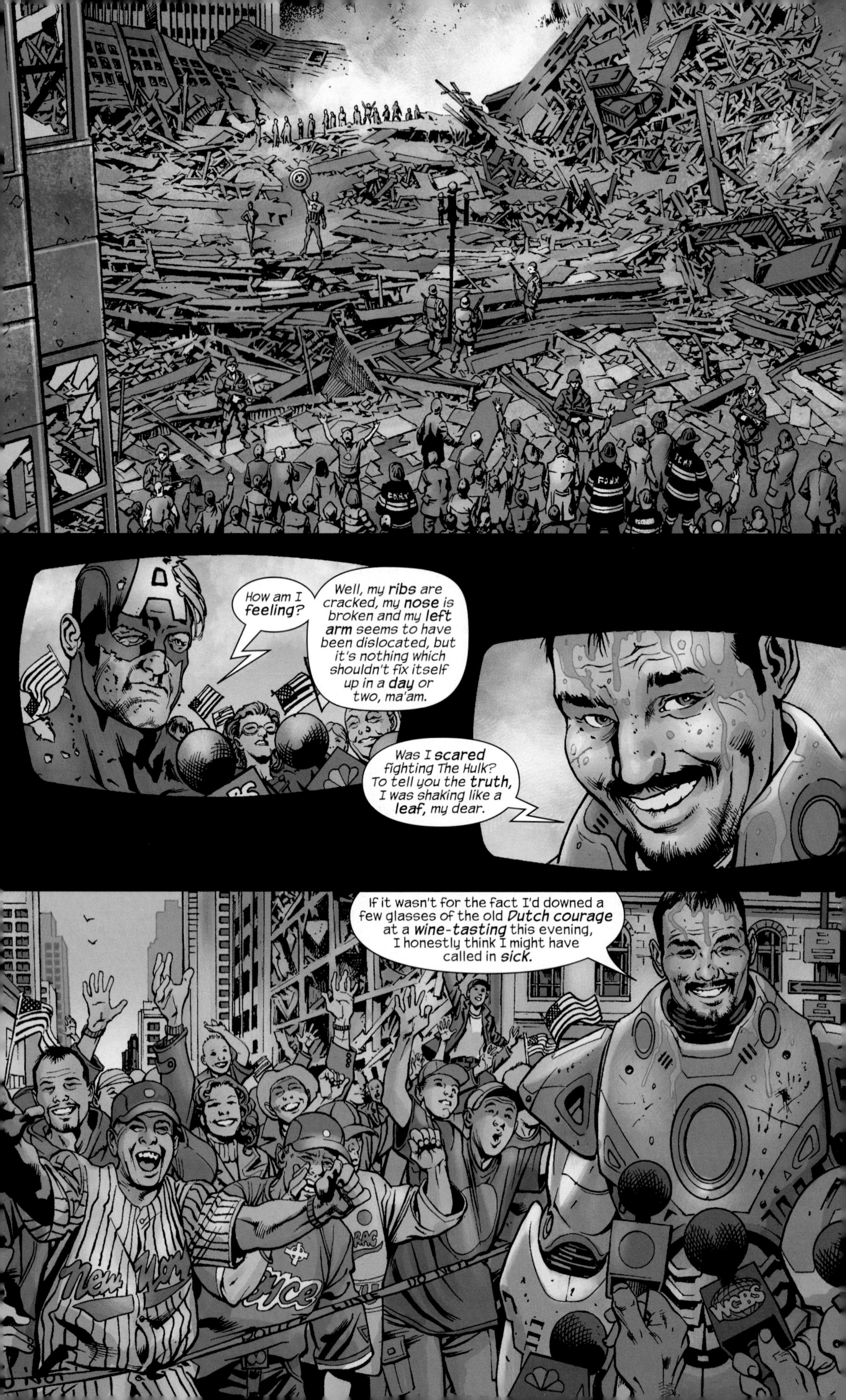
How am I feeling?
Well, my ribs are cracked, my nose is broken and my left arm seems to have been dislocated, but it's nothing which shouldn't fix itself up in a day or two, ma'am.
Was I scared fighting The Hulk? To tell you the truth, I was shaking like a leaf, my dear.
If it wasn't for the fact I'd downed a few glasses of the old Dutch courage at a wine-tasting this evening, I honestly think I might have called in sick.

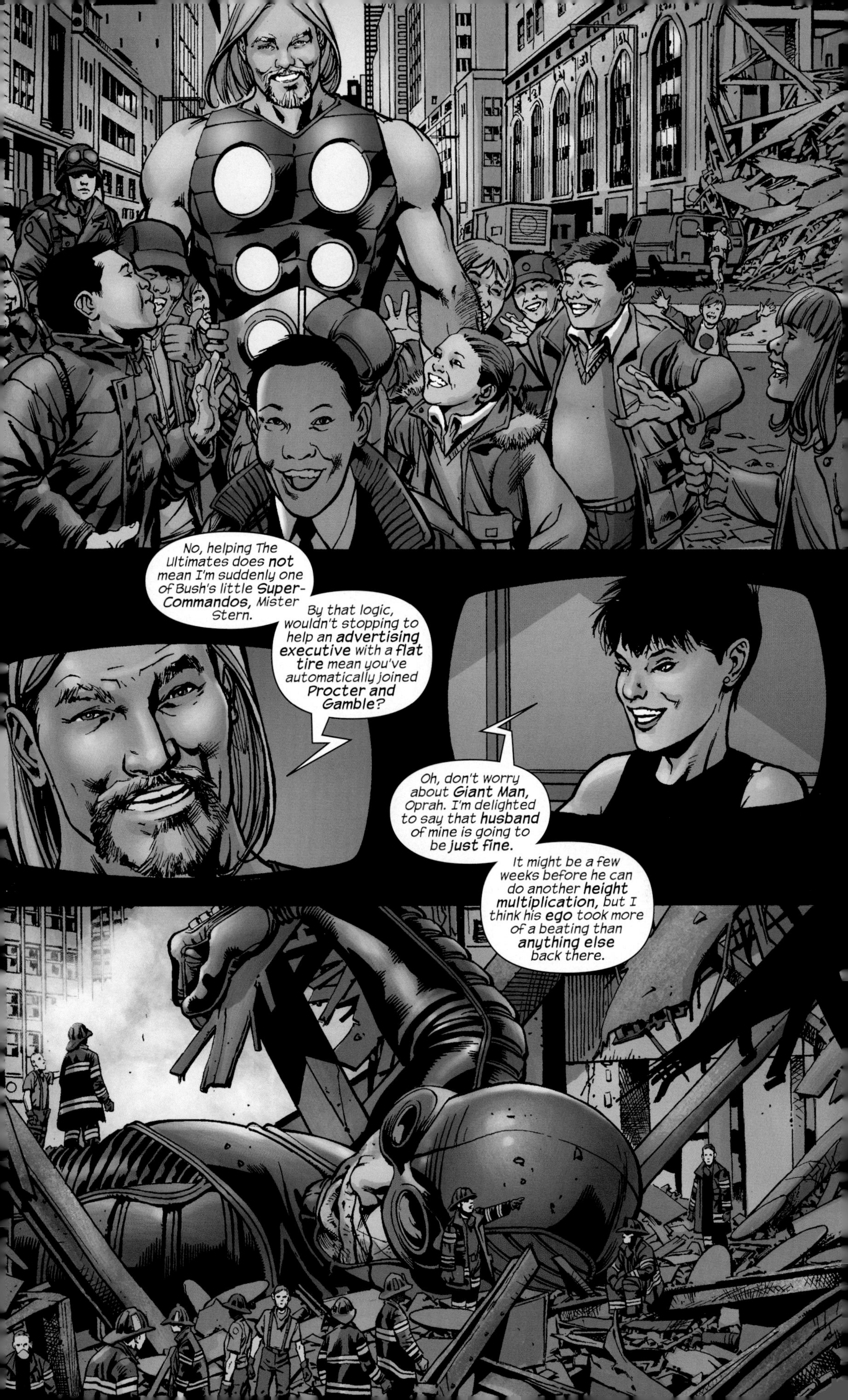
No, helping The Ultimates does not mean I'm suddenly one of Bush's little Super-Commandos, Mister Stern.
By that logic, wouldn't stopping to help an advertising executive with a flat tire mean you've automatically joined Procter and Gamble?
Oh, don't worry about Giant Man, Oprah. I'm delighted to say that husband of mine is going to be just fine.
It might be a few weeks before he can do another height multiplication, but I think his ego took more of a beating than anything else back there.

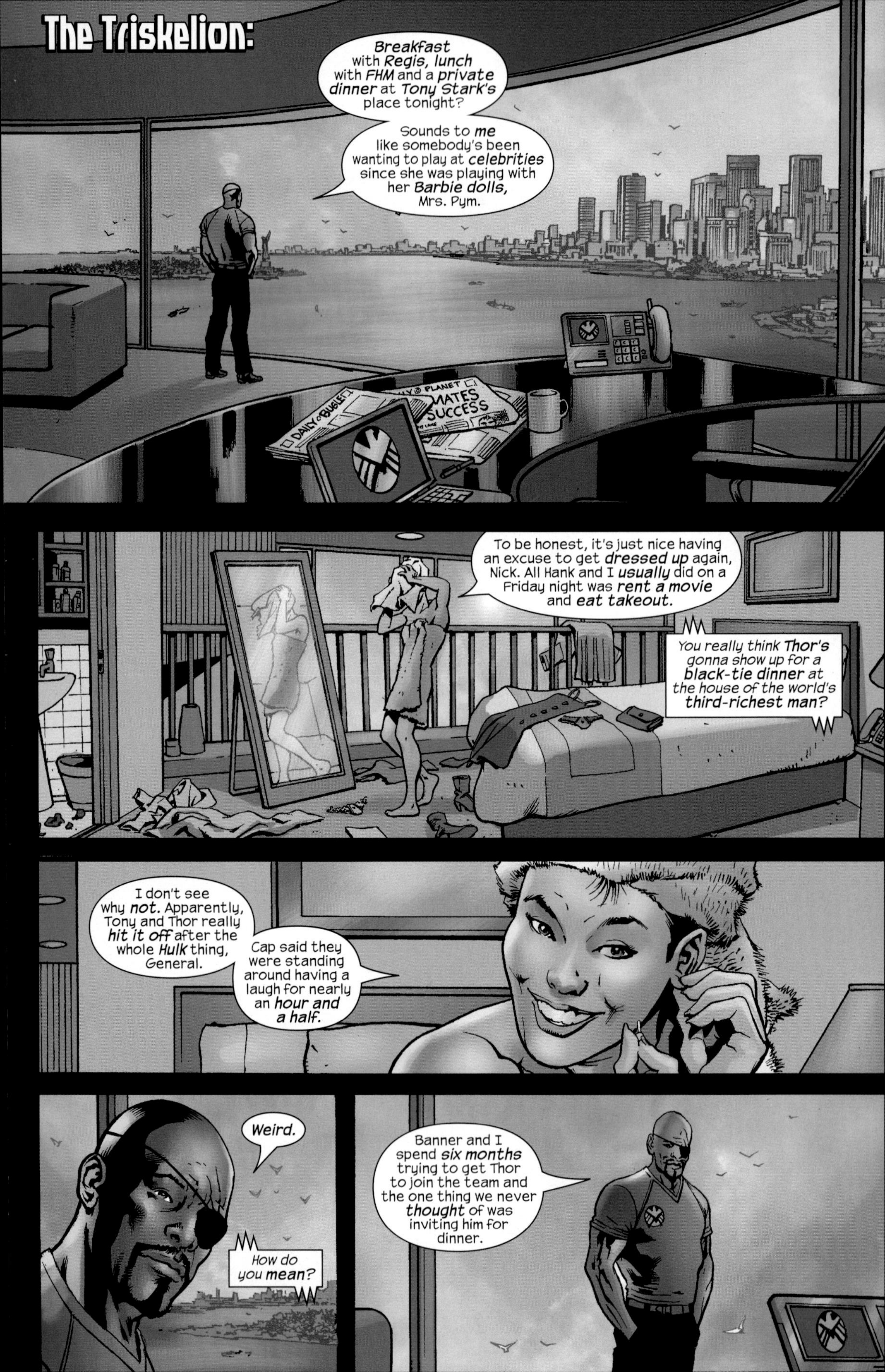
The Triskelion:
Breakfast with Regis, lunch with FHM and a private dinner at Tony Stark's place tonight?
Sounds to me like somebody's been wanting to play at celebrities since she was playing with her Barbie dolls, Mrs. Pym.
To be honest, it's just nice having an excuse to get dressed up again, Nick. All Hank and I usually did on a Friday night was rent a movie and eat takeout.
You really think Thor's gonna show up for a black-tie dinner at the house of the world's third-richest man?
I don't see why not. Apparently, Tony and Thor really hit it off after the whole Hulk thing, General.
Cap said they were standing around having a laugh for nearly an hour and a half.
Weird.
How do you mean?
Banner and I spend six months trying to get Thor to join the team and the one thing we never thought of was inviting him for dinner.

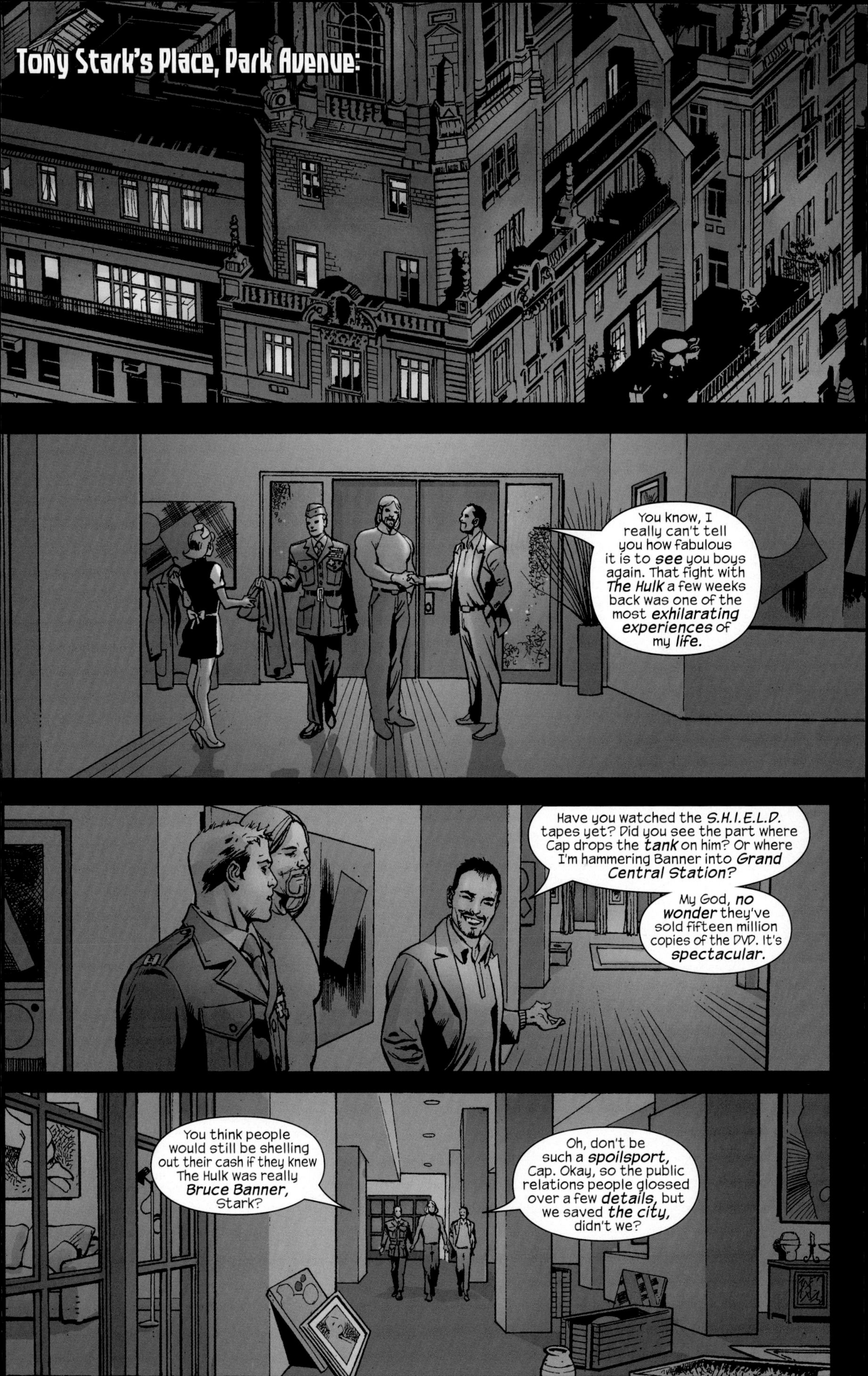

Tony Stark's Place, Park Avenue:
You know, I really can't tell you how fabulous it is to see you boys again. That fight with The Hulk a few weeks back was one of the most exhilarating experiences of my life.
Have you watched the S.H.I.E.L.D. tapes yet? Did you see the part where Cap drops the tank on him? Or where I'm hammering Banner into Grand Central Station?
My God, no wonder they've sold fifteen million copies of the DVD. It's spectacular.
You think people would still be shelling out their cash if they knew The Hulk was really Bruce Banner, Stark?
Oh, don't be such a spoilsport, Cap. Okay, so the public relations people glossed over a few details, but we saved the city, didn't we?

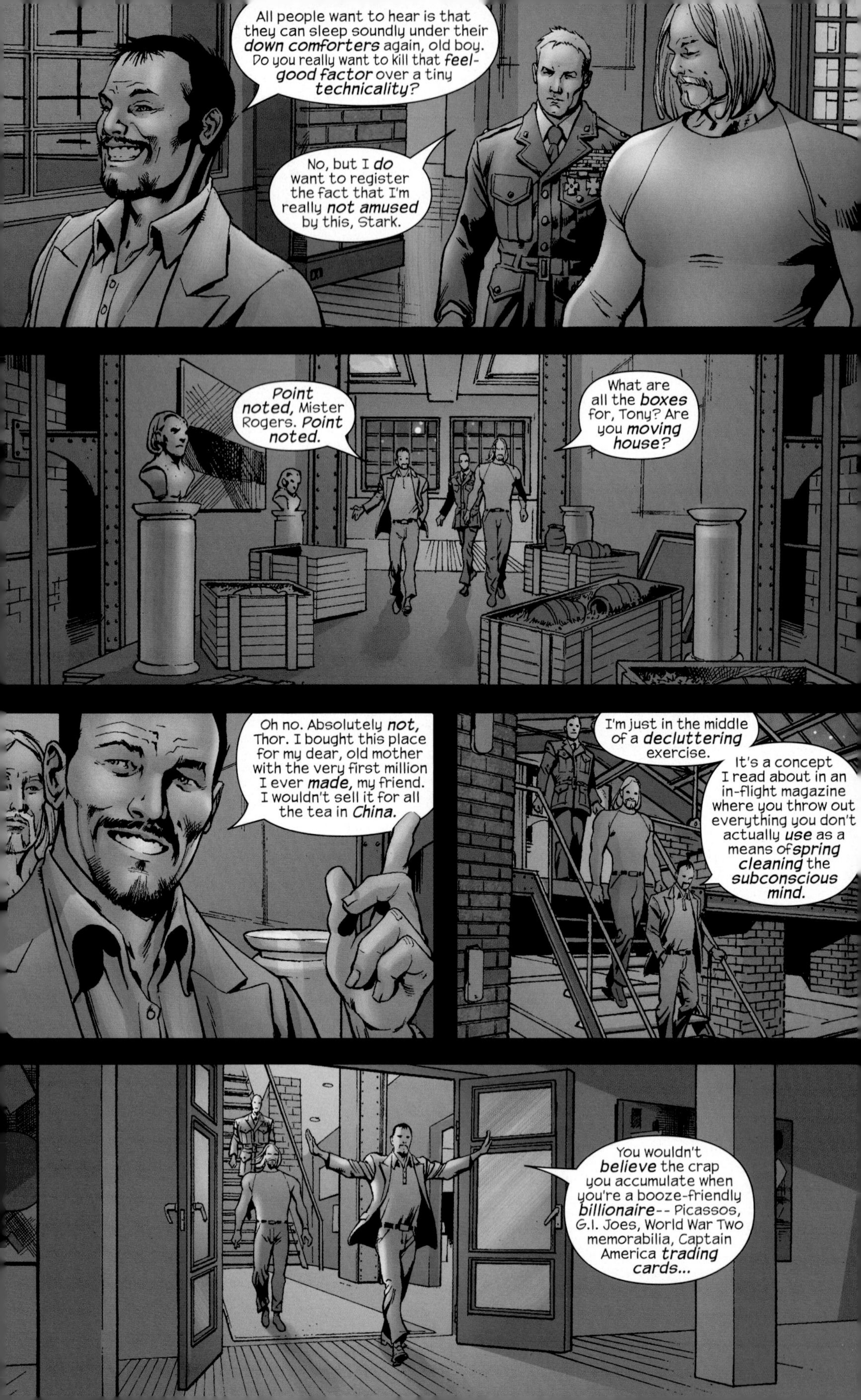
All people want to hear is that they can sleep soundly under their down comforters again, old boy. Do you really want to kill that feel-good factor over a tiny technicality?
No, but I do want to register the fact that I'm really not amused by this, Stark.
Point noted, Mister Rogers. Point noted.
What are all the boxes for, Tony? Are you moving house?
Oh no. Absolutely not, Thor. I bought this place for my dear, old mother with the very first million I ever made, my friend. I wouldn't sell it for all the tea in China.
I'm just in the middle of a decluttering exercise.
It's a concept I read about in an in-flight magazine where you throw out everything you don't actually use as a means of spring cleaning the subconscious mind.
You wouldn't believe the crap you accumulate when you're a booze-friendly billionaire-- Picassos, G.I. Joes, World War Two memorabilia, Captain America trading cards...

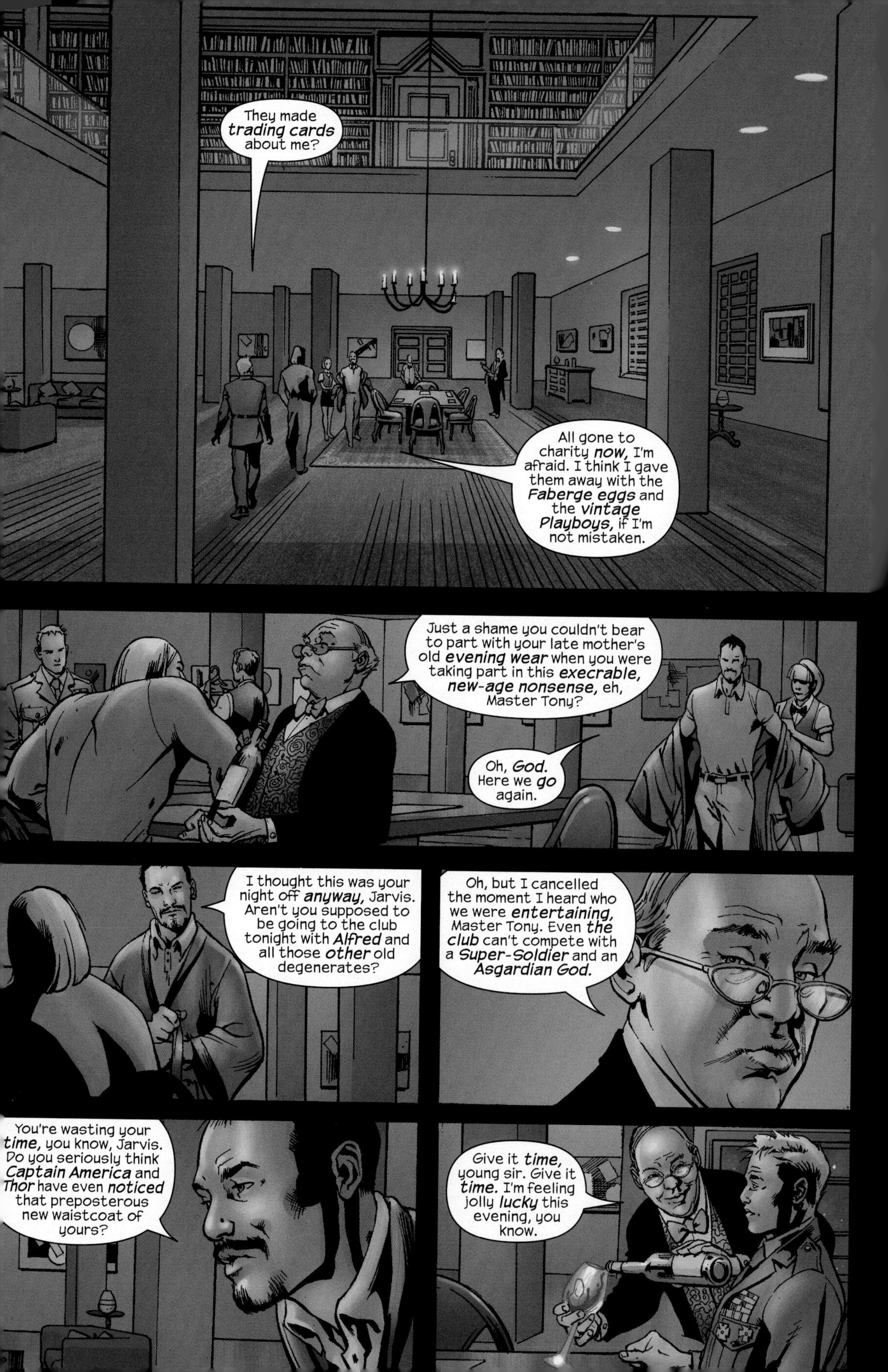
They made trading cards about me?
All gone to charity now, I'm afraid. I think I gave them away with the Faberge eggs and the vintage Playboys, if I'm not mistaken.
Just a shame you couldn't bear to part with your late mother's old evening wear when you were taking part in this execrable, new-age nonsense, eh, Master Tony?
Oh, God. Here we go again.
I thought this was your night off anyway, Jarvis. Aren't you supposed to be going to the club tonight with Alfred and all those other old degenerates?
Oh, but I cancelled the moment I heard who we were entertaining, Master Tony. Even the club can't compete with a Super-Soldier and an Asgardian God.
You're wasting your time, you know, Jarvis. Do you seriously think Captain America and Thor have even noticed that preposterous new waistcoat of yours?
Give it time, young sir. Give it time. I'm feeling jolly lucky this evening, you know.

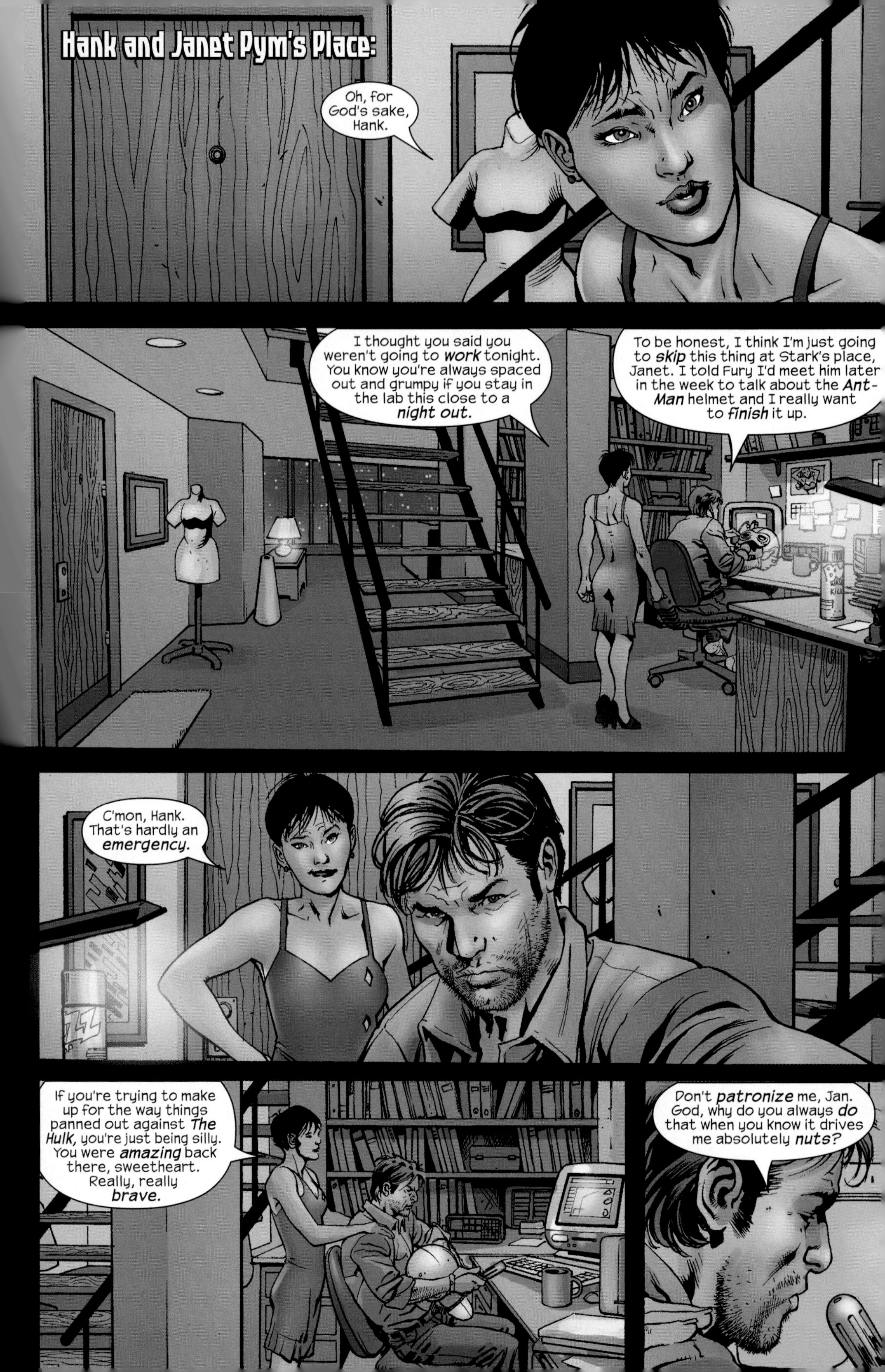
Hank and Janet Pym's Place:
Oh, for God's sake, Hank.
I thought you said you weren't going to work tonight. You know you're always spaced out and grumpy if you stay in the lab this close to a night out.
To be honest, I think I'm just going to skip this thing at Stark's place, Janet. I told Fury I'd meet him later in the week to talk about the Ant-Man helmet and I really want to finish it up.
C'mon, Hank. That's hardly an emergency.
If you're trying to make up for the way things panned out against The Hulk, you're just being silly. You were amazing back there, sweetheart. Really, really brave.
Don't patronize me, Jan. God, why do you always do that when you know it drives me absolutely nuts?

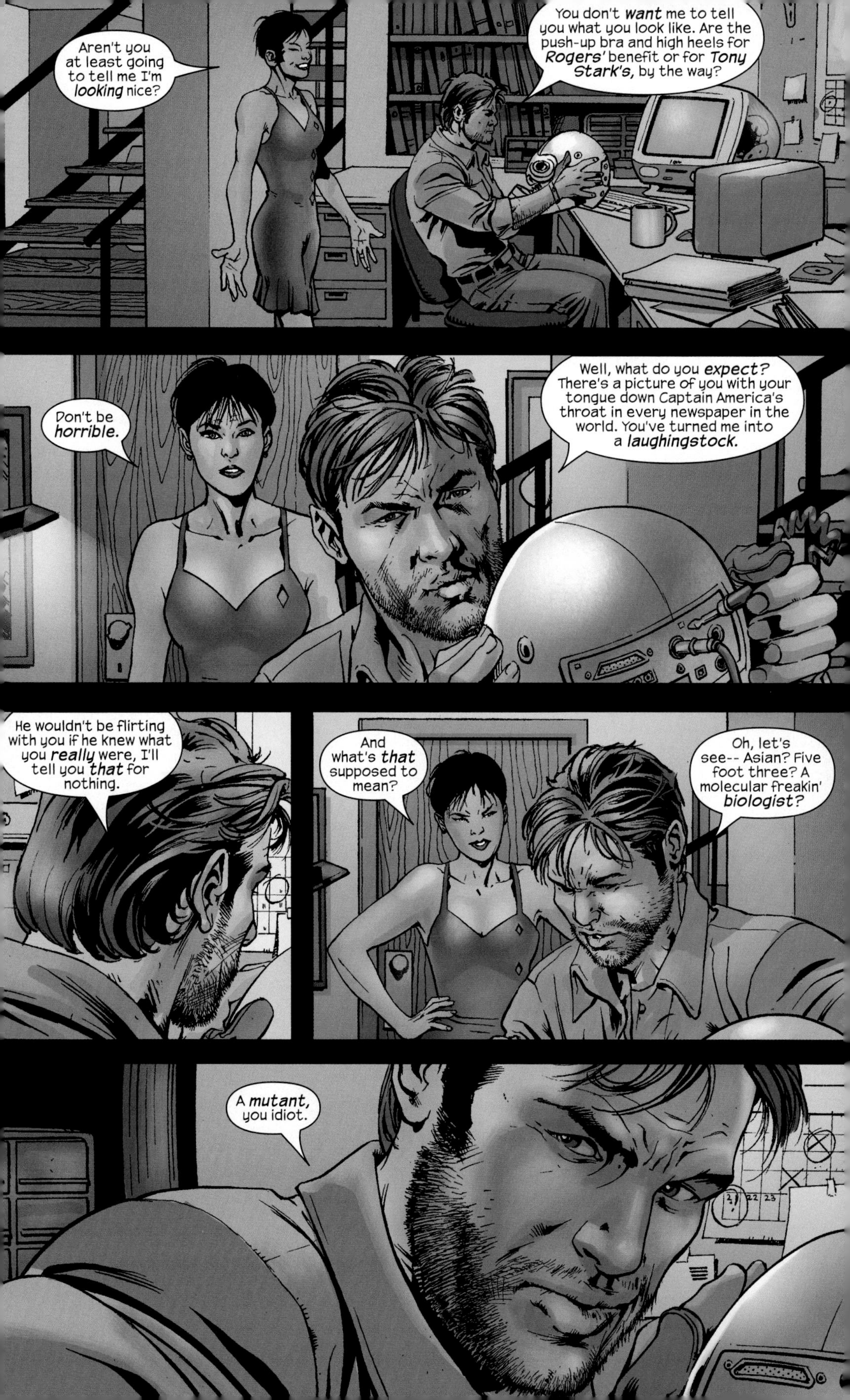
Aren't you at least going to tell me I'm *looking* nice?
You don't ***want*** me to tell you what you look like. Are the push-up bra and high heels for ***Rogers'*** benefit or for ***Tony Stark's,*** by the way?
Don't be ***horrible.***
Well, what do you ***expect?*** There's a picture of you with your tongue down Captain America's throat in every newspaper in the world. You've turned me into a ***laughingstock.***
He wouldn't be flirting with you if he knew what you ***really*** were, I'll tell you ***that*** for nothing.
And what's ***that*** supposed to mean?
Oh, let's see-- Asian? Five foot three? A molecular freakin' ***biologist?***
A ***mutant,*** you idiot.

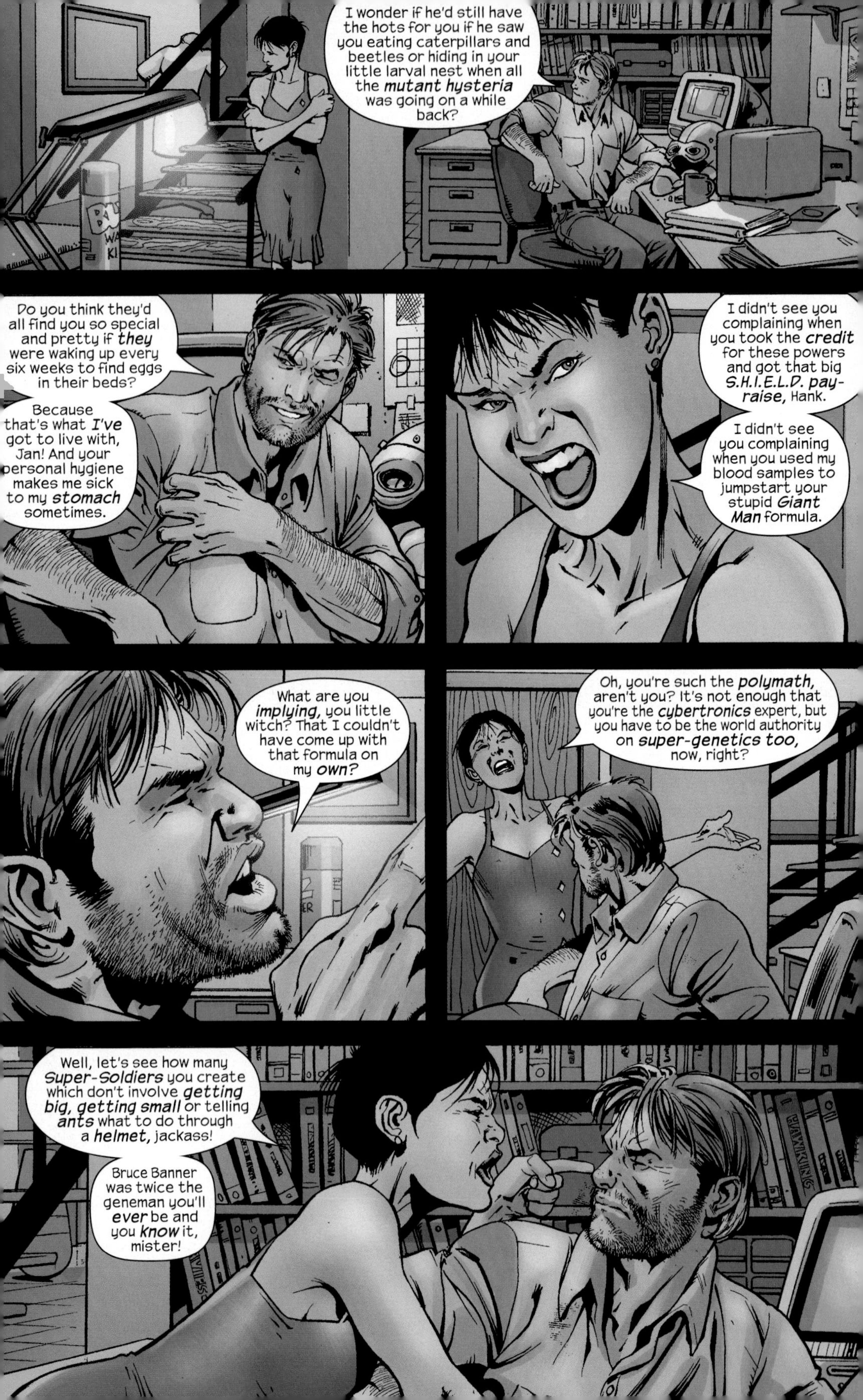
I wonder if he'd still have the hots for you if he saw you eating caterpillars and beetles or hiding in your little larval nest when all the *mutant hysteria* was going on a while back?
Do you think they'd all find you so special and pretty if *they* were waking up every six weeks to find eggs in their beds?
Because that's what *I've* got to live with, Jan! And your personal hygiene makes me sick to my *stomach* sometimes.
I didn't see you complaining when you took the *credit* for these powers and got that big *S.H.I.E.L.D. pay-raise,* Hank.
I didn't see you complaining when you used my blood samples to jumpstart your stupid *Giant Man* formula.
What are you *implying,* you little witch? That I couldn't have come up with that formula on my *own?*
Oh, you're such the *polymath,* aren't you? It's not enough that you're the *cybertronics* expert, but you have to be the world authority on *super-genetics too,* now, right?
Well, let's see how many *Super-Soldiers* you create which don't involve *getting big, getting small* or telling *ants* what to do through a *helmet,* jackass!
Bruce Banner was twice the geneman you'll *ever* be and you *know* it, mister!

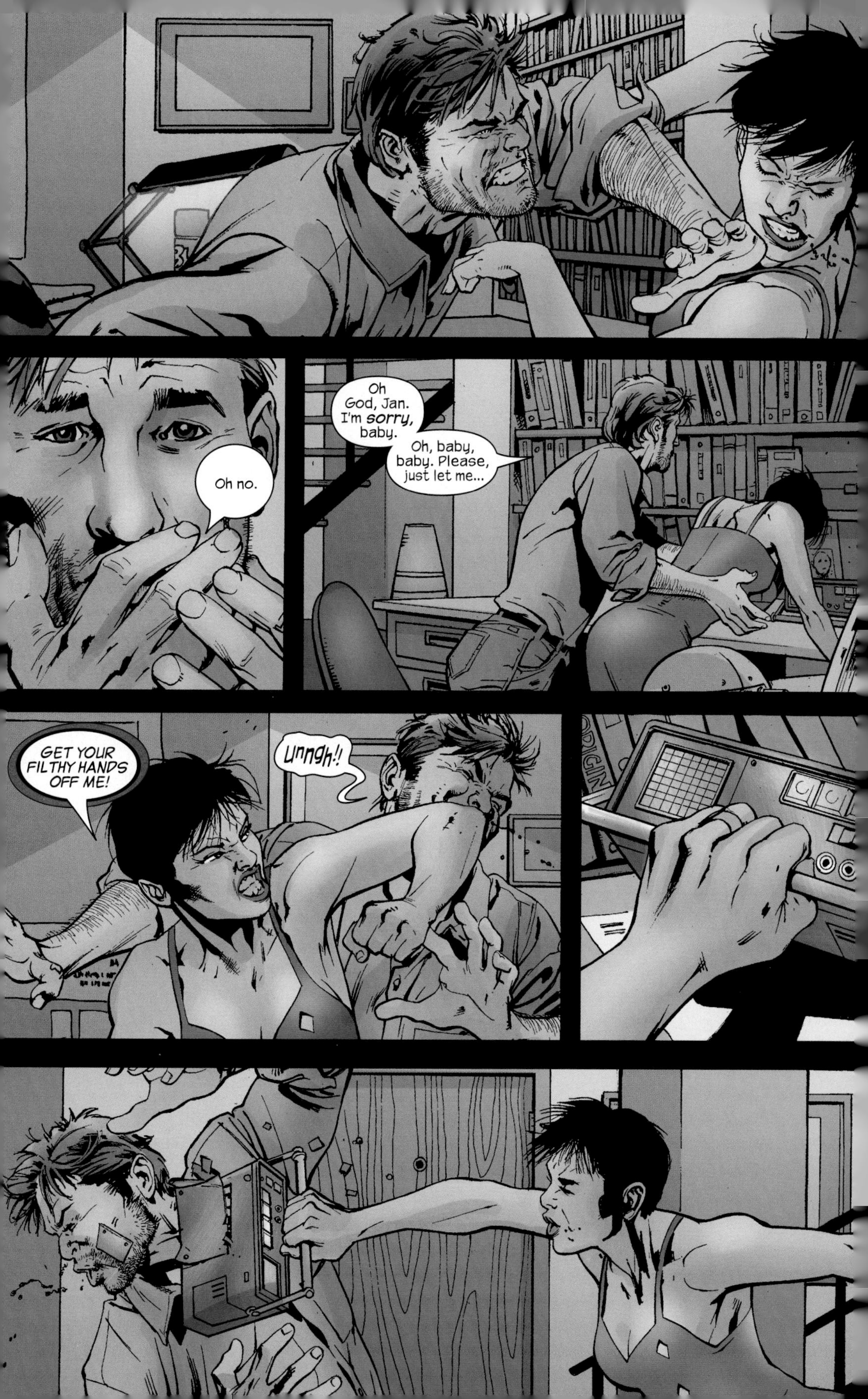
Oh no.
Oh God, Jan. I'm *sorry,* baby.
Oh, baby, baby. Please, just let me...
GET YOUR FILTHY HANDS OFF ME!
Unngh!!

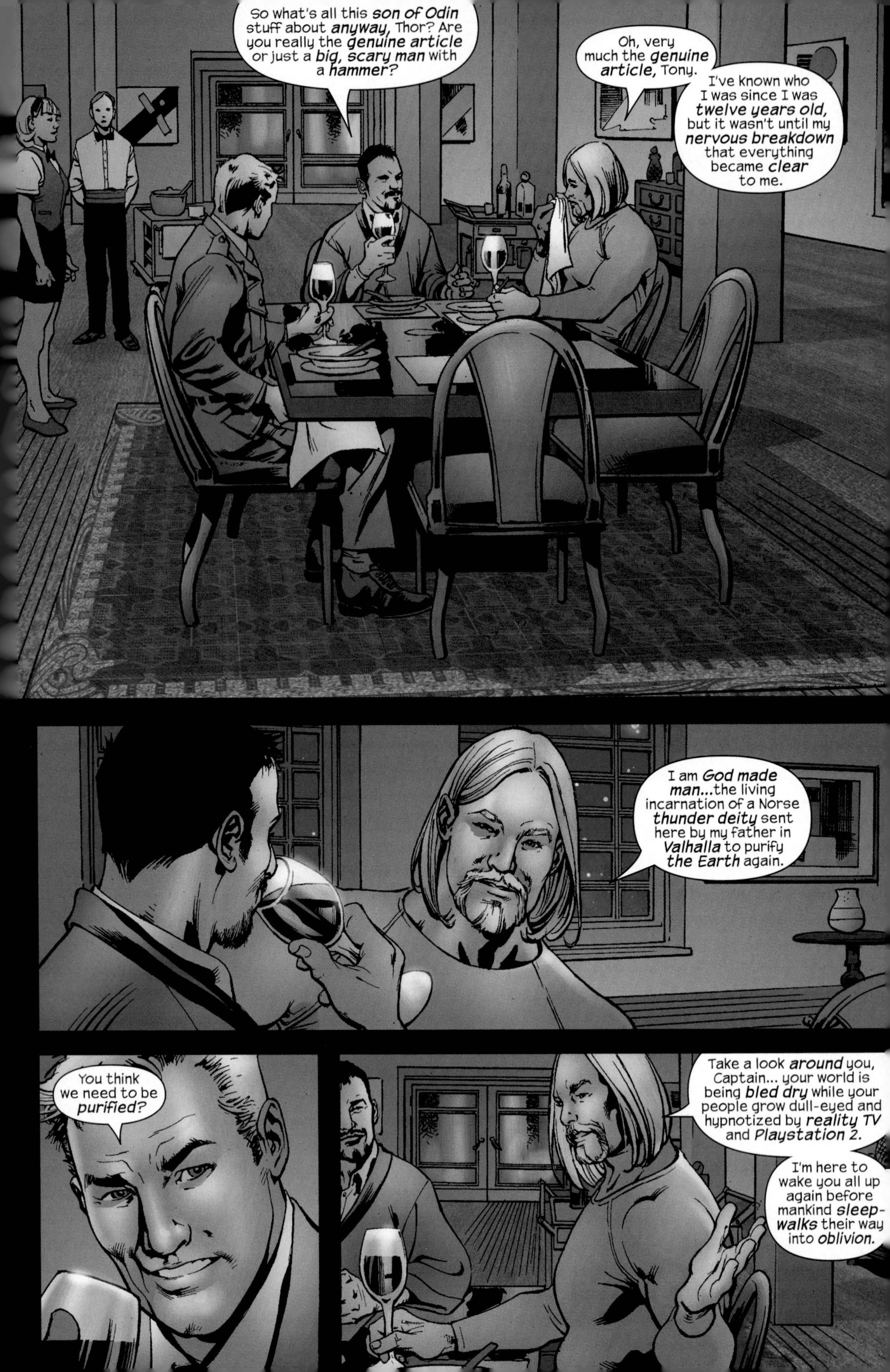
So what's all this son of Odin stuff about anyway, Thor? Are you really the genuine article or just a big, scary man with a hammer?
Oh, very much the genuine article, Tony.
I've known who I was since I was twelve years old, but it wasn't until my nervous breakdown that everything became clear to me.
I am God made man...the living incarnation of a Norse thunder deity sent here by my father in Valhalla to purify the Earth again.
You think we need to be purified?
Take a look around you, Captain... your world is being bled dry while your people grow dull-eyed and hypnotized by reality TV and Playstation 2.
I'm here to wake you all up again before mankind sleep-walks their way into oblivion.

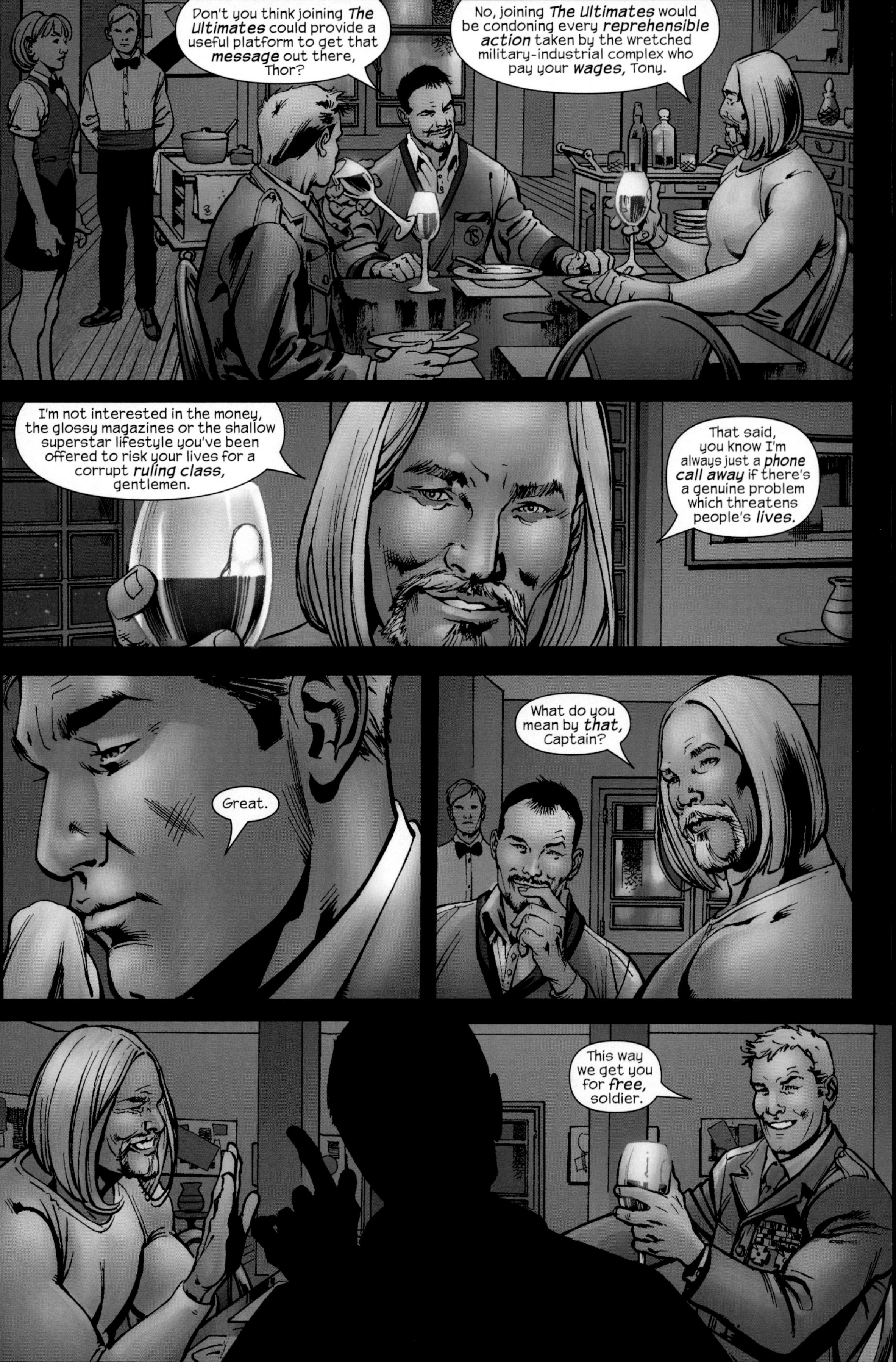
Don't you think joining The Ultimates could provide a useful platform to get that message out there, Thor?
No, joining The Ultimates would be condoning every reprehensible action taken by the wretched military-industrial complex who pay your wages, Tony.
I'm not interested in the money, the glossy magazines or the shallow superstar lifestyle you've been offered to risk your lives for a corrupt ruling class, gentlemen.
That said, you know I'm always just a phone call away if there's a genuine problem which threatens people's lives.
Great.
What do you mean by that, Captain?
This way we get you for free, soldier.

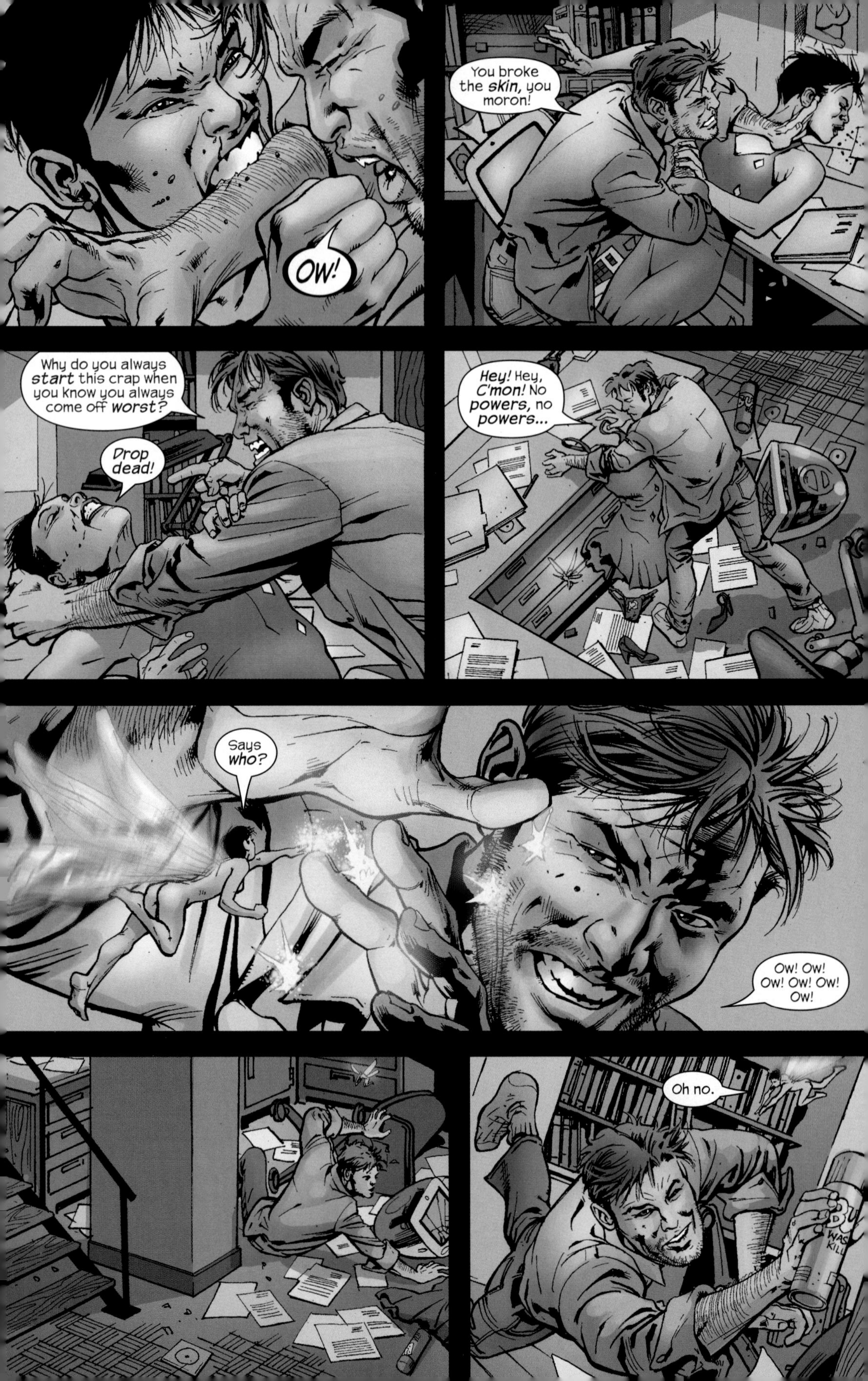
OW!
You broke the skin, you moron!
Why do you always start this crap when you know you always come off worst?
Drop dead!
Hey! Hey, C'mon! No powers, no powers...
Says who?
Ow! Ow! Ow! Ow! Ow! Ow!
Oh no.

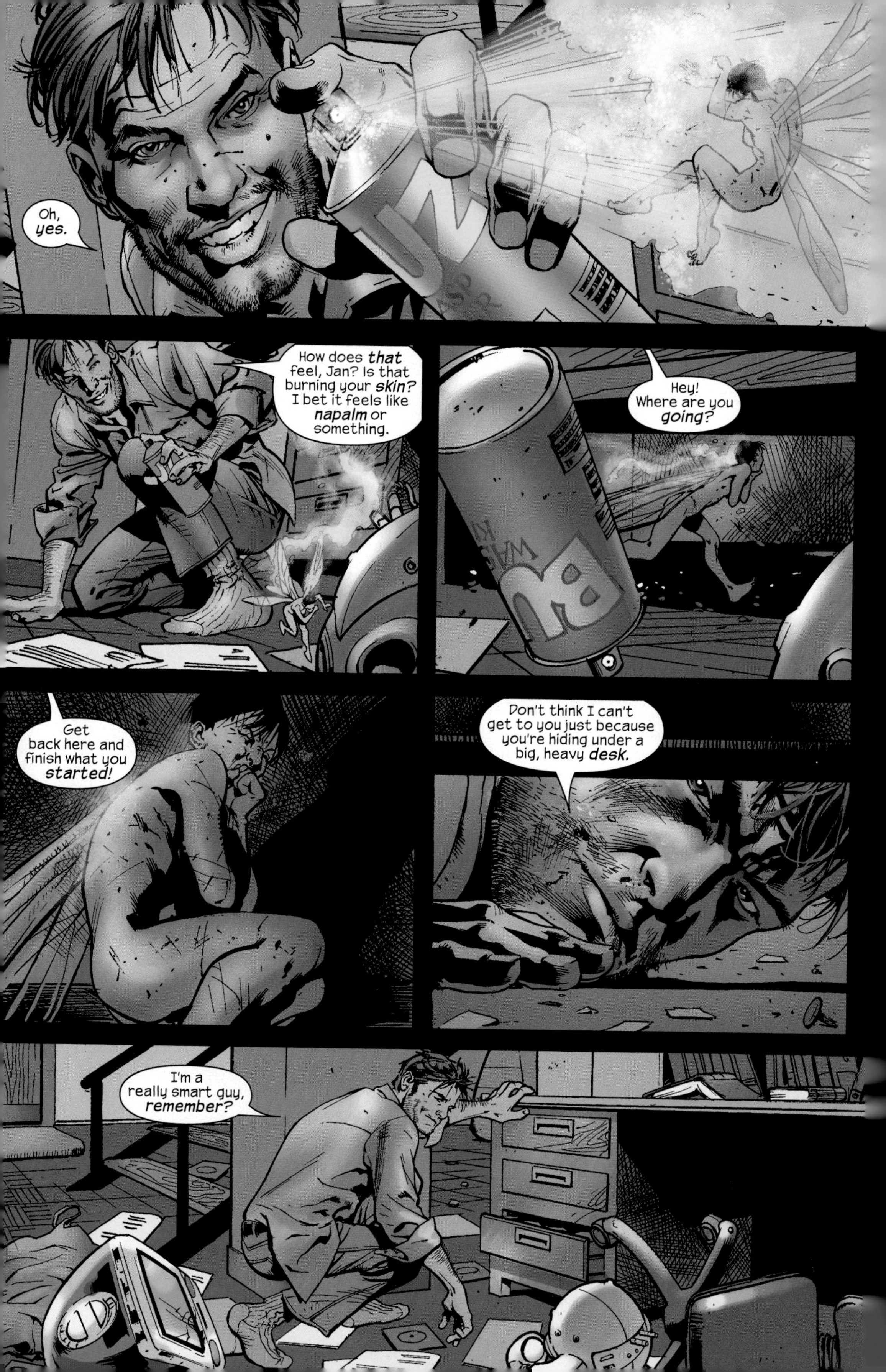

Oh, *yes.*
How does *that* feel, Jan? Is that burning your *skin?* I bet it feels like *napalm* or something.
Hey! Where are you *going?*
Get back here and finish what you *started!*
Don't think I can't get to you just because you're hiding under a big, heavy *desk.*
I'm a really smart guy, *remember?*

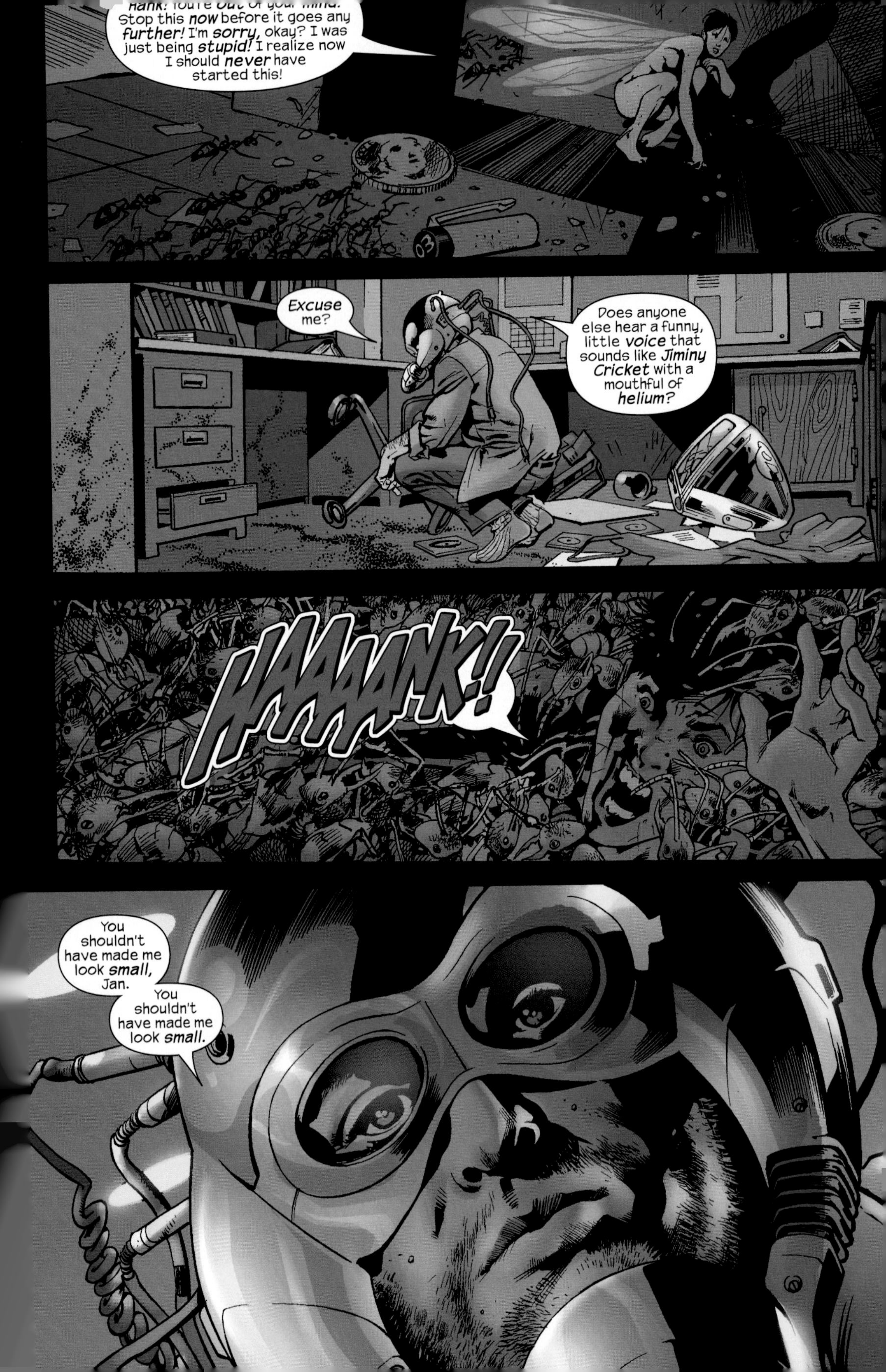
Stop this *now* before it goes any *further!* I'm *sorry,* okay? I was just being *stupid!* I realize now I should *never* have started this!
Excuse me?
Does anyone else hear a funny, little *voice* that sounds like *Jiminy Cricket* with a mouthful of *helium?*
HAAAANK!!
You shouldn't have made me look *small,* Jan.
You shouldn't have made me look *small.*

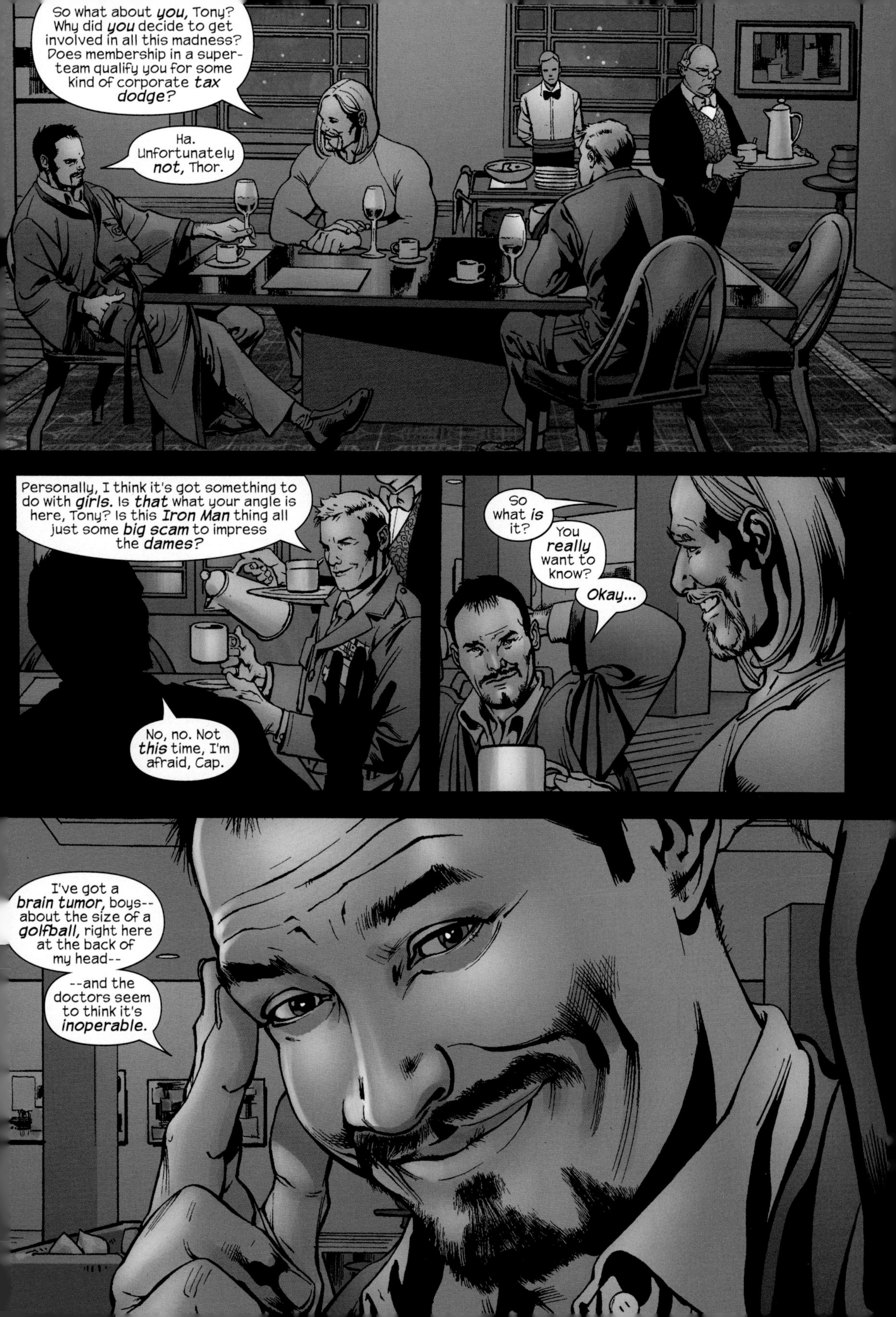
So what about you, Tony? Why did you decide to get involved in all this madness? Does membership in a super-team qualify you for some kind of corporate tax dodge?
Ha. Unfortunately not, Thor.
Personally, I think it's got something to do with girls. Is that what your angle is here, Tony? Is this Iron Man thing all just some big scam to impress the dames?
No, no. Not this time, I'm afraid, Cap.
So what is it?
You really want to know?
Okay...
I've got a brain tumor, boys-- about the size of a golfball, right here at the back of my head--
--and the doctors seem to think it's inoperable.

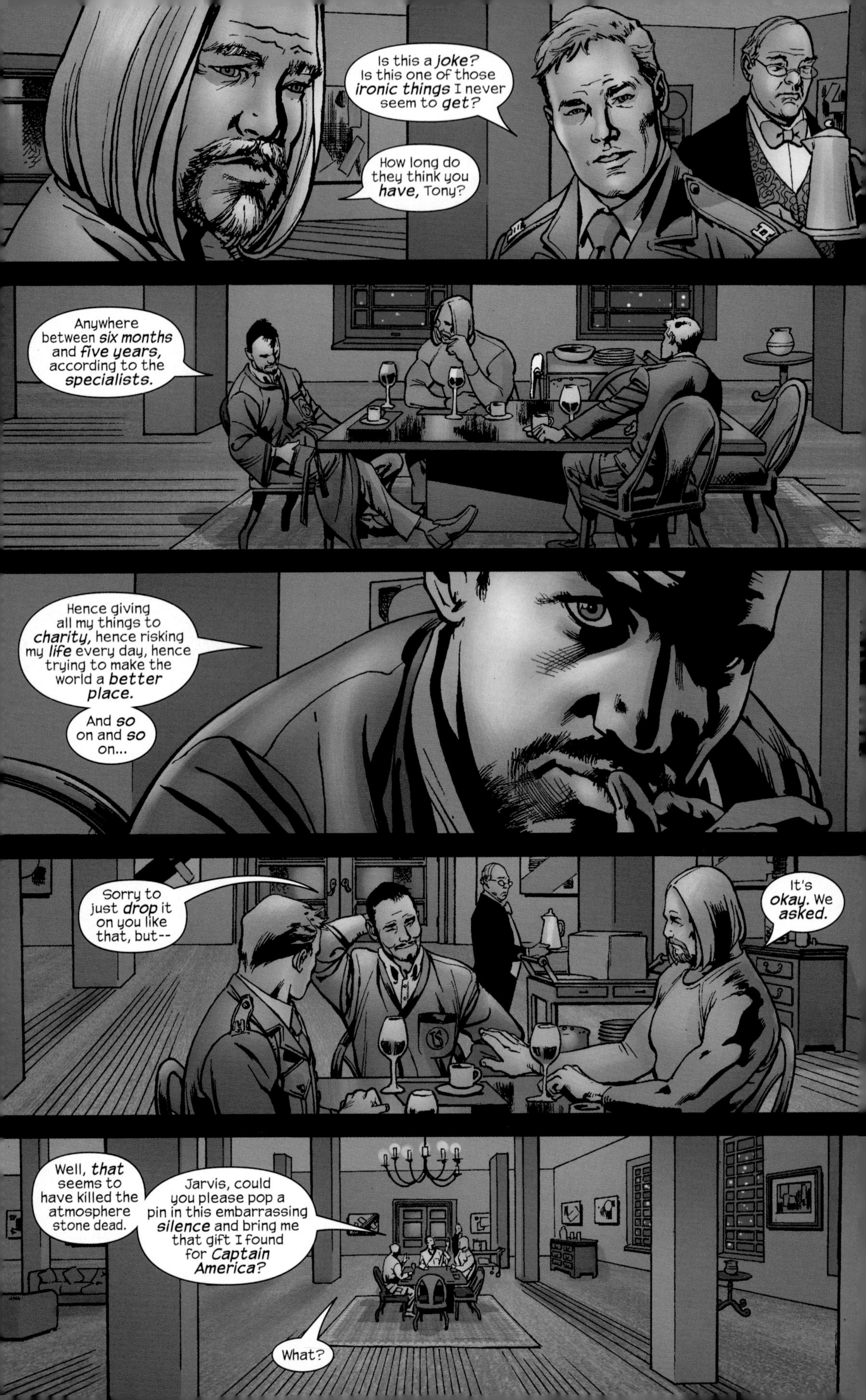
Is this a *joke*? Is this one of those *ironic things* I never seem to *get*?
How long do they think you *have*, Tony?
Anywhere between *six months* and *five years*, according to the *specialists*.
Hence giving all my things to *charity*, hence risking my *life* every day, hence trying to make the world a *better place*.
And *so* on and *so* on...
Sorry to just *drop* it on you like that, but--
It's *okay*. We *asked*.
Well, *that* seems to have killed the atmosphere stone dead.
Jarvis, could you please pop a pin in this embarrassing *silence* and bring me that gift I found for *Captain America*?
What?

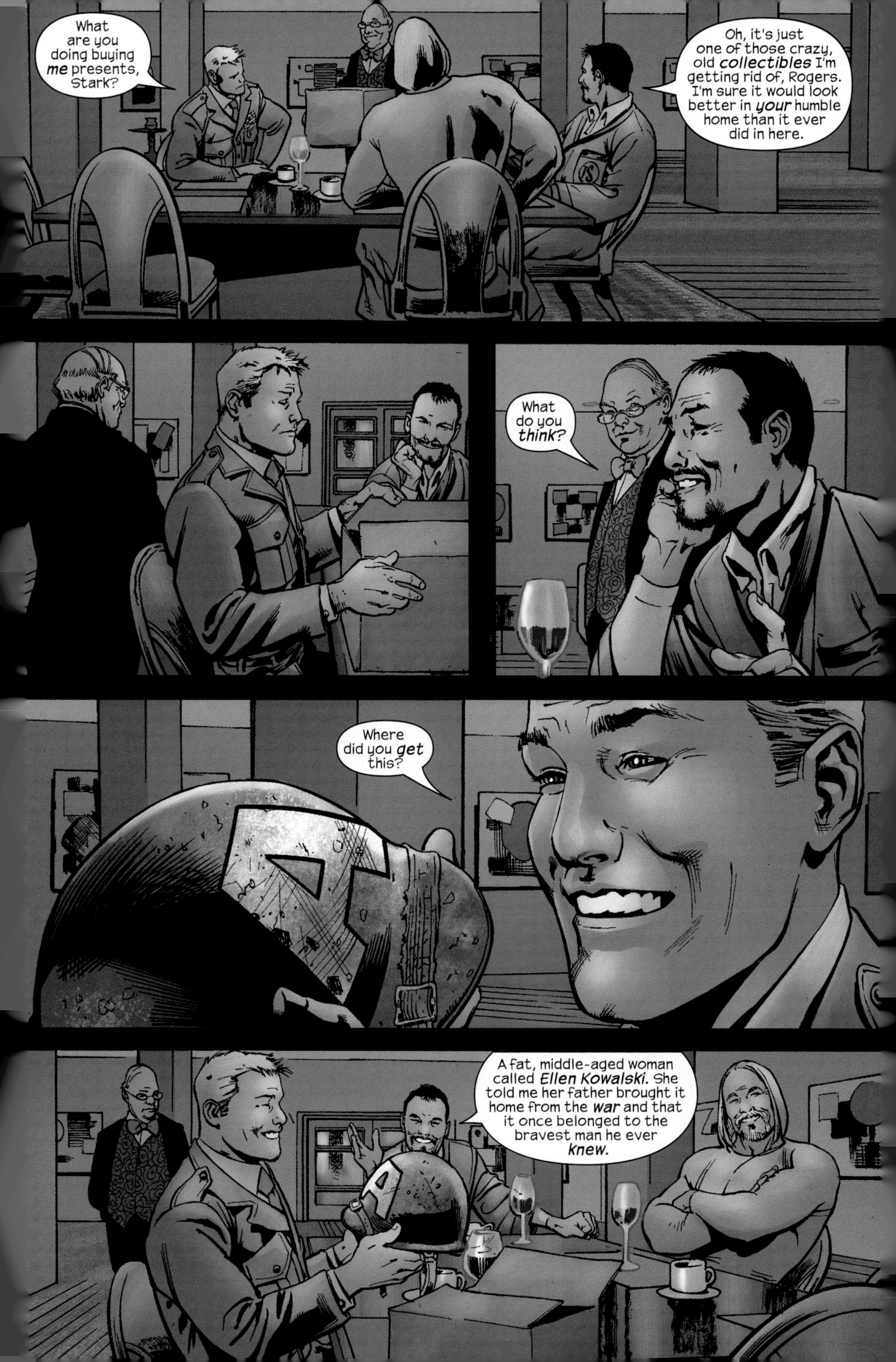

What are you doing buying *me* presents, Stark?
Oh, it's just one of those crazy, old *collectibles* I'm getting rid of, Rogers. I'm sure it would look better in *your* humble home than it ever did in here.
What do you *think?*
Where did you *get* this?
A fat, middle-aged woman called *Ellen Kowalski.* She told me her father brought it home from the *war* and that it once belonged to the bravest man he ever *knew.*

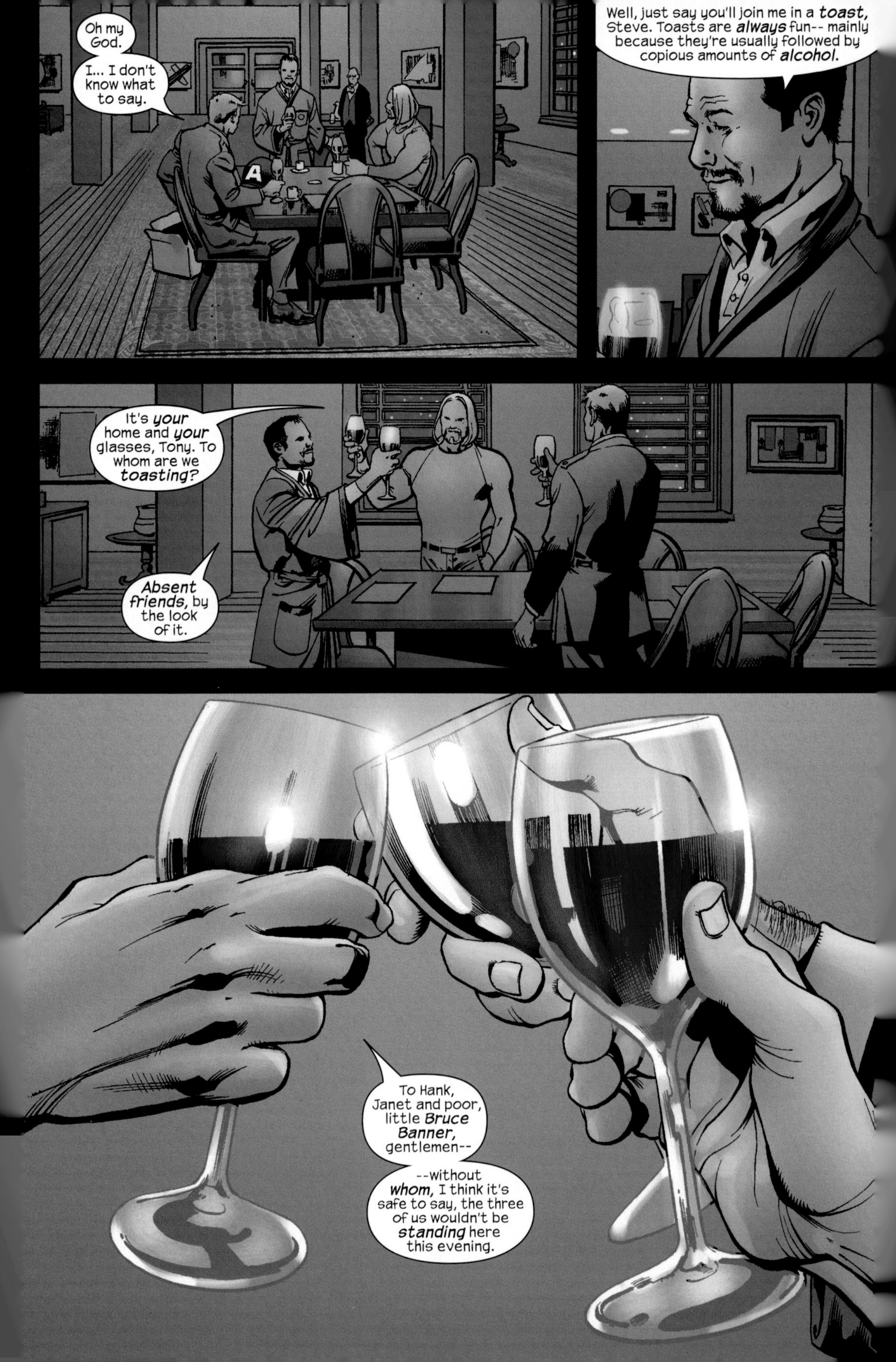
Oh my God.
I... I don't know what to say.
Well, just say you'll join me in a *toast*, Steve. Toasts are *always* fun-- mainly because they're usually followed by copious amounts of *alcohol.*
It's *your* home and *your* glasses, Tony. To whom are we *toasting*?
Absent friends, by the look of it.
To Hank, Janet and poor, little *Bruce Banner*, gentlemen--
--without *whom*, I think it's safe to say, the three of us wouldn't be *standing* here this evening.

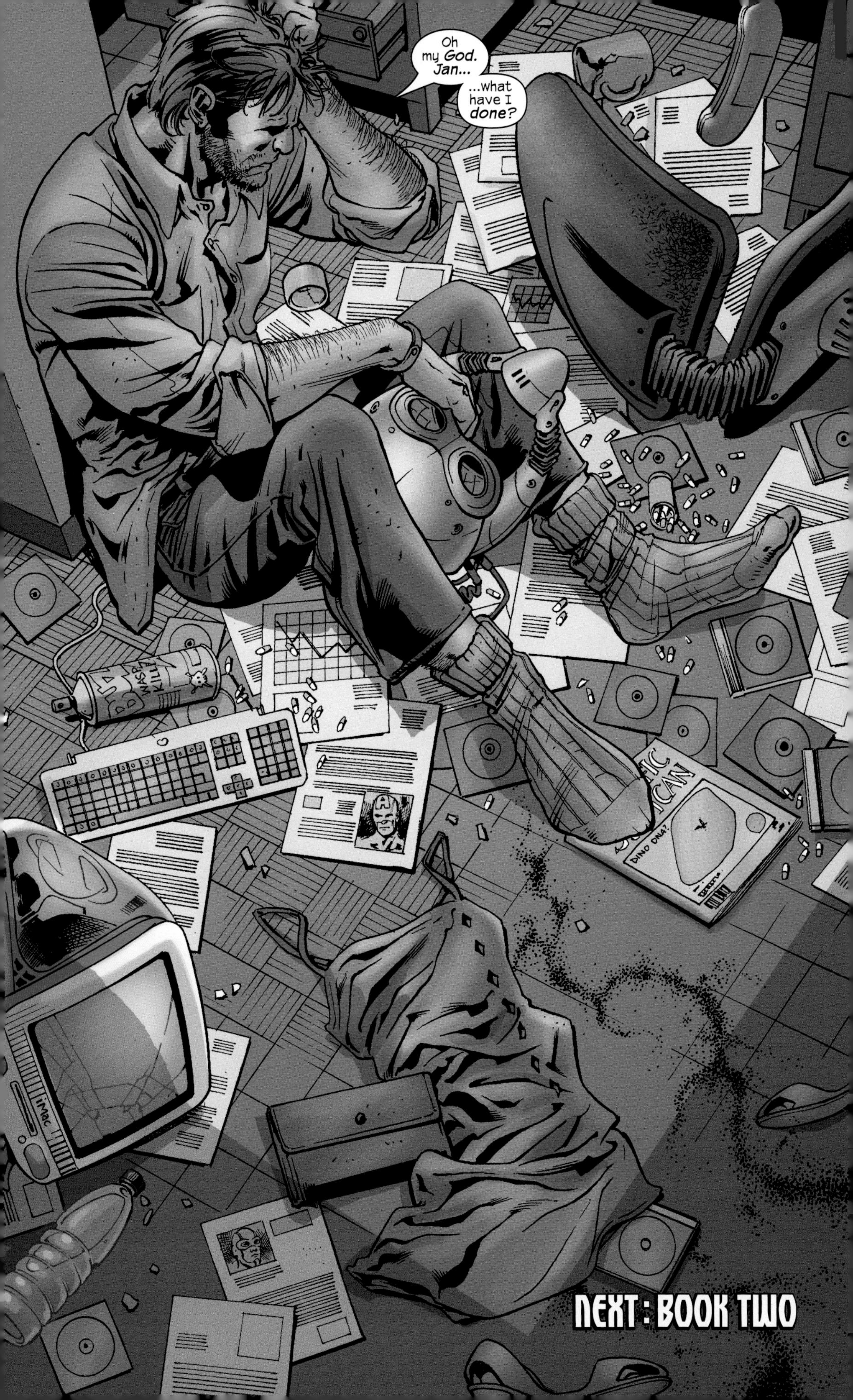
Oh my God. Jan...
...what have I done?
NEXT : BOOK TWO

ISSUE 1

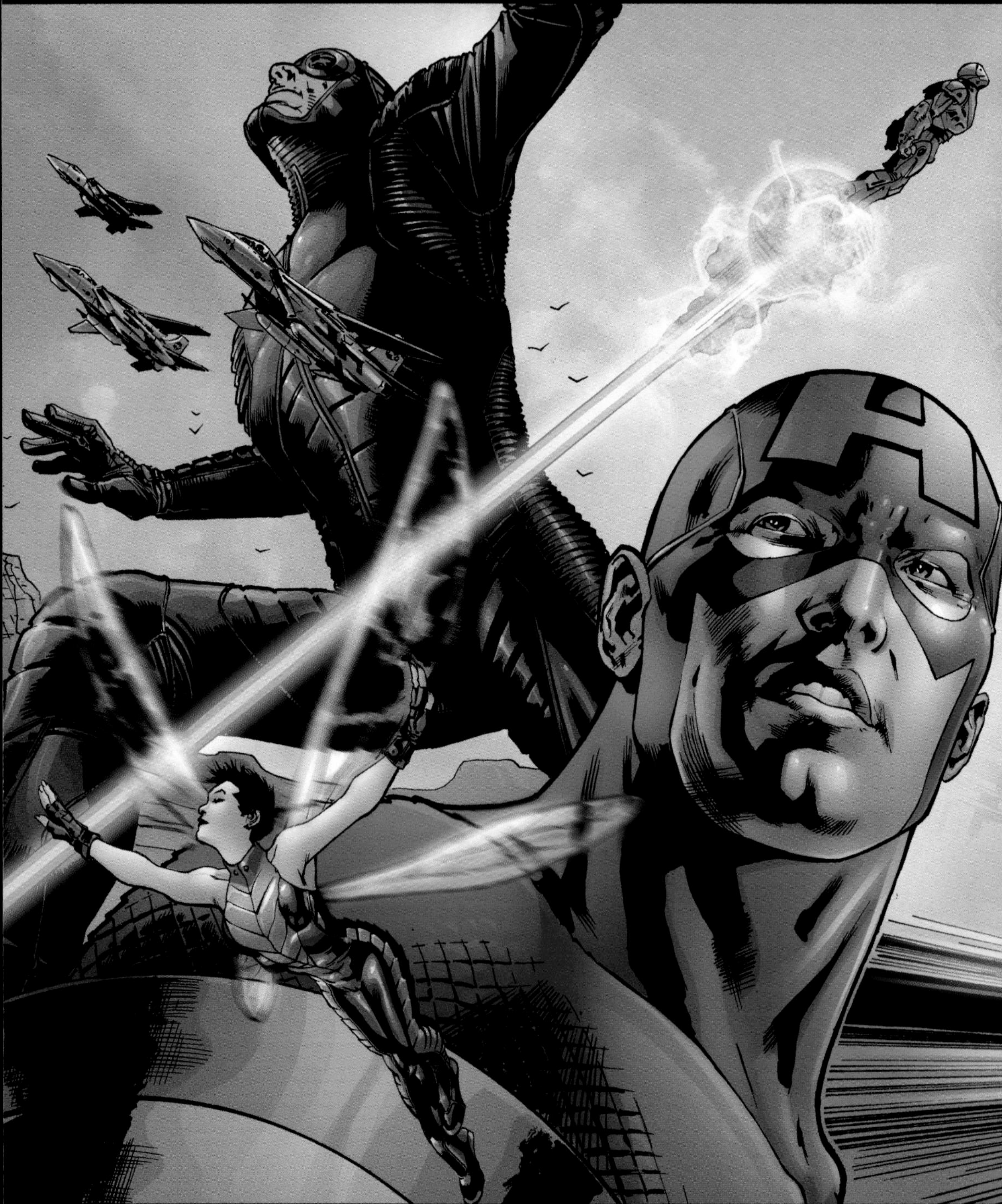

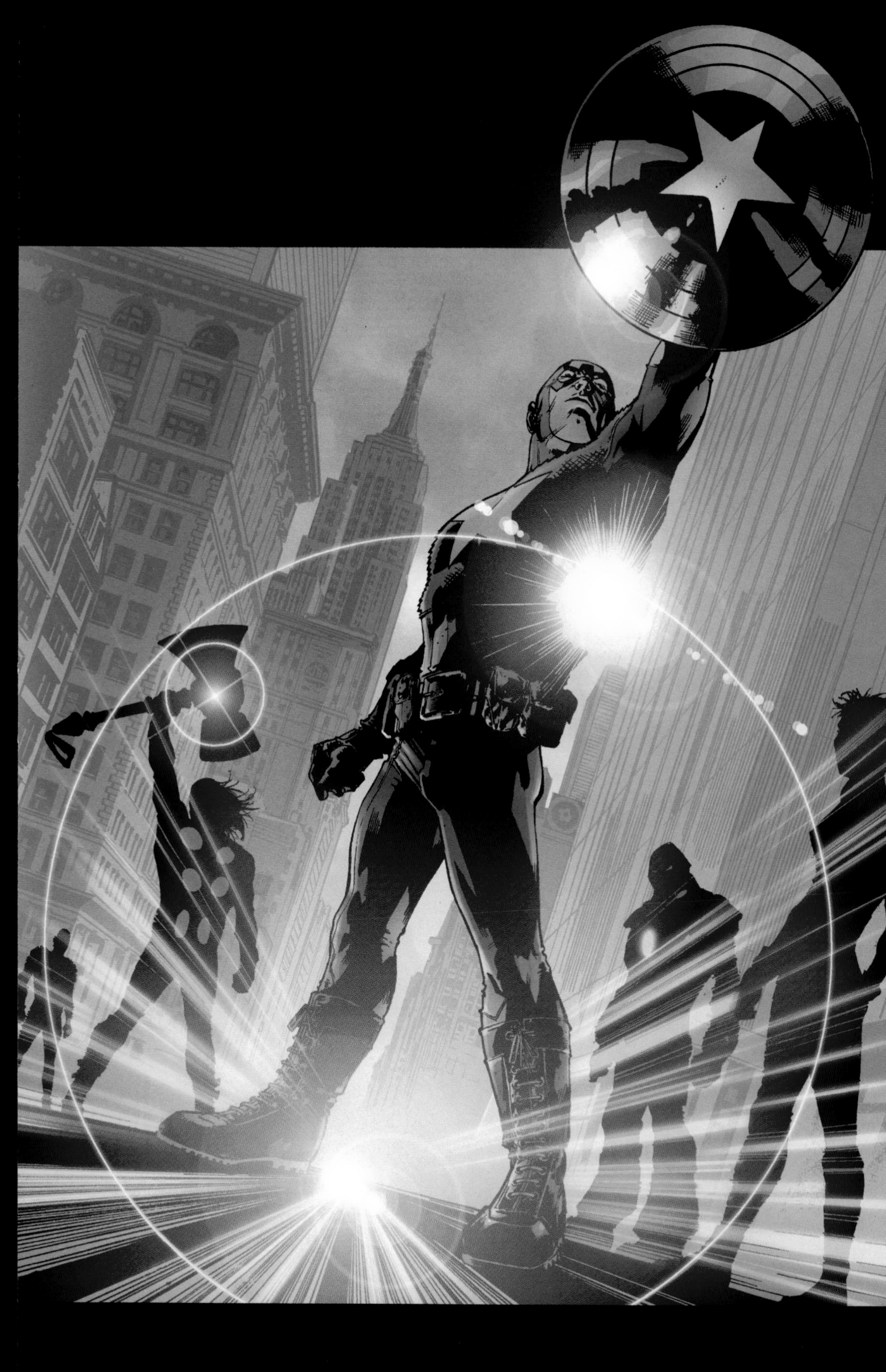

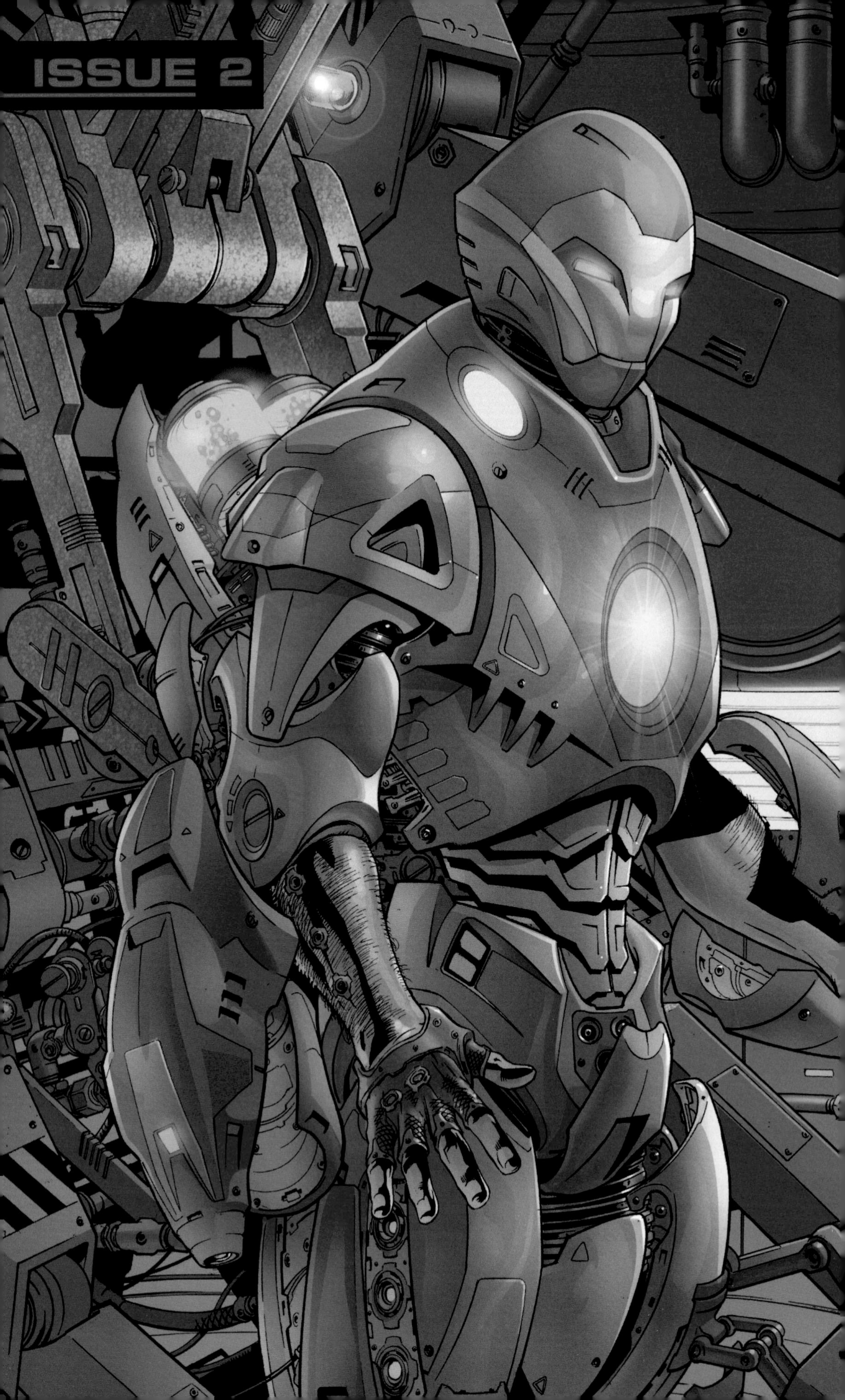
ISSUE 2

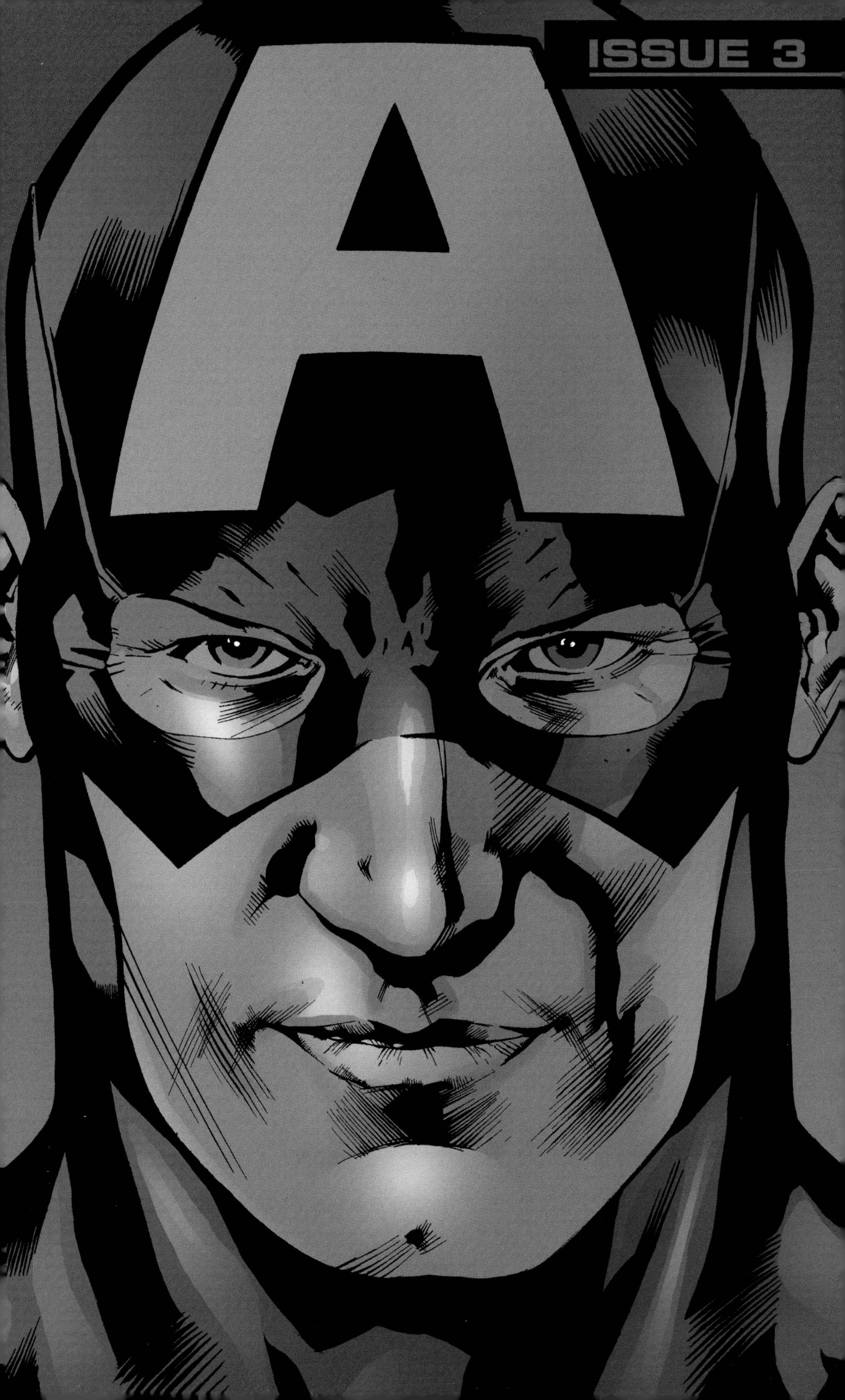
ISSUE 3

ISSUE 4

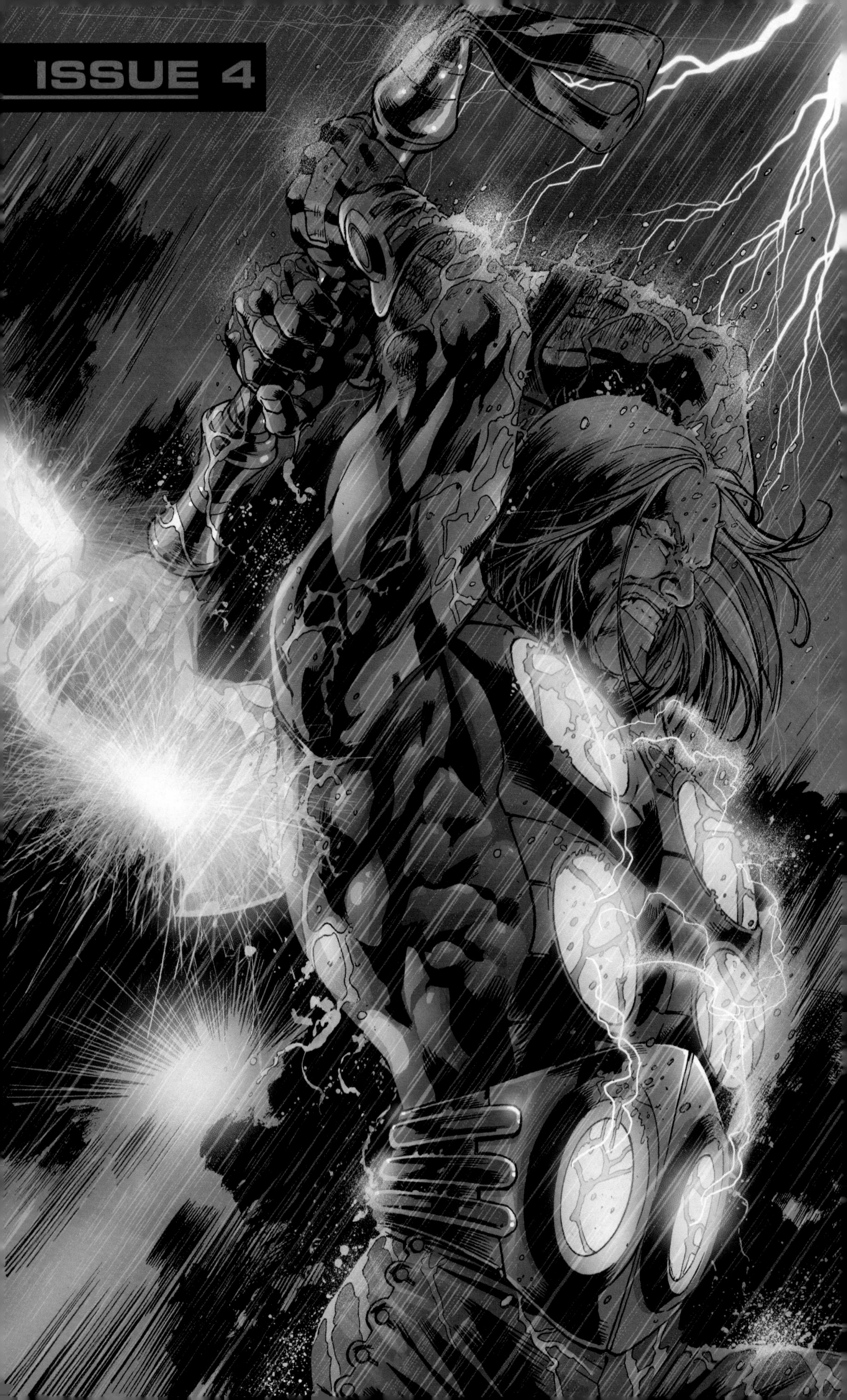

ISSUE 5

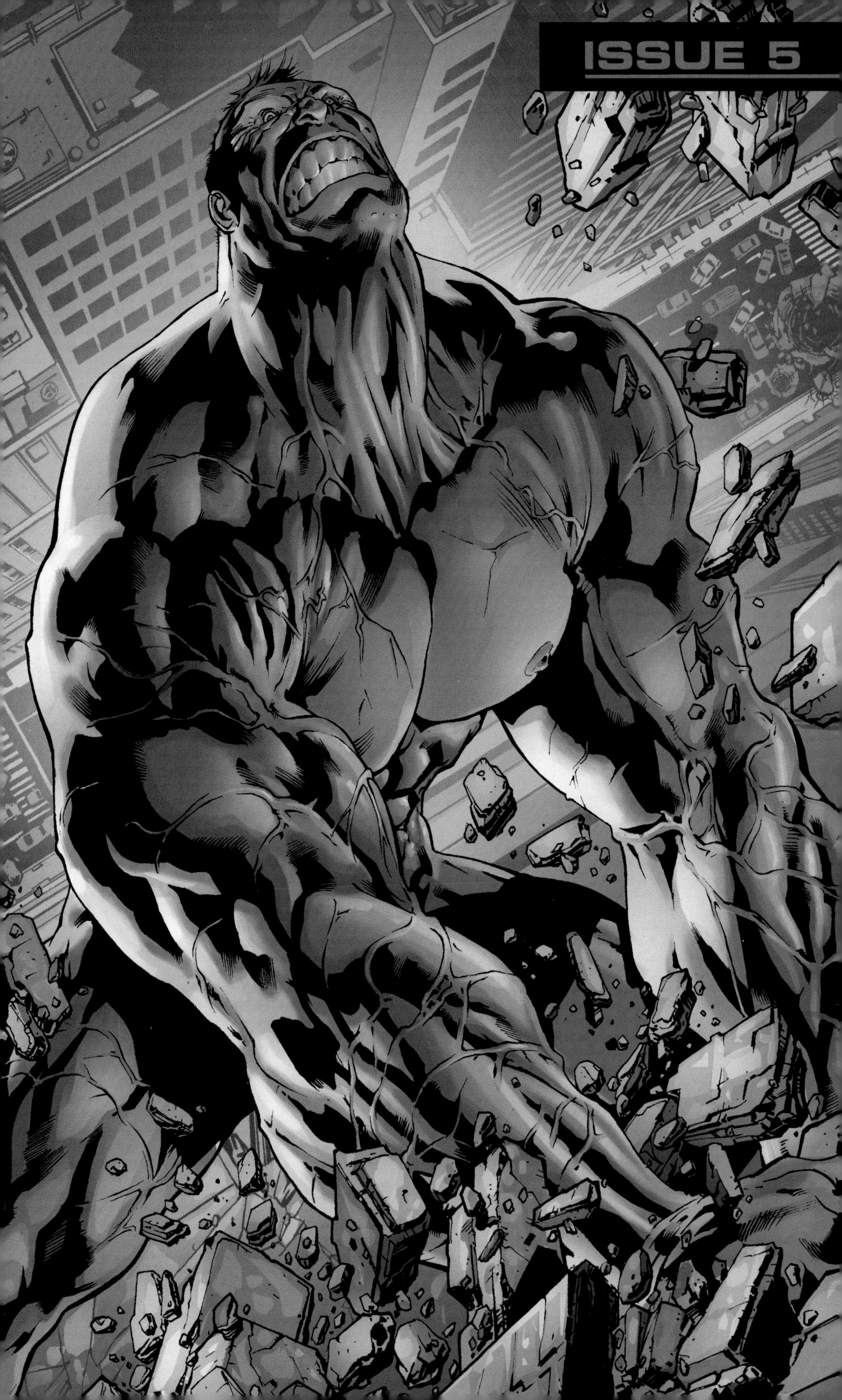

ISSUE 6

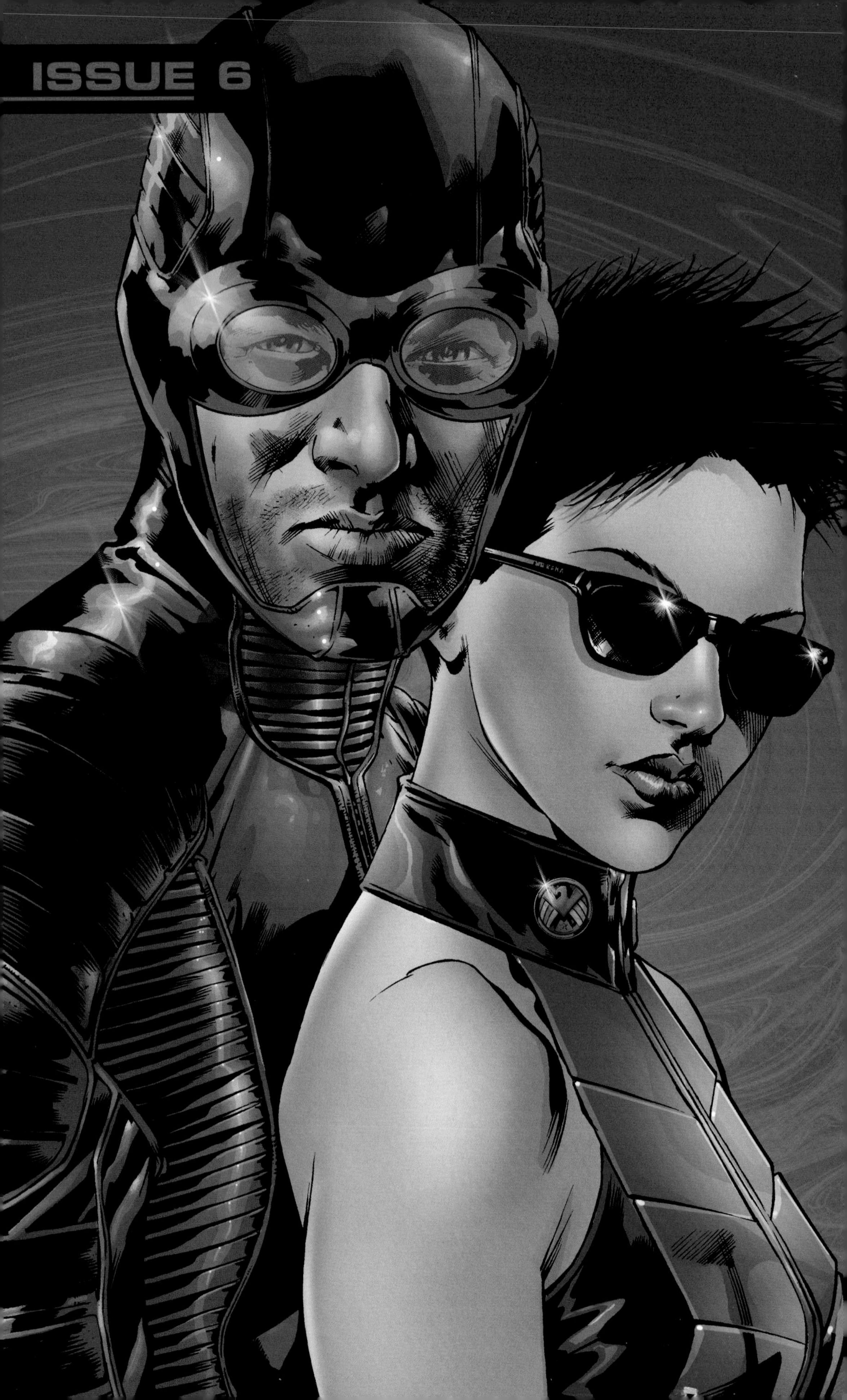

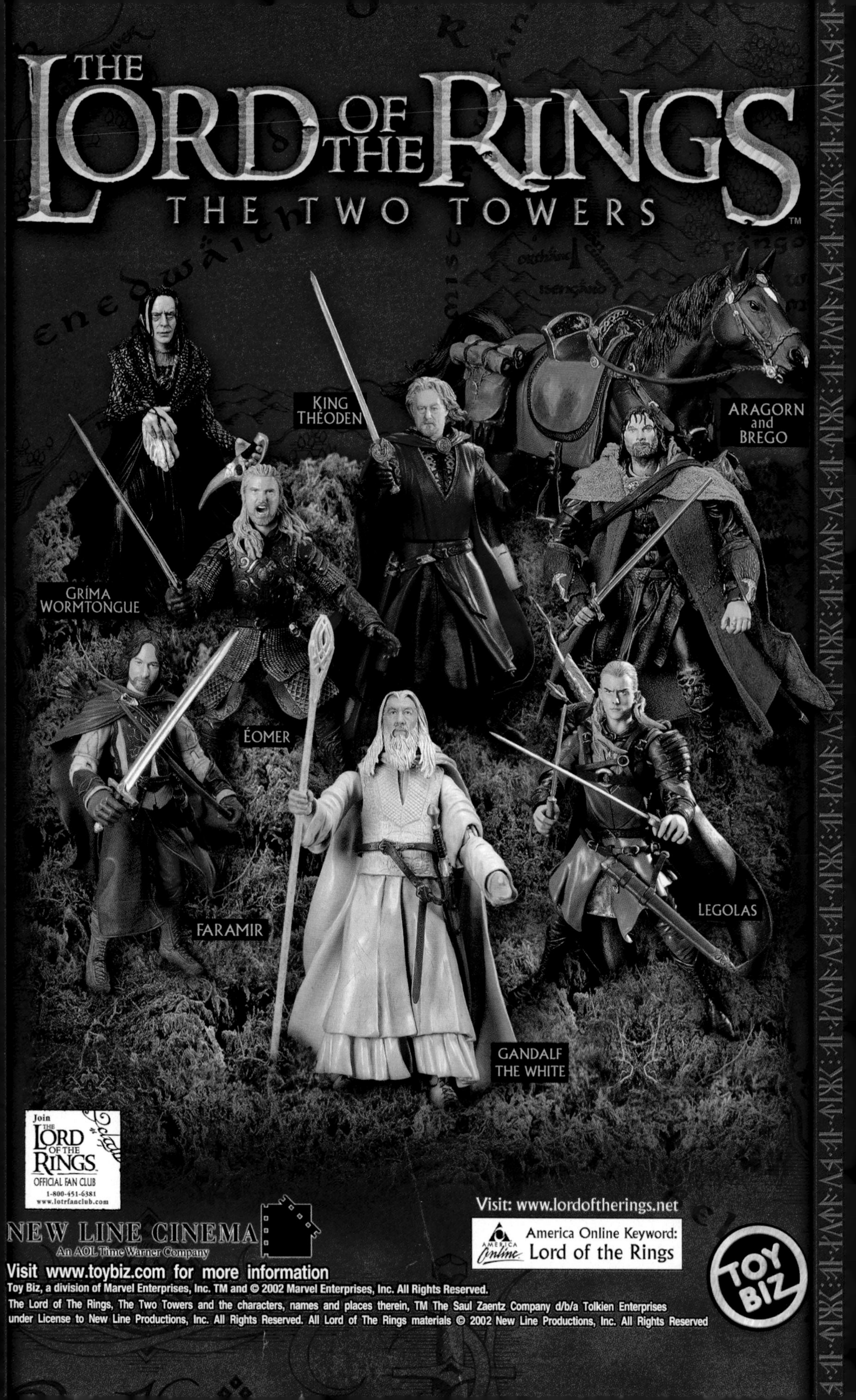
THE LORD OF THE RINGS
THE TWO TOWERS™
KING THÉODEN
ARAGORN and BREGO
GRÍMA WORMTONGUE
ÉOMER
FARAMIR
LEGOLAS
GANDALF THE WHITE
Join THE LORD OF THE RINGS OFFICIAL FAN CLUB
1-800-451-6381
www.lotrfanclub.com
Visit: www.lordoftherings.net
NEW LINE CINEMA
An AOL Time Warner Company
America Online Keyword: Lord of the Rings
TOY BIZ
Visit www.toybiz.com for more information
Toy Biz, a division of Marvel Enterprises, Inc. TM and © 2002 Marvel Enterprises, Inc. All Rights Reserved.
The Lord of The Rings, The Two Towers and the characters, names and places therein, TM The Saul Zaentz Company d/b/a Tolkien Enterprises under License to New Line Productions, Inc. All Rights Reserved. All Lord of The Rings materials © 2002 New Line Productions, Inc. All Rights Reserved